THE IRISH SHORT STORY FROM GEORGE MOORE TO FRANK O'CONNOR

Deborah M. Averill

UNIVERSITY
PRESS OF
AMERICA

LANHAM • NEW YORK • LONDON

Copyright © 1982 by

University Press of America,™ Inc.

4720 Boston Way
Lanham, MD 20706

3 Henrietta Street
London WC2E 8LU England

Library of Congress Cataloging in Publication Data

Averill, Deborah M.
   The Irish short story from George Moore to Frank
O'Connor.

   Bibliography: p.
   Includes index.
   1. Short stories, English–Irish authors–History and
criticism. I. Title.
PR8807.S5A9   823'.01'099417   81–40188
ISBN 0–8191–2133–9   AACR2
ISBN 0–8191–2134–7 (pbk.)

All University Press of America books are produced on acid-free
paper which exceeds the minimum standards set by the National
Historical Publications and Records Commission.

To my Father and Andy
and to the memory of my Mother

.

ACKNOWLEDGMENTS

I am grateful to the following publishers and agents for permission to quote passages from the works indicated:

Colin Smythe, Ltd.: The Irish Short Story, ed. Patrick Rafroidi and Terence Brown.

Viking Penguin, Inc.: Dubliners, by James Joyce. Copyright © 1969 by The Viking Press, Inc.

A. D. Peters & Co., Ltd.: Spring Sowing and The Mountain Tavern, by Liam O'Flaherty. Reprinted by permission of A. D. Peters & Co., Ltd.

Curtis Brown, Ltd.: Vive Moi!, by Sean O'Faolain. Copyright © 1964 by Sean O'Faolain; The Finest Stories of Sean O'Faolain ("Fugue," "The Patriot," "A Broken World," "A Born Genius," "Lovers of the Lake"). Copyright © 1957 by Sean O'Faolain; The Talking Trees, by Sean O'Faolain ("Feed My Lambs," "The Kitchen," "'Our Fearful Innocence'"). Copyright © 1968, 1969, and 1970 by Sean O'Faolain. Reprinted by permission of Curtis Brown, Ltd.

Joan Daves: An Only Child, by Frank O'Connor. Copyright © 1958, 1959, 1960, 1961, by Frank O'Connor; "In the Train" and "The House That Johnny Built," by Frank O'Connor. Copyright © 1936, 1944 by Frank O'Connor. Reprinted by permission of Joan Daves.

A. D. Peters & Co., Ltd.: The Lonely Voice and Collection Two by Frank O'Connor. Reprinted by permission of A. D. Peters & Co., Ltd.

Alfred A. Knopf, Inc.: The Stories of Frank O'Connor. Copyright © 1944, 1945, 1946, 1947, 1948, 1950, 1951, 1952 by Frank O'Connor.

CONTENTS

PREFACE

This book was written to fill a need for an introductory study of the Irish short story, an important genre that has not received enough attention from scholars. Intended for teachers and students who are not specialists in Irish literature, the book surveys the origins and development of the modern Irish short story from George Moore, the founder of the genre, to Frank O'Connor, its greatest practitioner. Much historical and biographical background material is included, as well as many references to previous critical commentary on the subject. Suggestions are given for further reading and research.

The Introduction to Part One traces historical conditions in the nineteenth and early twentieth centuries that contributed to the development of the Irish short story, and mentions some of the earlier fiction writers who tried to capture Irish life in stories and tales as well as longer works. It also briefly sketches the rise of the modern short story in Russia and Europe, and offers some theoretical speculations about the genre.

Chapters 2-5 are relatively brief treatments of the four writers who contributed most to the emerging short story tradition: George Moore, James Joyce, Seumas O'Kelly, and Daniel Corkery. Each chapter provices biographical and critical commentary followed by an overview of the writer's achievement in the short story and detailed discussions of selected stories. Recurrent themes and techniques are pointed out, and comparisons are made among the writers. Particular attention is given to the relationship between the individual and the community in the stories and to the use of oral narrative techniques.

In Part Two, a short Introduction (Chapter 6) fills in the historical background for the post-Revolutionary period and summarizes some common experiences and attitudes of the three major short story writers of this period, Liam O'Flaherty, Sean O'Faolain, and Frank O'Connor. Chapters 7, 8, and 9 follow a pattern similar to Chapters 2-5, but are much longer and more detailed. The organizational strategy provides a chronological survey of each writer's career; an exploration of recurrent communal themes such as war, religion, family life, love and marriage; and some discussion of each writer's concept of form, his relationship to other Irish

writers, and his place in the Irish short story tradition.

I would like to thank Drs. Doris L. Eder and George
H. Ford, who gave me much valuable help with the earlier
version of this manuscript, which was my Ph.D. disserta-
tion at the University of Rochester; the staff of Rush
Rhees Library for their co-operation and efficiency;
and Beth Roberts, for her careful and diligent typing.
I am very grateful also to my family and friends for
their patience and support during the long period of
writing.

Part One

THE IRISH SHORT STORY TRADITION

Chapter One

INTRODUCTION

The Irish short story, which began its development
with the publication of George Moore's The Untilled
Field in 1903, is essentially a modern art form. Its
techniques were derived not so much from Irish sources
as from foreign ones, especially Russian and French
stories of the late nineteenth century. Nevertheless,
the attitudes which Irish stories express are often
deeply rooted in the national experience. The genre
evolved in response to the peculiar frustrations and
conflicts of Irish life. Themes that recur in earlier
Irish fiction are re-examined and refined through the
astringent perspective of the short story writers.

Nineteenth-century Ireland produced a considerable
amount of fiction, but most of it is of poor quality.
Conditions were not favorable to a high level of cultural achievement. In addition to widespread poverty
and lack of opportunity, Irish society was characterized by uncertainty, demoralization, and sharp internal
contradictions. Because of their severe exploitation
under British law, the Irish people often regarded violence as the only remedy for their sufferings. But
they could not always agree among themselves in forming
national goals, and directed their violence not just
against the British, but also against each other.
Irish political nationalism in the eighteenth and nineteenth centuries culminated in several abortive uprisings, in which internal quarreling and betrayal contributed to the defeat. The unjust system of land ownership caused persistent tension between the owners,
often absentee, and the tenant farmers. Religion was
another major source of dissension in Irish life. The
Catholic majority regarded Protestantism as an alien
faith imposed by a conquering nation, while Protestants
whose families had lived in Ireland for several generations considered themselves as thoroughly "Irish" as
the natives. Political and religious differences were
aggravated by the large cultural gap between the Irish-
speaking and English-speaking populations. The Gaelic
culture was richly imaginative and poetic, as scholars
eventually discovered, but until the late nineteenth
century it remained virtually unknown to those who did
not speak Irish.

Several novelists in the first half of the

nineteenth century, including Maria Edgeworth, Gerald Griffin, and William Carleton, among others, attempted a serious, realistic depiction of Irish material. Although their achievements did not reach the standard of Jane Austen, the Brontës, Sir Walter Scott, and the other great English novelists of the period, their imperfect works mirrored the circumstances of Irish life at the time. The art of the Irish novelists was a hybrid one; English was an alien language, and Irish material could not easily be adapted to English literary conventions. (Stephen Dedalus, in Joyce's A Portrait of the Artist as a Young Man, cannot speak English "without unrest of spirit"; for him the language, "so familiar and so foreign, will always be . . . an acquired speech."[1]) Irish writers had to write primarily for an English audience, since there was little market for their work at home. Hence their works had a tendency to explain and justify Irish customs and behavior, and this didactic tone detracted from the purity of their art. The instability and lack of common purpose in Irish society also adversely affected the quality of Irish fiction.

The early nineteenth century was a period of cultural transition. The Protestant Ascendancy, which had ruled the country and kept the Catholic population in subjection for over a hundred years, began to lose its political and economic power after the Act of Union in 1800 dissolved the Irish Parliament and merged it with Westminster. At the same time the Anglo-Irish were developing a growing interest in Gaelic culture, an interest which eventually led to the Protestant-inspired Renaissance. Catholics began to find the political leadership they had lacked in men like Daniel O'Connell, who by arousing the peasants to the verge of civil war won Catholic Emancipation in 1829, with the final repeal of the oppressive Penal Laws. For the first time Catholics also began to produce some significant literature written in English. Irish was dying out and English replacing it as the native language.

Maria Edgeworth was the chief literary spokesman for the Protestant point of view in the early nineteenth century. Her Castle Rackrent (1802) was the first novel about Irish life to be written in English. The daughter of an Anglo-Irish landowner, she spent her girlhood in England but returned to Ireland at fifteen to help her father manage his estate, and remained there the rest of her life. Her father, though a loyal unionist, was a compassionate landlord who worked to improve the condition of his tenants. As his agent, Maria learned a great deal about the operation of the estate and the lives of the peasants. She never fully understood the peasant mind, however, and her Irish novels deal primarily with the gentry, especially with their responsibilities and failures as landlords. Like other Irish novelists of the period, she was writing for English readers, and her novels are flawed by distracting explication and sermonizing. (Some of this is contained in the lengthy prefaces and notes her father wrote for her books.)

Besides her novels, Miss Edgeworth wrote several collections of stories. Most of these were intended as illustrations of the ideas about education that she and her father shared and practiced on the younger Edgeworth children. The Parent's Assistant (1796), Early Lessons (1801), and Moral Tales (1801) are collections of educational stories directed at children of various ages. Popular Tales (1804) is directed at a broader audience, adults in the humbler social classes. This collection is also didactic; the stories depict conflicts between virtue and vice, emphasizing the pragmatic virtues which are most likely to bring success and contentment to ordinary people: hard work, persistence, considerateness, generosity, and humility. Most of the stories are set in England, but a few take place in Ireland.

Contemporary conditions in Ireland were very troublesome to Miss Edgeworth. Her Ireland--the Ireland of the Ascendancy--was dying, and she did not understand the new forces that were emerging. Her literary productivity depended very much on her father's encouragement and support, and after his death in 1817 she wrote little of importance, concentrating instead on managing the estate. The 1820's and '30's were years of declining economic conditions, peasant unrest, and local eruptions of violence fostered by secret agricultural societies. In a letter to her brother she explains why she could no longer write novels about Ireland.

> It is impossible to draw Ireland as she
> now is in the book of fiction--realities
> are too strong, party passions too vio-
> lent, to bear to see, or care to look at
> their faces in a looking glass. The peo-
> ple would only break the glass, and curse
> the fool who held the mirror up to nature--
> distorted nature, in a fever. We are in
> too perilous a case to laugh, humor would
> be out of season, worse than bad taste.
> Whenever the danger is past, as the man

5

in the sonnet says, "We may look back at
the hardest part and laugh." Then I shall
be ready to join in the laugh. Sir Walter
Scott once said to me, "Do explain to the
public why Pat, who goes forward so well
in other countries, is so miserable in his
own." A very difficult question: I fear
above my power. But I shall think of it
continually, and listen, and look, and
read.[2]

Miss Edgeworth felt that violence would bring the peasants not liberty but only a deeper enslavement, since
they could not stop quarreling among themselves. Her
withdrawal into silence was the only response she could
make to the harsh realities that were threatening her.

Although Maria Edgeworth attempted to provide a
realistic portrait of Irish life in some of her novels,
some other Protestant novelists of the period, most
notably Samuel Lover and Charles Lever, wrote superficial, farcical tales which portrayed the Irish peasant
as a blundering buffoon for the amusement of English
readers. These writers continued in fiction the bur-
lesque "stage-Irish" tradition established by seven-
teenth- and eighteenth-century playwrights. Catholic
novelists in the nineteenth century reacted strongly
against this distortion of peasant life and attempted
to correct the false image of Irishmen that was preva-
lent in England. Because they were the first of their
people to give voice to their heritage in English, the
Catholic novelists experienced conflicts of identity
even more acute than those of the Protestants.

Griffin and Carleton, both Catholics from rural
peasant families, lacked the cultural advantages that
Maria Edgeworth had. Griffin was the son of a poor
farmer in Limerick. The only formal education he
received was in a hedge school. He went to London at
twenty (1823) to try for success as a writer, since the
literary capital was opening up to Catholics. Griffin
stayed in London for three years, working at journalism
and other occupations, but felt rootless and homesick
there. After publication of his first novel, he
returned to Limerick and stayed there except for short
business trips to London. His Irish novels (the most
famous is The Collegians, 1830) provide much greater
insight into the lives of the peasants than do the
novels of Maria Edgeworth. One of his favorite themes
is the peasant attitude to violent crime and the established law. He often deals with contemporary conflicts

6

like the Tithe Wars of the 1830's, when Catholics violently resisted the law that required them to give
financial support to the Church of Ireland.

Griffin also published several collections of
stories and tales. While living in London, he conceived
the idea of writing tales depicting Irish customs and
scenery, similar to the currently popular regional tales
of Scott and others. Using anecdotes supplied to him
by his family and friends in Ireland, he wrote enough
stories for two volumes, Holland-Tide and Tales of the
Munster Festivals (1827). He also produced two later
collections, Tales of the Neighborhood (1835), which
anticipates The Untilled Field in its use of characters
who appear in more than one story, and the posthumous
Tales of the Jury Room (1842), which uses as a narrative
frame a group of sequestered jurors telling each other
stories to pass the time. Griffin's tales vary considerably in length; most are relatively long, and some
are actually short novels. Not all of them are realistic. Many are retellings of Gaelic folktales containing
magical or supernatural occurrences. His plots are
often contrived, improbable, and melodramatic, with a
tendency to digress in the wrong places; the characters
are stereotyped, and the diction is clumsily weighted
with circumlocutions and Latinate phrases, though he
does at times write colorful and convincing peasant
idiom.

After vacillating for many years between attitudes
of enthusiasm and detachment towards Ireland, Griffin
like Maria Edgeworth found it necessary to withdraw
from Irish affairs. Though he had confronted the violence of Irish life more fully than any previous writer,
he was disturbed at its extent. An unhappy love for a
married woman probably also affected his choice. Drawn
to the more peaceful existence that religious life
could offer, he entered a Christian Brothers monastery
in 1838 and died there two years later from typhoid
fever.

Most modern critics consider Carleton the best of
the nineteenth-century Irish novelists, though his background was even more obscure than Griffin's. He
belonged to an Irish-speaking peasant family in Ulster,
where Catholics were despised by the Protestant majority. As a youth he trained for the priesthood in a
hedge school, but was too much of a maverick to take
holy orders. When he was twenty-four (1818), he left
home to try his fortune in Dublin. Once there he
rejected his religious training, turned Protestant, and

7

married the niece of a Protestant schoolmaster who had connections with the government. Many of his writings are inconsistent, supporting whatever political opinions were most advantageous for him at the time. In his best work, however, he sheds his acquired identity and reverts to the world of his youth. His best-known work is not a novel but a collection of stories in several volumes, Traits and Stories of the Irish Peasantry (1830-33), dealing with the hidden world of the Irish-speaking peasants. Other collections of stories include Tales of Ireland (1834) and Tales and Sketches (1845).

In an introduction which he wrote in 1854 for a later edition of Traits and Stories, Carleton discusses some of the problems and frustrations Irish novelists have encountered. He says that in English literature since the time of Shakespeare, the Irishman has been presented to the English in a false light.

> It is well known that the character of an Irishman has been hitherto uniformly associated with the idea of something unusually ridiculous, and that scarcely anything in the shape of language was supposed to proceed from his lips but an absurd congeries of brogue and blunder. The habit of looking upon him in a ludicrous light has been so strongly impressed upon the English mind, that no opportunity has ever been omitted of throwing him into an attitude of gross and overcharged caricature, from which you might as correctly estimate his intellectual strength and moral proportions, as you would the size of a man from his evening shadow.[3]

Carleton explains that the Irishman's colorful speech results from the translation of Gaelic linguistic patterns into English. He says that although most English prejudice against the Irish results from ignorance, unfortunately there is one valid cause for this disparaging attitude: the lack of an Irish national literature. Because Ireland lacks publishers and markets for their work, most Irish writers have been forced into exile. But he is hopeful that the popularity of Traits and Stories and similar recent works in Ireland is an encouraging sign for the future of Irish literature. Carleton concludes with a detailed description of the true character of the Irish peasant, and affirms that he has presented an honest, accurate portrayal of peasant life in _Traits and Stories_.

Despite its many flaws, _Traits and Stories_ provides the best and most complete account available of life in Gaelic Ireland before the Famine. Carleton explores many of the themes that would recur in the work of later Irish novelists and short story writers-- the peasant attitudes toward politics, religion, crime and violence, the land, family life, courtship and marriage. He is often excessively melodramatic or sentimental, but he is also capable of objective realism, humor, and satire. Since he was reacting against the "stage-Irish" tradition, his attitude towards his material is seldom condescending.

Carleton's stories, like most nineteenth-century Irish stories, are long, digressive, and often poorly constructed. When he is not using peasant dialect, his style tends to be stilted and ornate. The impulse behind his writing is more didactic than aesthetic. He constantly interrupts his narrative to comment or interpret his material for the reader. Problems of narrative method did engage his attention, however. The first few stories in _Traits and Stories_ are linked by a device taken from the oral tradition--a group of people sitting around a fire in a pub telling each other stories in their own characteristic dialect. But after the fifth story, he abandons this scheme, because it "would ultimately narrow the sphere of his work, and perhaps fatigue the reader by a superfluity of Irish dialogue and its peculiarities of phraseology," and because he wants to "leave himself more room for description and observation."[4] In subsequent stories he uses a more omniscient point of view. He creates a broad picture of Irish life through the accumulation of detail; stories are loosely connected by recurrent themes and character types, but without a deliberate general design.

In his excellent study of the nineteenth-century Irish novelists, Thomas Flanagan sees Carleton as the embodiment of the deepest conflicts in Irish culture. The ambivalence we have examined in Edgeworth and Griffin is particularly acute in him.

> His conversion to Protestantism was, one
> might say, accidental and issuing from
> his circumstances. Yet his attitude
> toward life in Gaelic Ireland was deeply
> ambivalent, and from this ambivalence
> issues the best of his work. Toward his

material he directed at all times the artist's eye, which is at once loving and skeptical. In many ways his transformation from Billy Carleton, the poor scholar on the road, to Mr. William Carleton of Dublin was an escape from the crushing power not merely of material things but of his own heritage, from the haunted past, the obsessions, hatreds, and dark isolation of his own people.[5]

Carleton's rich but erratic talent exhausted itself prematurely, and in his last years his writing deteriorated.

During Carleton's years in Dublin, he became involved with an emerging literary movement in which both Protestants and Catholics participated. The first stage of the movement began with the founding of The Dublin University Magazine in 1833. The editors belonged to the Ascendancy and landlord class, but they tried to rise above politics and improve cultural standards in Dublin. They printed translations from European literature and also gave young Irish writers an opportunity to publish their work. Carleton was closely associated with the magazine from 1835-41. A more radical magazine, The Nation, was founded in 1842 by a group of young men, including James Clarence Mangan, Thomas Davis, and Charles Gavan Duffy, dedicated to the cause of Irish independence. This group and their supporters became known as the "Young Irelanders." At first they supported O'Connell in his campaign, begun around 1840, to repeal the Act of Union, but eventually they split from him because he was too pro-Catholic and pragmatic to suit their idealistic stance. They wanted to unite Protestants and Catholics of all classes in a new concept of Irish identity that would encompass all the traditions. The group became increasingly political and in 1848 initiated an unsuccessful rising.

Carleton contributed to The Nation but never fully identified with the principles of the Young Irelanders. In 1847, when most of his friends were dead and his talent was slackening, he wrote in a letter to a newspaper, "I am not a Young Irelander, nor in a political sense at least, an old one. I am no Republican, no Jacobin, no Communist, but a plain, retiring literary man who wishes to avoid politics."[6] The letter, which indicates his growing need to withdraw from public life, suggests the continuing reluctance of many Irish writers to be drawn into political controversies.

The catastrophic Famine, which began in 1845, produced drastic changes in Irish society and created a cultural void that lasted for the next half-century. Prior to the Famine, economic conditions were precarious; the population had been steadily increasing and the size of the farms decreasing as farmers subdivided their holdings among their children. Exorbitant rents and taxes contributed to the widespread destitution. Agriculture was badly managed and peasants relied on the potato as their main source of food. During the Famine years the population decreased rapidly as thousands died of starvation and thousands more emigrated in desperation. Afterwards, anti-British feeling intensified, as the Irish deeply resented England's refusal to provide adequate assistance. The Irish also became fiercely determined to reform their agricultural system. Instead of subdividing land, Irish farmers began to consolidate it. It became common practice that one son would inherit the land and the others would emigrate. Emigration, which before the Famine had been fairly infrequent and unpopular, continued in large numbers until well into the present century. The Irish custom of late marriages also dates from the Famine; sons were not in a position to marry until they had inherited their fathers' farms.

Though Irish economic conditions began to improve in the 1850's, and political activity increased, Ireland's cultural life deteriorated. As Thomas Flanagan points out, the relationship between literature and politics in Ireland had always been somewhat "incestuous." The high value placed on political commitment produced a nationalistic literature which was "rigid and brittle," its artistic standards subordinated to political ends, and after the Famine, politics smothered literature almost completely. Describing the cultural atmosphere that Joyce and other modern writers rebelled against, Flanagan says:

> In the years which followed 1850, the despair was universal. . . . Ireland in those years worked out the dark, final terms of her fate. . . . Subservient to an alien and indifferent power, its spiritual life confined by the ordinances of a harsh and provincial church, the strict and sombre history of its tragic past appropriated by demagogues and clowns, the best of its young men driven into the underground courses of hopeless conspiracy, the island accepted passively the nightmare of its history. Seen in

this context, Joyce's non serviam is less
the mutinous refusal of the artist to
accept social responsibility than the necessary assertion of individuality against
the abnormal claims imposed by a particular culture.[7]

This belief that the Irish national experience was an
"abnormal" one persisted among many modern Irish writers
besides Joyce, including the short story writers.

Several political movements in the latter half of
the century prepared the way for the achievement of
Irish independence in 1922. At the same time, though
literature was at a low ebb, the work of scholars and
translators was making accessible the huge body of
Celtic literature that inspired the Renaissance.

The Fenian movement was begun during the 1860's by
Irishmen who had emigrated to America during the Famine.
They formed a secret military organization called the
Irish Republican Brotherhood which planned and carried
out an unsuccessful rising in Ireland (1867). At first
the Fenian movement, condemned by the Church, was unpopular among Irish people, but when the leaders of the
rising were executed or exiled they acquired the status
of martyrs and their cause gained considerable popularity. The Fenians had some impact on Gladstone and the
English Parliament; by 1870 a Land Bill had been passed
providing for dual ownership of land by landlords and
tenants, and the Church of Ireland had been disestab-
lished.

After 1870 Irish politics was dominated by the Home
Rule movement, led in Parliament by a Protestant,
Charles Stuart Parnell, and by the Land League, founded
in 1879 by Michael Davitt, a former Fenian, to secure
peasant ownership of the land through such means as rent
strikes and armed violence. Parnell, a highly skillful
politician, managed to make the Home Rule question the
primary issue in Parliament during the 1880's. As president of the Land League he also worked with Davitt to
achieve the Land Act of 1881, which provided for fair
rents, fixed periods of tenure, and free sale of land.
Parnell's career was destroyed in 1890, however, when
Captain William O'Shea sued his wife for divorce on the
grounds that she had committed adultery with Parnell.
He died from stress and exhaustion in 1891, at the age
of 45. The scandal bitterly divided the Irish people
(the Christmas dinner scene in Joyce's Portrait of the
Artist effectively dramatizes the polarization of

12

feeling) and, although a Home Rule Bill was introduced
into Parliament in 1893, it was defeated. The Land
League was more successful; the British government lent
tenants money to purchase their farms and by the early
1900's the landlord system had virtually ended. Parliament eventually passed the Home Rule Bill in 1914, to be
implemented after World War I, but by then it was too
late.

Towards the end of the nineteenth century the
rediscovery of Celtic culture laid the groundwork for
the Renaissance. One important stimulus was the publication in 1878 of Standish O'Grady's History of
Ireland's Heroic Period. The work recreated the Ireland of the Celtic period and gave the Irish people a
new historic awareness of themselves. After O'Grady's
book appeared, the translators, including George Sigerson, Douglas Hyde, and others, began making more and
more Celtic literature available to non-Irish speakers.
In 1893 Hyde helped to found the Gaelic League, an
organization dedicated to reviving the Irish language
as well as the culture, and in 1899 he published The
Literary History of Ireland. Hyde and his supporters
argued that Irish literature should be written only in
Irish, not in English.

The fall of Parnell in 1890 resulted in a twenty-
year lull in political activity which proved very fruitful for literature. Groups of young Irish writers,
mostly Protestant, were formed in London and Dublin to
encourage the creation of a new national literature in
English. Their first publication was Poems and Ballads
of Young Ireland (1888), a collection to which W. B.
Yeats contributed among others.

The flowering of the Renaissance from such modest
beginnings is one of the great phenomena of literary
history. Under the energetic and visionary leadership
of Yeats, AE, Lady Gregory, and others, the emerging
literary movement gave the Irish people a revitalized
sense of pride and national identity which carried over
into the political sphere and contributed to the rebellion against England. The Renaissance, essentially
Protestant and aristocratic, could not be completely
identified with political nationalism, however. Tension
often existed between Yeats and his colleagues and the
nationalists, many of whom were Catholics from poor or
middle-class backgrounds. The theater which Yeats
founded with Lady Gregory, Edward Martyn, and George
Moore, after 1904 called the Abbey Theater, was frequently a source of public controversy. The plays

appealed to an elite audience and sometimes offended the nationalists as well as the general population. In the best-known instance, J. M. Synge's Playboy of the Western World, produced in 1907, caused a week of rioting at the theater because of its frank presentation of peasant traits.

The controversies Yeats and his friends were involved in were usually cultural rather than political, and the political events in Ireland during the early twentieth century were often deeply troubling to them. The Easter Rising of 1916, an armed rebellion against British authorities led by poets and intellectuals, including Patrick Pearse, Thomas MacDonagh, and James Connolly, took the country as a whole by surprise. The rebels occupied some public buildings for a few days and proclaimed an independent Irish Republic. As in the Fenian rising, the rebels did not win popular support until their leaders were executed by the British, and then the country rallied around them.

Irish nationalists took advantage of England's involvement in World War I to further their goals. In 1919 they set up their own Parliament in Dublin, with Eamon DeValera as President, and reaffirmed the 1916 Proclamation. They declared that British soldiers and authorities had no legal right to be in Ireland. The Irish Republican Army was formed to engage in clashes with British soldiers and police. England retaliated by sending over the Black and Tans, a group of brutal mercenary soldiers much hated by the Irish people. In 1922 a truce was signed establishing the Irish Free State. Since the Treaty excluded Northern Ireland and required an oath of allegiance to England, extreme nationalists (Republicans) found it unacceptable and the country was plunged into civil war. By 1923 the Republican side had been defeated and the country settled down to peaceful pursuits, but the bitter feeling engendered by the Civil War lingered for many years afterwards.

The literary Renaissance was romantic in outlook. It drew inspiration from Celtic literature, mythology, and folklore, celebrated aristocratic and peasant traditions, and was antipathetic to the middle-class. Poetry and drama were the predominant genres, and prose fiction was of secondary importance. A few collections of stories were published, however, that prepared the way for the later emergence of the form. The stories of Somerville and Ross (Edith Somerville and her cousin Violet Martin) are not "short stories" in the modern sense; they are humorous, slapstick tales intended primarily for entertainment, but they do show a thorough knowledge of Irish life and peasant dialect, and unlike many earlier stories they are carefully constructed. The authors belonged to the Anglo-Irish gentry and their class-consciousness is a limitation in their work, as it was in the stories of Kipling, one of their primary models. The cousins collaborated on several books, including three volumes of stories about Major Sinclair Yeates, an Englishman of Irish ancestry living in the West of Ireland: Some Experiences of an Irish R. M. (1899), Further Experiences of an Irish R. M. (1908), and In Mr. Knox's Country (1915). Some Renaissance poets, like Yeats and James Stephens, also wrote stories, but these too cannot be considered "short stories" in the strictest sense, as they lack serious realism and particularity.

Much more important to the development of the modern Irish short story was the publication of George Moore's The Untilled Field in 1903. The Untilled Field represents a seminal contribution not just to the Irish short story, but to the evolution of the short story in the English language. James Joyce's Dubliners (1914) and the stories of Seumas O'Kelly and Daniel Corkery followed Moore's book and provided links in the growing tradition, which was most fully realized in the work of the post-Revolutionary writers Liam O'Flaherty, Sean O'Faolain, and Frank O'Connor. These short story writers differed from the Renaissance poets and dramatists in some significant ways. They were all Catholics (Moore was later converted to Protestantism), and all except Moore were from middle- or working-class families. Their stories were realistic in mood and dealt mainly with contemporary Irish Catholic society rather than the aristocratic tradition or mythology and folklore. The mundane perspectives of their stories countered the more romantic and heroic perspectives of the poetry and drama.

The art form that Moore adapted to Irish material had its origins abroad, in the mid-nineteenth century. E. A. Poe and Nathaniel Hawthorne in America, and Nikolai Gogol and Ivan Turgenev in Russia, were among the earliest short story writers; their works provided models and inspiration for a host of later writers in many countries.

One early volume of short stories was particularly influential in Ireland and elsewhere: Turgenev's The Hunting Sketches (1852), a collection of stories about the daily lives of Russian serfs. All the stories are narrated by a compassionate, intelligent landowner who observes the peasants as he wanders around the countryside on hunting trips. The form of the stories is what some writers have called "organic" or "slice-of-life," evolving naturally from the material rather than being artificially imposed on it. The plots are structured not on contrived patterns of suspense or adventure, but on the patterns of ordinary life. Though the book contains little explicit social protest--Turgenev like many later short story writers deliberately avoided abstract polemic--its portrayal of the suffering and exploitation of the serfs helped bring about their emancipation.

The art of the short story was given a powerful impetus towards the end of the century by two masters of the form, Guy de Maupassant in France and Anton Chekhov in Russia. The two writers usually employ contrasting storytelling methods; Maupassant's stories are straightforward, objective narratives with a fairly prominent plot element, while Chekhov's are "organic" like Turgenev's--relatively plotless and inconclusive, depending instead on atmosphere and characterization for their effect. Maupassant, a protegé of Flaubert and the Naturalistic movement, deals primarily with the more primitive and sordid emotions of the peasants and bourgeoisie; frequent themes are cruelty, sexual exploitation, and social hypocrisy. Chekhov's themes are more subjective and psychological; he often portrays the frustration of characters caught in a sterile provincial existence.

The short story did not develop its demanding modern standards in England and the United States as early as it did in Russia and Europe. In the English-speaking countries it was for a long time a popular but not highly artistic genre. Until well into the twentieth century, English short story writers worked in the shadow of Rudyard Kipling, whose stories are dominated by an intrusive, moralistic, class-conscious narrator. American stories were turned out according to the slick magazine formula, perfected by O. Henry, that called for a highly contrived plot and gimmicky ending. Though the Irish contributed virtually nothing to the formal development of the short story in the nineteenth century, it was George Moore who first introduced the Russian organic type of story into the English language, years before Katherine Mansfield introduced it in England (1917) or Sherwood Anderson in America (1919). Moore was thoroughly schooled in Russian realism and French Naturalism and found these models more congenial to his purposes than the English fiction of the time.

Many attempts have been made to define the modern short story, but because it is such an open, flexible, individualized genre, a generally accepted definition has not been found. Some of the major disagreements have centered on whether the short story is a relatively new genre or an ancient one, and whether the short story is merely a shorter, more superficial version of the novel or a separate genre, fundamentally different in its view of reality.

The relationship between the Irish short story and the ancient folk culture is substantial, and it will enter into our discussion of Irish stories. Even more important, however, is the relationship between the short story and the novel. The modern short story, with its individual viewpoint and its high level of craftsmanship, has more in common with the novel than with the folktale. A good short story expresses its author's personal vision and is a realistic, carefully structured, unified work of art, employing techniques of compression and implication, and often tending towards symbolism or poetic lyricism.

Recent writers and critics have often defended the view that the short story offers an essentially different vision of life from the novel. Alberto Moravia, for example, has worked out thought-provoking definitions that emphasize the contrast between the two genres. He says that the organization of a novel, including its plot and character development, depends on its ideological or thematic content, whereas the short story is not patterned on an ideology. Short story characters are "caught at a particular moment, within narrow limits of time and space, and act in function of a determined event which forms the object of the short story." Characters in a novel, on the other hand, have "a long, ample and tortuous development that unites biographical with ideological data, and they move in a time and space that are both real and abstract, immanent and transcendent." Because of these contrasting qualities, the short story and the novel have very different effects on the reader. The short story has a special charm

> deriving from a literary art which is un-
> questionably purer, more essential, more
> lyrical, more concentrated and more abso-
> lute than that of the novel. Whereas, by
> way of compensation, the novel provides a
> deeper, more complex, more dialectical,

17

more polyhedric and more metaphysical
representation of reality than the short
story.[8]

Some writers have taken a more extreme view than
Moravia's and have asserted that the novel is outmoded,
and that the short story is a more valid art form in
the twentieth century. Elizabeth Bowen sees a resemblance between the short story and the cinema, both relatively new genres.

> The new literature, whether written or
> visual, is an affair of reflexes, of imme-
> diate susceptibility, of associations not
> examined by reason: it does not attempt
> a synthesis. Narrative of any length in-
> volves continuity, sometimes a forced con-
> tinuity: it is here that the novel too
> often becomes invalid.[9]

A similar view has been expressed by Nadine Gordimer,
who believes that the short story is thriving while the
novel is dead, because the "kind of creative vision" in
a short story is more appealing for the modern reader.
The short story has always been an open, experimental
form; though it requires strict discipline, it allows at
the same time a "wider freedom" than the novel does.

> Short-story writers have known--and solved
> by the nature of their choice of form--
> what novelists seem to have discovered in
> despair only now: the strongest conven-
> tion of the novel, prolonged coherence of
> tone, to which even the most experimental
> of novels must conform unless it is to fall
> apart, is false to the nature of whatever
> can be grasped of human reality.

Gordimer emphasizes the lack of stability and consistency in modern life; she compares the quality of human
contact to "the flash of fireflies, in and out, now
here, now there, in darkness. Short-story writers see
by the light of the flash; theirs is the art of the only
thing one can be sure of--the present moment."[10] Many
other writers have echoed the statements of Bowen and
Gordimer, and have agreed that the short story is the
most appropriate literary form for the restless, uprooted, fragmented consciousness of modern man. Though perhaps controversial, these perceptions are enlightening
when applied to the Irish short story, which evolved in
a particularly tormented and unstable society.

The problems inherent in defining the short story as a genre are reflected in the available scholarship on the Irish short story. Little general agreement exists among scholars as to what qualities characterize the Irish short story tradition, or whether a distinct and recognizable tradition even exists. One of the earliest writers to delineate an Irish tradition separate from the English was H. E. Bates, in The Modern Short Story (1941). Bates asserts that the poetry, violence, and religious consciousness of the Irish genius have contributed significantly to the quality of English literature and particularly to the modern English short story.

> The Irish short story has been bred of vastly different qualities from the English. Where art and people fight for existence, whether against religious, moral, or political tyranny or against plain indifference, and where such art is naturally poetic and such people are naturally and proudly belligerent, the tendency of all expression is bound to be revolutionary.[11]

Bates adds that the strongest influences on Irish literature have been the Irish language, politics, and the Catholic Church. The "sense of sin" inculcated by the Church has exerted particular pressure. The "struggle between the artist and religion, between religion and experience," has consistently affected the short story writers.

> In all of the writers of stories discussed in this chapter, from Moore to O'Faolain, there can be seen, in some degree, an expression of the struggle between beauty and sin, between the legacy of moral superstition and the physical loveliness of life, a struggle that gives them all the attitude of men sensuously grasping and caressing at the flesh of life while fearfully glancing over their shoulders for the dark swirl of the benighting cassock.[12]

Bates mentions several volumes which he considers of major importance in the development of the Irish short story. He begins with The Untilled Field, to which "the modern Irish short story might be said to owe its existence." The fresh, down-to-earth realism of Moore's book probably influenced Joyce's Dubliners,

19

the next significant landmark. In the post-Revolutionary period the best writers were O'Flaherty, O'Faolain,
and O'Connor. Naming each of their first collections
of stories, respectively, Bates says, "These volumes
are, then, the structure on which the Irish short story
is built: The Untilled Field [1903], Dubliners [1914],
Spring Sowing [1924], Midsummer Night Madness [1932],
Guests of the Nation [1931]."[13] The transposition of
ordinary life and the absence of contrivance in these
volumes anticipated the form not only of the contemporary Irish short story but of the English and American
as well. Though he omits O'Kelly and Corkery from his
discussion and so fails to note their influence on
later writers, Bates's chapter perceptively defines several recurring themes in the Irish short story and demonstrates the impact of its organic form on short story
development in the English language.

A substantial argument for the existence of an
Irish short story tradition has been advanced more recently (1964) by Vivian Mercier. He observes that the
Irish are "particularly gifted" for the short story
genre and "paradoxically weak in the novel."[14] Of the
major twentieth-century Irish fiction writers who tried
both forms, most abandoned the novel for the short
story; Moore and Joyce are the primary exceptions.

Mercier explains the Irish gift for short story
writing by stressing the influence of the Gaelic oral
tradition on Irish literature. Short tales called
eachtra or seanchas comprised a popular genre among
Irish storytellers. The oral quality in Irish fiction
can be traced beginning with Castle Rackrent, which is
narrated in idiomatic oral style. The later peasant
novelists like Griffin and Carleton used oral dialect
because "the brogue" was more natural for them than
standard English. Unlike Maria Edgeworth, Griffin and
Carleton were well acquainted with Gaelic folklore.
Other nineteenth-century Irish writers were influenced
by the oral tradition to varying degrees.

Modern short story writers who lived in the era of
the Gaelic Revival, like Corkery, O'Connor, and O'Faolain, deliberately learned to speak the language. Paradoxically, O'Flaherty, the only native Irish speaker of
the group, is "the least oral in his approach to narrative"; he writes "more for the eye than he does for the
ear or the speaking voice."[15] The fact that O'Flaherty
can write fluently in Irish may make him less likely to
model his stories on oral patterns. The two Irish writers most concerned with restoring the oral quality to

the short story are Moore and O'Connor. Joyce is the only story writer of the group who shows no awareness of a listening audience.

Mercier describes in detail the theatrical atmosphere of a traditional ceilidhe or story-telling session, still in vogue among native Irish speakers, to account for the highly dramatic quality of the Irish short story; he concludes that "the Irish short story has constantly revitalized itself through renewed contact with the oral tradition."[16]

Bates's theory of the Irish short story emphasizes thematic characteristics, while Mercier's emphasizes narrative techniques. The arguments of subsequent critics also demonstrate this dichotomy of viewpoints. Declan Kiberd offers a thesis similar to Mercier's; he believes that

> the short story has flourished in those countries where a vibrant oral culture is suddenly challenged by the onset of a sophisticated literary tradition. The short story is the natural result of a fusion between the ancient form of the folk-tale and the preoccupations of modern literature.[17]

Many of the Irish short story writers, like Corkery, O'Kelly, O'Flaherty, O'Faolain, and O'Connor, grew up in regions where the oral folk culture still existed, and these writers were also familiar with great works of the modern literary tradition. It was natural they would turn to the short story.

> By nature of its origins, the form was admirably suited to the task of reflecting the disturbances in Irish society as it painfully shed its ancient traditions. . . . The short story is particularly appropriate to a society in which revolutionary upheavals have shattered the very idea of normality.[18]

Like Mercier, Kiberd describes the Gaelic oral tradition and the kinds of stories that were most commonly told. He points out that although the modern short story often imitates oral techniques, its purpose is essentially different, as it expresses not communal attitudes but the personal, individual viewpoint of the author. "The folk-tale was impersonal, magical, and recited to a

21

credulous audience in a public manner. The short story is personal, credible, and written in private for the critical solitary reader."[19] Not all Irish story writers were influenced by the oral tradition; examples Kiberd gives of those who were not include Moore (he overlooks Moore's deliberate imitation of oral techniques), Joyce, John McGahern, and some of the Irish language writers.

Another very recent theory, presented by David Norris, takes the thematic rather than the technical approach. His argument somewhat resembles Bates's emphasis on the Irish writers' rebelliousness and their portrayal of the conflict between "beauty and sin," or "moral superstition and the physical loveliness of life." Norris's thesis is more cogent and comprehensive than Bates's, however. He defines the central theme of the Irish short story as

> the conflict between the individual's capacity for developing an imaginative response to his environment, and those forces I have characterized . . . as "authority structures"--which can be either the acknowledged public focus of organizational power represented by Church and State and their respective officers, or more frequently the subtle unacknowledged and internalized restrictions on personal growth inherent in us all. It is the universal tension between the dynamic and the static, between the accepting respectable members of conventional society, and the outsider, the individualist.[20]

The value system shared by the short story writers judges characters by their ability "to respond positively, imaginatively, even creatively to the life that surrounds them." Norris agrees with Bates that this independent attitude developed in response to the long resistance against British oppression and authoritarianism. The writers whom he surveys to illustrate this central theme include Somerville and Ross, Moore, Joyce, Padraic O'Conaire, O'Kelly, Corkery, O'Flaherty, O'Faolain, O'Connor, and Mary Lavin. These writers treat the theme with varying degrees of sophistication--some imitate the oral tradition more closely and show more awareness of their audience than others--but it is pervasive in the work of them all. Kiberd's and Norris's theories are indebted to the earlier theories of O'Faolain and O'Connor, which will be discussed in the chapters on these writers.

While all of these theories contain helpful insights, none is completely satisfactory. The theories about the impact of the oral tradition are too limited, as not all of the stories use oral techniques. Irish short story writers have employed as great a variety of techniques as have writers from other countries. The thematic approach, on the other hand, carries the danger of being too broad. The recurrent central themes are not exclusive to the short story, as they can also be found in other Irish genres. One important question considered by O'Faolain and O'Connor but not adequately addressed by any of the critics mentioned above is why the Irish have been more successful with the short story than with the novel.

In the following chapters I will not try to defend a single thesis about the Irish short story, but will emphasize several recurrent distinguishing characteristics of the genre. In classifying the stories and showing their interrelationships, I have found a thematic approach more fruitful than an arrangement based on formal techniques, as the themes recur more consistently and universally, and they can be more easily related to the social conditions in which the short story arose. But as formal elements are also indispensable to a story's total meaning, I have included some discussion of each writer's concept of short story form, with special attention to oral techniques.

One of the broadest and most pervasive themes in the Irish short story is the conflict between the individual and the community. This relationship is of course important in the literature of any country, but in Ireland it is more intense and is accompanied by greater ambivalence. The extraordinary pressures and restrictions which the Irish community imposes on its members result in frequent rebellions and struggles to assert personal freedom. At the same time, even the most determined individualists are deeply attached to some aspects of Irish life--perhaps the beauty of its landscape or its timeless rituals and traditions--and they are aware of their need for acceptance by their own people. They are torn, and often seek reconciliation with the community they have rejected. This broad theme can be broken down into several aspects of community life most frequently depicted as sources of conflict in the stories--nationalism and war, land ownership, crime and the legal system, religion, and the more personal areas of family life, courtship, and marriage. Community life in all of these areas is affected by social change and upheaval, the clash between the traditional and modern ways of life. Emigration and exile are also important aspects of the Irish national experience; individuals sometimes seek permanent escape from the community, but not without intense inner conflict.

This preoccupation with the conflict between the individual and the community resulted from the difficult relationship that existed between Irish fiction writers and their society. The vacillation between social involvement and withdrawal that we have already observed in nineteenth-century writers like Edgeworth, Griffin, and Carleton was also experienced by the modern short story writers, as their efforts to write realistically about the virtues and faults of Irish life met with hostility from the Irish public and made the writers acutely aware of the narrowness and intractability of their material. The writers' increasing preference for the short story over the novel can be attributed to social factors. The characteristics of the modern short story described earlier in this chapter--its emphasis on intuitive rather than rational or abstract truth, on brief flashes of revelation or insight rather than on sustained, continuous development--gave it a particular appeal for writers who lived in a disrupted, transitional society. Most Irish writers regarded their society as peculiar, self-defeating, and out-of-step with other western societies, and they could not achieve the stable, universalized view of Irish life that the novel demands. The short story allowed them to express their fluctuating, inconsistent moods by focusing on particular, non-ideological characters and on brief moments or fragments of experience.

Successive generations of Irish short story writers can be grouped according to their characteristic attitude to Irish communal life, with the qualification that their attitude may change from one story to another. Broadly speaking, the stories of the Renaissance period represent two antithetical viewpoints on Irish life. The stories of Moore and Joyce reflect a feeling of hopelessness about Ireland's future and a belief that escape from the country is necessary for personal fulfillment. O'Kelly and Corkery, writing at a slightly later time, express in their stories a spirit of national reawakening and a strong feeling for Ireland as a nurturing "home" rather than as a place to flee from. The stories of O'Kelly and Corkery are consequently more romantic than those of Moore and Joyce, but the romanticism is grounded in a realistic awareness of the faults

and limitations as well as the virtues of Irish people.
The post-Revolutionary generation, which included
O'Flaherty, O'Connor, and O'Faolain, experienced an almost overwhelming tension between these two viewpoints.
They were severely disillusioned by the Civil War, censorship, and other factors that will be discussed in
Chapter 6, but their participation in the nationalistic
movement had left them too fully committed to turn away
from Ireland completely. Their stories reveal a strongly ambivalent and complex attitude towards their native
country.

In setting the limits for this study, I have included only those writers who made a substantial contribution to the development of the modern Irish short story,
a highly artistic genre distinct from tales and other
short narratives. For this reason I have excluded writers like Griffin, Carleton, Somerville and Ross, Yeats,
and Stephens. Because of their inaccessibility to most
readers outside Ireland, I have also excluded the Irish-
language writers like Padraic O'Conaire, though their
stories are often of high quality. I have ended with
Frank O'Connor, whose contribution to the tradition was
greater than anyone else's, but it by no means stops
with him. It would require a separate work to give an
adequate account of the many fine short story writers
who followed O'Connor: Samuel Beckett, Michael McLaver-
ty, Bryan MacMahon, Mary Lavin, James Plunkett, and a
large group of younger writers. In each of the following chapters, I will examine biographical, autobiographical, and critical material as a prelude to a detailed
examination of the stories. The stories are grouped in
a way that approximately reflects each writer's chronological development and at the same time allows exploration of his most characteristic themes, his concepts of
short story form, and his relationship to the Irish
short story tradition. As this book is intended as an
introduction to the subject and not as an exhaustive
analysis, I have mentioned many sources for further reading and have suggested some possibilities for future
research, especially in comparisons among the writers.
Some excellent critical studies are available on individual writers, but very few comprehensive or comparative
studies have been made, and there are many gaps in our
understanding of this important genre.

Notes

1 James Joyce, A Portrait of the Artist as a Young Man (New York: Viking, 1971), p. 189.

2 Quoted in Thomas Flanagan, The Irish Novelists: 1800-1850 (New York: Columbia University Press, 1959), p. 103.

3 William Carleton, Traits and Stories of the Irish Peasantry, 10th edition, Vol. I (London: William Tegg, n.d.), p. i.

4 Ibid., p. 144.

5 Flanagan, p. 275.

6 Quoted in ibid., p. 327.

7 Ibid., p. 336.

8 Alberto Moravia, "The Short Story and the Novel," Short Story Theories, ed. Charles E. May (Ohio: Ohio University Press, 1976), pp. 150-51.

9 Elizabeth Bowen, "The Faber Book of Modern Short Stories," in ibid., p. 152.

10 Nadine Gordimer, "The Flash of Fireflies," in ibid., pp. 179-80.

11 H. E. Bates, The Modern Short Story: A Critical Survey (London: Thomas Nelson and Sons, 1941), pp. 148-49.

12 Ibid., pp. 150-51.

13 Ibid., p. 161.

14 Vivian Mercier, "The Irish Short Story and Oral Tradition," The Celtic Cross: Studies in Irish Culture and Literature, ed. Ray B. Browne et al. (Purdue: Purdue University Studies, 1964), p. 98.

15 Ibid., p. 105.

16 Ibid., p. 115.

17 Declan Kiberd, "Story-Telling: The Gaelic Tradition," The Irish Short Story, ed. Patrick Rafroidi and

Terence Brown (Gerrards Cross, Buckinghamshire: Colin Smythe, 1979), p. 14.

[18] Ibid., p. 15.

[19] Ibid., p. 19.

[20] David Norris, "Imaginative Response Versus Authority Structures. A Theme of the Anglo-Irish Short Story," in ibid., p. 40.

Chapter Two

GEORGE MOORE

The Untilled Field drew on a variety of influences,
both Irish and non-Irish, but ultimately represented an
original, seminal contribution both to Irish literature
and to the art of the short story. Although the work
does contain some artistic flaws, its level of craftsmanship is remarkable, considering that Moore was pio-
neering a new Irish genre. The themes and techniques
that Moore experimented with were to have a widespread
impact on younger writers.

Moore, a prolific novelist, published other volumes of stories, but they do not match the achievement
of The Untilled Field. In 1895 he published Celibates
(republished in substantially revised form as Celibate
Lives in 1927); in these stories the Irish background
is not so concrete as in The Untilled Field, and the
form is more diffuse. The stories in A Story-Teller's
Holiday (1918) are modelled on traditional folk-tales
and lack the serious realism of The Untilled Field.

The inspiration for The Untilled Field came from
Moore's involvement with the Irish literary revival.
Although he belonged to the Irish Catholic gentry and
owned an estate in County Mayo, he had rejected Irish
cultural nationalism as a young man and had lived for
many years as an expatriate in France and England. His
early works about Ireland--Parnell and His Island (1887)
and Confessions of a Young Man (1888)--were sharply critical of the country. In 1899, while living in London,
he was asked by W. B. Yeats and Edward Martyn to assist
with the founding of the Irish Literary Theater. At
first he was skeptical about the dramatic revival, but
he grew increasingly excited about it and after much
vacillation returned to live in his native country until
1911.

For the first few years of his return, Moore was
actively involved in the Irish language revival and the
dramatic movement. Disagreements with Yeats and Martyn
caused him to sever his formal connection with the theater, however, and for the remainder of his stay he concentrated on writing prose works: The Untilled Field,
his novel The Lake, and the satirical autobiography Hail
and Farewell, which expresses his disillusionment with
Irish affairs and his hatred of the Catholic Church.

29

Moore's anti-Catholic sentiment had grown so intense by 1903 that he became a Protestant.

The artistic concept of The Untilled Field was discovered in the process of writing. The earliest stories--"The Wedding Gown," "Almsgiving," "The Clerk's Quest," and "So On He Fares"--represented Moore's contribution to the Irish language revival. They were composed at the suggestion of his friend John Eglinton in imitation of Turgenev's The Hunting Sketches, and were to be translated into Irish to serve as models for young Irish-speaking writers. The Irish edition (1902) sold only a few copies, however, and Moore's interest in this project gave way to "a desire to paint the portrait of my country."[1]

Because they were intended for translation, the earliest stories were written in standard English, but most of the later stories were written in an idiomatic oral style that Moore called "Anglo-Irish." As his artistic conception became clearer, his anti-Catholic thesis grew more pervasive. He continued to revise the book through several subsequent editions, and the final 1931 edition is considerably different from the 1903 version.

Moore's choice of Turgenev's The Hunting Sketches as the model for The Untilled Field suggests the affinity that he felt for the Russian writer. The influence of Turgenev on the development of the Irish short story was probably greater than any other foreign influence. The attraction was not entirely one-sided; some of the inspiration for The Hunting Sketches had come from Turgenev's reading of Maria Edgeworth's stories about Ireland. There are many reasons for this national affinity. Turgenev's Russia, like Ireland, had experienced exploitation of peasants by an indifferent and decadent landlord class, and violent peasant uprisings against the landowners; both countries had suffered under a repressive, authoritarian form of government; in both there was a powerful undercurrent of national feeling, love for the native landscape and the traditional peasant culture. Moore had felt both a personal and a literary attraction to Turgenev for many years. They shared the experiences of disillusionment with their countries and exile, and in 1888 Moore wrote an essay expressing preference for Turgenev's literary methods over the Naturalism of Zola.

The Hunting Sketches influenced the overall design of The Untilled Field as well as the technique of

individual stories. (Moore's title was derived from
another work of Turgenev's, Virgin Soil.) Many of the
stories in each volume are linked by a common setting,
by recurring characters, and by repetition of a central
theme. In both books the form is organic; plot is
subordinate to atmosphere and characterization. Both
provide insight into the peasant mind, its religious
consciousness and intimacy with the land. Both use
landscape symbolically to reflect inner moods and feelings, and both convey a sense of the sadness and pathos
of human life.[2]

Ultimately, however, The Untilled Field is very
different in both theme and technique from The Hunting
Sketches. One of the most striking contrasts is in the
kind of national feeling expressed. Moore discusses
the dissimilarity of Russian and Irish national attitudes in Hail and Farewell, when he is recalling his
indecision about whether to return to Ireland in 1899.

> I began to think of the soul which Edward
> Martyn had told me I had lost in Paris
> and in London, and if it were true that
> whoever cast off tradition is like a tree
> transplanted into uncongenial soil.
> Tourgueniff was of that opinion: "Russia
> can do without any one of us, but none of
> us can do without Russia"--one of his
> sentimental homilies grown wearisome from
> constant repetition, true, perhaps, of
> Russia, but utterly untrue of Ireland.
> Far more true would it be to say that an
> Irishman must fly from Ireland if he
> would be himself. Englishmen, Scotchmen,
> Jews, do well in Ireland--Irishmen never;
> even the patriot has to leave Ireland to
> get a hearing.[3]

Many nineteenth-century Russian writers besides Turgenev
contemplated exile as a possible alternative to the
oppressive atmosphere at home. But Russian society,
despite its faults, was more coherent, stable, and self-
assured than Irish society. As a result, Russia produced some of the greatest novels of the century, while
Ireland produced only a few imperfect novels. In
Russia, exile was sought mainly by the upper classes,
and was often only temporary, whereas in Ireland after
the Famine emigration was a common choice among the
peasants as well as the gentry. Turgenev is more hopeful about the future of Russia than Moore is about the
future of Ireland.

The distinctively Irish theme of The Untilled
Field is summarized in a letter from Moore to his publisher: "All that tends to diminish, to impoverish and
to humiliate life is the sin against the Holy Ghost and
the theme of my book is that the excessive Catholicism
that prevails in Ireland tends to diminish the vitality
of the human plant."[4] The ramifications of this theme
have been summarized very well by Brendan Kennelly.

> Behind Irish puritanism and repression
> stretches a long, dark history of methodi-
> cal English tyranny and futile Irish pro-
> test that helps to account for the emo-
> tional and moral climate of The Untilled
> Field. . . . The lamentable change in
> Christianity from an inspired love of
> creation to a resolute distrust of life is
> the central theme. . . . Other pathetic
> features follow from this: the atmosphere
> of unrelieved poverty and squalor; the
> frustration of all ideals; the suppression
> of individual thinking; the hysterical
> fear of sex as the supreme evil of which
> man is capable; the confusion of servility
> with obedience, furtive inhibition with
> virtuous self-denial, caution with wisdom;
> the fear of full expression and hence the
> distrust of the artist. . . . Co-existing
> with this theme of stagnation is the theme
> of escape--especially to America, the land
> of promise where it seems possible to ful-
> fill these aspirations so tragically
> stifled in Ireland.[5]

At times Moore's hatred of Catholicism results in excessive polemic, but the attitude expressed in his best
stories is more subtle and balanced. In spite of his
insistence on the need for escape, his treatment of his
Irish material is not entirely unsympathetic. At times
he seems fascinated by certain qualities in the Irish
character. Herbert Howarth remarks that "two moods
intersect in The Untilled Field: sympathy with what is
generous, naive, and brave in the Irish; a protest
against the forces that enfeeble and depopulate Ireland."[6]

The revisions that Moore made in The Untilled Field
after 1903 in general enhanced its artistry by eliminating some of the more mechanical unifying devices, com-
pressing the polemical passages, and emphasizing character rather than theme.[7] When he was writing the

original version, he insisted that it had greater unity than it actually did have. He asserted, in a letter to his publisher, that "the book is a perfect unity, and I hope it will not be reviewed as a collection of short stories." He also suggested as a subtitle for the volume, "A Novel in Thirteen Episodes."[8] The original London edition began and ended with two polemical "frame" stories, "In the Clay" and "The Way Back," both concerned with the difficulties Irish artists encounter in dealing with their material. Moore dropped these stories from subsequent editions. In the Preface to the 1903 Leipzig (Tauchnitz) edition, he comments that the stories "seemed to be less deep-rooted in the fundamental instincts of life than some of the others."[9] He later combined the two into a single story, "Fugitives," which ends the 1931 edition. Other revisions included the breaking up of the long story "Some Parishioners" into four stories, and a rearrangement of several stories to produce a more effective grouping. These revisions suggest that Moore was moving away from his concept of the book as a "novel," towards a recognition of the unique potentialities of the short story form. His "portrait" of Ireland was actually a series of loosely related portraits, each reflecting a different point of view.

The 1931 edition of The Untilled Field opens with two stories about exiles, "The Exile" and "Home Sickness," both set in Mayo. These stories, Moore says, set him thinking of the villages near Dublin, and the next four stories concern the strict priest Fr. Maguire and his parish outside Dublin: "Some Parishioners," "Patchwork," "The Wedding Feast," and "The Window." To counterbalance the harshness of Fr. Maguire, Moore then portrayed the gentle, pathetic figure of Fr. MacTurnan.[10] The two Fr. MacTurnan stories are "A Letter to Rome" and "A Play-House in the Waste." The latter story is linked to the next one, "Julia Cahill's Curse," by the narrative device of oral dialogue and by their characterization of passionate young women who violate the sexual mores of the community. The four earliest stories follow: "The Wedding Gown," "The Clerk's Quest," "Almsgiving," and "So On He Fares"; the middle two of these are urban stories set in Dublin, and the others are generalized fables. Two polemical, anti-Catholic stories end the volume, "The Wild Goose" and "Fugitives." The volume thus begins and ends with a strong emphasis on the need for exile. Moore experiments with a variety of narrative viewpoints, including omniscience, limited omniscience, oral storytelling, and first-person narration.

In "The Exile," Moore explores some of the deepest
emotional conflicts of the Irish character, between the
attachment to religion, family, and the land, and the
need for love and personal happiness. The story concerns the Phelan family, Pat, an elderly farmer, and
his two sons, James and Peter. James, the elder, is
practical and efficient, while Peter is dreamy, incompe-
tent, and unsure of his vocation. James wants to marry
Catherine Ford, a neighbor who could help him run the
farm, but she loves Peter and will marry no one else.
Peter has considered the priesthood and when he sees
that he is standing in his brother's way, he enters the
seminary at Maynooth. Catherine still refuses to marry
James, however, and enters a convent instead. James
grows increasingly depressed and thinks about emigrating. Eventually both Peter and Catherine decide they
do not have religious vocations; they agree to marry,
work the farm, and care for Pat, and James departs on
the boat for America.

"The Exile" consists of a series of dramatized
scenes with a minimum of narration and description.
The scenes blend together so that even though there are
large gaps of time in the narrative, it seems to flow
continuously. The setting is not depicted in detail but
is briefly sketched; details are carefully chosen to
reinforce character and theme. The simple, idiomatic
style effectively renders the mental world of the peasants and captures the oral quality that Moore desired.
By shifting the point of view from one character to
another, Moore arouses sympathy for each of them; no
individual is blamed for the unhappy situation. Moore
is able to understand the peasants' minds and at the
same time maintain his objectivity.

The virtues as well as the inadequacies of Irish
life are illustrated in "The Exile." The Phelans have
a strong sense of family loyalty. The brothers are con-
siderate of each other, and they take for granted that
one of them must stay home to care for their father and
the farm, their heritage from previous generations. But
Ireland cannot offer a full life to many of its young
people, and James's decision to emigrate follows a pattern common in his community.

One apparent irony of the story is that the wrong
son is forced to leave. The reader feels that James is
Pat's favorite son, and that James and Catherine together could make a success of the farm. Peter does not
love Catherine as deeply as James does and probably
would be just as content living away from home. But

34

Moore implies that in a way it is more appropriate for Peter to stay in Ireland than for James to do so, since Peter's incompetence and aimlessness are qualities bred and tolerated by the stagnant Irish environment.

The attitude to religious life expressed in the story is that it is an escape from the real world, supported by the labor of others. When old Pat Phelan is riding to the convent to tell Catherine about Peter's return from Maynooth, he is struck by the contrast between the empty and neglected land outside the convent and the flourishing garden within. As he stands in the convent parlor waiting to see Catherine, he reflects that the religious life is much easier than the life outside, with its anxiety and loneliness, and for a moment he wonders if he should bring Catherine "back to trouble."

With his peasant shrewdness Pat realizes that the nuns are reluctant to let Catherine go because she is the only one who can successfully operate their dairy. In many other ways Catherine embodies the best qualities of Irish women. She has a strong instinctive grasp of reality that enables her to make the choice that is right for her and pursue it. She loves Peter partly because of his helplessness. He is a challenge for her, and she is determined to make something of him. He is her vocation.

Catherine's grasp of reality is associated with a capacity for visionary experience. Her decision to leave the convent is made independently, even before she knows of Peter's decision, because she sees a vision in the convent garden. She tells the Reverend Mother that she has seen a ship waiting to take James to America and Pat sitting alone at home, and she feels a "call" to look after the old man. This capacity to reach deeper levels of reality through visionary experience is a quality of the Irish mind that intrigues Moore.

Catherine and James both seek exile--she in the convent, he in America--because Irish life has not fulfilled their emotional needs. Peter's decision to marry Catherine permits her to return joyfully from exile and build the life she wants, but Ireland cannot provide many such opportunities, and James must break with his past and seek a new life elsewhere. The story ends on a sad note; Moore does not assure us that James will find happiness in America. Because he has been forced to leave a home and way of life that he loves, he will probably spend his life as a discontented, rootless man. The sadness of emigration is heightened in this case by the strength of Irish family loyalty and love for the land, virtues which survive even in the midst of poverty and neglect.

"Home Sickness," one of Moore's finest stories, presents an almost inverse situation, the return home of an Irishman after many years in America. James Bryden has worked for thirteen years as a bartender in a Bowery slum. He returns to his native village to recover from an illness, falls in love with a village woman, Margaret Dirken, and agrees to marry her. He cannot proceed with the marriage, however; he grows increasingly disenchanted with the submissiveness and apathy of the villagers and longs for the activity of the Bowery. Finally he returns to America permanently, marries, and raises a family. But in his old age, as he faces death, his American life recedes in his mind, and his most persistent memory is an image of Margaret and the village.

Moore's technique in this story is somewhat different from his technique in "The Exile." The entire story is narrated in the third person from Bryden's point of view; as a result the language, though still idiomatic, is closer to standard English and the perspective on Ireland is more distanced. Moore's criticism of Irish life is harsher than in "The Exile." The contrast between the Irish and American settings is one of the main structural features of "Home Sickness." Moore avoids oversimplifying this contrast; America is described not as a paradise, but as a place where people must work so hard that their health may be destroyed.

Bryden's inner feelings are conveyed symbolically, through details of the setting and landscape. Because of his illness and the long absence, he is in an over-wrought, susceptible state when he arrives. His first impression of the village, which like the rest of Ireland has been victimized by the landlord system, is one of deterioration and neglect. His first night in Mike Scully's house, where he has taken a room, is disturbing. He is possessed by an intense, nervous loneliness, evoked by the unfamiliar sounds of geese cackling, a dog howling, and even Mike breathing beside his wife.

The experiences of Bryden's first night in the village foreshadow his eventual departure. Although his discomfort is mitigated during his convalescence by the peacefulness of the surroundings, the kindness of the

36

Scullys and their neighbors, and the relationship with
Margaret, we retain our original impression that he is
out of place in Ireland. Except for Margaret, he takes
little interest in the lives of the villagers.

The marriage to Margaret offers Bryden a good
chance for financial security, since he has saved some
capital and she will inherit money from an uncle. It is
not so much the poverty of the village that repels him,
but the submissiveness of the villagers, and particularly their passive acceptance of Church authority. The
puritanical and intolerant parish priest represents the
life-denying forces in Ireland. He objects to courtship before marriage and breaks up evenings of dancing
and merrymaking that Bryden has organized. Bryden cannot help comparing the "weakness and incompetence" of
the Irish unfavorably with the "modern restlessness and
cold energy" of the Americans. One morning he leaves
for America abruptly, with a great sense of relief,
though he does not admit to himself or Margaret that he
will not return.

Once back in America, Bryden realizes that he
belongs there. He feels a "thrill of home" that he did
not feel in Ireland, and wonders why the smell of the
bar seems "more natural than the smell of fields, and
the roar of crowds more welcome than the silence of the
lake's edge."[11] America is a more satisfactory home for
Bryden as an active, vital man seeking material and emotional fulfillment. Yet his return there does not fully
resolve his inner conflict. After his wife has died and
his children have married, he is haunted not by memories
of his family life but by a memory of Margaret and the
village. Moore suggests in the final paragraph that the
imagination dwells more on what we have lost than on
what we have achieved or possessed.

> There is an unchanging, silent life within
> every man that none knows but himself, and
> his unchanging, silent life was his memory
> of Margaret Dirken. The bar-room was for-
> gotten and all that concerned it, and the
> things he saw most clearly were the green
> hillside, and the bog lake and the rushes
> about it, and the greater lake in the dis-
> tance, and behind it the blue line of wan-
> dering hills.[12]

This image of a remembered landscape, representative of
all the attraction Ireland holds for him, has become
more real than his memories of his American life.

This story, with its careful balance between the two homelands, illustrates beautifully the ambivalence which Moore felt towards Ireland. He implies that even though escape is necessary for economic and emotional survival, the emigrant is haunted by dreams of returning home. His mind retains compelling memories of the beauty and peace of the landscape and the special traditions of Irish life. The insight which Moore captured in this story was absorbed and modified in various ways by later writers.

Although religion is a major factor in both "The Exile" and "Home Sickness," the clergy are not portrayed in depth. The characters of Fr. Maguire and Fr. MacTurnan are rendered more fully, and Moore succeeds in making them appear human in spite of his anticlericalism. Fr. Maguire is zealous, authoritative, and puritanical, but he is humanized by the capacity for remorse and self-criticism that he reveals in conversations with his uncle, Fr. Stafford. Maguire's interference in his parishioners' lives has unfortunate consequences; in "Patchwork," his refusal to marry a young couple because they cannot pay his fee results in their living in sin for one night, and in "The Wedding Feast," his arrangement of an unsuitable marriage between a wild, passionate woman and a dull man results in the woman's rejection of her husband and flight to America.

Fr. Maguire appears at his best in his project of building a new church, which absorbs much of his energy through all four stories about him. His shrewd, materialistic temperament enables him to raise funds and manipulate his workmen effectively. One of Moore's best stories, "The Window," describes Maguire's dealings with Biddy M'Hale, an old woman who donates a stained-glass window to the church and then sees visions in it. Biddy, a deformed spinster, has saved money from raising poultry. She becomes increasingly obsessed with her window and withdraws further and further from reality into a state of visionary ecstasy. The story is similar to a story of Turgenev's, "Living Relics," in which a dying woman, Lukeria, sees visions of Christ comforting her. But Lukeria's temperament is sweet and gentle, while Biddy is as shrewd and obstinate as Maguire himself. Moore's depiction of the battle of wills between Biddy and Maguire over how her money will be spent is a masterpiece of characterization.

The window is an elaborate symbol closely linked to Biddy's own needs and aspirations. Modeled on a picture by Fra Angelico, it shows Christ surrounded by the women who loved him, and the souls of the damned in flames; joy and sorrow are mingled. The blue of the Virgin's cloak is linked to a blue ribbon Biddy used to wear blackberrying as a girl and to a blue cloak she starts wearing to the church. During Mass she hears harp music and singing from the window and sees Christ crowning and embracing her. The vision represents her dream of immortality and compensation for everything she has missed in life.

Moore remarked in a letter that "the old woman who puts up a window in her church and hears the saints singing is intended to represent Ireland."13 Biddy embodies his mixed feelings about the country; on one level, she is an unkempt, crazy old woman regarded mainly as a nuisance by Fr. Maguire and her neighbors, but on another level she attains the spiritual transcendence of the medieval saints. Moore carefully controls the point of view so that Biddy's experience is seen from both the outside and the inside. Though other people cannot understand her happiness, Moore leaves no doubt that her visions are real to her and that she is ecstatically happy. She is typical of those who remain in Ireland--the old, the sick, the feeble-minded--while the healthy young people emigrate. Visionary ecstasy provides a possible way of escape for those who cannot escape physically.

Fr. MacTurnan is also a kind of visionary. His parish is one of the poorest and most desolate in Ireland, and both stories about him concern his impractical schemes for improving the lives of his parishioners. He represents the best type of Irish priest--gentle, compassionate, self-effacing. In "A Letter to Rome," he is disturbed by the frequent emigration of young people. Aware that the clergy live better than anyone else, he has the inspiration to write to the Pope, suggesting that Irish priests be allowed to marry and repopulate the country with Catholics. His isolation has made him more independent of convention than other priests. An ascetic man for whom celibacy is a gratification rather than a sacrifice, MacTurnan is embarrassed and troubled when he thinks of one of his parishioners as a possible wife. The Bishop summons him to explain the letter, but when he sees how naive and sincere MacTurnan is, he remarks kindly, "'You have borne the loneliness of your parish a long while.'"14 Although the tone of the story is gently ironic and humorous, MacTurnan is treated sympathetically, and serves as a counterbalance to the portrayal of Fr. Maguire.

Despite Moore's sympathy for some of his characters and for some aspects of Irish life, the dominant impression we get from The Untilled Field is one of pathos and desolation. This mood is reasserted in "The Wild Goose," the longest story in the collection. Much of it is tediously polemical, but it also contains some fine lyrical passages. The protagonist Ned Carmady, an Irishman who left as a boy, has spent his life engaged in a variety of occupations all over the world. Like James Bryden, he has carried with him an indestructible memory of his native country. He returns to Ireland, courts and marries an Irish girl, and becomes involved in nationalist politics. His marriage eventually fails because he is restless and because his pious Catholic wife is offended by his attacks on the clergy. As his ties with Ireland grow weaker, he decides to leave for South Africa to fight in the Boer War.

At the time Ned is preparing to leave Ireland, the national consciousness is epitomized for him in the song of a shepherd which he hears while wandering in the countryside near his home.

> "A dolorous land of nuns and rosaries!"
> and as if in answer to his words the most
> dolorous melody he had ever heard came
> out of the mist. "The wailing," he said,
> "of an abandoned race." And he wandered
> on calling to the shepherd, but the mist
> was so thick in the hollows that neither
> could find the other.[15]

Later, Ned tells his wife,

> "It is the song of the exile, the cry of
> one driven out into a night of wind and
> rain, a prophetic echo. A mere folk-tune,
> mere nature, raw and unintellectual; and
> these folk-tunes are all that we shall
> have done, and by these, and these alone,
> shall we be remembered."[16]

The tone of melancholy despair in this passage suggests Moore's most characteristic attitude to Ireland.

If we compare the above passages to a similar one from Turgenev's story "The Singers," we immediately see the difference in national feeling between the two writers. In "The Singers," the narrator hears two peasants compete in a singing contest at a local tavern; the one who wins captures the spirit of Russia in his song.

40

Rarely, I confess, have I chanced to hear
such a voice; it was a little overworked,
and it rang as if it were slightly cracked;
at first it even had a hint of something
painful about it, yet there were in it, as
well, an uncounterfeited, profound passion,
and youth, and strength, and sweetness, and
some sort of enticingly heedless sorrowing.
A Russian soul, true and ardent, sounded
and breathed in it, and simply plucked at
your heart, plucked right at its Russian
chords. . . . He sang, and from every sound
of his voice there was wafted something
near and dear and unencompassably vast, as
though the familiar steppe were unrolling
before us, receding into the infinite
distance.[17]

Turgenev and Moore both perceive an intimate relationship between the landscape and the song, but for Turgenev the song evokes a passionate love for Russia and a
feeling that the Russian spirit is youthful and vigorous, whereas for Moore it evokes distaste and a feeling
of abandonment and exile. The image of Ned and the
shepherd calling to each other in the mist but unable
to find each other symbolizes not only Moore's inability
to reconcile himself permanently with Ireland, but also
the essential loneliness of the human condition. The
setting of mist, hills, and bogs provides a suitable
image for this mood of hopelessness; the shepherd's song
is a distillation of many centuries of suffering and
defeat.

Although the quality of Moore's writing in The
Untilled Field is uneven, at his best he achieved the
pure, organic form that succeeding Irish short story
writers would emulate. He introduced a standard of
craftsmanship not found in the work of Carleton and
other earlier Irish fiction writers. Moore took advantage of the flexibility of the short story genre to
experiment with several narrative methods. There is an
oral quality in many of the stories, but some of his
best narrative effects--as in "Home Sickness," for exam-
ple--do not depend on oral techniques. The "models" he
provided for younger writers stimulated technical experimentation and variety.

Moore brought his highly individual outlook to
characteristic Irish themes: religion, nationalism,
attachment to the land, family and community relationships, and exile. The attitudes expressed in The

41

<u>Untilled Field</u> vary from story to story. The short story genre was well suited to conveying Moore's vacillation towards Ireland. A fairly consistent viewpoint does emerge from the collection as a whole, however. In the long run Ned Carmady proves to be the character most closely identifiable with Moore himself, for whom exile was the inevitable choice.

Notes

[1] George Moore, The Untilled Field (Macmillan of Canada: Maclean-Hunter Press, 1931/76), p. xviii.

[2] See Eileen Kennedy, "Turgenev and George Moore's The Untilled Field," English Literature in Transition, 18 (1975), 145-59. See also George Moore in Transition: Letters to T. Fisher Unwin and Lena Milman, 1894-1910, ed. Helmut E. Gerber (Detroit: Wayne State University Press, 1968), chs. 7 and 8.

[3] George Moore, Hail and Farewell: Ave, I (New York and London: D. Appleton, 1920), p. 3.

[4] George Moore in Transition, p. 260.

[5] Brendan Kennelly, "George Moore's Lonely Voices: A Study of his Short Stories," George Moore's Mind and Art, ed. Graham Owens (Edinburgh: Oliver and Boyd, 1968), pp. 153-54.

[6] Herbert Howarth, "Dublin 1899-1911: The Enthusiasms of a Prodigal," in ibid., p. 85.

[7] See George Moore in Transition, pp. 273-79.

[8] Ibid., pp. 247, 249.

[9] Quoted in Kenneth B. Newell, "The 'Artist' Stories in The Untilled Field," English Literature in Transition, 14 (1971), 123.

[10] See The Untilled Field, p. xviii.

[11] Ibid., p. 48.

[12] Ibid., p. 49.

[13] Joseph Hone, The Life of George Moore (New York: Macmillan, 1936), p. 246.

[14] The Untilled Field, p. 148.

[15] Ibid., p. 276.

[16] Ibid., p. 277.

[17] Ivan Turgenev, The Hunting Sketches, tr. Bernard

Guilbert Guerney (New York: New American Library, 1962), pp. 251-52.

Chapter Three

JAMES JOYCE

James Joyce's Dubliners is acknowledged to be a
landmark among modern short story collections, but its
relationship to the Irish short story tradition is not
as widely recognized. Dubliners was written at least
partially in reaction to The Untilled Field and some of
Moore's other works, and in turn Joyce's book affected
the work of younger Irish writers, though not as substantially as we might expect. Within exclusively
urban limits, Joyce treats several of the Irish themes
we have examined in Moore and earlier writers. The
earliest stories of Dubliners were written in 1904,
during the months when Joyce was reaching his decision
to leave Ireland and live permanently in exile. Most of
Dubliners was completed in Trieste in 1905, although
three stories--"Two Gallants," "A Little Cloud," and
"The Dead"--were added later.

Like his protagonist Stephen Dedalus in A Portrait
of the Artist as a Young Man, Joyce had to break his
ties with family, country, and church before he could
attain enough freedom and detachment to proceed with his
creative work. In his letters to Nora Barnacle, written
while he was courting her and making plans to leave the
country, he tries to explain some of the circumstances
of his early life which led to his rejection of Irish
conventions and institutions. He says that he had to
reject the idea of home as well as the accepted social
order and Christianity; his own home life was ruined by
his father's spendthrift habits, and his mother's death
from cancer convinced him that she was a victim of her
family and the "system." He also expresses his hatred
of the Catholic Church and asserts that he "cannot enter
the social order except as a vagabond."[1] The death of
Joyce's mother, which had occurred in August 1903, was
the event which confirmed his resolution to leave Ireland; her disease became symbolic for him of all the
life-denying forces there. In another letter to Nora,
he insists on his need for independence and says of Ireland, "There is no life here--no naturalness or honesty.
People live together in the same houses all their lives
and at the end they are as far apart as ever."[2]

Other factors in Joyce's decision to live abroad
were his incompatibility with contemporary Irish writers
and his hostility to the Irish language revival and the

esthetic ideals of the Renaissance. He admired Yeats's
work but his attitude to the older poet was arrogant
and presumptuous. He refused the role of protégé,
although he did receive some assistance from Yeats,
Lady Gregory, and other Irish literary figures. The
first stories in Dubliners were composed at the suggestion of George Russell, editor of The Irish Homestead,
who wrote Joyce requesting a contribution to the magazine that would be simple and rural and would not shock
the readers. "The Sisters" did not exactly meet
Russell's specifications but he published it anyway in
August, 1904, followed by "Eveline" in September and
"After the Race" in December. The antagonism which
Joyce showed towards Irish writers was particularly
severe towards George Moore. Joyce did not actually
meet Moore during his years in Dublin, and felt hurt
that Moore never invited him to any of his gatherings.
Moore made several derogatory remarks about Joyce's
family background and his early work.

Joyce insisted that in writing Dubliners he had
undertaken something that no Irish writer had attempted
before. In a letter to his brother Stanislaus, he
speculates about the reaction of the Dublin papers to
his stories and says irritably, "Of course do not think
that I consider contemporary Irish writing anything but
ill-written, morally obtuse formless caricature."[3] He
read The Untilled Field in November, 1904, shortly after
leaving Dublin, and if he saw any similarities between
Moore's methods and intentions and his own, he did not
admit them. He wrote to Stanislaus that the book was
"stupid."

> A woman alludes to her husband in the
> confession-box as 'Ned.' Ned thinks &c!
> A lady who has been living for three
> years on the line between Bray and Dublin
> is told by her husband that there is a
> meeting in Dublin at which he must be
> present. She looks up the table to see
> the hours of the trains. This on DW and
> WR where the trains go regularly: this
> after three years. Isn't it rather stupid
> of Moore. And the punctuation! Madonna![4]

Joyce was interested enough in the book to reread it in
September, 1905, but his reaction this time was even
more extreme.

> I read that silly, wretched book of Moore's
> 'The Untilled Field' which the Americans

> found so remarkable for its 'craftsman-
> ship.' O, dear me! It is very dull
> and flat, indeed: and ill-written.[5]

Despite Joyce's refusal to acknowledge the debt, he was
thoroughly familiar not just with The Untilled Field but
with most of Moore's work, and was considerably influenced by it.[6] Though Dubliners may not have been deliberately modeled on The Untilled Field, there are numerous resemblances between the two works.

In a comparison of Joyce's book with Moore's, it
is difficult to distinguish the immediate from the more
distant influences. Some of the similarity between the
two books probably resulted not so much from direct
borrowing as from their common admiration for French
and Russian realistic fiction. From the French Natura-
lists both writers derived their emphasis on seemingly
trivial or sordid facts of daily life. Joyce was particularly attracted to Flaubert. From the Russians the
Irish writers derived the organic form of their stories
as well as their representation of local customs and
national traditions as universally significant.

Although Joyce read Russian literature as widely
and enthusiastically as Moore did, his taste was somewhat different. He found Turgenev too sweet and gentle-
manly, and preferred Lermontov and Tolstoy.[7] (Scholars
have also noted a strong resemblance of mood between
Joyce's stories and Chekhov's, though Joyce said he had
not read Chekhov when he wrote Dubliners.[8]) Nevertheless, Turgenev's The Hunting Sketches, whether directly
or indirectly, had a formative influence on Dubliners.
Joyce seemed to recognize this affinity in later years.
Speaking with a young Irish writer, Arthur Power, in
1921, Joyce compared himself with Turgenev much as Moore
had done in Ave. Joyce advised Power to write in his
own tradition rather than imitate an alien one; all
great writers, Joyce insisted,

> were national first, and it was the inten-
> sity of their own nationalism which made
> them international in the end, as in the
> case of Turgenev. You remember his
> Sportsman's Notebook, how local it was--
> and yet out of that germ he became a great
> international writer. For myself, I always
> write about Dublin, because if I can get
> to the heart of Dublin I can get to the
> heart of all the cities of the world.[9]

47

Dubliners, like The Untilled Field, resembles The Hunting Sketches in its structural connection of a group of stories through a shared location, overlapping characters, and repetition of a central theme. All three writers wanted to achieve a unity that extended beyond the individual stories to the work as a whole, but that did not require the continuous plot and character development of a novel. The works also have in common their impressionistic narrative method and their use of the inconclusive ending.

Joyce's immediate debt to Moore can be seen more clearly in the themes of Dubliners than in its structure or style. Both Dubliners and The Untilled Field portray Ireland as a stagnant or paralyzed country whose citizens lead unproductive, futile lives, both criticize the role of the Irish Church, and both describe efforts of Irishmen to escape. Several scholars have explored in detail the parallels between the two books. Brendan Kennelly concludes that in The Untilled Field "Moore began to examine a certain sickness at the very heart of Irish society which Joyce later examined at far greater depth."[10] Karl Beckson agrees that Moore "provided the groundwork for Dubliners" and "forged a vision of Ireland that anticipated Joyce's in a variety of ways and provided an alternative to the romantic idealism of the Celtic revival."[11]

One significant difference in the themes of the two books is that The Untilled Field expresses a greater optimism about the possibility of escape than does Dubliners. Some characters in Moore's book do manage to escape or transcend the restrictions of Irish life. He offers some hope of release even to characters who remain in Ireland, either through imaginative liberation or through religious ecstasy--as in the case of Biddy M'Hale, the old woman who sees visions of saints in a stained-glass window. Joyce's characters, in contrast, remain inert, trapped, and spiritually torpid.

That Dubliners belongs within the Irish short story tradition is evident not only from Joyce's debt to Moore, but also from his own statements of artistic purpose. His permanent exile and international reputation have sometimes obscured the fact that Dubliners was originally intended as a contribution to Irish literature, for the edification of Irish readers. Joyce made this clear in his correspondence with Grant Richards, with whom he had arranged to publish Dubliners in 1906. Richards had requested some minor alterations of wording to appease the printer, but, in a letter of May, 1906,

Joyce insisted on the need for stylistic precision.

> My intention was to write a chapter of
> the moral history of my country and I
> chose Dublin for the scene because that
> city seemed to me the centre of paraly-
> sis. . . . I have written it for the
> most part in a style of scrupulous mean-
> ness and with the conviction that he is
> a very bold man who dares to alter in
> the presentment, still more to deform,
> whatever he has seen and heard.[12]

A few days later his increasing exasperation led him to
define his purpose further.

> The points on which I have not yielded
> are the points which rivet the book
> together. If I eliminate them what
> becomes of the chapter of the moral his-
> tory of my country? I fight to retain
> them because I believe that in compos-
> ing my chapter of moral history in exactly
> the way I have composed it I have taken
> the first step towards the spiritual
> liberation of my country. Reflect for
> a moment on the history of the literature
> of Ireland as it stands at present written
> in the English language before you condemn
> this genial illusion of mine which, after
> all, has at least served me in the office
> of a candlestick during the writing of the
> book.[13]

In June he wrote to Richards:

> It is not my fault that the odour of
> ashpits and old weeds and offal hangs
> round my stories. I seriously believe
> that you will retard the course of civili-
> zation in Ireland by preventing the Irish
> people from having one good look at them-
> selves in my nicely polished looking-glass.[14]

Richards finally refused to publish Dubliners at that
time, and the book did not appear until 1914.

This correspondence helps to define Joyce's attitude to Ireland during this period of his life. A year
earlier, in a letter to Stanislaus, he had described his
intention in writing Dubliners as at times "plainly

mischievous," and had refused to elaborate on his motives.[15] But in his letters to Richards he presented himself as an Irish writer addressing his countrymen, with the purpose of exposing whatever is false, corrupt, and sterile in their lives in order to liberate them spiritually and advance their civilization. He had sufficient faith in this larger purpose to find in it emotional support during the composition of the stories.

The narrative method of Dubliners involves a careful grouping of the stories and an elaborate symbolic pattern. These techniques reinforce the unity achieved by the common setting and central theme. The stories are grouped into four categories which correspond to the stages of growth in an individual's life: childhood, adolescence, maturity, and public life. There are many repeated images and motifs which link the stories to each other. Struggles of characters to escape their confining circumstances are related to a pattern of directional symbolism that is consistent throughout the collection. Movements eastward suggest a quest for freedom and a fuller life. Moral paralysis is represented not just by physical inaction, but also by aimless circuitous movement and frustration of attempts to escape eastward.[16] A cluster of images is associated with this underlying pattern, as Florence Walzl has demonstrated.

> Though the symbols are numerous and complex, those imaging paralysis are recognizable in situations of immobility, insensibility and arrest. Also, since Joyce views paralysis as a kind of living death, or rather succession of deaths, emotional, psychological, or spiritual, details of darkness, cold, night, winter, and blindness image this process. . . . In contrast, the motif of life, which for Joyce meant vital action or escape, is symbolized by images of growth, light, motion, water, or flight.[17]

Other related symbolic patterns include images of enclosure (dark rooms, coffins, etc.) versus open space, images of color and music, an elaborate motif of religious and sacramental imagery, and abundant allusions to Irish history and mythology. The effect of this careful organization in Dubliners is an extraordinary unity not matched by any other collection of Irish stories before or afterwards.

The narrative viewpoint of Dubliners is generally detached and ironic, though in some stories (notably the stories of childhood) the mood is more subjective. As in Moore's stories, Joyce's narrator regards the characters with varying degrees of sympathy. He observes rather than judges them, rendering their thoughts and feelings sensitively while at the same time maintaining his ironic distance. The language and style are appropriate for the character being described. Joyce managed to achieve simultaneously a scrupulous realism and a complex symbolism. He did not try to create the effect of a human voice speaking to an audience, as Moore did. The style of Dubliners bears little resemblance to oral storytelling. Another technical difference is that Joyce treats time in an extremely compressed manner. Moore's stories often encompass a relatively long period of months or even years, suggesting the effects of passing time, while most of Joyce's stories take place in one day or less, stressing the significance of the present moment and creating an effect of timelessness.

Joyce's arrangement of his stories into groups reflecting the stages of normal human growth contributes to the irony of Dubliners, since his characters' growth has been arrested or distorted. The stories of childhood ("The Sisters," "An Encounter," "Araby") describe a sensitive and lonely boy's ambivalence towards the paralyzing forces that threaten to engulf him. These stories, the only ones in Dubliners narrated in the first person, are more subjective than the later stories; Joyce can partially identify with the boy. Like Ulick in Moore's story "So On He Fares," a fatherless boy who leaves home to escape his mother's unloving cruelty, Joyce's unnamed boy protagonist lacks a warm family life. An orphan, he lives with an aunt and uncle with whom he has little in common.

The original Irish Homestead version of "The Sisters" is merely a brief, self-contained sketch, but the final revised version incorporates themes and motifs that are developed throughout Dubliners, and it serves as a fitting prologue to the book.[18] In this story the boy's complex reactions to the death of an old priest, Fr. Flynn, reveal the diseased spiritual condition of Dublin.

Because the boy is more sensitive and intelligent than those around him, he sees the inadequacy of their conventional values and rejects them. He is angered by the opinions of his uncle and a family friend, Old

51

Cotter, that his friendship with Fr. Flynn is unhealthy
and that he should play with boys his own age, exercise,
and take cold baths. In response to this disapproval,
the boy has become reticent and introverted, determined
not to betray his true feelings. It was his need for
an intellectual companion and mentor that attracted him
to Fr. Flynn, but the priest's moral sickness threatens
to damage his psyche more deeply than the other characters could do.

Joyce's narrative method involves raising a question at the beginning about Fr. Flynn's condition, with
Old Cotter's remark that there is something "queer" and
"peculiar" about him, and then dropping hints and fragments of information without filling in the gaps. The
reader's comprehension parallels that of the boy himself, as he probes his own memories and dreams about the
priest as well as the conversations of other people
about him. The words of the priest's sister at the
wake confirm that he actually did have a mental breakdown brought on by guilt over breaking a chalice, was
found laughing madly in a confession box, and was
retired from his duties. The priest's illness is physical as well as mental, and little distinction is made
between the two. His paralysis is the final stage of a
long deterioration and is symbolic of the moral and
spiritual paralysis of all the Dubliners. His physical
repulsiveness, which Joyce depicts graphically, mirrors
his moral repulsiveness.

Since Joyce leaves so much unexplained in the
story, there has been much critical disagreement about
the fundamental nature of Fr. Flynn's illness and his
relationship with the boy. Some critics have suggested
that there may be a homosexual element, but this does
not seem to be a major factor, as it is in "An Encounter." The priest is also linked symbolically with sim-
ony (worldliness), though we are not told whether he
was actually guilty of it, and with the gnomon, a geo-
metrical figure suggestive of a lack or incompleteness
in his character. What seems most important is his
overscrupulousness about his priestly duties, and his
attempt to instill this in the boy. With Jansenistic
severity he reviews intricate doctrinal issues and questions the boy on them until he becomes confused and
tongue-tied. Fr. Flynn's obsession with literal doctrine is a perversion of his true spiritual role as a
priest. As Edward Brandabur points out, the relationship has a destructive, sado-masochistic quality. "The
boy seeks the characteristically human activities of
knowledge and friendship; his relationship with the

52

priest corrupts both activities and dehumanizes him."[19]
The boy is strongly tempted to acquiesce in the "pleasant and vicious" state of paralysis, as his dream
about hearing the priest's confession implies, but he
is also drawn to active fulfilling life. His relief at
the priest's death is the relief of a still healthy
nature escaping the domination of a sick one. "I felt
even annoyed at discovering in myself a sensation of
freedom as if I had been freed from something by his
death."[20]

The underlying symbolic patterns in the story
enrich its meaning and connect it with the stories that
follow. In the system of directional symbolism the relative absence of movement, not just eastward but in any
direction, images the boy's dependent passivity, though
he does dream of visiting a distant oriental place.
His quest for freedom becomes more active in "An Encounter," when he journeys eastward towards the Pigeon
House, and in "Araby," when he visits an oriental
bazaar. Several images of enclosure are associated with
Fr. Flynn (his small, dark, fireless room, the confession box, the coffin) as are the colors green and brown,
which have negative connotations throughout Dubliners.
In contrast, cheerful images such as sunlight, Christmas, and bright theatrical posters suggest the free,
joyful existence the boy seeks. The chalice which the
priest breaks and which lies "idle" on his breast in
death represents the failure of his vocation and is connected with the secular eucharist of sherry and crackers
which the boy is offered at the wake.

Fr. Flynn is the only priest in Dubliners characterized in detail, but the priests who are mentioned
briefly--in "Araby," "Ivy Day in the Committee Room,"
and "Grace"--seem equally inert and deteriorated. By
comparison Moore's priests appear relatively sane and
healthy. Both Fr. Maguire and Fr. MacTurnan are active,
energetic men, comfortable in their vocations, ascetic
and dedicated. Though Fr. Maguire has many faults, he
is not degenerate, as Fr. Flynn is. To get a more complete idea of Joyce's attitude towards the clergy, we
must look not in Dubliners but in his novels.

The characters in the stories of adolescence
("Eveline," "After the Race," "Two Gallants," "The
Boarding House") are not teenagers but young adults trying to discover their mature role in life. They lack
inner strength and conviction, however, and remain
arrested at the adolescent stage of development. Joyce
views these characters with much greater ironic distance

than the child characters. Of the four stories, "Eveline" deals with the conflict most characteristic of Irish national experience, the choice between remaining in Ireland or emigrating in search of a better life.

"Eveline," written while Joyce was preparing to leave Ireland, draws on several details of his own life and in some ways parallels his own situation. It was probably also influenced by Moore's novel Evelyn Innes and its sequel Sister Teresa, which describe a young woman's search for freedom.[21] Eveline is portrayed at a crucial moment in her life, when she must decide whether to run away from Ireland with Frank, her suitor-- an act necessary for her to develop into a mature woman--or to remain trapped at home to care for her widowed father and younger brothers and sisters. Joyce carefully delineates the inner conflicts which cause her indecision, so that the significance of her final choice can be fully realized. In contrast to Nora Barnacle, who did run away with her lover James Joyce, and to the characters in Moore's emigration stories, Eveline in the end cannot summon the strength to overcome the paralyzing influence of her environment. The story is told in the third person from Eveline's point of view, and the vocabulary and idiom are consistent with her thought processes. There is no authorial intrusion until the very end.

As in "The Sisters," images of arrest and enclosure are abundant. Eveline's small, gloomy bourgeois house symbolizes the confinement and suffocation of her character. Much of her inner vacillation takes place as she is sitting by a window, watching the evening grow darker. This posture suggests the paralysis which has overtaken her life, her inability to act on her dreams. The falling darkness foreshadows the destruction of her hopes. "Her time was running out but she continued to sit by the window curtain, inhaling the odour of dusty cretonne."[22] The dust which pervades Eveline's house is a recurrent image of emotional and spiritual death. The house is anachronistic; it has not kept pace with the changes that have taken place in the neighborhood, and it images Eveline's inability to outgrow her past.

Gradually Joyce exposes the meaninglessness of the bonds which tie Eveline to an almost intolerable home life. Her mother is dead and her father threatens her in his fits of drunken violence. None of her brothers or sisters can protect her from him. She clings to the familiar, not because it gives her what she needs, but because she cannot face the unknown. Home at least offers a certain degree of security, and she has a few happy childhood memories that she cannot relinquish. She has also let herself be bound by a promise to her dead mother to keep the home together.

Eventually it is revealed that Eveline's mother went insane and died because of the destructive conditions of her life. As Eveline remembers what her mother's life was like, she experiences a moment of terror which compels her to leave the window and go to the quay. (The quay is east of Dublin, in keeping with the directional symbolism.)

> She stood up in a sudden impulse of terror. Escape! She must escape! Frank would save her. He would give her life, perhaps love, too. But she wanted to live. Why should she be unhappy? She had a right to happiness. Frank would take her in his arms, fold her in his arms. He would save her.[23]

Frank, an open-hearted, manly sailor, has offered her love, respectability, and a new home in Buenos Aires ("good air," in contrast to the dusty air of Ireland). Joyce's portrayal of Frank suggests that Eveline would have a real chance for happiness with him. As in other stories in Dubliners, images of ships, the sea, and travel represent adventure and a renewal of life. But at the last minute, when Eveline must board the ship, she holds back. She clings to her sterile religious faith for guidance, and asks God not to give her courage to live, but to show her her "duty." She cannot take the necessary risk. "All the seas of the world tumbled about her heart. He was drawing her into them: he would drown her."[24] The metaphor implies that she fears sexual experience as well as the uncertainty of a new life.

Despite her anguish, Eveline's inability to break from her past and strive for maturity dehumanizes her. She has evaded her own moral responsibility and surrendered to external orthodoxy. At the end of the story, Joyce shifts the point of view so that we see her from the outside, as she would look to an observer. "She set her white face to him, passive, like a helpless animal. Her eyes gave him no sign of love or farewell or recognition."[25] The sympathy which the reader feels for her during most of the story is destroyed at the end by the harshness of the author's comment. Once she has ceased her struggle to escape, Eveline's moral nature no longer interests us.

The irresolution of the characters in the stories of adolescence becomes stagnation in the stories of adult life ("A Little Cloud," "Counterparts," "Clay," "A Painful Case"). These characters, deeply entrenched in their routines of home and work, have a chronic sense of frustration and unfulfillment. They struggle briefly to escape, but without success. The characters in "A Little Cloud" and "A Painful Case" have greater insight into their situations than do the characters in the other two stories, but they all remain paralyzed.

"A Little Cloud," written in 1906, was the last story added to Dubliners except for "The Dead" (1907). It reflects a somewhat different attitude towards Ireland from the attitude presented in "Eveline," though both stories evoke a mood of frustration and paralysis. Little Chandler, a law-clerk with an undeveloped penchant for literature, resembles the dreamy, ineffectual clerks of Gogol and other Russian writers. There is also a more immediate prototype for him in Moore's story "The Clerk's Quest," one of the few urban stories in The Untilled Field. Both stories begin with the clerk sitting at his desk by a window, bogged down by his daily routine.[26]

Like Eveline and many other characters in Dubliners, Little Chandler experiences a crisis in his life which briefly offers hope of escape but in the end merely deepens his sense of entrapment. He meets an old friend, Gallaher, who has become a successful journalist in London and has returned to Dublin for a short visit. The meeting stimulates Little Chandler to daydream about escaping to London (east of Dublin) and beginning a distinguished career as a poet. When he meets Gallaher later in a pub, he realizes that his friend has become vulgar and lewd. The London world is not necessarily superior to the Dublin world. Emboldened by the whiskey he has been drinking, Little Chandler asserts his masculinity; he taunts Gallaher for his failure to marry and boasts of his own wife and child. But after he leaves Gallaher and returns to his small house, we realize that it is, like Eveline's house, a prison. He is trapped by financial obligations and oppressed by his nagging, hostile wife. His movements around Dublin have been roughly circular, and his quest to move eastward has failed.

The narrator's viewpoint in this story is at the same time more omniscient and more sympathetic than in

"Eveline." We are given no details of Eveline's appearance, but we see Little Chandler from the outside as well as the inside. Physical description portrays him as vain, fastidious, and somewhat effeminate. His appearance is consistent with his personality. He has a rudimentary capacity for creative response, but he is immature and his imaginative powers are slight and undeveloped.

Little Chandler's relationship to his surroundings is one of almost perpetual discomfort. The streets of Dublin make him anxious and ill-at-ease; although he sometimes tries to overcome his timidity, his efforts are ineffectual, and he remains isolated.

> It was his habit to walk swiftly in the
> street even by day and whenever he found
> himself in the city late at night he hur-
> ried on his way apprehensively and exci-
> tedly. Sometimes, however, he courted
> the causes of his fear. He chose the
> darkest and narrowest streets and, as he
> walked boldly forward, the silence that
> was spread about his footsteps troubled
> him, the wandering silent figures troubled
> him; and at times a sound of low fugitive
> laughter made him tremble like a leaf.[27]

Little Chandler is a stranger in his own city, unable to participate in its hidden, instinctual life and unable to escape. His fantasy about becoming a poet in London gives him a brief sense of superiority over his fellow citizens, but it also reveals the triteness of his mind. He imagines himself a member of the Celtic school and his self-praise is expressed as a series of clichés that parody the ideals of the Renaissance. To the reader he appears as an absurd, pathetic figure.

Little Chandler is even more uncomfortable in Corless', the fashionable pub where he has arranged to meet Gallaher, than he is in the streets. The atmosphere of noise and bustle confuses him. His habits are abstemious, and the whiskey and strong cigar that Gallaher gives him go quickly to his head. His spirit of adventure begins to sour as he realizes how vulgar and shallow Gallaher is, and his puritanical nature is offended by his friend's lewd stories about European cities. Roused by so many unaccustomed stimuli, Little Chandler experiences a moment of intense personal crisis.

> He felt acutely the contrast between his
> own life and his friend's, and it seemed
> to him unjust. Gallaher was his inferior
> in birth and education. He was sure that
> he could do something better than his
> friend had ever done, or could ever do,
> something higher than mere tawdry journa-
> lism if he only got the chance. What was
> it that stood in his way? His unfortunate
> timidity! He wished to vindicate himself
> in some way, to assert his manhood.[28]

His belittlement of Gallaher's bachelorhood is an attempt to prove himself the better man, but he succeeds
only in making himself look ridiculous. His timidity
is a form of emotional paralysis that he will never
overcome.

The scene at Little Chandler's house provides a
deflating contrast with his earlier fantasies; we realize he is incapable of a genuine relationship with
anyone. His domineering wife is angry with him for coming home late and forgetting to stop at the store, and
she leaves him in charge of the baby while she goes out.
Everything in the house looks mean to him, and resent-
fully he wonders if it is too late to escape from his
house and go to London like Gallaher. He tries to read
a juvenile poem of Byron's in one of the books that he
has kept since his bachelor days, but his poetic mood
is destroyed by the baby's crying. The poem suggests
an ironic resemblance between Little Chandler's house
and the "narrow cell" or grave where the poet's beloved
lies. Little Chandler's once-romantic feeling for his
wife has also turned cold. As the child's crying dis-
tracts him, he realizes that he is a "prisoner for
life"; his rebellion exhausts itself in a scream of impotent rage at the child, followed by surrender and
remorse as his wife returns, reprimands him with hatred
in her eyes, and turns her attention to soothing the
child.

Little Chandler is a more sympathetic character
than Eveline. Perhaps because he had been living in
exile for two years when he wrote "A Little Cloud,"
Joyce does not indicate in this story that mere physical escape from Ireland will bring fulfillment, as he
does in "Eveline." Gallaher has become even more shallow and crude during his years in London. Despite his
moral paralysis, Little Chandler is clearly superior to
Gallaher in refinement and sensitivity. Little Chandler also differs from Eveline in that escape offers her

a real chance for love and happiness, while his dream of escape is unrealistic from the start, as he lacks the talent to become a poet and is already caught in an unhappy marriage. He does not regress to the level of a "helpless animal," as Eveline does, but remains acutely aware of his failings. Since he is more irrevocably trapped and more fully human than Eveline, we feel greater compassion for him.

The stories of Irish public life deal with several of its most characteristic aspects: politics and nationalism in "Ivy Day in the Committee Room," cultural activity (concerts) in "A Mother," and alcoholism and religion in "Grace." All of these subjects are brought together and combined with the more personal subjects of love and marriage in the superb final story, "The Dead." Whether it is considered apart from or in conjunction with the rest of Dubliners, "The Dead" must be judged one of the finest short stories in any language.

"The Dead" reflects even more than "A Little Cloud" the change that had gradually taken place in Joyce's attitude to Ireland. Exile had softened his intransigence. In a letter to Stanislaus written in September, 1906, he suggests that his condemnation may have been too harsh, since he has not reproduced in Dubliners any of the attractive qualities of Dublin, such as its insularity and hospitality. He also praises the natural beauty of Ireland. Although Joyce continues the letter by saying he could not rewrite Dubliners in a different spirit from the one that originally inspired him, his comments reveal a growing ambivalence.[29] In "The Dead," he partially compensates for the harshness of earlier stories by depicting traditional Irish hospitality, by praising life in the West of Ireland, and by allowing Gabriel Conroy to achieve a sense of identity with his country.

The scope of the story is broader than that of earlier stories in Dubliners; Gabriel has a greater intelligence and capacity for self-awareness than any previous character. Like several other characters, he is portrayed away from the familiar atmosphere of his own home, in a special situation which produces a crisis in his life. The story takes place in three settings: the annual dance at the home of Gabriel's aunts; the journey afterwards through the streets to the hotel where Gabriel and Gretta, his wife, have decided to spend the night; and the scene at the hotel when Gabriel, overcome by desire for his wife, learns that she is thinking not of him but of Michael Furey, a former suitor who died because of his love for her. The shock precipitates a moment of vision in which Gabriel escapes from the limitations of his ego, sees his true relationship to all other men, and transcends the loneliness that he has experienced.

Most of the story is narrated in the third person from Gabriel's point of view, although some of the earliest incidents take place in his absence. The first few paragraphs are narrated from an extremely restricted point of view, that of Lily, the young domestic servant. Soon after Gabriel arrives we begin to see things through his eyes, though we do not identify with him completely until the end. This shift in point of view provides a transition from the other stories in Dubliners. Lily thinks in clichés and cannot see beyond the limits of her everyday life. Gabriel's perspective, in contrast, eventually broadens to include the whole universe.

Most of the party guests are similar to characters in Joyce's earlier stories—culturally backward, materialistic, addicted to eating and drinking. Yet there is an atmosphere of festive warmth and hospitality that is lacking in earlier stories; almost everyone is genuinely enjoying himself. Gabriel feels like an outsider, however, and is ill-at-ease during most of the party. As a teacher and intellectual he feels superior to the ordinary people around him but also fears that he will be misunderstood by them and appear foolish. He is enclosed in his condescending egotism but is not secure.

Gabriel's conversation with Miss Ivors, a nationalistic teacher, is particularly upsetting to him because she is more candid than the other guests and challenges some of his assumptions about the cultural inferiority of Ireland. She chides him for publishing a review in a pro-British newspaper, and invites him to visit the Aran Islands the following summer instead of going on a cycling tour of the continent, as he has planned. When she accuses him of not taking enough interest in his own heritage, he bursts out rudely, "'I'm sick of my own country, sick of it!'"[30] Gabriel's alienation is not limited to the party but characterizes his whole attitude to Irish life.

References to other places and other times as preferable to the present place and time are frequent in the story. At times during the evening Gabriel feels a strong impulse to escape elsewhere. He worries particularly about the after-dinner speech he has to make, and as dinnertime approaches he withdraws to a window:

> Gabriel's warm trembling fingers tapped
> the cold pane of the window. How cool it
> must be outside! How pleasant it would
> be to walk out alone, first along by the
> river and then through the park! The
> snow would be lying on the branches of
> the trees and forming a bright cap on
> the top of the Wellington Monument.31

This physical image of escape into cool solitude is
repeated once more just before he begins the speech. In
addition to physical escape there are other forms of
evasion in the story. Gabriel also escapes the present
situation by daydreaming frequently about the past--his
boyhood, his dead mother, and his marriage.

Preoccupation with other places and times, and particularly with the past, characterizes not just Gabriel
but virtually everyone at the party. The conversation
often turns to the superiority of the past over the
present. For example, when the guests are discussing
opera during dinner, most of them agree that older singers were better than the contemporary ones. Frequent
references to death and dead people throughout the story
contribute to the general feeling that a superior, irre-
coverable past is intruding on the present.

Gabriel succeeds in capturing this feeling in his
trite and sentimental speech. Comparing the new "skeptical" and "thought-tormented" generation to the older
one (he has Miss Ivors' rude early departure in mind) he
says that the newer generation lacks humanity, hospitality, and kindly humor, and that the present age is "less
spacious" than the earlier one. But, he continues, it
is debilitating to brood too much on memories. "We have
all of us living duties and living affections which
claim, and rightly claim, our strenuous endeavors."32
Gabriel's speech becomes ironic in relation to the rest
of the story, since he does not follow his own advice
but allows himself to be intimidated by his wife's past.

The journey to the hotel in the early morning, a
physical release from the atmosphere of the party, contributes to Gabriel's emotional release. Not realizing
that she has been roused by memories of her former
lover, Gabriel recalls his wife's distant grace and
beauty as she stood on the stairs listening to Bartell
D'Arcy, the tenor, sing "The Lass of Aughrim." Gabriel
plans to make love to her passionately in the hotel.

61

The description of the gloomy, foreboding dawn contradicts the gaiety of mood, however, and anticipates his
later disillusionment.

The hotel represents for Gabriel a chance for new
adventure, for renewal of his love affair with his wife.
"As they stood at the hotel door, he felt that they had
escaped from their lives and duties, escaped from home
and friends and run away together with wild and radiant
hearts to a new adventure."[33] The small, dark hotel
room, illuminated only by a shaft of light from the window, recalls the tomblike houses of "The Sisters," "Eveline," "A Little Cloud," and other stories, yet has larger implications. It suggests, besides a tomb, an
internalization of experience, a transition from the
social to the personal realm. This constriction of setting is followed by a rapid expansion of the boundaries
of Gabriel's mental world, as his wife's revelation
makes him see his own role as petty and ludicrous.

The ending of "The Dead" (which is much indebted to
George Moore's Vain Fortune[34]) is full of ambiguities
and has been interpreted in a variety of ways. Florence
Walzl points out that her predecessors tended to view
the ending in one of two ways; those who analyzed the
story in context with the rest of Dubliners saw Gabriel's vision as a negative revelation of his own spiritual death, the culmination of the paralysis theme,
while those who analyzed the story separately saw the
vision more positively, as an experience of maturation
and rebirth. Ms. Walzl argues, mainly through an analysis of imagery in "The Dead" and in the rest of Dubliners, that Joyce deliberately made the ending ambiguous.
Referring to Gabriel's vision, she asserts, "Paradoxical
images of arrest and movement, darkness and light, cold
and warmth, blindness and sight, are used in this conclusion to recall both the central paralysis-death theme
of Dubliners as a collection and the rebirth-life theme
of 'The Dead' as a narrative." One example of this
ambiguity can be found in the directional symbolism. In
one sense, it is consistent with earlier stories; the
east (Continent) is the direction of escape for Gabriel
and the west is associated with the graveyard and death.
But "it soon becomes evident that Joyce is developing,
side by side with this east-west symbolic pattern,
another one that is opposite in certain ways. In this
system the east suggests the old, traditional, and
effete; the west, the new, primitive, and vital."[35] The
ambiguity is also developed in the contrasting characters, Gabriel and Michael, who confront each other in
the final vision. According to Ms. Walzl, Gabriel is an

"everyman" figure in many ways similar to earlier protagonists in Dubliners. Michael represents the traditional Gaelic Ireland that Gabriel has dismissed and
rejected. In one sense Ireland has betrayed Gabriel,
as she betrayed earlier characters; in another sense
Gabriel, the Dubliner, has betrayed Ireland. More universal symbols like the association of Michael and
Gabriel with archangels and the ubiquitous snow confirm
the ambiguous roles of the two characters. Ms. Walzl
concludes that Joyce constructed the "great final ambiguity" of the ending in order to "resolve the problem in
logic which arose from his changed viewpoints" towards
Ireland.36 Her argument, though persuasive, is unsatis-
fying, since it allows two radically different and
incompatible readings of the story. We may also question her identification of Gabriel as an "everyman" figure, since he emerges as a unique and intelligent personality.

It is possible to see "The Dead" as a suitable and
consistent finale for Dubliners without seeing Gabriel's
vision as a completely negative one of paralysis and
spiritual death. The dominant effect of the snow imagery at the end of the story is that it silently but
inexorably forms connections--among parts of Ireland
(moribund Dublin and the vital West) and among all the
souls of men, living and dead--creating an almost mystical vision of human interdependence and involvement.
Gabriel's paralysis, like that of other characters in
Dubliners, makes him withhold himself from intimacy and
from full participation in the here-and-now. Just as
the other characters in Dubliners are enclosed and withdrawn, Gabriel encloses himself in a manipulative egotism which is really a form of evasion. As Homer Brown
suggests, Gabriel's attempt to manipulate his wife's
feelings is the culmination of a series of efforts
throughout the evening to exploit other people, to make
them subservient to his ego. His failure with Gretta
forces him to recognize the separate inner lives of
other people.

> Gabriel's discovery of other people and his
> new sympathy for them is an imaginative
> identification with their thoughts and feel-
> ings. Paradoxically the breakdown of his
> illusion of control over them is a break-
> down of the barriers between them and leads
> to a new mode of knowledge.37

The painful "death" that Gabriel experiences at the end
of the story is the surrender of the egotistical

illusion of self-sufficiency. His identity merges with the real world which he has stood aloof from. The West of Ireland and his "journey westward" become symbolic of the primal instinctive life he shares with all other men, living and dead. The absence of irony and identification of the narrator with Gabriel at the end of the story are further evidence of this resolution.

Gabriel achieves not spiritual death but spiritual liberation and maturity, the condition which Joyce told Grant Richards he envisioned for Ireland as a whole. The relief of the boy in "The Sisters" at the priest's death, Eveline's impulse to escape so that she can give and accept love, and Little Chandler's fantasy of escaping to a place where he can express his creative self are incomplete stages in the process. The stories of childhood and "The Dead" are the most subjective stories in Dubliners, probably because they are the only stories in which the protagonists are still capable of growth. The narrator identifies fairly closely with the child but regards the adolescent and adult characters with varying degrees of ironic detachment. Gabriel himself is regarded ironically until he succeeds in escaping from the limitations of his ego, accepting the reality and separateness of other people, and acknowledging the mortality which everyone shares and which gives value to moments of intense and passionate life. Gabriel's liberation is experienced not as joyful release but as painful awareness followed by resignation; Joyce suggests that the process of maturation is a difficult one, and that escape from egotism also involves acceptance of our insignificance and eventual annihilation.

In examining the paralysis within areas of Irish life such as nationalism, religion, the family, and marriage, Moore and Joyce agree on several of its causes. They both regard the influence of the past on the present as deadening and view the circumstances of Irish history as peculiar and debilitating. Both criticize the role of Irish Catholicism in suppressing instinctive vitality, though the criticism is more explicit in Moore's stories than in Joyce's. Both usually see Irish family life and marriage as empty of real warmth and love. As in the case of many earlier writers, their feelings toward Ireland are ambivalent, but they both finally reject the country and regard its future as hopeless. In their stories as in their lives, the need for some form of escape is pervasive and urgent. Failure to escape results in waste of human potential.

As has been suggested, there are also some

important differences between Moore's stories and Joyce's. Although both writers see Ireland as a desolate, lonely country, in Moore's stories fulfillment is possible, either through emigration or through a rich spiritual existence within Ireland that compensates for the loneliness. In most of Joyce's stories fulfillment is not possible; the characters are too trapped to emigrate, and Dublin is devoid of spiritual compensations. Only in "The Dead" does a character achieve genuine release. Gabriel Conroy reaches a level of self-transcendence attained by few characters in literature. His vision takes him mentally far beyond the particular Irish environment that formed his character.

A more obvious difference between the two writers is in the level of craftsmanship they achieved. Dubliners is regarded as a modern masterpiece, while The Untilled Field is seldom read except by scholars. The term "organic form," while appropriate for Moore, does not really do justice to the elaborate patterning and symbolism of Joyce's stories. As his style became more and more intricate and allusive, he found the short story too confining a genre. After "The Dead" he stopped writing stories and devoted himself to his increasingly complex novels.

Despite the substantial influence which Dubliners had on short story development in other countries, the Irish story writers who followed Joyce often found his methods uncongenial. They tended to reject as too extreme his view of Ireland's paralysis and his exclusively urban perspective, and though they sometimes imitated his techniques, they usually preferred a style that was conversational rather than heavily symbolic. They seldom attempted to establish the kinds of explicit interconnections among stories that both Moore and Joyce had used to unify their collections. Nevertheless, Dubliners set a high standard against which later Irish short story writers had to measure their work.

Notes

[1] James Joyce, _Letters_, II, ed. Richard Ellmann (London: Faber and Faber, 1966), p. 48.

[2] Ibid., p. 53.

[3] Ibid., p. 99.

[4] Ibid., p. 71.

[5] Ibid., p. 111.

[6] See B. K. Scott, "Joyce's Schooling in the Field of George Moore," _Eire-Ireland_, 9, no. 4 (1974), 117-41.

[7] Richard Ellmann, _James Joyce_ (New York: Oxford University Press, 1959), pp. 215, 217.

[8] Ibid., p. 171. See also T. O. Beachcroft, _The Modest Art: A Survey of the Short Story in English_ (London: Oxford University Press, 1968), pp. 179-80, and Marvin Magalaner and Richard M. Kain, "Dubliners and the Short Story," _James Joyce's Dubliners: A Critical Handbook_, eds. James R. Baker and Thomas F. Staley (Belmont, Ca.: Wadsworth, 1969), pp. 19-23.

[9] Quoted in Ellmann, p. 520.

[10] Brendan Kennelly, "George Moore's Lonely Voices: A Study of his Short Stories," _George Moore's Mind and Art_, ed. Graham Owens (Edinburgh: Oliver and Boyd, 1968), p. 159.

[11] Karl Beckson, "Moore's _The Untilled Field_ and Joyce's _Dubliners_: The Short Story's Intricate Maze," _English Literature in Transition_, 15 (1972), 291. See also Eileen Kennedy, "Moore's Untilled Field and Joyce's Dubliners," _Eire-Ireland_, 5, no. 3 (1970), 81-89, and John Raymond Hart, "Moore on Joyce: The Influence of _The Untilled Field_ on _Dubliners_," _Dublin Magazine_, 10, no. 2 (1973), 61-76.

[12] _Letters_, II, p. 134.

[13] Quoted in Ellmann, p. 230.

[14] Quoted in ibid., p. 230.

[15] _Letters_, II, p. 99.

[16] See Brewster Ghiselin, "The Unity of Dubliners," Twentieth Century Interpretations of Dubliners: A Collection of Critical Essays, ed. Peter K. Garrett (Englewood Cliffs, N.J.: Prentice-Hall, 1968), p. 58.

[17] Florence L. Walzl, "Pattern of Paralysis in Joyce's Dubliners: A Study of the Original Framework," College English, 22 (1960-61), 223.

[18] See Marvin Magalaner, Time of Apprenticeship: The Fiction of Young James Joyce (London: Abelard-Schuman, 1959), pp. 72-87.

[19] Edward Brandabur, "The Sisters," Dubliners: Text, Criticism, and Notes, eds. Robert Scholes and A. Walton Litz (New York: Viking, 1969), p. 341.

[20] Dubliners, p. 12.

[21] See Albert J. Solomon, "The Backgrounds of Eveline," Eire-Ireland, 6, no. 3 (1971), 23-38.

[22] Dubliners, p. 39.

[23] Ibid., p. 40.

[24] Ibid., p. 41.

[25] Ibid.

[26] See Scott, pp. 129-30.

[27] Dubliners, p. 72.

[28] Ibid., p. 80.

[29] Letters, II, p. 166.

[30] Dubliners, p. 189.

[31] Ibid., p. 192.

[32] Ibid., p. 204.

[33] Ibid., p. 215.

[34] Ellmann, p. 260.

[35] Florence L. Walzl, "Gabriel and Michael: The Conclusion of 'The Dead,'" in Dubliners, p. 431.

[36] Ibid., p. 443.

[37] Homer Obed Brown, James Joyce's Early Fiction:
The Biography of a Form (Cleveland and London: Press of
Case Western Reserve University, 1972), p. 99.

Chapter Four

SEUMAS O'KELLY

Seumas O'Kelly and Daniel Corkery are both unjustly
neglected writers whose work contributed significantly
to the evolution of the Irish short story. Committed
nationalists, they stayed in Ireland and worked actively
for Irish independence. Their stories represent a radical shift in outlook from those of Moore and Joyce.
They introduced to the Irish short story a mood of
acceptance of Irish life and affection for Irish peasants that recalls the affection of much earlier writers
like Carleton and Turgenev for their people.

The stories of O'Kelly have a distinctive charm
and gently ironic humor that anticipate in many ways
the stories of Frank O'Connor. O'Kelly's love for the
peasants, traditions, and landscape of Ireland is tempered by a realistic awareness of the hardship and loneliness of Irish life. His best-known story is his masterpiece, "The Weaver's Grave," but he wrote several
others that deserve to be ranked with the best in Irish
literature.

O'Kelly, whose exact birth-date is unknown, was
slightly older than Joyce but wrote most of his stories
several years after Dubliners was completed. The son of
a grain-merchant, O'Kelly grew up in Loughrea, a small
town in Galway. His formal education was limited, but
he learned Irish and read widely on his own. The influence of his native surroundings was profound, as Anne
Clune points out. "O'Kelly's youth, spent in the vicin-
ity of the Clanrickarde estate and the poor lands of
East Galway had given him an intense awareness of poverty, deprivation, and the evils of emigration and depopu-
lation."[1] As a young man, O'Kelly developed an interest
in journalism, which he saw as a means of effecting the
reform and regeneration of Ireland. He became editor
of a newspaper in Cork and, after brief stints with several papers in Kildare and Dublin, eventually succeeded
Arthur Griffith as editor of the Sinn Fein newspaper
Nationality, published in Dublin. His health had been
poor for several years as a result of rheumatic fever,
and in 1918 he suffered a heart attack and died during
a riot at the newspaper office. A very good-natured and
popular man, he was given a hero's funeral.

Four volumes of O'Kelly's short stories have been

published: a slight early volume, By the Stream of Killmeen (1906); Waysiders (1917); and two posthumous volumes, The Golden Barque and the Weaver's Grave (1919) and Hillsiders (1921). He also published a volume of fantasy tales, The Leprechaun of Killmeen (1918). The publication dates do not necessarily reflect the order of composition; the stories in Hillsiders, for example, were first published serially in 1909, and Waysiders and The Golden Barque combine early and late work. In addition to stories he wrote novels (The Lady of Deerpark, 1917, and Wet Clay, 1922), poetry, and plays, several of which were produced at the Abbey Theater. His premature death prevented his full development as an artist, and the quality of his work is uneven.

That O'Kelly's best work was done in the short story form indicates his need for refuge from the pressures of political involvement. Like many Irish writers before and after him, he could not successfully express his artistic gifts until he withdrew from public controversies. Eamon Grennan sees O'Kelly as a man with two voices, public and private. The private voice was expressed mainly in his stories, the public in his journalism and at times in his novels and plays. When he attempted to use his public voice in creative works, the result was usually artistic failure. To succeed as an artist O'Kelly had to retreat from politics

> into a world of total privacy and to con-
> centrate upon single human lives occupied
> with the simplest and so the most profound
> business of living in a landscape that is
> not cluttered with political abstractions.
> This form is, of course, the short story
> and it is in his devotion to it that the
> genuine artist in O'Kelly is liberated
> towards his proper achievement.[2]

The traditional, rural world of O'Kelly's stories is a world which could not survive in the twentieth century, but it provided a symbolic refuge for his imagination.

As a child O'Kelly was fascinated by the oral folk tradition, and it helped to shape his mature art. George Brandon Saul comments that O'Kelly "had absorbed into his gift the finest qualities of the wandering hearthside storyteller and heightened them by his faculty for dramatization."[3] O'Kelly's early exposure to the oral tradition also strengthened his appreciation of Irish community life. Eamon Grennan draws attention to this quality in comparing O'Kelly with one of his

70

primary influences, Turgenev. Since they were not peasants themselves, both writers achieved an objective viewpoint, but O'Kelly's treatment of the peasants has a "unique tenderness" that distinguishes him from Turgenev. "He is like a man moving silently through the house of old relatives, allowing as he does so an entire community to define itself in its own terms."[4] O'Kelly's "concept of community" may also be compared with Carleton's. Both writers admire the courage and determination of peasants to survive oppression and extreme poverty. In both writers, the desire to praise and elucidate the peasants' virtues for outsiders sometimes leads to sentimentality. O'Kelly's gentle humor is a special quality not found in Carleton or other earlier writers, however.

In relating O'Kelly to the short story tradition begun by Moore and Joyce, we can perceive a continuity as well as some marked contrasts. O'Kelly has much in common with Moore, especially. They both treat the loneliness of Irish life and the close relationship between the peasants and the land. O'Kelly's attraction to Moore is particularly apparent in an early sketch, "The Land of Loneliness," from By the Stream of Killmeen. The story contrasts the present desolation of the land with the heroic glory of the past. The description of the deteriorating villages and neglected fields echoes Moore, though O'Kelly puts the blame on British oppression rather than on the Catholic Church. When the narrator describes an old Galway man who tells stories of the past, the comparison with The Untilled Field becomes explicit.

> He looked over the deserted country with
> that same strained look as before, and I
> was struck with the thought that the old
> man's eyes had a great look or similarity
> to the country around--that similarity
> which I subsequently read Mr. George Moore
> had also noted from one of his sketches
> in that singular book, The Untilled Field.[5]

Moore's story "The Exile" shows that he at least partially understood the peasant instincts that O'Kelly later portrayed intimately; James Phelan's deep attachment to the farm he grew up on is broken when he emigrates, and the story implies that America has nothing to compensate for his loss of the land. O'Kelly differs from Moore, however, in his acceptance of what Moore had rejected. For Moore, the loneliness of Irish life could only be overcome by spiritual transcendence or

71

emigration; for O'Kelly, loneliness could be overcome by deepening traditional bonds with the land and the community.

This view of Irish community life is fully rendered in the group of early stories collected in Hillsiders, one of the few Irish collections to follow the example of The Hunting Sketches and The Untilled Field in its use of overlapping characters, settings, and incidents. The common setting includes the impoverished western town of Boherlahan, and the village of Kilbeg. One story, "The Apparitions of Oul' Darmody," is a comic "ghost" story; another, "The Elks," is a sentimental story describing a daring rescue at sea, and should be compared with the sea stories of Corkery and O'Flaherty. The remaining four stories are more closely interrelated; they deal with the suffering and loneliness of old people, and the communal ties that help individuals to preserve their dignity and spirit. The community encourages individualism within strict limits of acceptability. "Hannah" concerns a charwoman whose fears that she will be retired from her job cleaning the church are allayed by a compassionate priest; in "The Prodigal Daughter," Miss Mary Hickey leaves Kilbeg, where she has enjoyed much social homage, to live on a farm with her nephew, but she is so forlorn there that she returns, partly on foot, to the village; when Winnie O'Carroll in "The Miracle of the Tea" learns that relatives are coming to visit, she feels embarrassed that she has no money to buy tea for them; she finds some by an accidental "miracle" and involves the whole village in an uproar. The best story in Hillsiders is "Nan Hogan's House," which describes the intense attachment of a spirited old woman to her home.

Nan Hogan lives alone in a small cabin in Kilbeg. All her children have either died or emigrated, and her only remaining interest in life is in waging a perpetual battle with the rest of the village, and particularly with Sara Finnessy, whose son ran away with Nan's cherished eldest son. Nan becomes ill and Tim O'Halloran, the relief agent, arranges for her to be sent to the poorhouse hospital, much against her will. At the hospital Nan meets Maura Casey, a homeless woman working there as an aide, and tells her about her house and the village. One day Maura leaves the hospital and takes possession of Nan's house in Kilbeg; she has led a wandering life and has always longed for her own home. When Nan hears what has happened, she cures herself through sheer will power and returns to her house. The two women argue over possession until Tim O'Halloran

72

cleverly uses Sara Finnessy as a common enemy to unite
them. They decide to live in the house together and
enjoy the companionship which they both lacked before.

The story is told in the third person by a narrator thoroughly familiar with the virtues, idiosyncra-
cies, and past histories of the villagers. He speaks
as a sympathetic but detached observer. He does not
reveal the characters' inner thoughts but describes them
as they appear to each other and to the village as a
whole. This technique, similar to the technique that
Frank O'Connor would later develop, establishes a good-
humored, conversational tone and draws the reader into
the situation. Although the narrative pace is leisurely, we do not feel that words are wasted. The story is
a fine example of integrated organic form.

O'Kelly uses caricature to portray the villagers,
but it is affectionate rather than critical. The odd-
ness of the peasants is evidence of their individualism
and the strength of character which has enabled them to
survive. At the beginning of the story a neighbor discovers Nan on the floor, overcome by illness. In spite
of her weakness, her "uncompromising head and shoulders
rose out of the pillows, and her one fearless steel-grey
eye took Mrs. Paul Manton in with steady and frank dis-
pleasure."6 This physical description of Nan captures
the fierce antagonism that she thrives on.

The portrayal of the setting is similar to the portrayal of character. Houses are described as if they
were extensions of human personality. The world of
Kilbeg is an intensely human and personal world.

> Kilbeg in its construction had never come
> under the tyranny of the architect or the
> conventionality of the engineer. There was
> no designing, no mapping and planning, no
> consideration of aspect, and no surveying
> of the site. The houses were put up by the
> people according as they were wanted, and
> under conditions of the most perfect indi-
> vidual liberty. One cabin, so to speak,
> did not care a snap for the other, and
> showed it. If you were a sociable person,
> for instance, you hooked your habitation
> on to a number of others. If you were of
> a retiring disposition you planted yourself
> away in from the road or went down into a
> dip in the ground. If you were aggressive
> or overbearing you put your house on a

> commanding view, and if you were nasty
> and wanted to be disagreeable you built
> your cabin in front of your enemy's door,
> so that he would have to walk about your
> house to get in or out of his own, and
> the movements of his family would be
> under your constant observation.[7]

In a humorous way O'Kelly suggests a close interaction between character and environment. Peasant ruggedness grows out of ruggedness of landscape, and the peasants build cabins that express both their individualism and their integration into community life.

The historical consciousness of the peasants is very acute; when Nan is sent to the poorhouse hospital the whole village is deeply disturbed. The people fear the hospital because it reminds them of the hardships and injustices of the Famine years, when few people returned from the poorhouse once they had entered it. The poorhouse car is "an emblem of death and pestilence and horror, a black vulture that hovered over places where the people lay broken, a thing that had direct descent from the Famine."[8] This deeply ingrained historical memory is one source of the strong sense of community that the peasants share. What George Moore saw as "pathetic submission" and James Joyce saw as "paralysis," O'Kelly sees as a defiant survival instinct.

Maura Casey is an outsider in Kilbeg, and as such is mistrusted by the villagers, but her obvious need for a home and the care she devotes to Nan's house soon bring about her acceptance. Because she has led a wandering life and has been exposed to many hardships, Maura thoroughly appreciates her new home and clings tenaciously to it. When Nan returns to the village she is at first determined to drive Maura out; Maura grows miserable at the thought of taking to the roads again. But, as Nan sees that Maura is a capable homemaker and nurse as well as a sympathetic listener, she relents and accepts the new companionship. The villagers approve the turn of events because they know Nan will be well cared for. They feel protective of her in spite of her antagonism, because they know all the sorrows she has lived through. Nan and Maura both escape from the poorhouse and all that it represents back <u>into</u> the community--not away from it.

The concept of home which O'Kelly presents in this story reveals much about his artistic vision and represents a further similarity to Frank O'Connor. A home within a close-knit, traditional community offers shelter and protection against harsh forces which threaten to destroy the life instinct and even life itself. Loneliness is a very real factor in the lives of O'Kelly's characters, and they must somehow keep it at bay if they are to sustain their vitality and avoid despair. Survival requires not emigration but strengthening of ties to home, community, and nation; even an antagonistic relationship with neighbors is better than no relationship. The community does not cause loneliness, as it does in most of Moore's stories and all of Joyce's; rather it helps the individual to overcome loneliness by providing him with physical security and emotional support. At the same time O'Kelly recognizes, with sadness, that the communal traditions are dying out. Many of the young people have left home, and Kilbeg is inhabited mostly by the old.

Waysiders is a more uneven collection than _Hillsiders_, and it deals with a greater variety of subjects. There are several comic and fantasy tales, the best of which is "The Can with the Diamond Notch," a story of an avaricious shopkeeper outwitted by tinkers. Two stories probe the subject of death: "The White Goat" resembles O'Flaherty's stories about human cruelty to animals, and "A Wayside Burial" is a meditation on mortality and the sorrows of Irish history. Religious attitudes are reflected in several stories; "The Rector," though not one of the better stories, provides insight into O'Kelly's views. He presents the Catholic Church not as an oppressive, life-denying institution, as Moore and Joyce do, but as an institution vitally connected with national and community life.

In "The Rector" O'Kelly attacks the attitudes of the Protestant Ascendancy. The Anglican Rector, a native of Ulster who has moved to an inactive parish in the West, is dour and pessimistic and has erected inflexible barriers between himself and the locality. He withdraws from the life around him into a mental world of sterile theological controversies. When he sees some Catholic peasants on the road he gives them "the look of a man who stood outside of their lives, who did not expect to be recognized, and who did not feel called upon to seem conscious of these peasant folk."[9] By using the Rector as a protagonist, O'Kelly suggests that outsiders who erect religious and social barriers miss much of the essential life of Ireland. In contrast to the Rector, the Catholic peasants are lively, optimistic, and warm-hearted. His self-imposed isolation and rigidity are defenses against his dim suspicion that the

75

Irish national spirit might transcend religious differences, that "there might be all unconscious among these people a spirit of common country, of a common democracy, a common humanity, that forced itself to the surface in course of time."[10]

The two stories of emigration in Waysiders, "Both Sides of the Pond" and "The Building," also illustrate the contrast between O'Kelly's views and those of earlier writers. Both stories depict America as a place that corrupts young immigrants. Denis Donohoe, the protagonist of "Both Sides of the Pond," is a young peasant turf-cutter. He and his mother eke out a difficult existence in a primitive cabin near the bog. Most of the story describes a journey Denis must make to town, to sell a cartload of turf. On his way he stops at a cabin to visit Agnes, a girl he admires, but she has gone to the post-office. When he stops there again on his way home, he learns that Agnes' sister in Australia has sent her the money to emigrate there, and he is overcome by gloom. In despair he emigrates to New York and degenerates into a cheap entertainer in a Bowery bar.

The "pond" is the Atlantic Ocean, which separates the two settings of the story: the remote, mountainous region of Galway where Denis and his mother live, and the night club in the Bowery. The description of the Irish setting stresses the intimate relationship between the peasant and the landscape. The bogland around Denis' cabin is "a sweep of country that had, they said, in the infancy of the earth been a great oak forest, across which in later times had roved packs of hungry wolves, and which could at this day claim the most primitive form of industry in Western Europe."[11] Continuity with the ancient past provides a source of pride that is absent from Moore's landscapes. Turf-cutting is regarded not as empty drudgery but as a venerable occupation that provides warm, pleasant fires for the hearths of Irish homes.

Denis himself is admirable for the strict discipline of his life. On the journey into town, he has the strength of mind to ignore his hunger and take pleasure in the companionship of his donkey and the beauty of the dawn. In the town he tolerates silently the haggling and disparagement of his customers and finally sells the turf for only a few shillings, enough to buy essential supplies for his mother and himself.

As in Moore's story "The Exile," in this story

Denis' decision to emigrate is motivated by the loss of
his beloved. His attachment to Ireland centers on
Agnes, as James Phelan's does on Catherine. Denis'
reaction to the news of Agnes' decision is conveyed
through a drastic change in his behavior. Before stopping at her house he sings a Gaelic folk-song, reminiscent of the song in Turgenev's "The Singer." The song's
ancient refrain expresses the peasant's timeless immer-
sion in his environment. As he leaves the cabin Denis
travels in silence, now alienated from the landscape.

> Overhead the sky was winter clear, the
> stars merry, eternal, the whole heaven
> brilliant in its silent, stupendous song,
> its perpetual Magnificat; but Denis
> Donohoe made the rest of the journey in
> a black silence, gloom in the rigid fig-
> ure, the stooping shoulders, the dangling
> legs; and the hills seemed to draw their
> grim shadows around his tragic ride to the
> lonely light in his mother's cabin on the
> verge of the dead brown bog.[12]

O'Kelly does not deny that the land can be desolate when
human relationships fail; Denis' environment offers him
little opportunity for love. Emigration seems the
obvious choice, but the scene in the Bowery demonstrates
that it is the wrong choice for Denis.

The nightclub scene, much shorter than the Irish
one, provides an abrupt contrast in mood. This scene is
very melodramatic and so inferior artistically to the
rest of the story that Eamon Grennan omitted it in his
edition. Denis has altered considerably. As a nightclub singer he performs not genuine Gaelic music but
cheap parodies in a false brogue. His Irish identity
has been vulgarized and merged indiscriminately with
other national identities. The disciplined purity and
simplicity of his earlier life have given way to cynicism and dissipation. The scene invites comparison
with Moore's "Home Sickness," in which a Bowery bar provides James Bryden with a kind of fulfillment that was
not possible in Ireland. Although O'Kelly shares with
Moore the realization that Ireland is a lonely place,
he disagrees about the advantages of leaving home.

Six of the stories in The Golden Barque and the
Weaver's Grave are interrelated accounts of life along
the Midland canal and aboard the canal boat, the "Golden
Barque." These are mostly stories of intense passions
and some are uncharacteristically dark; for example,

betrayed love in "Michael and Mary," bitter enmity over a woman in "Hike and Calcutta," and perversely selfish avarice in "The Derelict." Powerful as these stories are, they are considerably overshadowed by the novella "The Weaver's Grave," the last work that O'Kelly completed before his death.

"The Weaver's Grave" combines several of the themes treated earlier into a mature, comprehensive vision of Irish culture. The plot is a simple one. Mortimer Hehir, the weaver, has died. He is one of the two remaining people with rights to burial in the ancient graveyard Cloon na Morav (the Meadow of the Dead), and his widow (and fourth wife) has brought two old men to identify the gravesite: Meehaul Lynskey, the nail-maker, and Cahir Bowes, the stone-breaker. With them are two young gravediggers, twin sons of the caretaker. When, after much searching and arguing, the old men cannot find the grave, the widow visits the invalid Malachi Roohan, the cooper, the last man who will be buried in Cloon na Morav. He gives her a philosophical discourse instead of helpful information, however. She returns to the graveyard and suggests that they suspend the search until the next day, but just as they are leaving, Cahir Bowes triumphantly remembers the grave-site. During the day an attraction has developed between the widow and one of the gravediggers, and it appears that they will achieve a fulfilling love.

The narrative emits the aura of Gaelic Ireland, and the colorful dialogue captures Gaelic speech patterns. O'Kelly makes good use of his skills as a dramatist; besides the lively dialogue, there are many striking visual poses and gestures. The tone is similar to that of "Nan Hogan's House"--casual, good-humored, and appreciative, but with an elegaic undertone. The story is divided into five sections, each unfolding and enlarging the central theme as well as advancing the plot at a leisurely pace. The classical structure incorporates many contrasts and symmetries: the older generation versus the younger one, the rivalry of the two old men, the mirror image of the twin gravediggers, the open space of Cloon na Morav versus the stuffy sickroom of Malachi Roohan. The action takes only a few hours, but within this span are compressed many centuries of Irish tradition and a broad philosophical view of human existence.

Like the graveyard in "A Wayside Burial," Cloon na Morav becomes a symbol for a dying culture and the vicissitudes of Irish history. Paradoxically, it also represents the irrepressible individualism and dynamism we have seen reflected in the architecture of Kilbeg, in Hillsiders. One source of the intimacy between the Irish peasant and the landscape is this custom of personalizing and naming every feature of it. The weathered, eccentric, animated character of Cloon na Morav seems to derive from its inhabitants. "The ground was billowy, grotesque. Several partially suppressed insurrections--a great thirsting, worming, pushing and shouldering under the sod--had given it character."13 It is very different from the newer cemetery, whose orderly arrangement and conventional inscriptions suggest the triviality of modern civilization.

The old men in the story are also associated with dying traditions, but are vital and intense. Each of them has a strong interest in geneology and a rich store of anecdotes and memories of local families. Each has worked at a manual craft or trade made obsolete by machine technology. O'Kelly's method of caricature is to connect the physical appearance with the trade: Cahir Bowes is bent forward from the waist and he peers constantly at the ground, and Meehaul Lynskey makes frequent hammering gestures and sees the world with eyes that are "small and sharp, but unaccustomed to range over wide spaces."14 As if they sense that this will be their last productive day on earth, Cahir and Meehaul enjoy the outing to the full, and each is determined to triumph over the other. O'Kelly's compassion for old people is central to his artistic vision; he recognizes that their difficult ways, their contentiousness, their childish egotism and petulance have resulted from a lifetime of hard struggle and are expressions of a defiant spirit resisting neglect, bodily decay, and approaching death. His old people are the last of a vanishing race, and the younger generation seems bland and colorless by comparison.

The weaver's widow is a somewhat mysterious personality. Her meditation as she walks to Malachi Roohan's house gives us some information about her relationship with the weaver. Since she was much younger than he and was his fourth wife, their marriage was relatively passionless, and it was dominated by his obsession with his grave, which for him represented his family pedigree and special position in life. The widow ponders the irony that the weaver, who took such a proprietary and authoritative interest in Cloon na Morav, has neglected to leave instructions for locating his own grave. She is anxious to see him properly buried, partly out of a superstitious fear that his turbulent soul will wander otherwise, and partly out of a respectable sense of duty. She is a kind of surrogate for O'Kelly himself in her placid, unresentful tolerance of the vanity and crankiness of old men.

Malachi Roohan proves to be the most extraordinary old man of all. He is feeble, shrivelled and grotesque, but he clings ferociously to life. His remaining vitality is concentrated in his intense blue eyes and powerful voice, and his connection with the living world is symbolized by the rope which he uses to raise himself in bed. Like the other old men he is fiercely independent and resists offers of help. He rouses himself from senile confusion long enough to conduct a lucid, passionate discourse on the unreality of life. "'The world is only a dream, and a dream is nothing at all! We all want to waken up out of the great nothingness of this world.'"[15] This sense of the illusory quality of life is developed in many ways throughout the story, and contributes to its elegaic mood. To all the old men the past, which they remember only in elusive fragments, is more real than the present, and the only tangible thing that will confirm their reality after death is the grave.

As the widow returns to Cloon na Morav, she has an experience that seems to bear out what Malachi Roohan has said, and illustrates the wonder and mystery of life. Instead of seeing the gravediggers as indistinguishable twins, she sees them as individuals and feels strongly attracted to one of them. "The most subtle and powerful of all things, personality, sprang silently from the twins and made them, to the mind of the widow, as far apart as the poles."[16] David Norris comments that "The bleakness of the old man's prophecy seems to operate subliminally on the widow, wakening her to experience like a frosty disintegration of the soil that allows new growth."[17] The dream of love is also part of the illusion of life; O'Kelly suggests that only those things which engage the imagination most deeply are worth living for. It seems fitting that the widow should be rewarded with a romantic love for patiently discharging her obligations to the weaver. The story ends in a joyous mood as the grave is located and dug, Cahir gloats over Meehaul, and the gravedigger passionately kisses the widow.

In its exploration of the universal themes of love and death, "The Weaver's Grave" offers many points of comparison with Joyce's great story "The Dead." Both stories contrast the older generation with the younger,

and a passionless marriage with a passionate love relationship; both offer a perspective on the dead and their
relationship to the living, and a sense of the ambiguity
and illusion of life. But the differences in treatment
of these elements epitomize the differences in the writers' views. In "The Dead" the past is a source of
paralysis which keeps the characters from living fully
in the present; in "The Weaver's Grave" it is a source
of enrichment, deepening the characters' identity
through family and community traditions. Though both
stories describe vanishing cultures, Joyce's symbolic
world is effete and corrupt, whereas O'Kelly's retains
vitality and a coherent system of values. O'Kelly's
vision is more reassuring and optimistic than Joyce's,
as new love emerges from death and the human cycle
begins again.

Notes

1 Anne Clune, "Seumas O'Kelly," The Irish Short Story, ed. Patrick Rafroidi and Terence Brown (Gerrards Cross, Buckinghamshire: Colin Smythe, 1979), p. 144.

2 Seumas O'Kelly, A Land of Loneliness and Other Stories, ed. Eamon Grennan (Dublin: Gill and Macmillan, 1969), p. 6.

3 George Brandon Saul, Seumas O'Kelly (Lewisburg: Bucknell University Press, 1971), p. 77.

4 A Land of Loneliness, p. 3.

5 Ibid., p. 25.

6 Seumas O'Kelly, Hillsiders (Dublin: Talbot Press, 1921), p. 88.

7 Ibid., pp. 91-92.

8 Ibid., p. 101.

9 Seumas O'Kelly, Waysiders: Stories of Connacht (Dublin: Talbot Press, 1924), p. 105.

10 Ibid., p. 111.

11 Ibid., p. 37.

12 Ibid., p. 50.

13 A Land of Loneliness, p. 145.

14 Ibid., p. 147.

15 Ibid., p. 174.

16 Ibid., p. 181.

17 David Norris, "Imaginative Response Versus Authority Structures," The Irish Short Story, p. 53.

Chapter Five

DANIEL CORKERY

Although Daniel Corkery has much in common with
Seumas O'Kelly--his nationalistic views, his attachment
to the religious traditions and landscape of Ireland,
his affection for peasants and compassion for the poor
and afflicted--there are some significant differences
in the artistic visions of the two writers. Corkery,
writing exclusively about the region around Cork,
depicts urban as well as rural scenes. His work is
darker in mood, less humorous and sociable in tone, than
O'Kelly's. Within his limited range he provides
insights into some aspects of the Irish consciousness
that earlier writers did not adequately treat.

Corkery's career extended through the Revolution
and Civil War into the post-Revolutionary period. He
continued to write short stories long after O'Kelly had
died and Joyce had given up writing stories for novels.
As an articulate nationalist, Gaelic enthusiast, and
established writer, he had a considerable influence on
the next generation of Irish writers. Born into a
family of carpenter-craftsmen in 1878, he spent virtually his entire life in the area of Cork; the prospects
of exile did not attract him. After briefly attending
St. Patrick's College in Dublin, he taught for many
years in Cork elementary schools, and actively encouraged his pupils (one of whom was Frank O'Connor) to
learn Irish. He also helped to organize, in 1908, the
Cork Dramatic Society, a group inspired by the Abbey
Theater Movement. Both O'Connor and Sean O'Faolain knew
him well as young men and benefited from his guidance
and support in their early literary efforts, though
they later became estranged from him. In 1929 he
received an M.A. from the National University of Ireland
and in 1931 became Professor of English at University
College, Cork. After his retirement he served terms in
the Irish Senate and the Arts Council. He never married, and died in 1964 while living with his niece in
County Cork. In addition to a novel (The Threshold of
Quiet, 1917), poems, plays (some produced at the Abbey),
and works of criticism, his writings include four volumes of short stories: A Munster Twilight (1916); The
Hounds of Banba (1919); The Stormy Hills (1929); and
Earth out of Earth (1939). A fifth volume, The Wager
and Other Stories (1950), contains stories which Corkery
selected from the earlier volumes.

The judgments expressed in Corkery's critical writings are strongly colored by his political views and as a result are often biased or unsound. In fact his own work violated his precepts, since he wrote in English rather than Irish and published his stories in England and America. Nevertheless, his criticism is helpful at times in illuminating his short stories. The introductory chapter of his book on Synge, Synge and Anglo-Irish Literature (1931), is particularly relevant not just as a guide to his own artistic attitudes, but as a statement of ideas that stimulated or antagonized younger writers. He argues in this chapter, much as Carleton did in his introduction to Traits and Stories, that Anglo-Irish literature cannot truly be called a "national literature" because it has been written mainly for foreign readers and judged by foreign critical standards. Because of the circumstances of Irish history, Corkery asserts, Irish literature in English has not had a "normal" development in the way that other national literatures have. Normal literature "lives or dies" by the judgments of its own people, not by the judgments of outsiders, and it "is written within the confines of the country which names it. It is not dependent on expatriates."[1] In most countries expatriation is the choice of only a few writers, and is usually only temporary. But almost all the Anglo-Irish writers have been expatriates, and usually for life. The main reason is that no market exists for their work at home. Because this state of affairs has existed since the beginnings of Anglo-Irish literature in the eighteenth century, contemporary Irish writers have no "normal" tradition to fall back on. Instead Irish material has consistently been distorted to entertain alien audiences.

Corkery disparagingly reviews Anglo-Irish "colonial" literature from Castle Rackrent to Shaw's John Bull's Other Island. He says that even Catholic peasant writers like Griffin wrote essentially for English audiences, and thus distorted their material. He praises the Abbey Theater writers because they attempted to "express Ireland to itself." But as the theater movement lost momentum after 1922, writers began turning once again to English and American markets.

One obstacle affecting the writers' efforts to "express Ireland to itself" is the lack of a definite national consciousness. The Irish mentality is characterized by flux and uncertainty. While the education of an English child supports what he observes around him, and "practically all the literature he reads focuses for him the mind of his own people," the education of an Irish child produces self-doubt and conflict.

> No sooner does he begin to use his intellect than what he learns begins to undermine, to weaken, and to harass his emotional nature. For practically all that he reads is English. . . . It does not therefore focus the mind of his own people, teaching him the better to look about him, to understand both himself and his surroundings. . . . Instead of sharpening his gaze upon his own neighborhood, his reading distracts it, for he cannot find in these surroundings what his reading has taught him is the matter worth coming upon. His surroundings begin to seem unvital.[2]

This view of the Irish national consciousness is remarkably similar to Stephen Dedalus' in A Portrait of the Artist; Stephen believes that the Irish conscience is "uncreated," and that it is the mission of the artist to create it. Corkery accounts for the lack of good fiction, and particularly of good novels, in Irish literature by saying that writers do not have sufficient grasp of the "distinctive vitality" of the Irish environment; their writings lack emotional relevance to the Irish people.

In his own stories Corkery attempted to capture the vitality and emotional relevance that he felt were lacking in Irish fiction. The themes of his stories are often drawn from the three powerful forces which he thought comprised the Irish national being and were not sufficiently recognized by Irish writers: religion, nationalism, and the land. The Irish religious consciousness is "so vast, so deep, so dramatic, even so terrible a thing, occasionally creating wreckage in its path, tumbling the weak things over, that when one begins to know it, one wonders if it is possible for a writer to deal with any phase whatever of Irish life without trenching upon it." Nationalism is an equally deep and pervasive force in Irish life, "drawing sanction, as it does, from hundreds of battlefields, slaughterings, famines, exoduses, as well as from hundreds of heroic lives and the piety of verse."[3] Attachment to the land, although not as widespread a force as the other two, nevertheless must be taken into account. A much larger percentage of Irishmen work on the land than Englishmen. Corkery compares the prominence of the

85

struggle for land ownership in Irish literature to the prominence of the freeing of the serfs in Russian literature.

Corkery shares with Moore and O'Kelly a deep interest in the oral tradition, and he asserts that Irish literature of the future will be revitalized by contact with the popular oral literature that is cherished by Irish people but not widely known elsewhere. He says that the Celtic Renaissance has run its course and can develop no further; the new literature will grow from intimate knowledge of life in "the huts of the people." This prophecy was fulfilled by Corkery himself and by his successors; in the next generation, the short story was to become the genre that most effectively captured the lives of ordinary Irish people.

Corkery achieved his greatest artistic success in his short stories. The propaganda that colors his critical writings is absent from most of his stories. Perhaps, like O'Kelly, he can be regarded as a man with two voices, public and private, who found that in the short story he could best express his private self. Benedict Kiely provides a good description of Corkery's art: "Corkery's attitude [in the stories] is primarily contemplative and his writing has always been happier in dealing not with the aggravations of controversy, but with the cloistral, candle-lit places of the soul." Kiely notes Corkery's violent reaction against "the Irish storytellers who saw the common people of Ireland, very simply, as comic relief"; instead the people in Corkery's stories go "into places where the shadows of moral responsibility are as bewildering and terrifying as the mists on the stormy mountains."[4]

Comparing Corkery and Joyce, Kiely points out that both writers dealt with religion and nationalism, but Corkery accepted the conditions that Joyce rejected. Corkery's acceptance required a certain narrowness of outlook, and "implied also a definite denial of much of the past and present of the life of Ireland."[5] Corkery himself noted that he and Joyce shared a preoccupation with religion, but said that Joyce had "gone astray-- although [the Irish religious texture] nearly succeeded in holding him fast."[6]

The characters in Corkery's stories live mostly in the tenements of Cork city or in the mountains along the Cork-Kerry coast. They are more solitary than O'Kelly's characters, though the community still plays an important role. Corkery is especially sensitive to the love-hate relationship between man and the land and to the religious superstition and awareness of evil in the Irish mind. He explores the perverse, violent, destructive side of human nature more fully than O'Kelly does. He did not write comic or fantasy tales, and although some of his stories are humorous, his tone is more often sombre and reflective.

The characteristic themes discussed above dominate Corkery's first collection, A Munster Twilight, which contains some of his best work. Several stories explore the interaction between individuals and the community in the laneways and tenements of Cork. These stories emphasize the poverty and hardship of the characters' lives and their nearness to death. Although the community often supports the individual, it can also be a source of bitterness and enmity. "The Return" portrays a sailor who has killed a mate in a fight, and who seeks an evening of companionship in a lodging-house before taking his own life. Six interrelated stories comprise "The Cobbler's Den," a gathering place for local gossips. The setting resembles that of O'Kelly's "The Shoemaker," though the stories are very different in mood. The gossips in Corkery's story include the cobbler, a blind man (one of Corkery's favorite symbolic types), and Maggie Maw, a warm-hearted, maternal woman. The situations encompass many aspects of tenement life: a reminiscence of a devastating flood; a portrait of a simple woman driven mad by inherited American money; a wake for a son dead in America; the departure of a resident shamed by the return of his estranged wife; a plot of revenge against a woman who makes money insuring her neighbor's lives; the accidental drowning of a child. Many families have been diminished by emigration and some of the emigrants have returned to Ireland. As in O'Kelly's work, America is regarded as a place of greed and corruption.

Corkery's attitude to emigration is most graphically conveyed in the lyrical story "Storm-Struck." Since the story shows a relationship between emigration and love, it should be examined within the context of Moore's emigration stories, Joyce's "Eveline," and O'Kelly's "Both Sides of the Pond." The protagonist, John Donovan, returns home to a fishing village in Cork after being blinded in a mining accident in Montana. He intended to earn enough money in America to marry his sweetheart, Kitty Regan, but when he returns to his parents' house after the accident he learns that she is unhappily married to someone else. Embittered by his blindness and the loss of his beloved, he spends most

of his time wandering the cliff-tops near the sea, with
a local boy as his guide. One day he is caught by a
storm while sitting alone on the cliffs; he cries out
fearfully for the boy, who is not there; instead he is
rescued by a woman who leads him home. When they are
near his house she runs away from him to avoid discovery, and he realizes she is Kitty Regan. He sits all
night by the window in his room listening, and as if he
hears something, whispers an invitation of love which
is not answered. Kitty Regan is found half-conscious
and exhausted the next day in the hills between John's
village and her husband's. Whether she actually stood
outside John's window during the night remains a
mystery.

The story is narrated in a conversational, idiomatic style. Like many of Moore's and O'Kelly's stories,
this one is told from the point of view of an observer
who is familiar with details of the village life but
who cannot see into the characters' minds. For example,
he can only speculate about the reasons for John's love
of the cliffs: "Perhaps he remembered west and east in
the touch of the wind."7 The effect of this narrative
method is to suggest that John's burdensome inner
thoughts are inaccessible to those who have not shared
his experiences.

In this story Corkery presents emigration as an
evil much worse than the poverty that motivates it.
John's first impulse after the accident is to go home,
where he is secure. His American adventure has changed
him permanently, however. At home, his preference for
silence and solitude suggests deep inward suffering.
He holds aloof from the rest of the village. The
rugged, windswept cliffs are more congenial to his mood
than the village gathering places. He seems to possess
terrible knowledge hidden from others.

The storm scene has many symbolic overtones.
Kitty Regan, the person he cares about most deeply, rescues him from his terrified isolation. Later, his
vigil by the window symbolizes all his futile yearning
for love and companionship, and the empty future that
awaits him. His blindness has given him a capacity for
poetic insight, and his feelings are distilled into a
delicate metaphor at the end of the story: "In the
crowd of gossips that gathered in Lavelle's public-
house discussing the event, he began to jest about the
storm-birds that seek shelter from the storm at the
lighthouse-keeper's window, how they do not have the
courage to enter when the window is opened to them."8

John, the "lighthouse-keeper," is watchful and solitary. The fact that he jokes about the incident to gossips in the pub reveals the extent of his bitterness.

Although John Donovan escapes the physical danger of the storm, he does not escape the loneliness caused by his blindness and the loss of love. His family and the community give him a certain amount of support, but they cannot sustain him emotionally in the way that Kilbeg sustains Nan Hogan. He must finally be content with the insights of the solitary imagination.

John Donovan prefers the rugged, windswept cliffs because the landscape corresponds to a quality deep within himself. This close relationship between man and the land is probably the most essential element in Corkery's vision, and it informs some of his finest works. Sean Lucy comments on the relationship between character and natural setting in Corkery's stories. He

> was attracted to imagination and to will, and fascinated when these came together in obsession. The focus of story after story is on a man gripped by a vision, more or less real, and led beyond the ordinary everyday boundaries of his life. In a natural setting, particularly a wilder and more challenging setting, the individual human being shines out more strongly and more strangely than in the city, and Corkery has given us that strength, without denying the narrowness that often goes with it, and has given us the strangeness, without flinching from some of its more gross and grotesque manifestations.[9]

Several other stories in A Munster Twilight treat the relationship between man and the land. "The Spancelled" recounts a love affair between a man and woman both trapped by land inheritance laws; "Solace" captures the fierce spirit of an eighteenth-century bard and his family evicted from their farm; in "Joy" a change in the land laws allows an old man evicted from his farm and exiled to the city many years earlier to purchase a new farm. The most disturbing and powerful of the stories in the collection is "The Ploughing of Leaca-Na-Naomh," which treats the conflict between land-hunger and religious superstition.

The story concerns an old Gaelic family that owns a remote farm in the mountains. Behind the farm is a

leaca--a field jutting out from the side of the mountain. According to local legend it is a holy place, the
burial ground of the saints, and therefore must not be
ploughed. The landowner, a determined farmer with a
passion for cultivating all available land, conceives
the idea of ploughing the leaca. He suggests it repeatedly to one of his servants, a half-witted fool named
Liam Ruadh. The fool at first is shocked by his master's heresy, but gradually the idea takes hold and he
counters by suggesting that the master's spirited stallion, Griosach, be harnessed to the plough. They finally agree to go through with the foolhardy plan. On the
appointed morning, the farmhands gather fearfully to
watch. The leaca is too distant to see clearly, but
when they hear a mating call from a mare in the stable
who was supposed to be harnessed with Griosach, they
realize that Liam Ruadh has harnessed him with another
stallion. The mare's call causes the stallions to
fight and drag the fool over the edge of the leaca to
his death.

The narrative technique of this story is more complex than that of "Storm-Struck." The narrator is an
outsider, a Gaelic enthusiast who has travelled into
the mountains in search of an old Irish family, many
years after the incident took place. Intrigued by the
wasted appearance of the landowner, now an old man, the
narrator senses that some tragedy has destroyed him and
elicits the story from an old farmhand who was an
observer of the ploughing. The story has a forceful
impact on the narrator; he flees at once from the mountains to escape the knowledge of evil he has gained
there. The narrative device of passing on the tale
from one person to another until it acquires the quality
of a legend is derived from the oral tradition and gives
the story the authenticity of myth. The narrator also
acts as translator, since the story is told to him in
Irish; he uncovers the hidden Gaelic world for outsiders.

The mood of the story is ominous and awesome. In
the first paragraph, the narrator establishes his theme
in a stark, poeticized style, influenced by Gaelic
storytelling style, that emphasizes the primal struggle
between man and the land.

> With which shall I begin--man or place?
> Perhaps I had better first tell of the man;
> of him the incident left so withered that
> no sooner had I laid eyes on him than I
> said: Here is one whose blood at some

> terrible moment of his life stood still,
> stood still and never afterwards regained
> its quiet, old-time ebb-and-flow. A word
> or two then about the place--a sculpted-out
> shell in the Kerry mountains, an evil-
> looking place, green-glaring like a sea
> when a storm has passed.10

The glen where the farm is located is a dark and evil
place, except for the leaca, which glimmers "like a gem"
with sunlight long after it has faded elsewhere. The
imagery suggests the holiness of the leaca and the
depravity of the men who want to desecrate it.

The conflict between the master and Liam Ruadh is
as elemental as the conflict between the master and the
land. The characters are described as if they are blind
natural forces; they are shaped by the landscape to
such an extent that they seem part of it, as the old
farmhand tells the narrator. "'The tree turns the wind
aside, yet the wind at last twists the tree. Like wind
and tree, master and fool played against each other,
until at last they each of them had spent their
force.'"11 The operation of evil in the minds of the
master and the fool has an appearance of inevitability.
Once the sacrilegious idea has entered their heads, it
cannot be stopped.

The ploughing takes place in a chilly dawn, after
a snowfall. The moonlight, whiteness of the snow, and
chilliness of the air symbolize the intense moral dread
the observers feel; they are as silent and still as statues. When they see Liam about to be dragged over the
cliff, their fear erupts in an outburst of chaotic shouting, followed by prayers for his soul. The master's
reaction is not described, but we know from the earlier
characterization of him that he is devastated by
remorse. As in "Storm-Struck," Corkery makes us feel
the intensity of a character's mood without revealing
his inner thoughts. The atmosphere of mystery and awe,
reminiscent of the mysterious atmosphere Turgenev
achieves in stories like "Bezhin Meadow," is an essential aspect of the author's vision.

That the incident has a powerful impact even many
years later is demonstrated by the narrator's decision
to escape immediately after he hears it. He does not
explain his reasons for leaving, and the reader must
interpret the ending for himself. The extraordinary
reactions of the narrator and other characters suggest
that violating the sanctity of the leaca for material

gain is a heinous betrayal of the ancient Gaelic religious spirit. The knowledge of this evil and the tragic death that results from it is a burden almost too great to bear. The narrator flees physically from the glen but carries with him the memory of what he has seen and heard.

In both "Storm-Struck" and "The Ploughing of Leaca-Na-Naomh," characters are overwhelmed by hidden knowledge which makes them isolated and aloof from other men. Although the moral judgments are not explicitly stated, Corkery implies a judgment against these characters for allowing material desires to overcome their commitment to Gaelic spiritual values--John Donovan leaves Ireland to earn money, and the farmer ploughs the leaca to increase his crop. In each case, after the betrayal the imagination becomes obsessed with a burdensome vision.

Irish nationalism is the central theme of the stories collected in The Hounds of Banba, all of which describe the guerrilla warfare in Ireland during the rebellion. Corkery was the first of the writers discussed so far to participate actively in the war. Benedict Kiely sees in these stories the same contemplative quality that is present in Corkery's work as a whole; they are "quiet studies of people normally quiet but provoked by peculiar circumstances into the approval of violence. They are stories of contemplatives in revolution."[12] Corkery's nationalism is clearly evident in these stories. They are marred by propaganda and their artistic quality is not as high as in some of his other work. According to George Brandon Saul they are his "lamest set of tales."[13] These stories have a historical importance, however, since they served as models for the war stories of O'Faolain and O'Connor and defined the ethos that these writers reacted against. In The Hounds of Banba the guerrilla warfare against England is idealized and otherwise ordinary characters are transformed and ennobled through their participation in the cause. Corkery describes several types of people caught up in the struggle: a retarded man in "A Bye-Product"; a shy farm boy in "The Aherns"; a nunlike girl in "The Price"; a university student in "Seumas." Some of the stories concern relationships between the older generation of nationalists, the Fenians, and the young Volunteers: "The Ember," "Cowards," and "On the Heights."

One of the better war stories, "On the Heights," is representative of themes and techniques used throughout

92

the collection. A young revolutionary soldier flees
high into the mountains on his bicycle to escape pursuing British soldiers and the threat of imprisonment.
At first the wild mountain terrain makes him feel lost
and desolate, though he is safe from his pursuers. He
soon finds refuge in an isolated cottage occupied by an
Irish-speaking couple and the husband's elderly, bedrid-
den father. The couple receive the stranger reluctantly; they are afraid he will bring trouble to the house.
They keep his identity hidden from the old man. That
night the soldier sleeps in the same bed with the old
man because it is the only place there is room for him.
In the morning he learns that he has spoken his dreams
aloud in his sleep, and that the old man is a former
Fenian who shares his dreams for Ireland's future. The
two are united in comradeship by a bold nationalistic
vision which the timorous couple do not possess.

The soldier narrates his story in the first person.
(Several narrators in the collection are young guerril-
las on the run.) The rapid pace and excitement of the
opening section, describing his flight from the British,
create a mood of challenge and expectation. The excitement is succeeded by bewilderment as he nears the top
of the mountain pass. A cloud bringing a heavy rain-
storm blots out all the familiar landmarks, and he feels
desolate and exposed.

As in "Storm-Struck" and "The Ploughing of Leaca-
Na-Naomh," rugged landscape evokes the protagonist's
inner disturbance. He welcomes with great relief the
first signs of human habitation; his discovery of the
cottage represents his reintegration into the human community. But the soldier's expectations are disappointed
by the lukewarm reception he is given at the cottage.
It is not just human contact that he needs, but the
more profound and spiritual communion which the old
Fenian provides. This relationship is strengthened by
physical contact; the soldier awakes in the morning to
find the old man gently touching his face. Their mutual
commitment to the Irish cause sets them apart from ordinary people. The story ends in a mood of renewed enthusiasm and joy. There is no note of disillusionment
with the war, as there would later be in the stories of
O'Flaherty, O'Faolain, and O'Connor. The physical
escape from capture and imprisonment is also a psychological release from the effects of British oppression.
The flight serves as the prelude to a rediscovery of
the national spirit and renewed commitment to the cause.

Corkery compensates for the narrowness of vision

in The Hounds of Banba in his next collection, The
Stormy Hills, which explores a wider range of subjects
than either of the earlier volumes. There are two sea
stories, "The Awakening" and "The Eyes of the Dead,"
and one of Corkery's few stories about the clergy, "The
Priest." The latter is an interesting study of the
elderly Fr. Reen, who has withdrawn from active involvement with his very poor parishioners. A long ride at
night to visit a dying man reawakens his guilt that he
has not done enough to improve his parishioners' lives.
He does manage to arouse a spiritual consciousness in
the old man, but the sight of his primitive home and his
squabbling heirs makes the priest flee in repulsion.
He is unable to confront the squalor of his parish.
There are also several other stories about old people.
As in O'Kelly's stories, Corkery's elderly characters
seek ways of clinging to life and warding off the threat
of uselessness and neglect by the community. Among the
best of these are "The Emptied Sack," a pathetic account
of an old man who has just lost his occupation, and "The
Rivals," the story of two old storytellers who try to
outdo each other even in death, like the old men in
"The Weaver's Grave." Predictably, the best stories in
the collection concern man's feeling for the land. "The
Wager" and "The Ruining of Dromacurrig" reflect the
deterioration of the gentry. "The Stones" is a grim,
haunting story of the superstitions associated with the
mountain landscape and their insidious effect on the
minds of local people. "Carrig-an-Afrinn" ("Rock-of-
the-Mass") evokes the intense emotions associated with
the long struggle in Ireland for possession of the land.
It is the story of Michael Hodnett, an elderly peasant,
who has successfully reclaimed the land at considerable
human cost.

On the occasion of a family reunion, Hodnett tells
for the first time the whole story of his move from
Carrig-an-Afrinn, a barren farm near the mountains, to
Dunerling East, a much better lowland farm neglected
and abandoned by the gentry, and of his unrelenting
effort to reclaim it. He has always cherished a special
feeling for Carrig-an-Afrinn, and especially for the
rock-pile which gave it its name, where Mass was said
secretly in the Penal days. On the day he leased
Dunerling East he heard a legend that angels guard the
places where Mass was said, and this gave him a superstitious dread of moving. Although Dunerling East has
become thriving and productive, much has been lost
along the way. In the early years several of his family, including his wife and favorite son, overworked
themselves and died.

94

The story is well constructed. The family reunion provides an intensified situation that shows what has become of Hodnett's family and land, and stimulates his memories of earlier times. His remaining children and two American visitors make up a receptive audience, and as the old man talks they gain a better appreciation of what he has been through. Part of the story is told in the third person by an omniscient narrator, part in Hodnett's own words, and part through the dialogue of his family; these multiple perspectives allow the reader to evaluate the story compassionately yet objectively.

The contrast between the two farms has broad symbolic implications. Carrig-an-Afrinn, though bleak and harsh, has a religious aura dating back to the dark days of the Penal Laws. Hodnett's character was formed by his youthful experience there, and he has always felt that it is his true home. Its value is spiritual, while that of Dunerling East is material. Although he has fought with all his strength to improve it, Dunerling East has no emotional associations for him, and provides no comfort when he is troubled. As in other stories Corkery suggests that the Irish character identifies more deeply with the rough mountain landscape than with the moderate plains.

As Hodnett relates his story, the extent of his loss becomes clear. His own character and will were so strong that in waging his war he unintentionally tyrannized over his family and drove them beyond their limits. Besides his wife and eldest son, three other children died, one of whom went mad first. His oldest surviving daughter has also been deranged by her labors. "Her cheeks were thin and haggard, colourless, her hair grey, and her eyes stared blankly at the life moving before them as if it were but an insipid and shadowy thing when compared with what moved restlessly, perhaps even disastrously, within the labyrinths of her own brain."[14] As his farm prospered and he gained more leisure to reflect, Hodnett became subject to fits of depression, and only the thought of Carrig-an-Afrinn sustained him. At the end of the story his son reveals to one of the Americans that the mass rocks have been blasted away to widen the road; he dreads that his father will find out. It is ironic that the old man who devoted his energies to progress should have his emotional anchor destroyed by the "progress" of modern Ireland. Corkery implies, as in other stories, that to sacrifice ancient Gaelic spiritual roots for material gain exacts a terrible price. This moral judgment does not intrude on the story, however; it is an essentially objective portrait of a ferocious, indomitable peasant who embodies all the energy and ambivalence of the Irish character.

Earth out of Earth is even more varied in content than The Stormy Hills, but it shows a considerable decline in Corkery's artistic powers. He attempts some technical experiments, such as telling a story in epistolary form, without much success. A few new subjects are introduced. Some of the better stories in the collection are narrated from a child's point of view: "Vision," "Children," and "The Lilac Tree." There are also some fairly good stories about old people: "The Old Stevedore," "--As Benefits Forgot," "Death of the Runner," and "Refuge." One story about a returned emigrant, "Understanding," recalls Moore's "Home Sickness" in its portrayal of Peter Farrell, a man who has suffered a nervous collapse and has returned to Ireland to convalesce. Farrell also goes back to America when he has recovered. There are several mediocre stories about religion, the sea, tenement life, and other subjects, and in general the collection contributes little to Corkery's artistic stature. Although at his best Corkery could produce short stories of high quality, he lacked a capacity for growth and adaptation, and his artistic vision, like his political views, remained static.

The above discussion reveals some differences in outlook between Corkery and O'Kelly as well as some obvious similarities. Both writers succeed in uncovering aspects of the Irish mind which were not adequately explored by earlier writers--the peasant's attachment to the land and to religious, national, and communal traditions. Both writers accept their subject matter with affection and enthusiasm. Although they both recognize sources of loneliness and frustration within Irish society, they do not express the strong antipathy towards Ireland that Moore and Joyce expressed. They look to Ireland's past to provide inspiration for her future and regard efforts to leave the country as misguided. They suggest that escape from stifling or destructive circumstances can be achieved by a liberating identification with the communal and national spirit.

The main differences of perspective between Corkery and O'Kelly can be seen in the moods of their stories, in their characterizations, and in their symbolic treatment of settings. O'Kelly is primarily interested in the constructive interaction between individual and community which is essential for emotional as well as physical survival. He often uses affectionate humor as a method of breaking down barriers between people and creating an atmosphere of tolerance and sociability. He describes places and buildings primarily as images of social relationships. Corkery also recognizes the individual's need for strong community ties, but his most characteristic stories deal with solitary characters, particularly with the mental desolation and moral disorder found in people whose ties with community or family have been broken or violated in some way. His rugged settings image the primitive depths of the self. His probing of the Irish conscience is often brooding and reflective.

Our examination of stories by Moore, Joyce, O'Kelly, and Corkery has revealed enough connections among them to justify regarding these writers as the founders of a coherent and distinct Irish short story tradition. From a technical standpoint, these stories are diversified; they employ many different kinds of plots and narrative methods. Oral techniques are used frequently, but with varied effects--O'Kelly's narrators are often humorous and sociable, for example, while Corkery's are thoughtful and solitary. And many of the stories, most notably Joyce's, but also some by other writers, rely on techniques that are not at all oral. Joyce's elaborate symbolic and structural devices set him apart technically from the other writers.

It is not so much in their techniques but in their attitudes and themes that the relationship among these writers, as well as their relationship with earlier Irish writers like Edgeworth and Carleton, can be seen most clearly. Although they differ in their degree of sympathy towards their Irish material, the short story writers share a common recognition of the powerful and contradictory forces in their heritage--a land that is hauntingly beautiful but does not provide an adequate living; a religion that offers rich spiritual rewards but demands the repression of vital sensual instincts; a traditional community that can give firm support to the individual but can also brutally ostracize anyone who violates its rigid standards; a nation that dreams of freedom and national pride, but undermines and betrays the efforts of its best men. All four writers, regardless of their political or religious convictions, found it necessary to withdraw from the violence and turbulence of Irish public life to do their best creative work. The short story genre appealed to them because of its concentration on a circumscribed,

private world, and its relative freedom from propaganda and abstraction. They could focus on such subjects
as the tension between the individual and his local
community, or the loneliness and need for fulfillment
in individual lives, without the necessity of presenting
a consistent, comprehensive view of a society which was
often disrupted and unsure of its values. These four
writers determined the direction that the Irish short
story would follow in the post-Revolutionary era.

Notes

Daniel Corkery, Synge and Anglo-Irish Literature (Cork: Mercier Press, 1931/66), p. 3.

Ibid., pp. 14-15.

Ibid., pp. 19-20.

Benedict Kiely, Modern Irish Fiction: A Critique (Dublin: Golden Eagle Books, 1950), pp. 2-3.

Ibid., p. 9.

Synge, p. 20.

Daniel Corkery, The Wager and Other Stories (New York: Devin-Adair, 1950), p. 174.

Ibid., p. 178.

Sean Lucy, "Place and People in the Short-Stories of Daniel Corkery," The Irish Short Story, ed. Patrick Rafroidi and Terence Brown (Gerrards Cross, Buckinghamshire: Colin Smythe, 1979), p. 169.

The Wager, p. 179.

Ibid., p. 185.

Kiely, p. 2.

George Brandon Saul, Daniel Corkery (Lewisburg: Bucknell University Press, 1973), p. 36.

The Wager, p. 65.

Part Two

MASTERS OF THE IRISH SHORT STORY

Chapter Six

INTRODUCTION

The emergence of the short story as the most important genre in post-Revolutionary Ireland resulted in
part from an international trend, and in part from
Irish cultural conditions. During the twenties writers
in the United States, England, and elsewhere often
turned to the short story as a highly artistic and
refined genre that could succinctly express the prevail-
ing mood of the time. This generation of writers--the
"lost generation"--experienced severe disruption of
their lives during World War I, when many of them fought
for abstract ideals which they failed to achieve, and
afterwards they felt alienated from a world of rampant
materialism and disintegrating values. Uprooted both
physically and spiritually from their home communities,
they often sought a more meaningful life in exile, but
found foreign societies unsatisfactory too, and longed
nostalgically for the security of childhood that they
could not recover. Many avoided social involvement and
lived as bohemians or withdrew to isolated rural areas.
The situation changed somewhat in the thirties as many
writers again became active in social causes.[1] The
short stories of the twenties, by Anderson, Fitzgerald,
Hemingway, Faulkner, Mansfield, Coppard, Lawrence, and
others, reflect the writers' disillusionment. Their
stories often portray rootless and isolated characters
at odds with society. Having rejected conventions and
abstract principles, these characters must rely on
their own intuitions for guidance, and as a result
their attitudes are often ambivalent and uncertain.

Irish writers of this generation shared in the general alienation, but they also felt that Irish culture
was peculiar and unrepresentative, that they had to confront greater frustrations and contradictions than were
found elsewhere. Irish society did not keep pace with
changes in other countries. While the rest of the world
was engaged in World War I, Ireland was fighting its
own private war of independence. After the war the pol-
icies of the Free State government fostered Ireland's
cultural provincialism and isolation from world affairs.
Writers were treated with deep distrust.

The primary tasks undertaken by the new government
were necessary but mundane--the establishment of an
efficient administration and civil service system, the

modernization of a backward, largely agricultural economy, and the consolidation of Irish independence from England. Until 1932 the country was headed by William Cosgrave, leader of the pro-Treaty party (Fine Gael), and for much of this time extreme nationalists refused to recognize the government. But eventually Eamon DeValera and his Republican followers began to participate actively in the political process, and their party (Fianna Fail) won control of the government in 1932 and has stayed in power with only a few interruptions since then. The remaining political ties with England were gradually dissolved; in 1937 a new Constitution was passed creating the nation of Eire, and in 1949 the separation from England was completed with the formation of the Irish Republic and withdrawal from the Commonwealth. Ireland's economy has remained heavily dependent on England's, however.

From the time of the Treaty, Irish government and society exhibited certain attitudes that were disturbing to many writers and intellectuals. The internal quarreling and bitterness that were legacies of British rule, though temporarily overcome during the Revolution, recurred in the aftermath of the Civil War. Timothy Coogan recalls this atmosphere of disillusionment.

> The comradeship, the national "oneness"
> of the independence movement, was broken.
> I have seen hardened, cynical old men with
> tears in their eyes as they told how,
> instead of friendship, bitterness grew;
> instead of self-sacrifice, selfishness;
> instead of order, chaos; instead of progress,
> destruction. Art and politics diverged.[2]

Irish political parties were suspicious of each other, and among the people as a whole the disrespect for authority which had developed under British rule persisted.

Ireland's internal problems contributed to its isolationist attitude. Irish neutrality during World War II brought protests from England and the United States, as well as from Irish writers and other citizens who believed their country should not turn its back on the world. During the war Irish life stagnated more than before. The press was censored and the mood within Ireland was harshly repressive. The policy of isolationism lasted until 1955, when Ireland joined the United Nations and committed itself to participation in international affairs.

The cultural insularity of Ireland was even more extreme than its political insularity. Government leaders envisaged a Gaelic state that would be a model of purity and virtue in a corrupt world. Irish was made the official language and until very recently was a required subject in the schools. The government was heavily influenced by the Catholic Church, which had been a dominant force in Irish political life since the days of the Penal Laws. The Church's support was one reason for the victory of the Free State forces over the Republicans and the acceptance of the Treaty by the majority of Irish people. One of the earliest acts of the new government was to pass a law forbidding divorce. DeValera's party later became reconciled with religious leaders and incorporated into the 1937 Constitution a provision recognizing the special position of the Church as the spiritual leader of Ireland. The Irish educational system was run by the Church, and the clergy held a highly respected and influential position in the community. One unfortunate effect of this influence was the tendency towards puritanism and intolerance in Irish society. The reasons why Irish Catholicism developed these traits are complex; the monastic tradition, the isolation of the Irish Church from European Catholicism, and the long, determined struggle to preserve itself against British suppression were contributing factors. The cultural atmosphere after the Revolution is described by Donal McCartney.

> The "addiction to goodness" was every-
> where evident, and everybody was going
> about everybody else's business. The
> Bishops' pastorals and the sermons of
> the priests were obsessed with the evils
> of "company-keeping," the heathenism of
> modern dancing and the dangers of the
> foreign newspapers and books.[3]

Irish women who committed sexual transgressions were severely persecuted and those who became pregnant often fled the country. Young people repelled by the stifling social climate emigrated in large numbers, and the emigration rate remained at a high level until the sixties.

The atmosphere of post-Revolutionary Ireland was particularly deleterious for the writers. The Irish public was generally apathetic towards literature, and openly hostile towards literature that criticized Ireland too harshly. Although writers of the Renaissance period had found publishers for their work in Ireland, after the Revolution there was no commercial literary publisher until the founding of the Dolmen Press in 1951. Irish writers once again had to seek foreign publishers, as they had done in the nineteenth century. Even more devastating was the impact of censorship. The Censorship Act of 1929 set up a Board to recommend banning books, magazines, and newspapers that were indecent or obscene and lacked redeeming artistic merit, or that advocated unnatural methods of birth control. Censorship at that time was of course not, unique to Ireland--Joyce's Ulysses was banned in England and the United States after its publication in Paris--but whereas England and the United States liberalized their censorship laws in the thirties, Ireland's law was severely enforced. The Censorship Board blatantly abused its power and suppressed the work of nearly all Irish writers who portrayed Irish life realistically, as well as works by many of the best foreign writers. John Kelleher, writing in 1945, comments on this perversion of the Act's original intention.

> For it is plain by now that the censor's hand falls most heavily, not on the purveyor of obscenity, but on the non-conforming writer. He is indeed outlawed. The action against his book is taken in secret. He has no appeal from the decision of the Board. He cannot expect the justice of a speedy trial, for his book may be banned as soon as it appears, or not till after the important first three or four months. . . . But most maddening of all is his knowledge that the very law under which he is penalized has been openly perverted by the censors themselves.[4]

As a consequence of this persecution, more and more Irish writers went into exile, including Liam O'Flaherty, Sean O'Casey, Samuel Beckett, Francis Stuart, and others. In 1946 the Censorship Act was amended to provide for an Appeal Board, but severe censorship persisted until the late fifties, when the Censorship Board became somewhat more lenient. The situation has continued to improve, but even today the Board exercises considerable power.

In the last two decades Irish society has become much more liberal. Church and state play a less dominant role in individual lives, sexual behavior has become more uninhibited, and writers are often treated tolerantly and even respectfully. In fact, the government has provided tax incentives to encourage creative

artists from other countries to take up residence in
Ireland. The country still has some serious social
problems, however; the continuing violence in Northern
Ireland is the most obvious manifestation of trouble.
Cultural apathy and provincialism are still fairly per-
sistent and widespread.

During the post-Revolutionary period many novels
were produced, by O'Flaherty, Brinsley MacNamara,
Peadar O'Donnell, Francis Stuart, and others, but many
of these are flawed and in general they are surpassed
in quality by the short stories. The major short story
writers of the period, O'Flaherty, Sean O'Faolain, and
Frank O'Connor, shared some experiences and attitudes
that distinguished them from their predecessors. All
three grew up in the atmosphere of idealism and nationalistic fervor that preceded the Revolution, joined
actively in the struggle for independence, and saw their
high hopes for the country defeated by brutality and
fanaticism during the Civil War, and by the anti-intellectualism of the new Irish Free State. Their lives
reveal a pattern common to Irish writers of their generation: involvement in public causes and controversies
as young men, followed by withdrawal into a more private
way of life, with frequent periods of travel or residence abroad which gave them a more cosmopolitan outlook. Because of their intense inner conflict between
commitment and alienation, their attitudes to Ireland
are more complex and inconsistent than those of their
predecessors. All three possessed an acute historical
consciousness and they had to define and redefine their
historical insights before they could fully understand
their own identity.

All three writers experimented with other genres
but found the short story more congenial to their purposes. They tried to write novels--O'Flaherty wrote a
large number and considered himself primarily a novel-
ist--but were more successful with the shorter form.
O'Faolain and O'Connor theorized at length about the
special qualities of the short story and the reasons
why the Irish could write stories better than novels.
They both agreed that Irish society was too narrow and
rigid to give the novelist enough scope.

In the hands of these three masters the Irish
short story realized its potential and acquired an
international audience. Their stories are essentially
traditional in method, not experimental; their techniques are borrowed more often from earlier fiction
than from contemporary sources. The dominant mode of

the stories is a kind of poetic realism, sometimes
lyrical, sometimes satiric, sometimes objective and
dramatic. The oral style used by Moore and others continued as a common narrative method, but other methods
were tried as well, and no single narrative technique
distinguishes the work of these writers. Their connection with each other and with the Irish short story tradition can be seen more clearly in the themes of their
stories; the broadest underlying theme is still the
relationship between the individual and the community,
the tension between a need for belonging and a need for
freedom from communal restrictions.

The traditional subject areas that we have examined in earlier writers--nationalism, religion, the
land, the family, love and marriage--recur also in the
stories of this generation, but with an altered perspective arising partly from intervening social change.
These writers focus more often than their predecessors
on the middle-class; of the three, O'Flaherty writes
most often of rural life, but he also portrays the rising merchant class, the influx of tourists, and other
social changes that affect traditional Irish life.
O'Faolain and O'Connor pay tribute to the rural traditions that are rapidly disappearing, but their primary
subject is the Catholic middle-class that is gaining
influence in Irish towns and cities. Their treatment
of these subjects alters during successive phases of
their careers or even from one story to the next.
O'Flaherty's work shows limited development, but
O'Faolain and O'Connor continued to grow and explore
new dimensions throughout their careers. Their late
work (especially O'Faolain's) reflects the recent liber-
alization of Irish society in their decreased emphasis
on communal restrictions and in their frank treatment
of such touchy subjects as mental illness, sexual aberration, and clerical celibacy. The subject of emigration and exile is treated differently too, as higher
income and access to rapid transportation enable the
modern Irishman to leave and reenter the country much
more easily; exile becomes a more internalized concept.

Despite the exploration of some new attitudes, subjects, and techniques in the later stories of all three
writers, the artistic quality is generally not as high
as in their earlier work. They all produced their
greatest stories during the period when they were most
deeply engaged with Irish social conflicts, when their
quarrel with Ireland was most intense. As they became
more detached and tolerant, their work lost some of its
passion and drama.

Notes

1 See Malcolm Cowley, Exile's Return: A Literary Odyssey of the 1920's (New York: Viking, 1951/62).

2 Timothy Patrick Coogan, Ireland Since the Rising (New York: Frederick A. Praeger, 1966), p. 167.

3 Donal McCartney, "Sean O'Faolain: 'A Nationalist Right Enough,'" Irish University Review, 6, no. 1 (1976), 83.

4 John V. Kelleher, "Irish Literature Today," The Atlantic Monthly, 175 (March, 1945), 73.

Chapter Seven

LIAM O'FLAHERTY

i

The publication of Liam O'Flaherty's stories in
the twenties initiated a phase of Irish literature in
which the short story would surpass poetry and drama as
the preferred genre. In spite of problems with censorship and hostility from the Irish public, O'Flaherty
and his contemporaries Sean O'Faolain and Frank O'Connor
wrote short stories prolifically and produced many that
rivalled the best stories in other countries. O'Flaherty spent much of his life in exile, but like Joyce
wrote almost exclusively about Ireland. In a simple,
direct, and vigorous style he portrayed the life of the
Aran Islands, the West of Ireland, and occasionally
Dublin. In addition to a biography, two autobiographies, and some miscellaneous books, he wrote fifteen
novels and thought of himself primarily as a novelist,
but most critics agree that his best achievement lies
in his short stories. The short story was the most
appropriate form for expressing his vision of Irish
life. His attitude to Ireland was more complex and
ambivalent than that of the earlier writers we have considered. He experienced many personal and cultural conflicts that could not be fully resolved in his novels
but could be briefly illuminated in his stories.

The influence of the Aran Island culture on
O'Flaherty's work was more profound than any later
influence. He was born on Inishmore, largest of the
islands, in 1896. At that time Aran peasants lived in
extreme poverty, in a manner that pre-dated the Famine.[1]
O'Flaherty's family was large and one of the poorest.
His mother, a gentle and imaginative woman, relieved
the hard struggle for existence by telling her children
fantastic and humorous tales. From her O'Flaherty
absorbed much of the island folklore, and as a child he
liked to make up lurid, violent stories that shocked
his mother and teachers. His father was stern and
remote, a rebellious nationalist who had been a Fenian
and Land-Leaguer. Most of O'Flaherty's siblings emigrated to America.

Because it was anachronistic, Aran culture embodied
many contradictions. The islanders were devoutly Catholic and respected the authority of the priest, but they

111

also clung superstitiously to ancient pagan charms and
cures. There was also a conflict between the Irish and
English languages; English was more practical, especially for those planning to emigrate, but Irish was associated with national identity and pride. O'Flaherty's
family spoke English until, at age seven, he rebelled
and insisted that they speak Irish. This conflict was
to pursue him in later years, when he wrote some
stories in Irish but was discouraged by their failure
to sell. A social conflict of more recent origin existed between the peasants and the rising commercial
class, the "gombeen men" who exploited them as ruthlessly as the landlords had done. O'Flaherty disliked
the commercial life of towns and preferred the native
peasant culture and the wilder, more remote areas of
the islands. He regarded the traditional life of Aran
as a special world, different from the rest of Ireland.
His earliest experiences thus instilled in him a sense
of an irreconcilably divided culture, what Patrick
Sheeran has called "a broken world, the two halves of
which hardly belonged to the same time or place."[2]

Religion and nationalism were strong early influences which O'Flaherty later found it necessary to
reject. Under pressure from family and friends, he
spent several years studying for the priesthood at
Rockwell, a seminary in Tipperary. When he refused to
take his vows he was accused, probably justly, of using
the seminary to obtain a free education. He also
briefly attended seminaries in Blackrock and Dublin.
His religious training produced an intense anti-cleri-
calism; in his autobiography Shame the Devil he says
that even as a child he felt ashamed when his relatives
and neighbors thought he had a religious vocation. "I
despised the priesthood and thought it was more noble
to do the ordinary chores of our society as a lusty
male, to till the earth, to be strong and brave at sea,
to marry and beget children, to raise one's voice with
authority in the councils of one's fellows."[3] His break
with Catholicism was similar to Joyce's "non serviam,"
and it was not until late in his career that his anticlericalism softened to any degree.

O'Flaherty's attitude to nationalism was more complicated. During his school years he was an enthusiastic Republican, but after attending University College,
Dublin, for a year, he left abruptly in 1915 to join
the British Army. This act outraged his relatives even
more than his rejection of the priesthood, but his war
experience broadened his outlook and enabled him to outgrow the narrow fanaticism of Irish nationalists. He

was shell-shocked during the war and suffered from nervous fears for a long time.

After the war O'Flaherty broadened his experience still further by wandering around the world and working at a variety of jobs. These experiences are recounted in his autobiography Two Years. Two manifestations of twentieth-century civilization particularly intrigued him: Communism and machine technology. Underlying both interests was his concern for the welfare of the poor and his dream of man's evolution towards perfection.

These progressive ideals conflicted with some of O'Flaherty's deepest feelings, however. He shared the Aran peasants' conservative caution and resistance to change. The conflict was aggravated by his mental instability, which at times worsened to mental illness. He could not give lasting allegiance to any social causes, and ultimately chose the artist's stance of isolation. In Two Years he describes a night of agonizing personal crisis, when he had to choose between reconciling himself with his people or affirming his freedom.

> Should I still hold with what remained
> of the spiritual fetishes of my people
> or cut adrift completely and stand all
> my life alone? . . . What horror! What
> loneliness! No hunger of an empty, food-
> entreating belly gives such an ache as
> the coward heart, which cries for com-
> fort in distress. An outcast hermit, who
> makes a god of thought and eschews all
> contact with the material empire of this
> earth, denies its gods, spits on its
> honours, and turns his cold, loveless
> eyes from mother, wife, child, friend,
> compatriot! Such must I become if I must
> win the empire of the mind which has no
> limits, whose beauties are unfathomable,
> eternal since they are not chained to
> time, and terrifying in their mystery.[4]

On the verge of a nervous collapse, he returned from his wanderings to spend a few months recuperating on Aran, but he was still regarded as an outcast and this was his last extended visit to his home. Afterwards he could return there only in his imagination.

The months O'Flaherty spent on Aran were followed by a brief period of activity as a Republican in Dublin.

The extent of his participation in the Civil War is not known, but one incident became famous: in 1922, with a group of unemployed men, he captured the Rotunda, a public building, and hoisted a red flag. After three days he surrendered the building to avoid bloodshed. He says in Shame the Devil that this incident probably broke his mother's heart and helped cause her death a few months later. It also intensified his ostracism from his people, who thought of him as a Communist, an atheist, and a public menace.

O'Flaherty achieved his first literary success in London, under the guidance of Edward Garnett, an editor at Jonathan Cape. In 1924 he returned to Dublin, hoping to establish himself there. This proved to be one of the most disillusioning periods of his career.[5] His attitude towards other Irish writers was arrogant and self-serving. He identified himself with a group of young writers, including Austin Clarke and F. R. Higgins, who rebelled against the Establishment led by Yeats and AE. He also met the writer Margaret Barrington; she divorced her husband to marry O'Flaherty and they had a daughter, but the marriage lasted only a few years.

Together with some of his friends, O'Flaherty founded a monthly magazine, To-morrow, which published only two issues, August and September, 1924. The main reason for its failure was the powerful influence of the Jesuits, who probably objected to some heresies in a story by Lennox Robinson in the first issue. This was O'Flaherty's first painful encounter with censorship. After the demise of To-morrow, he continued to publish his opinions in letters to The Irish Statesman and elsewhere. The earliest of these letters express a hope for the future of Irish literature. In October, 1924, he writes in praise of the life, passion, and virile force in Irish culture and says that these qualities are more important than philosophy and scholarly disputation; the violence of Irish life is a sign of vitality. "Ours is the wild tumult of the unchained storm, the tumult of the army on the march, clashing its cymbals, rioting with excess of energy."[6] By the following June his views have become somewhat more critical, though they are still predominantly hopeful. He says that the time is right to make a beginning in building up a national culture that will be internationally respected. Whether an Irish culture will exist in the future is still in doubt, however. "The younger generation alone can decide whether in twenty years' time we will be still a nation of bigoted and intolerant people

114

or whether we are going to build up a civilization distinctly our own, a civilization and a culture that will make us a force in Europe."[7] The note of doubt gradually hardened into a mood of severe disillusionment as his own work came increasingly under attack by the Irish press.

The result of O'Flaherty's disillusionment with the Dublin literary scene was his withdrawal from it. This withdrawal is consistent with his lifelong habit of retreat from difficult situations, but as has been suggested it also conforms with a pattern followed by many Irish writers of his generation. By 1927 he had given up hope of leading a new literary movement in Ireland. In his last letter to The Irish Statesman, written in December, 1927, he concludes that the Irish people are "too hopelessly sunk in intellectual barbarism to be capable of being saved by a single man."[8] He left Ireland and from 1927-32 lived mostly in England and the United States. In 1929 the Censorship Act was passed and most of his books were banned.

An article O'Flaherty wrote for The American Spectator in 1932 provides a strongly worded statement of his reactions to censorship and the ignorance of the Irish reading public. He begins by describing in Swiftian style the presence of dung and filth in small Irish towns, and continues in a vein that echoes Swift and Joyce.

> Unclean offal of any sort, whether in my neighborhood or in the minds of people with whom I have association, is strongly distasteful to me. So is poverty, ungracious tyranny and ignoble suffering. In my work I have been forced in honesty to hold up a mirror to life as I found it in my country. And, of necessity, the mirror shows the dung about the pretty altars. So a censorship has been imposed upon my work, since it is considered sacrilegious by the Irish Church that I should object to the sordid filth around the altars.

Though O'Flaherty bitterly condemns the priests and the bourgeoisie, he is much gentler in his attitude to the mass of Irish people. He considers them victims enslaved to the will of those in power. His affection for his people and the personal tragedy of his ostracism emerge poignantly as the article continues.

> I am censored and abhorred by the illiterate ruffians who control Irish life at present. There is hardly a single newspaper in Ireland that would dare print anything I write. There is hardly a bookshop in Ireland that would dare show my books in its windows. There is hardly a library that would not be suppressed for having my books on its shelves. Outside Dublin not a single organization would dare ask me to address them. Yet I claim that Ireland is the only country where I feel of any consequence as a writer. It is the only country where I feel the youth and freshness of Spring among the people, where I feel at one with my mates, where I sing with their singing and weep with their weeping, where I feel that I am a good workman doing a useful job and honored for my craft.[9]

The passage describes eloquently the frustration that Irish writers experienced as the long-awaited political freedom brought a stifling of free artistic expression.

Anger and frustration are apparent in much of O'Flaherty's writing published in the late twenties and early thirties. Increasing disillusionment combined with marital problems brought him by 1933 to the brink of a severe emotional crisis. Shame the Devil describes this crisis and his struggle to regain his creativity by seeking refuge in Brittany. When he arrives there, his imaginary alter-ego reminds him of the particular relationship with nature, especially with its harsher aspects, that he needs to regain his inner vitality and well being.

> Here is the earth in all its nakedness, without flowers or trees or birds to make it tame and friendly. There is the sea, sombre and dangerous in the light of evening. There is the air, grown cold, to give you an indication of the storms that buffet man. But all that is good if you accept it as good. If you fear it and turn aside from it to hide in the artificial sewers of cities, that means you have lost contact with life, that it has become an alien. The earth, the sea and the air are man's substance and his sustenance. What man builds on earth and

116

> his contraptions for mastering the ele-
> ments are ephemeral and alien to nature.
> Renew your friendship with nature. In
> that lies your chance of regaining peace.[10]

Despite his fascination with machines and human "progress," O'Flaherty essentially regarded urban civilization as alien to man. Observation of natural cycles and
the instinctive behavior of peasants and animals gave
him simplified objective images for his erratic subjective states and helped him to come to terms with himself.

The creative outburst described in Shame the Devil
was to become a more and more infrequent phenomenon in
O'Flaherty's later years. Since 1937, when his best
novel, Famine, was published, he has published only two
mediocre novels and a small number of short stories.
Little is known about his life during this time. He
spent the World War II years in North and South America,
and afterwards kept moving about, living for brief periods in Ireland, but primarily in France and England.
For the past few years he has resided mainly in Dublin;
perhaps recent changes in Irish society have enabled
him to feel more comfortable there.

O'Flaherty's career gives the impression of unfulfilled potential. The extraordinary cultural contradictions which he inherited may at least partially account
for his erratic temperament. The contrast between the
stark, primitive world that formed his sensibility and
the intellectually and technologically complex world
that he encountered in his travels probably contributed
to his sense of rootlessness and dislocation. The hostility of his people to his work was one of the severest
ordeals he had to face, since his best writing was
inspired by love for them. He seems most fully himself
when he is contemplating imaginatively the landscape
and inhabitants of Aran.

Most of O'Flaherty's short stories were written in
the twenties and early thirties, though he continued to
produce stories sporadically until the fifties. His
published collections include Spring Sowing (1924); The
Tent (1926); The Mountain Tavern (1929); Two Lovely
Beasts (1948); Duil (1953; stories written in Irish);
The Stories of Liam O'Flaherty (1956; mostly reprints
with a few new stories); The Pedlar's Revenge (1976;
previously uncollected stories mostly published in
periodicals between 1924 and 1953); and several limited
and selected editions. Because the majority of

O'Flaherty's stories were written within a five year period (1924-29), his work lacks the diversity and development found in the work of O'Faolain and O'Connor. There are, however, some observable differences of theme and style between his early and late stories.

Except for scattered comments in his letters to Edward Garnett, O'Flaherty has written almost nothing about the art of the short story or his concept of the genre. Remarks in his letters indicate that he considered the stories less important than his novels. His letters of 1924 express irritation that his stories were received better than his first novel, Thy Neighbour's Wife. He says that at times writing the stories bores him, since they "seem to advance according to a formula," but at other times they satisfy "an instinct for love of writing."[11] His novels preoccupied him intellectually, while the stories fulfilled a primarily instinctual need.

The atmosphere of O'Flaherty's novels is strikingly different from that of his short stories. John Zneimer has theorized that the stories reflect an altered state of consciousness. "If the novels are marked by violence and melodrama and fury, O'Flaherty's short stories are best marked by their qualities of calmness, simplicity, and detachment."[12] Violence and anguish are still present, but are treated differently from the way they are treated in the novels. Zneimer views O'Flaherty as a divided self, alienated and weighed down by a sense of the evil and futility of life, who could be reconciled to himself only by a process resembling religious conversion, a "shift from one center of consciousness to another,"[13] from the world of the novels to the world of the short stories.

James O'Brien has also commented on this change, noting that the novels are dominated by "oversized Dostoevskian figures" whose "dreams of perfection, twisted and fanatic as they generally are, represent man's upward movement to a perfection implicit in the evolutionary process," whereas the characters in the stories are uncomplicated peasants or animals. Like many other critics, O'Brien recognizes the difficulty of accounting for the simplicity and directness of O'Flaherty's best stories. "Somehow by stripping away the covering of civilization and the superstructures of reason, he penetrated to a bedrock of experience." O'Flaherty may have seen a stability and permanence in the instinctive peasant life of Aran that was lacking in his own temperament and in the modern world. His state of mind while writing the stories represents "almost a total surrender of the author's personality to the nature of things outside himself."[14]

O'Flaherty's novels were intended to provide a comprehensive intellectual view of modern society, and because he could not achieve intellectual wholeness, most of the novels were failures. The stories were more successful because they did not require an intellectual framework. They provided a refuge for his imagination, a timeless, elemental world to which he fled when the sickness and despair of civilization threatened to overwhelm him.

Although their distinctive characteristics derive from the Aran background, O'Flaherty's stories share some common ground with stories by other writers. His earliest stories were written under the spell of Maupassant, whom he read avidly.[15] Both writers depict the passion and violence of the peasant; both expose man's greed and cruelty towards other men or animals. O'Flaherty also resembles D. H. Lawrence, another protegé of Edward Garnett's, in his recognition of modern man's need to revitalize his instincts through contact with nature. He shares with Hemingway his mystique of physical courage and endurance as the noblest response to a hostile universe. At times, especially in his later stories, O'Flaherty also portrays characters similar to Sherwood Anderson's "grotesques," people whose growth has been stunted by a narrow provincial environment.

There is little indication from O'Flaherty's critical writing that he consciously saw himself as the inheritor of an Irish short story tradition. Except for some book reviews and an essay on Conrad, he wrote almost no commentary on the work of other writers. He read Joyce with much interest and expressed sympathy for his condition of exile,[16] but he did not publish his reaction to Dubliners or any of the other collections we have examined. (He did write some reviews of stories written in Irish by Padraic O'Conaire and others.) His refusal to theorize about the short story is consistent with his concept of story writing as an inspired, instinctive process. Nevertheless, there are many similarities of theme and form between his stories and those of earlier Irish writers.

Several of the characteristic Irish themes that we have traced in earlier stories recur also in O'Flaherty's work. Some of his stories are comic or fantasy tales. He examines many aspects of the traditional community, including its religious values, sexual mores, family life, treatment of children and old people, and attitude towards emigration and exile. In some stories characters live in harmony with the community, while in others they are frustrated and seek escape. He prefers to write not about social attitudes or psychological conflicts but about the relationship between man and nature, the harsh landscape and the treacherous sea. His characters are most fully tested in their efforts to survive and wrest a living from their environment. Many of his stories are about the behavior of animals threatened by human cruelty or natural forces; some contain no human characters at all.

O'Flaherty draws heavily on his Gaelic background and the oral tradition, but in a manner different from earlier writers. Perhaps because of his native ability in Irish, he does not self-consciously imitate oral narrative techniques, as do Moore, O'Kelly, and Corkery. His fluency in Irish is almost a handicap, since his transliteration into English sometimes produces awkwardness.[17] He borrows material freely from island folklore, particularly in animal stories. His distinctive style also owes much to the Gaelic influence. James O'Brien sees this influence in O'Flaherty's "directness of narrative, the simplicity of language, and an elemental concern with primary emotions."[18] A. A. Kelly sees it in the visual and aural quality of O'Flaherty's prose. His vivid visual imagination resembles that of the Gaelic storyteller, and his use of aural devices like repetition and rhythmic phrasing suggests that he wanted the stories to be heard as well as read.[19]

O'Flaherty's attitude towards artistic technique was very casual. He rejected the meticulous craftsmanship practiced by writers like Yeats and Joyce; he sometimes revised his stories but left many unrevised. In 1924 he wrote belligerently to Edward Garnett, "Dammit man, I have no style. I don't want any style. I refuse to have a style. I have no time for a style. I think a style is artificial and vulgar."[20] This refusal to take pains with his writing produced some atrocious flaws, but at their best his stories have an inspired originality and immediacy. He seldom uses sophisticated devices like flashbacks, intricate symbolism, or irony. Many of the stories are lyric sketches that take place in a timeless present and are narrated from a detached, unobtrusive viewpoint, though some stories are formally more elaborate and contain analysis and commentary. Except for their common setting, he makes no attempt to link stories with each other through overlapping

120

characters, plots, or other devices. His refreshing energy and simplicity are probably O'Flaherty's outstanding contribution to the Irish short story tradition.

ii

O'Flaherty's early stories, those collected in Spring Sowing and The Tent, include some of his best and most original work. Although he treats many of the themes that earlier writers treated, he achieves an arresting simplicity and lyrical intensity that has no precedent in Irish fiction.

Some of the subjects that were prominent in earlier stories are inappropriate to the mood of O'Flaherty's stories; as a result he treats them infrequently or poorly. He wrote several novels about war, including The Informer, Insurrection, and The Martyr, but only four war stories, two of which ("The Sniper" and "Civil War") appear in the early volumes. These stories convey the terror experienced by men engaged in gun battles. He also wrote only a few stories about urban or bourgeois life, none of which are memorable. He felt that cities are alien and destructive to man. "The Tramp," for example, suggests that the precarious freedom of the open road is preferable to the security of an oppressive urban environment.

Another subject which O'Flaherty treats in novels but seldom in the stories is clerical life. (His novels which characterize priests in detail include Thy Neighbour's Wife, The House of Gold, and Skerrett.) Two early stories describe characters in religious institutions who decide to leave the Church: "Benedicamus Domino" and "The Inquisition." Most of his portrayals of priests are harshly satirical. In "Offerings," a well-fed and complacent priest pretends to read his breviary while actually watching the accumulation of offerings at the wake of a poor man's child. O'Flaherty's anger is even more apparent in the savage and melodramatic caricature of a priest in "The Outcast." A young female parishioner with an illegitimate baby calls on the priest to plead for help, but he angrily banishes her from the parish, and she drowns herself. In only one story, "Charity," does O'Flaherty portray a priest with any degree of sympathy. Like war and urban life, the subject of religion raised complex social and moral issues which O'Flaherty probably felt were suitable for novels but not for short stories. Also, priests aroused his hostility and prejudice, so that he could not write about them objectively, and objectivity was essential to his storytelling method. He usually did not excel at satirical writing, as his tone often became too melodramatic or sarcastic.

The stories about rural peasant life are more central to O'Flaherty's artistic vision. Many of his early stories about the community life of peasants are humorous; they often turn on a character's efforts to outwit other characters. Stories of this type include "Selling Pigs," "A Shilling," "A Pot of Gold," "Colic," and "A Red Petticoat." They are related to his more serious stories about survival in that quick-wittedness is one means of warding off the effects of severe poverty. In "A Red Petticoat," for example, an ingenious widow whose four children are on the verge of starvation hatches a scheme of blackmail to buy food on credit; she knows that the shopkeeper has been having an affair with the tailor. The story contains some marvelously histrionic scenes of feminine sparring. O'Flaherty describes the colorful traits of tinkers in "The Tent" and "The Stolen Ass," but neither story matches O'Kelly's "The Can with the Diamond Notch." There are several stories, not all humorous, about the volatile anger of peasants: "Blood Lust," "The Fight," "The Struggle," "At the Forge." Exceptional among the early stories of peasant life is "Stoney Batter," one of only a few stories employing a first person narrator and imitating the oral narrative style. It anticipates the social conflicts of the later stories in its depiction of a pathetic ne'er-do-well dispossessed of his land by his bourgeois brother.

The subject of emigration and its effect on family life, treated in several later stories, occurs in only one early story, "Going into Exile," but it is one of O'Flaherty's masterpieces. It views the complex social issue of emigration with elemental simplicity. The plot encompasses only a single night and morning. A family of islanders, the Feeneys, host a night of dancing and merry-making for their two eldest children, Michael and Mary, who are leaving for America the following morning. After the guests have gone the family spend a last few hours together, and then Michael and Mary, accompanied by some of their family and friends, depart for the steamer to the mainland.

The narrator is omniscient and completely unobtrusive. The characters' emotions are rendered without commentary or analysis. Human experience is reduced to

essentials. The compression of time suggests the timelessness of the theme; past and future seem insignificant compared with the agonized moment of parting.

The story develops through a series of stark contrasts. It opens with a scene of companionship and fes-
tivity, as the crowd packs into the Feeneys' cabin for
the dance, and it concludes with a scene of desolation
and loss, and the mother calls frantically after her
departed children. At the beginning there is also a
contrast between human activity and the vastness and
stillness of nature; the natural background, described
with O'Flaherty's extraordinarily acute perception, contributes to a mood of inevitability. Through the cabin
door "a starry June sky was visible and, beneath the
sky, shadowy grey crags and misty, whitish fields lay
motionless, still and sombre."[21] Nature clearly reflects the deep sadness that the people try to disguise
with their merrymaking.

The traditional community plays a supportive rather
than a hostile role in this story. Since emigration is
a frequent occurrence among the islanders, and since
many of the emigrants never return, the people have
developed an almost ritualistic pattern of community
behavior to help the grief-stricken individuals endure
the departure. It is also traditional that the family
members stoically suppress their grief as much as they
can.

Despite the emphasis on communal response, O'Flaherty makes us aware of the feelings of individual family members. The characters do not have highly developed intellects, but although they have only a vague
understanding of what is happening to them, their emotions are profound. The father tries to keep up the
spirits of the guests while his mind is in agony, and
he senses inarticulately that a world in which such terrible separations are necessary is a "queer world."
Like her husband, Mrs. Feeney is "unable to think intel-
ligibly about her two children going away. Whenever
the reality of their going away, maybe for ever, three
thousand miles into a vast, unknown world, came before
her mind, it seemed that a thin bar of some hard metal
thrust itself forward from her brain and rested behind
the wall of her forehead."[22] The image of the bar of
metal effectively conveys her pain.

As might be expected, Michael's and Mary's feelings
about their departure are more ambivalent. Although the
young people are grief-stricken, they are also full of

123

anticipation about the prospects their new life will bring. Michael hopes to escape his father's life of poverty and squalor and use his strength to earn a good living. Mary thinks of the romantic men she will meet and the fine clothes and house she may someday have. She feels compassion for her mother's life of hard work and sacrifice but does not want to be trapped in the same kind of existence. Her stress produces a state of heightened apprehension and guilt in which every detail of her mother's appearance is fixed in her mind. She has been slightly afraid of her father since he whipped her for kissing a neighbor's son; the incident hints, without explicit theorizing, at the kind of repressive morality that would impel a healthy young woman to leave home. But O'Flaherty does not dwell on the reasons why the young people are emigrating. He focuses instead on the actual experience of parting.

After the young people have left, the mother and some village women who have stayed behind in the house begin to keen and utter customary phrases. But ultimately the communal responses are inadequate. The mother's grief as her children disappear down the road is too great for any consolation.

> She looked wildly down the road with
> dilated nostrils, her bosom heaving.
> But there was nobody in sight. Nobody
> replied. There was a crooked stretch
> of limestone road, surrounded by grey
> crags that were scorched by the sun.
> The road ended in a hill and then dropped
> out of sight.[23]

The bleak horizon marks the boundary of her limited world and images her sense of loss. Two old women try to comfort her by saying that time and patience cure everything, but their words seem meaningless in comparison with the terrible image of loss that O'Flaherty has created.

"Going into Exile" is a major landmark in the tradition of Irish emigration stories. It differs from earlier emigration stories like "Home Sickness" and "Both Sides of the Pond" in that it contains no opinions about emigration. It merely depicts the characters' states of mind at the moment of parting and relates these reactions to the vast ineluctable realities mirrored in the natural environment.

Many of the early stories deal more directly than

124

"Going into Exile" with the peasant's relationship to his harsh environment, either the land or the sea. In these stories the community's role is important, not for its conventions but for its support of the individual's struggle to survive against natural forces. "Spring Sowing" captures both the hardships and the joys of the peasant's life. It describes the first day of sowing potatoes for a newly married couple, Martin and Mary Delaney. Their masculine and feminine viewpoints are contrasted, as Martin thinks mainly of proving his manhood by outdoing the others, while Mary ponders a variety of womanly hopes and anxieties.

The description of nature in "Spring Sowing" is straightforward, and the only symbolism is of the most obvious kind, such as the parallel between sowing seeds in the spring and beginning a marriage. In "Going into Exile" nature evokes a contemplative, static mood; in "Spring Sowing," nature is an arena for energetic activity.

The sense of a shared communal life is prominent in this story as in "Going into Exile." All the able men, with their wives assisting them, begin their planting on the same day and use the same primitive methods their ancestors used. Their friendly rivalry helps them to sustain the arduous labor. The communal undertaking brings together not just different families but also different generations; Martin's grandfather, too old to work himself, watches Martin work and offers abundant advice. The sowing has a timeless, cyclical quality, in harmony with the rebirth of spring.

The most effective feature of this story is its rendering of the tension and ambivalence the young couple feel as they face a life of bondage to the soil. Though they are newlyweds and deeply in love, O'Flaherty does not romanticize their feelings. Mary is particularly apprehensive about what their marriage may bring. When she sees the fierce, unheeding look in Martin's eyes as he works to subjugate the earth, she becomes "suddenly afraid of that pitiless, cruel earth, the peasant's slave master, that would keep her chained to hard work and poverty all her life until she would sink again into its bosom."[24] But at other times during the day, she is filled with tender joy at her love for Martin and the beauty of the spring. In this story as in the similar story "Milking Time," contentment supplants fear; in other stories, however, a darker view of peasant existence is presented. Patrick Derrane in "Poor People" desperately tries to gather seaweed to fertilize

his fields, after getting a late start because of illness, but his work is interrupted by the death of his
young son. His life seems an endless round of misery
and hunger. Even in "Spring Sowing," the consolation
Mary feels for the hardship of her life is a dubious
one: "night would always bring sleep and forgetfulness."[25]

The most powerful and threatening force in the Aran
environment is the sea, and O'Flaherty found it deeply
inspiring. One of his most gripping stories, "The
Landing," dramatizes the efforts of fishermen to land
their curragh during a storm. The story is told from
the viewpoint of observers sitting on the shore. Only
one boat from the village is out fishing when the storm
rises unexpectedly, and as the boat returns to attempt
a landing, the villagers gather to watch and help. As
in other O'Flaherty stories, the whole life of the community is epitomized in the moment of crisis, and
through reliance on traditional skills and procedures
as well as on personal courage, the men make a safe
landing.

In spite of a few stylistic lapses, the technique
of this story is representative of O'Flaherty at his
best. Paul Doyle comments that it

> contains one of the most effective descrip-
> tions of a sea storm ever recorded in a
> short story. In passages worthy of Joseph
> Conrad, the reader not only sees but feels
> and tastes the fury of the wind and water
> and he understands and admires the endur-
> ance of men pitted against seemingly impos-
> sible odds.[26]

The vitality and sensuous immediacy of the style draw
the reader into the action. There is no narrator to
interpret or mediate between us and the experience.

Human responses are closely attuned to natural phenomena as the story moves through several stages of
intensity. Before the storm rises, two old women are
sitting on the shore watching the calm sea. The characterization emphasizes their conformity to the communal
life of the islands--they are all dressed alike and they
exchange familiar platitudes. One of them comments on
the paradoxical quality of the sea which both sustains
and destroys them. "'Sure, we only live by the Grace of
God, sure enough, with the sea always watching to devour
us. And yet only for it we would starve. Sure, many a

thing is a queer thing, sure enough.'"[27] The speech of
the women is casual. Their observations are uttered
more from habit than from genuine apprehension, since
no danger exists at the moment.

When the storm suddenly blows up, the tension
increases correspondingly. O'Flaherty depicts vividly,
especially through personification and sound imagery,
the battle between the people and the sea. The sea
seems to possess a diabolical life of its own. The people are acutely responsive to every natural sign, and
their behavior echoes the turbulent rhythm of the storm.

> The sea was getting rougher with every
> wave that broke along the rocky beach.
> It began to growl and toss about and
> make noises as if monstrous teeth were
> being ground. It became alive and spoke
> with a multitude of different yells that
> inspired the listeners with horror and
> hypnotized them into feeling mad with
> the sea. Their faces set in a deep frown
> and their eyes had a distant fiery look
> in them. They shouted when they spoke to
> one another. Each contradicted the other.[28]

The two wives of the men out fishing become the center
of interest, and they react with the hysteria that
everyone expects of them.

When the curragh rows into sight everyone's attention is riveted to it. The onlookers support the oars-
men with prayers, and the men go to the beach of the
rocky cove where the boat will land. At the critical
moment, everyone is carried away by an emotion that
transcends fear.

> The boat, the crew, the men on the
> beach, the women on the boulder were all
> mingled together for a wild moment in a
> common contempt of danger. For a moment
> their cries surmounted the sound of the
> wind and sea. It was the defiance of
> humanity hurled in the face of merciless
> nature.[29]

The boat's safe landing represents a momentary triumph
over nature. It is not an individual triumph, but a
communal one. Generations of experience have provided
the community with the knowledge and skill necessary to
land a curragh safely. The emotions the people feel

are also communal. Since everyone in the village makes his living the same way, the death of one person deeply affects the rest. In "The Landing" as in "Going into Exile" and "Spring Sowing," O'Flaherty pays tribute to the supportive communal spirit that O'Kelly praises in stories like "Nan Hogan's House," and that also informs many of Griffin's and Carleton's stories.

A more unusual method of finding sustenance, but one still endemic to Aran life, is described in "Trapped." Bartley Hernon, a man who makes his living by searching the cliffs at night for birds and eggs, is one day cut off from his return route by a freakish avalanche. He finally escapes by overcoming his panic and negotiating an extremely dangerous alternate route. The narrator is more intrusive than in other stories we have discussed, but not objectionably so. He occasionally breaks into the story to explain peasant characteristics and comment on Hernon's behavior.

The massive cliffs are described as carefully and observantly as the sea in "The Landing." They are not merely anonymous geological features, but have been explored and named by generations of islanders. O'Flaherty achieves an extraordinary effect of animation and cataclysmic change through subtle and delicate sound imagery.

> There was a dull rumble as the loosened rock fell with a thud against the slanting pile. Then there was silence for about half a second. Then the silence was broken by a slight snapping sound like the end of a dog's yawn. That sound changed into another and louder one, as of a soft mound bursting. Yet nothing seemed to move; until suddenly there was a tremendous crash. A cloud of dust rose in the air and the great pile of broken cliff hurtled down to the sea, casting rocks far out into the dark waters, where they fell with a pattering sound, while the bulk subsided to the base of the cliff and became still almost immediately.[30]

The abrupt contrasts between sound and silence, motion and stillness, contribute to the awe-inspiring mood.

Hernon is a gentle, passive man who lives entirely on a physical plane. Although he is usually fearless on the cliffs, he becomes panic-stricken and helpless

128

after the avalanche. The coming of night and the sound
of birds flying into the caves to roost heightens his
fear. When he tries to plan a way of escape, he can
think only of all the local men who have been killed on
the cliffs.

The fear of death paralyzes Hernon's mind until the
moon rises, and then he feels reassured, forgets his
fear, and negotiates with apparent ease the very difficult descent to the sea. The narrator expresses his
admiration. "His figure, bending and bounding, looked
wonderfully agile and beautiful in the half-darkness of
the pale yellow moonlight; the mysterious bounding figure of a cliff-man."31 Once at the bottom, he exults
in the accomplishment of what no man has done before,
and rapidly swims over a mile through shark-infested
water to the beach, thinking all the while of what the
village people will say about his feat.

In a way Hernon's escape from almost certain death
is more remarkable than the escape in "The Landing,"
because he achieves it alone and in a situation that
has no precedent in his experience. But the instincts
and skills acquired during many years on the cliffs see
him through the ordeal. Although the island community
does not play as obvious a role in this story as in the
others, nevertheless Hernon identifies himself with the
community and his anticipation of his triumphant return
to the village indicates that his individual escape is
a victory for everyone.

O'Flaherty's preference for wild and rugged terrain
recalls Daniel Corkery more than any other previous
story writer. Both writers view the harshness of nature
as a challenge to man, and they suggest that rough landscape appeals to a more elemental and profound level of
the mind than gentle landscape. But Corkery associates
natural objects with religious and moral values, as in
"The Ploughing of Leaca-na-Naomh" and "Carrig-an-Afrinn,"
whereas O'Flaherty regards nature simply as a blind,
indifferent force which man may temporarily conquer,
but which will eventually destroy him. O'Flaherty also
looks more closely than Corkery does at the brutal,
predatory aspect of nature.

By far the largest group of O'Flaherty's early
stories concerns the instincts of animals. These
stories, written at the suggestion of Edward Garnett,
have their precedent in Aran folklore rather than in
literary tradition. Most of them are not moral fables,
like Aesop's stories, but realistic and observant

depictions of animal behavior. There are many parallels
between O'Flaherty's animal and peasant stories. Both
types are concerned with survival instincts such as
mating, finding sustenance, and avoiding danger, and
both reflect admiration for courage, endurance, and
skill in the face of imminent death. Some but not all
of the animal stories contain human characters.

Many of O'Flaherty's animal stories describe animals or birds giving birth or raising their young:
"The Cow's Death," a remarkable story in which a cow
leaps over a cliff after the body of her stillborn calf;
"His First Flight"; "Three Lambs"; "The Lost Thrush";
"The Wild Goat's Kid." Others describe efforts of animals to escape human or animal predators: "The Rockfish"; "The Blackbird"; "The Hook"; "The Conger Eel";
"The Wounded Cormorant." There are also several ugly
stories about human cruelty or neglect towards animals,
a subject also treated by Maupassant: "The Wren's
Nest"; "Sport: The Kill"; "The Wild Sow"; and "The
Black Bullock."

O'Flaherty seems particularly intrigued by the
maternal instinct. "The Wild Goat's Kid" is a lyrical,
beautifully rendered story of a goat who has become separated from the herd and has gone wild on the cliff-
tops. When a predatory dog threatens her new-born kid,
she determinedly withstands its cunning attack and kills
it with her hooves.

The narrative viewpoint is almost completely objective, and the style is delicate and precise. The
description of the goat's pregnancy shows particularly
well O'Flaherty's gift for close observation.

> Towards the end of winter a subtle change
> came over her. Her hearing became more
> acute. She took fright at the least sound.
> She began to shun the sea except on very
> calm days, when it did not roar. She
> ate less. She grew very particular about
> what she ate.[32]

The simple, repetitive sentence patterns are appropriate
for the fundamental simplicity of the material.

The goat's instincts become attuned to her environment, and she enjoys her maternity in the solitude of
the cliffs, in "absolute freedom and quiet." The dog
represents the brutal, destructive side of nature, but
O'Flaherty makes no attempt to attach moral significance

to the conflict; it is simply a manifestation of larger creative and destructive cycles. The dog instinctively times his attack to coincide with the ominous night, and the goat's victory and escape coincide with the rebirth of dawn. The protracted battle is dramatized in such authentic detail that Paul Doyle has concluded, "O'Flaherty has obviously witnessed such a conflict; and the effect of his description is such that the scene could be no more completely captured or delineated."[33] As the story ends and the goat flees eastward with her kid, towards the rising sun, the joyful mood suggests a celebration of the freedom inherent in wildness and solitude, a freedom worth defending ferociously.

O'Flaherty's animals possess the same qualities of instinctive courage and skill as do his peasants, and they battle for their lives with equal determination. Like the stories about men escaping from danger or succumbing to death, the animal stories move us because they depict the primal life force that continually struggles and asserts itself against annihilation. By showing strong resemblances between human and animal instincts, O'Flaherty suggests that man fulfills himself most completely when he is immersed in his natural environment and guided by his deepest biological drives.

In these early stories O'Flaherty found a way of simplifying his complex relationship with Ireland and expressing his admiration and respect for the inhabitants of Aran. Religious and social themes are not prominent in these stories; they emphasize instead the courageous struggle for survival in a harsh and dangerous environment. The mood is somewhat fatalistic and violence and death are regarded as commonplace realities. Survival of individuals depends on communal experience and skill. Characters are not developed in depth as individuals but are identified with the community and with natural cycles.

The organic form of these stories grew out of O'Flaherty's artistic vision. His perception of the world in vivid contrasts and antitheses influences the structure of the stories. He often uses repetition as well as contrast for emphasis, and the sensuous freshness and immediacy of his style allows the reader to apprehend the material directly. To read these stories is to rediscover the primal innocence that civilization has obscured.

As we have seen, the period of the mid- and late-
twenties was a difficult one for O'Flaherty. His frustration with the Irish public and press affected the
mood of his third short story collection, The Mountain
Tavern. A. A. Kelly has pointed out that a high proportion of stories in the volume concern death.[34]
There are fewer humorous stories and more about outsiders and social conflicts. The admiration for peasant
life expressed in earlier stories is often replaced by
a more critical or ambivalent attitude, especially in
stories dealing with social themes. A more complex
technique is required to handle the greater complexity
of theme, and several of these stories are longer and
more elaborate than the early ones.

Despite these differences, there is considerable
continuity between this volume and the earlier collections. The two war stories, "The Mountain Tavern" and
"The Alien Skull," are similar to earlier ones in evoking the horror felt by soldiers. "The Mountain Tavern," set during the Civil War, uses the symbol of falling snow, perhaps borrowed from Joyce's "The Dead," to
suggest the purity and oblivion of nature in contrast to
human misery and hatred.

The theme of man's struggle against a harsh environment also recurs in The Mountain Tavern, though much
less often and sometimes in combination with other
themes. "The Oar" is a brief but powerful depiction of
fishermen fleeing from a storm. It has much in common
with "The Landing" but is darker and more paradoxical
in mood. Two curraghs are out fishing when a storm
blows up. They try urgently to reach shore, but one
boat capsizes. The sight of the drowning men haunts
the survivors as they reach shore safely. Since the
viewpoint is that of the fishermen rather than the people waiting on shore, the struggle has even greater dramatic immediacy than in "The Landing." Although human
foolhardiness is a motivating factor in "The Oar"--the
men keep fishing in spite of warning signs in the sky,
because they are greedy for a large catch--our admiration for their courage and skill is not lessened by the
fact that they invited their predicament.

O'Flaherty's familiar devices of contrast, repetition, and vividly sensuous imagery are combined with
superb artistry. His description of the sea just before
the storm foreshadows the drowning. There is a "heavy
silence," and "strange shadows" can be seen on the

water.

> Above, the Drowned Man's Leap stood;
> a proud cruel cliff with a jutting beak,
> from which water dripped down its bulging,
> mossy belly. And round the frail, swaying
> boats, other shadows crept up from the
> deep, shapes of sunken rocks, where fishes
> roamed in lairs and beds of clustering
> yellow weeds.[35]

The passage verges on symbolism without being overtly
symbolic. Repetition is used with particular effective-
ness to heighten the drama. "Now a motionless black
floor supported the motionless coracles. Now there was
no moon. Now a black mass filled the sky."[36] The repetition of "now" focuses attention on the urgency and
danger of the present moment; as each brief moment
passes, vast and threatening natural changes occur.

When the fishermen begin their battle to reach
shore, they draw on all the traditional skill and knowledge they possess. There is no time for thought; their
response is entirely instinctive. As in "The Landing,"
their emotions transcend fear. But nature is relentless
and chance determines which boat is capsized and which
is saved. Contrast and repetition help create a moving
symbol of the horror of death:

> First they saw an upraised oar, raised
> straight on high, its handle grasped by
> an upraised hand. Beneath it, they saw
> an upraised face in agony. The face looked
> up, with staring eyes, as if saluting
> Heaven with his upraised oar.[37]

Another lightning flash reveals the oar with no hand
grasping it, and a third flash reveals only the empty
sea. The image haunts and terrifies the men as they are
pulled onto the shore. The story convincingly expresses
the vulnerability of life, the nearness of death, and
the heroism of men who expend every effort to survive
in a vast, menacing universe. That some men live and
some die is determined by chance, but their fate seems
less important than their courage and their urgent will
to live.

The Mountain Tavern contains several stories about
the survival instincts of animals, including "Birth,"
"The Blackbird's Mate," "Prey," and "The Black Rabbit";
in comparison with the earlier animal stories these

133

seem somewhat mechanical and redundant, as if O'Flaherty had tired of the formula. But the unusual combination of an animal story with religious satire in "The Fairy Goose" produces a masterpiece. The story is taken almost unchanged from Aran folklore,[38] and is presented as a fable.

"The Fairy Goose" depicts the conflict between pagan and Christian beliefs in an island village. An old woman, Mary Wiggins, raises a gosling that does not develop like a normal goose and becomes a kind of pet. The villagers come to believe that the goose is a good fairy with power to cast spells and cure the sick. When Mary realizes she can make money from the goose, she sets herself up as a "woman of wisdom," and sells charms to the villagers. A jealous neighbor informs the priest, who arrives in a rage and denounces Mary Wiggins as a heretic. His cruelty towards the goose sets an example for several village youths, and later that night they stone her to death.

O'Flaherty describes the goose with the delicacy characteristic of his animal sketches. Her appealing mannerisms and affection for people are fully rendered, to strengthen the impact of the satire when she becomes the innocent victim of human greed and cruelty. "She was quite small, a little more than half the size of a normal, healthy goose. But she had an elegant charm of manner, an air of civilization and a consciousness of great dignity, which had grown out of the love and respect of the villagers."[39] The readiness of the people to believe the goose is a fairy shows that pagan superstitions are still influential among them, despite their Christianity. Their reverence for the goose appears as a harmless fantasy, however, until it brings out the greed in Mary Wiggins.

But even Mary Wiggins' exploitation seems relatively harmless compared with the hysterical reaction of the priest. The people fear him much more than the fairies and rapidly switch their allegiance when he arrives. O'Flaherty's portrayal of the priest is a harsh caricature, like his earlier caricatures in "Offerings" and "The Outcast." The narrator's tone is heavily sarcastic as he describes the goose's reaction to the terrifying figure. "The bird, never having known fear of human beings, never having been treated with discourtesy, was so violently moved by the extraordinary phenomenon of a man wearing black clothes, scowling at her and muttering, that her animal nature was roused and showed itself with disgusting violence."[40] The priest is as crude and violent as his parishioners; he strikes Mary Wiggins, destroys the goose's nest, kicks her and, feeling ashamed of his outburst, throws a stone at her as he leaves.

Consistent with its fable structure, the story ends with a moral: ever since the death of the goose, the people of the village have been "quarrelsome drunkards, who fear God but do not love one another."[41] As elsewhere, O'Flaherty in this story attacks a Christianity that is based on fear and hatred rather than love. He also satirizes the faults of the peasants: their gullibility, fickleness, and submission to authority; this kind of criticism is seldom found in his earlier stories. The anticlerical viewpoint expressed in "The Fairy Goose" is similar to that often expressed in Moore's stories, but without the explicit polemic that Moore indulges in.

Another anticlerical satire from The Mountain Tavern, "The Strange Disease," describes a priest's visit to a sick parishioner, a situation also used in O'Kelly's "The Sick Call" and Corkery's "The Priest." The stories differ considerably in purpose and mood, but in all three the sick call leads to a confrontation of the deeper realities of Irish life. In "The Strange Disease," the priest's discovery that his uncouth young parishioner is merely suffering from love-sickness triggers an angry outburst in which the priest's lovelessness and sour puritanism are exposed.

Several social themes besides religion are explored in the collection. In "Mackerel for Sale," O'Flaherty attacks the exploitation of peasants by commercial "gombeen men." He also looks more closely than in earlier stories at social problems connected with sex and marriage. His few attempts to write about middle-class sexuality are unconvincing and tedious. He is much more successful with his depictions of peasants' sexual attitudes in such stories as "The Painted Woman," "The Ditch," and "Red Barbara." Here, as in his religious stories, his viewpoint often bears some resemblance to that of George Moore. These stories are sordid and naturalistic, especially "The Ditch," which recounts the murder of a newborn baby by the mother's lover. Child-murder as a result of the Irish peasant's hysteria over sexual misconduct also occurs in Moore's "A Play-House in the Waste." In addition, O'Flaherty shares the compassion of Moore and other earlier writers for the loneliness of old people; "The Stream" and "The Stone" anticipate the many studies of old people in his later work.

The vacillation between positive and negative attitudes towards Ireland that we have observed in O'Flaherty affects the two stories of family life and exile in
The Mountain Tavern, "The Letter" and "The Child of
God." In "The Letter" Irish life is regarded as superior to life in exile, but in "The Child of God" exile
is preferable to the intolerance and hostility at home.

"The Letter" is reminiscent of O'Kelly's "Both
Sides of the Pond" in its view of America as a place
that corrupts young Irish people. O'Flaherty emphasizes
the natural simplicity and wholesomeness of peasant
life instead of its poverty and narrowness. The story
is told not from the emigrant's point of view but from
that of her peasant family. One afternoon as they are
working happily in their potato field, they receive a
long-awaited letter from their daughter Mary, who left
for America a few months before. At first they are
overjoyed when they see that she has enclosed a check
for twenty pounds, but they soon realize that she has
earned the money as a prostitute and has become miserable and lonely.

As he does frequently, O'Flaherty rhythmically
counterpoises human emotions against the natural surroundings. The family's perception of nature alters
with their emotions. At the beginning of the story
nature appears to be in harmony with man, but by the
end it has become alien and indifferent to human suffering. The entire story takes place in the field. The
choice of a field as the setting rather than a cabin or
another place is appropriate, since the field is the
place where the peasants have the closest contact with
the fertile earth that provides spiritual as well as
physical sustenance. O'Flaherty's preference for open-
air settings has been documented by A. A. Kelly, who
observes that three-fifths of his stories take place
outdoors. His indoor scenes are often "linked with
frustration, or abnormal states of mind and body resulting in a feeling of entrapment."[42] But "The Letter,"
like "Both Sides of the Pond," demonstrates that even
the most beautiful natural setting can fail to console
or sustain man in his deepest grief. The projection of
human moods onto the landscape is of course a common
literary device, but few writers have portrayed the
relationship with the immediacy and precision that
O'Flaherty achieves.

Because "The Child of God" emphasizes Irish social
conflicts, the natural background is of less importance
than in "The Letter." This relatively long story is

136

atypical in that it probes a subjective autobiographical subject, the antagonism between an artist and his native community. The subject had been treated previously by Moore in "In the Clay" and "The Way Back" as well as by Joyce in A Portrait of the Artist, and O'Flaherty's viewpoint is similar to theirs.

The protagonist, Peter O'Toole, rejects the priesthood to pursue a career as an artist and is eventually forced into permanent exile from his village. Even as a child he is different from the other children, sensitive and gloomy. His mother, who adores him and thinks he is a "child of God," determines that he will be a priest and not a farmer like his father. The family goes into debt to send him to the seminary. After doing well there for several years he is expelled, and his family is disgraced in the village. A year later he returns home unexpectedly for a visit, announcing that he has become an artist. His family and the villagers try to welcome him, but his behavior alarms them. He tells them he no longer believes in God, and he spends several months carousing with other young men and making sketches of the villagers. The incident which brings their hatred of him into the open and completes his ostracism is an old man's wake. The wake, attended only by young men who had insulted the old man while he was alive, turns into a drunken orgy. When the villagers observe Peter painting the scene, they react with violent outrage. Peter's father orders him to go away, the villagers stone his house, and the priest banishes him. He is compelled to go for good.

The first part of the story, leading up to the day when Peter returns to the village, is presented mostly in summary form with dialogue interspersed to illustrate crucial points. After Peter's return the narrative becomes more dramatic and immediate as the incidents preceding the wake are related. The point of view is generally objective, though we sometimes see into characters' minds, especially Peter's.

O'Flaherty gradually reveals the severe pressures that traditional peasant values and attitudes exert on an imaginative, sensitive individual. Peter's misguided ambition to enter the priesthood is understandable for an artist growing up in Irish society. Stephen Dedalus in Joyce's Portrait is attracted to the priesthood for reasons similar to Peter's. Priests, like artists, are set apart from others; unlike artists, they have power and authority and are treated reverently by the people. They also are surrounded by the trappings of religious

137

ceremony, which appeal to the artist's need for ritual, beauty, and sensuous gratification.

The peasants' suspicion and hostility towards a "spoiled priest" are brought out during the homecoming scene. The narrator comments on the reaction of Peter's parents to the changes they recognize in him.

> The two of them felt in their minds that this strange being, who had been their son, was so utterly remote from them that they were terrified of hearing anything of his past. It is impossible to explain the instinct of peasants, their aversion for anything unlike themselves and their intuition for sensing the presence in strangers of forces which are alien to their own natures.[43]

When they learn he no longer believes in God, they feel that their bond with him is broken. It is characteristic of O'Flaherty that he does not attempt to theorize about this narrow-minded attitude, but merely presents it as a powerful and immutable force that affects Peter's life.

Peter's own attitude towards the villagers fluctuates. As a man, he is emotionally involved with them and is torn between affection and defensive hostility. But he has also begun to view them with the artist's detachment, and he has an impersonal appreciation for their beauty. When the villagers come to his house to welcome him home, he is struck by their appearance. "He stood in the middle of the floor and they sat around the walls, strange, beautiful faces, all sombre and dignified; mysterious faces of people who live by the sea away from civilization; age-old people, inarticulate, pitiless yet as gentle as children."[44] He is inspired to express their primitive beauty in his paintings, to articulate what they cannot articulate themselves.

Peter views the degrading scene at the wake with this same objectivity and tries to capture it on canvas. John Zneimer explains Peter's alternate states of consciousness.

> As an artist he is cold and detached, and to that scene which in the normal man would evoke terror and horror he feels impelled to bring his vision. . . . He has been a part of the scene as a man, a

> leading participant in all the debauch-
> ery. But always the second self--the
> artist--is watching, and when the scene
> reaches the stage when no normal man can
> watch unaffected, the artist detaches
> himself and makes the scene the material
> for his art.[45]

This depiction of character through contradictory moods
is a technique we have observed in other O'Flaherty
stories. But because Peter is an artist and has a more
antagonistic relationship with his people, his emotional
vacillation is more extreme than that of the other characters, more like that of O'Flaherty himself.

In a curious shift of viewpoint, O'Flaherty describes the effect of the banishment not on Peter but
on his mother, left alone in her house while the father
is seeing Peter off. The scene is somewhat similar to
the ending of "Going into Exile," but much less effective. Perhaps because the subject is such a personal
one, O'Flaherty allows excessive sentimentality to
intrude.

"The Child of God" illustrates vividly a common
Irish theme--the hysterical resistance among Irish people to seeing themselves portrayed realistically in art.
In contrast to "The Letter," peasant life in this story
seems unhealthy and sterile, and exile seems essential
for Peter's well-being and his free development as an
artist. That O'Flaherty could write, at approximately
the same period, two such contradictory stories, demonstrates the complexity and inconsistency of his attitude
towards Irish life.

The culmination of O'Flaherty's most prolific period as a short story writer is his long story "The
Caress," which was written in the early thirties and
included in Shame the Devil as evidence of his recovery
from a nervous collapse. In "The Caress" O'Flaherty
combines masterfully several of the subjects that he
explored in The Mountain Tavern--sexual attitudes, marriage customs, old age, exile, the limitations of peasant life.

The protagonist Bartly Delaney, an old bachelor,
has been dominated by his mother all his life. After
her death he decides he wants to marry a young woman
who will give him sexual gratification and children.
He thinks that his money will get him an attractive
wife, but he is so withered and sexually repressed that

139

his self-delusion appears ridiculous. One night when
he is drunk, he decides inappropriately to seek the
hand of Mary Madigan, a beautiful young woman recently
returned from America. He and some drunken companions
visit her father's house, but while Delaney and Mary's
father are drinking and discussing financial arrange-
ments, Mary and her lover Martin Derrane meet outdoors
and decide to leave for America the next day. Inside
the house Delaney has become so drunk that he mistakes
Julia, Mary's half-witted elder sister, for Mary and
tries to caress her in the bedroom. An uproar occurs
when Michael, Mary's brother, returns home from the
night's fishing and catches Delaney pawing Julia.
Michael pushes Delaney into a pile of fish, where he
sprawls ignominiously. As his companions are taking
him home he keeps muttering drunkenly that he wants to
marry a young girl.

The powerful sense of contrast that O'Flaherty
employs in earlier stories is also evident in "The
Caress." There is an antithesis between older characters whose natures have been distorted and repressed--
Delaney and Julia--and characters who are young and full
of vitality. As in many of his later stories, O'Flaherty here shows compassion for repressed and unfulfilled
characters. The emphasis is not on the young lovers
who escape to America, but on the absurd old man left
behind. O'Flaherty's concern with those who are bereft
and lonely is evidence of his deep imaginative identification with Ireland, particularly with the inhabitants
of its most desolate regions, who cannot easily find
compensations for their losses and deficiencies.

Delaney represents a type of character frequently
produced by the narrow inbred island life. His attachment to his prudish widowed mother has thwarted his
sexual development, and when he finally decides he wants
a wife, he cannot court one in a normal way. O'Flaherty also implies that the prevalence of drinking and
crude materialism in Irish society stifles sexual development and romantic love, impelling many of the young
people to go away. But the portrayal of Delaney conveys
pity as well as repulsion.

> He was not dry and withered because of
> his age, but because he had never known
> the joy and exuberance of passion granted
> its fulfillment in action. His whole lank
> body, all hunched and twisted by hard
> work in the fields, told the same tale
> of frustration as his face; lean and

> hungry and unkempt, like a tree whose
> growth has been arrested by a sudden
> drought of the earth about its roots.[46]

Delaney is a silent and modest man when he is not drunk.

The plot, imagery, and setting reinforce the antithesis between Delaney and the youthful, vital characters. The story is fast-moving and dramatic; much of
it consists of colorful dialogue. This energetic activity contrasts with Delaney's impotent and befuddled
character. O'Flaherty uses imagery, especially animal
imagery, to relate character traits to the natural environment. Delaney is compared to a malodorous, rampant
goat and an overheated sheep, while his splendid young
companions are associated with a beautiful mare that
they stop to ride on the way to Madigan's.

During the scene at Madigan's house the contrast
between Delaney and Julia and the young people becomes
even more striking. Mary Madigan is an extremely beautiful girl, restless and passionate. She is disgusted
by Delaney's courtship and thinks only of Martin Derrane. Her lovemaking with Martin outside the house is
in harmony with the vast yet delicate beauty of the
natural setting, while the befuddlement of the characters indoors corresponds to the ugly, coarse side of
nature. Delaney's clumsy advances to Julia parody the
real lovemaking outside. The love between Mary and
Martin is so intense that it overcomes Martin's shame
at having no money of his own. Material values seem
insignificant. Their emigration will give them freedom
from family conflict and social censure.

Delaney's collapse into the pile of fish after his
encounter with Michael completes his degradation. The
dead fish symbolize his repulsive, deathlike lechery.
The story ends with Delaney stumbling around a field
while his companions interrupt their trip home to drink
some more. He still insists that he wants to marry a
young girl and has money and land to offer her. The
narrator's final comment epitomizes Delaney's distorted
nature. "It was like a grotesque dance, the drunken
leaping of that withered man."[47]

"The Caress" illustrates O'Flaherty's perception
at this stage of his career of the conflicting, often
antithetical forces at work in the Irish environment.
He does not analyze social attitudes in detail, but presents them as part of the environment, almost as natural
phenomena. Beauty and ugliness, passion and lechery,

141

fertility and impotence all coexist as manifestations
of the vast creative and destructive cycles of nature.
Although the environment contains vital, passionate
energy as well as grotesque sterility, it is still too
restrictive for many of the young people, and they must
escape it.

iv

An interval of almost twenty years passed between
the publication of The Mountain Tavern and "The Caress,"
and O'Flaherty's next collections, Two Lovely Beasts
and The Stories of Liam O'Flaherty (the latter contains
only a few new stories). A few of the late stories are
of high quality, but many of them are mediocre and in
general they evidence a decline in his creative powers.
Several of these stories were also published in Irish
versions, and Irish scholars have asserted that O'Flaherty's Irish style is more graceful and self-assured
than his English style.

It is difficult to speculate about the reasons for
O'Flaherty's lack of productivity in later years.
Patrick Sheeran believes that O'Flaherty's mental instability was the source of his creative drive. "His fear
of insanity was . . . an important stimulus to artistic
activity. In later life he grew to be more stable:
gentleness replaced violence and with it came an end to
his creative work."[48] The censorship and hostility of
the Irish public which drove him into exile may also
have dried up his inspiration, since his best writing
was motivated by love for his people and was directed
towards an Irish audience. It may be that, in contrast
to Joyce, he needed involvement in Irish life rather
than the distance and detachment of exile.

There are some noticeable differences in mood and
technique between O'Flaherty's early stories and his
late ones. The wildness and energy of the early stories
have diminished considerably, and there is no physical
violence. There are more stories about social conflict
and change, especially the intrusions of the modern
world on traditional Irish life, and fewer about man's
relationship with nature. We can observe in some of
these late stories a broader emotional range, more depth
of characterization, and greater moral ambiguity.
O'Flaherty places greater emphasis on the deprivation
and stagnation of Irish life; the characters are often
mentally deficient, ill, or elderly.

142

A few of the late stories are technically superior to the early ones. The plots are often more elaborate and are structured on social or psychological conflicts rather than on physical action. O'Flaherty relies more heavily on dramatic presentation than on narration and summary, and evidences skill at handling dialogue.

Several of the subjects that were treated negatively in earlier stories are not treated at all in the late ones--war, urban life, the role of the clergy. There are also none of the simple lyric sketches about man struggling against the land or sea, like "Spring Sowing" or "The Landing"; instead O'Flaherty incorporates the natural environment into a more comprehensive view of Irish life.

O'Flaherty returns to the comic genre which he used often in the first two volumes but not in The Mountain Tavern. "The Bath" is a satire on lawyers; "The Post Office" is a very funny satire on tourists trying to communicate with Irish country people. There is a lively story about tinkers at a fair, "The Challenge," and two about horse-races, "The Beggars" and "Grey Seagull."

Several animal stories are included, similar in form to earlier ones; the best of these is "The Hawk." Two stories about children, "The New Suit" and "Desire," are light in mood, but a third, "The Parting," is a darker, autobiographical study of a boy about to leave his island family to enter a seminary on the mainland. The boy feels anguish at the separation and resentment because he knows he is being made a priest to help rear his brother's children. The story is skillfully constructed; a parallel is drawn between the boy's situation and that of the family's bullock, who is being sent to the mainland for slaughter. "The Parting" demonstrates more control and objectivity than earlier autobiographical stories like "The Inquisition" and "The Child of God."

The subject of social change and its effect on Irish family life recurs more often in these later volumes. "The Eviction" is a pathetic story about the bitter ironies of Irish history. An elderly brother and sister are ruthlessly evicted from their estate by a man whose own family was evicted from their cottage by the brother many years before. Motivated by a desire for revenge, the man has risen from poverty to a position of financial power, and he has foreclosed on their property. His refusal even to let the old people take

143

a portrait of an ancestor with them shows his unrelenting hatred of the landlord class.

The rise of the bourgeoisie is also described in "Two Lovely Beasts," one of the best of the late stories. Colm Derrane, a peasant farmer, overcomes his poverty and becomes a wealthy shopkeeper, but to do so he and his family have to make a painful break with the traditions of their community. He reluctantly buys a second calf to help out a widow, Kate Higgins, whose cow has died and whose children are starving. Traditionally, no one in his community raises more than one calf, because the land is too poor and the cow's extra milk is supposed to be shared with the neighbors. But at Kate's urging Colm becomes obsessed with the challenge of raising both calves. To feed them, he denies the neighbors their milk and imposes severe economies on his own family, beating his wife into submission when she rebels. After saving enough to open a shop in his own community, he eventually sells the calves at a large profit and decides to open a shop in town, away from his neighbors. The plot is relatively elaborate, covering a period of about two years. The narrative method is dramatic and objective; much of the story is told through dialogue, and the narrator refrains from making judgments.

The focus of the story is primarily on Colm's changing relationship with his neighbors as he persists in his scheme. When he first buys the calf from Kate, they ostracize him and refuse to visit his house. A man named Gorum voices the community's attitude. "It's too wild and barren here for any one man to stand alone. Whoever tries to stand alone and work only for his own profit becomes an enemy of all."[49] Ironically even Kate Higgins reviles him, though she previously urged him to buy her calf. Colm's rise parallels Kate's downfall. She is unable to manage her money, some of her children die of starvation, and she ends up in an insane asylum. Colm rents her unused land to pasture his calves. When he first opens his shop, the people change their views and admire his courage and enterprise; they try to help him by doing business with him. But as he grows increasingly wealthy and rises too far above them, they denounce him again.

The story has been interpreted as an attack on capitalism, consistent with O'Flaherty's socialist views.[50] In his early stories he praises the communal spirit of the peasants that enables them to survive, and clearly expresses his hatred of the gombeen man in stories like

"Mackerel for Sale." But in "Two Lovely Beasts" the moral values are more ambiguous. Gorum seems hidebound and malicious in his attacks on Colm, and at the end of the story he joins with a group of intoxicated men to jeer and whistle at Colm's family. Colm is not presented as completely unfeeling and ruthless. He is concerned about his family and his neighbors, and goes through much inner debate before deciding to buy the calf. He possesses abundant energy and courage, qualities which O'Flaherty always admires. But as he begins to succeed, he is carried away by pride and ambition until at the end of the story, his eyes are "cold and resolute and ruthless." The moral conflict in this story is similar to that in Corkery's "Carrig-an-Afrinn." In both stories, strong men undertake ambitious and difficult enterprises to improve their family's material condition, but they succeed at great human cost, as people around them go insane or die. Both men are obsessed and ruthless, but they also have admirable traits, and the authors present them objectively without condemning them. Both authors seem to recognize that traditional ways perpetuate extreme poverty, and material progress is inevitable in Irish life. In O'Flaherty's story, World War II accelerates the process of change.

The problems arising from Irish sexual attitudes are also treated more frequently in O'Flaherty's later work. Several of the characters in these stories are sexually repressed or frustrated women who long for passionate fulfillment. They are pathetic and sometimes repulsive, but O'Flaherty portrays them with compassion. In "The Touch" a beautiful young woman is forbidden by her father to marry the man she loves and is instead forced into a loveless arranged marriage. "The Lament" describes a Connemara woman whose frustration has resulted in religious obsession and mental illness. A meeting with a handsome traveling journalist stimulates her fantasies of love. The story contains much debate about the conditions of life in the West of Ireland, and suggests that what looks beautiful to tourists can be lonely and oppressive to natives.

The best of O'Flaherty's late stories about repression is "The Wedding," which depicts the reactions of two unmarried middle-aged women to a wedding in their village. One of them, Nuala, is deranged and physically deformed. The other, Peggy, has returned to live in Ireland with her daughter after many years as a prostitute in America and has become an alcoholic. They both stay in Peggy's house while the wedding of two village people, also middle-aged, takes place. Nuala is

particularly jealous of the wedding because she has
invented the fantasy that the bridegroom is her lover.
At the end of the story the two women cry together for
the wedding they never had.

The entire story takes place in Peggy's house. As
has been suggested, O'Flaherty prefers open-air settings
and often uses interior scenes to suggest entrapment or
frustration. Details of the wedding are brought to the
house by Peggy's daughter, Girleen. The wedding in
many ways symbolizes the stagnant village environment.
The day is inauspiciously rainy and gloomy. Since most
of the young people have emigrated, weddings take place
very infrequently; this one is the first in five years.
The middle-aged couple are awkward and unattractive,
and it is implied that they are marrying for materialistic rather than romantic reasons. Helene O'Connor comments that the whole atmosphere of "The Wedding" is
sterile. All the characters are women without men.
Nuala is "only an extreme of the sterility that envelops
the entire village and its inhabitants."[51]

Most of the story is devoted to the characterization of Nuala. She is over fifty, but because of a
childhood disease her body failed to develop normally.
She is dirty and bedraggled and her manners are repulsive. Yet there is a latent beauty in her that we
glimpse occasionally. At one point she stares at herself in the mirror.

> Her countenance lost its expression of
> insanity and was no longer ghoulish.
> It became apparent that her features had
> been moulded by Nature with remarkable
> delicacy and in perfect proportion.
> Her delicate nostrils and the fine line
> of her mouth showed breeding.[52]

The physical description also suggests that Nuala is a
potentially passionate woman whose sexual drive has been
thwarted. When she raises her skirt to catch scraps of
food Girleen is giving her, she reveals startlingly
beautiful legs. "The sickness, which had ravaged her
face and her hands and unhinged her mind, had spared
this loveliness that lay hidden behind filthy rags,
longing for caresses."[53] Gestures such as scratching
her breasts and hugging herself reinforce the image of
thwarted sexuality.

Nuala's unfulfilled sexual needs distort her outlook. Her jealousy makes her foul tempered; she

repeatedly curses the bride and groom and hopes the marriage will be childless. She has fantasized that the bridegroom is her rightful lover because like her he is ugly and deformed, and because both of them were left behind when the other young people emigrated. When Peggy says she does not blame the young people for leaving such a dismal place, Nuala expresses her own bitterness at being denied the fullness of life.

> "All the lovely young people go away from the black, lonely places. They go marching east and west looking for the big towns where there is everlasting light and dancing and fine music. It was for the lovely young people that God made the world."54

Like most of O'Flaherty's characters, Nuala is highly responsive to changes in the natural environment. She exults in the rainfall, but feels defeated when the sun comes out just before the ceremony.

The mood of stagnation and futility in "The Wedding" is very different from the mood in most of O'Flaherty's early stories. His years in exile appear to have increased his consciousness of the backwardness and provincialism of Irish life, as opposed to the primitive beauty and wildness he emphasized earlier. Yet Nuala has certain traits in common with his earlier characters in her closeness to nature, her strong instinctive needs, and her spirited defiance.

Another social problem treated often in O'Flaherty's later work is the relationship between old people, their families, and the community. His recognition of the need elderly people feel for companionship and usefulness is similar to O'Kelly's perspective, and both writers frequently portray old people as spirited and individualistic, but O'Flaherty's depiction of old people is more pessimistic than O'Kelly's. He places more emphasis on their physical decrepitude, senility, and mistreatment by the young. "Life" and "The Old Woman" contrast old people with children, suggesting the cyclic quality of life and the sadness of mortality. "Galway Bay," an exceptionally fine late story, describes an old man's rebellion against his domineering daughter. Old Tom is an islander and former boat pilot. His wife is dead and his children have emigrated except for one daughter who has come home to care for him. He has signed over control of his land to her and her husband, but has kept control of his stock. When the daughter tries to sell his cow locally, he quarrels with her and takes the cow himself to the Galway fair, though he is over eighty. The story takes place during the boat trip from the island to the mainland, and dramatizes old Tom's encounters with local people and tourists. When he lands in Galway he feels lonely and helpless, and he regrets the quarrel with his daughter.

The story is a kind of elegy to the older generation of islanders and to the traditional life of Aran, and in this sense is similar to O'Kelly's "The Weaver's Grave." Old Tom has the pride and endurance that characterize the island people. He is shriveled and intermittently senile, but well-preserved. His remaining vitality is concentrated in his ferocious eyes; O'Flaherty compares him to a captured hawk. He is affectionate towards his fellow islanders but hostile to tourists, and tells a group of them defiantly, "We are a breed by ourselves. We are people of the islands and of all the land that does border on the Western sea. We want no foreigners to come interfering with us."[55] Other island characteristics that Tom possesses include his fondness for animals, boats, and the extraordinary scenery of Galway Bay, and his earthy colorful speech. The dramatic technique of the story enables O'Flaherty to do full justice to the vivid curses, insults, and banter of the island people. The tourists, representatives of modern civilization, to whom Tom is merely an eccentric character to gawk at, seem bland and superficial by comparison. Old Tom's rebellion exhibits something of the same courage and will that moved characters to defy their fate in earlier stories. Paul Doyle remarks that "in his loneliness and isolation he continues to manage his own life and to defy anyone who attempts to dominate him or take advantage of him. . . . The terror and misery of the human condition is balanced by a spark of fire, or by a gesture of control, which makes old Tom a heroic figure in the most unheroic conditions possible."[56]

The stories of O'Flaherty explore a broader emotional range and greater variety of attitudes than the stories of his predecessors. Nevertheless we feel that he did not reach his full potential as a short story writer. Perhaps he exhausted his material; there are only so many stories that can be written about life on the Aran Islands, and the rest of Ireland inspired him less. Or perhaps, as was suggested above, he lost his motivation to write. The introduction of some interesting new attitudes and insights in his late stories makes us regret that he did not explore them more fully.

148

The collections of stories that O'Flaherty did publish undoubtedly establish him as one of the great Irish short story writers. He occupies his place in the tradition because he found a way of transforming his extremely complex relationship with Ireland into stories of arresting and profound simplicity. The short story genre gave him, as it did other Irish writers, a vehicle for expressing his attitudes to Irish life in a compressed and purified form, without an elaborate intellectual framework. His achievement in the short story surpasses his achievement in the novel, and his earlier, simpler stories are superior to his later ones. His narrative method requires an empathetic identification of the author with his material. Although he sometimes employs a recognizable narrative voice that intrudes and comments on the story, the voice is usually a sympathetic one and speaks from within the community rather than from a distanced or ironic perspective. More characteristically, he dispenses with a narrator and presents his material in an immediate, objective style which relies on direct visual and aural perception.

The community functions within O'Flaherty's stories as both a source of support and a source of loneliness. He recognizes the unique attractions of the Aran culture, its closeness to nature, its timeless rituals, and its grasp of fundamental realities, but he also recognizes its repressiveness and the limitations it imposes on personal freedom and creativity. As in the work of O'Kelly and Corkery, his depiction of his native culture sometimes conveys a mood of sadness at the inevitable dying out of ancient traditions supplanted by the more prosaic and materialistic modern civilization.

O'Flaherty seems most comfortable when dealing not with psychological conflicts between individuals and society or with social change, but with timeless, cyclic conflicts between men and animals and their natural environment. He sees the harsh environment as a vast and terrifying yet beautiful arena for testing the courage and will to live in men and animals. In situations of life and death, the individual cannot afford to be at odds with the community but must rely on it for support. Without communal, traditional knowledge and skill, individual efforts would fail. In the stories of survival more than any others, O'Flaherty finds a way of escaping the loneliness and frustration of his life and reconciling himself imaginatively with the passionate, instinctive, natural life of his people.

Notes

[1] See Patrick Sheeran, The Novels of Liam O'Flaherty: A Study in Romantic Realism (Atlantic Highlands, N.J.: Humanities Press, 1976), pp. 13-77.

[2] Ibid., p. 42.

[3] Liam O'Flaherty, Shame the Devil (London: Grayson & Grayson, 1934), pp. 19-20.

[4] Liam O'Flaherty, Two Years (London: Jonathan Cape, 1930), pp. 218-19.

[5] See John Zneimer, The Literary Vision of Liam O'Flaherty (Syracuse: Syracuse University Press, 1970), pp. 1-25.

[6] Liam O'Flaherty, "National Energy," The Irish Statesman, 3 (October 18, 1924), 171.

[7] Liam O'Flaherty, "A View of Irish Culture," The Irish Statesman, 4 (June 20, 1925), 461.

[8] Quoted in Zneimer, p. 24.

[9] Liam O'Flaherty, "The Irish Censorship," in The American Spectator Yearbook, ed. G. Jean Nathan, Theodore Dreiser, et al. (New York: Frederick Stokes Co., 1934), pp. 132-33.

[10] Shame the Devil, p. 217.

[11] Quoted in Zneimer, p. 175.

[12] Ibid., pp. 146-47.

[13] Ibid., p. 150.

[14] James H. O'Brien, Liam O'Flaherty (Lewisburg: Bucknell University Press, 1973), pp. 93-94, 97.

[15] See Two Years, pp. 312-13.

[16] Liam O'Flaherty, A Tourist's Guide to Ireland (London: Mandrake Press, 1929), p. 55.

[17] See Maureen Murphy, "The Double Vision of Liam O'Flaherty," Eire-Ireland, 8, no. 3 (1973), 20-25.

[18] O'Brien, p. 95.

[19] A. A. Kelly, Liam O'Flaherty the Storyteller (New York: Barnes and Noble, 1976), pp. 52-63.

[20] Quoted in Sheeran, p. 104.

[21] Liam O'Flaherty, Spring Sowing (London: Jonathan Cape, 1924), p. 269.

[22] Ibid., p. 277.

[23] Ibid., pp. 286-87.

[24] Ibid., p. 13.

[25] Ibid., p. 19.

[26] Paul A. Doyle, Liam O'Flaherty (New York: Twayne, 1971), p. 51.

[27] Spring Sowing, p. 66.

[28] Ibid., p. 69.

[29] Ibid., p. 75.

[30] Liam O'Flaherty, The Tent (London: Jonathan Cape, 1926), pp. 208-9.

[31] Ibid., p. 213.

[32] Ibid., p. 70.

[33] Doyle, p. 57.

[34] Kelly, p. 116.

[35] Liam O'Flaherty, The Mountain Tavern and Other Stories (New York: Harcourt, Brace, 1929), p. 76.

[36] Ibid., p. 78.

[37] Ibid., pp. 82-83.

[38] See Sheeran, p. 48.

[39] The Mountain Tavern, p. 155.

[40] Ibid., p. 156.

[41] Ibid., p. 161.

[42] Kelly, p. 128.

[43] The Mountain Tavern, p. 256.

[44] Ibid., p. 260.

[45] Zneimer, p. 172.

[46] Liam O'Flaherty, The Pedlar's Revenge and Other Stories, ed. A. A. Kelly (Dublin: Wolfhound Press, 1976), p. 197.

[47] Ibid., p. 222.

[48] Sheeran, p. 67.

[49] Liam O'Flaherty, Two Lovely Beasts and Other Stories (New York: Devin-Adair, 1950), p. 15.

[50] See Doyle, pp. 111-13, and O'Brien, pp. 112-14.

[51] Helene O'Connor, "Liam O'Flaherty: Literary Ecologist," Eire-Ireland, 7, no. 2 (1972), 52.

[52] Two Lovely Beasts, p. 182.

[53] Ibid., p. 193.

[54] Ibid., p. 192.

[55] Ibid., p. 262.

[56] Doyle, p. 113.

Chapter Eight

SEAN O'FAOLAIN

When a reader turns from the stories of Liam
O'Flaherty to those of Sean O'Faolain, he enters a
strikingly different atmosphere--subtle, reflective,
and urbane rather than primitive and wild. O'Faolain's
academic background and his fondness for analysis and
evaluation contributed to the intellectual dimension of
his work. He articulated his views not just in his fiction, but also in numerous articles and books of criticism, biography, autobiography, travel, and social commentary. Despite several periods of residence in
exile, he was deeply committed to Irish culture and
fought for many years to improve the country's intellectual climate. In contrast to O'Flaherty, O'Faolain
wrote only a few novels and concentrated mainly on
short stories. His stories are longer and more elaborate than O'Flaherty's, and they explore a wider range
of characters and situations. There are many thematic
and formal connections between O'Faolain's stories and
those of his predecessors; he is very conscious of his
place in the Irish tradition.

Born John Whelan in Cork in 1900, O'Faolain was the
youngest of three sons in a policeman's family. His
autobiography Vive Moi! (1963) recounts his efforts to
escape the false standards imposed by his parents and
teachers, and to fulfill himself by basing his life on
imagination instead of convention. Although he often
felt resentment towards his family, his native city, and
Ireland, he learned to accept his background as part of
himself and to regard his Irish identity as a unique
advantage in his literary work.

O'Faolain's parents, both from peasant backgrounds,
were ambitious for their sons and lived a strictly
disciplined and frugal life in order to give them a
good education. His father, Denis Whelan, was an honest, hardworking, dutiful man, extremely loyal to the
British government that employed him, proud of its hier-
archies and social standards, and anxious that his sons
should become "gentlemen." O'Faolain admired his father
but was never able to feel close to him. His mother
also exhorted her sons to "'Rise in the world.'" A
melancholy, self-denying woman, she used her martyrdom
as a form of emotional blackmail against her children.
O'Faolain loved her as a boy but grew to pity her later.

"She was deeply pious, but it was not a happy piety. Her religious melancholy withered everything it touched, like a sirocco."[1] She respected education not for its own sake, but as a means of getting a good job. O'Faolain came to regard his family's parsimony and ambition as a kind of "shabby genteelism," leading to a "dull and disciplined degradation of life."[2]

Because of their material and emotional deprivation, O'Faolain and his brothers learned very early to rely on their imaginations. The Cork opera house was a particular source of delight to him as a boy. Religion was another source of imaginative stimulation. He loved the atmosphere of the Church, its images, statues, and rituals, which were his "first symbols and metaphors." His early religious training was not good preparation for life in the practical sense, but it provided an emotional support and source of joy. He experienced several religious crises in later life and recognized the inadequacy of his early training; while in Italy in 1946, he adopted Roman, as opposed to Irish, Catholicism, because he found it more life-giving. The aspect of Irish Catholicism which he criticizes most harshly is its puritanical attitude towards sexual matters.

O'Faolain attended the Lancasterian National School and the Preservation Brothers College, and regarded both schools as unsatisfactory because of their conventionality and repression of intellectual curiosity. His rebelliousness found a natural outlet in Irish nationalism. This interest was first aroused in his boyhood, during summer visits to relatives in the country, usually in Co. Limerick. The timeless and unchanging life of the country emancipated him from his parents' values. He felt a love for the rural landscape and people that he had never felt for the city.

Other significant events in the development of O'Faolain's nationalism included his viewing of Lennox Robinson's play Patriots, which made him realize that ordinary Irish life could be transformed into worthwhile literature, and the Easter Rising, which caused him to transfer his allegiance from the British government to the Irish martyrs. After his high school graduation, he attended summer school in West Cork to improve his fluency in Irish, and there he met a group of young people as enthusiastic as himself, including Eileen Gould, the girl he was later to marry. Her father, a native of Cork, enhanced O'Faolain's appreciation for the city by telling him stories about its traditions. Looking back on his life there, O'Faolain describes his ambivalence and eventual acceptance of his home town.

> I have loved, admired, feared and hated
> no city so much as you.
>   Do I then condemn my birthplace and
> spit it out of my mouth? The city was
> my shadow, and no man jumps off his own
> shadow. It was for twenty-six years my
> life; more than that it was Life--and
> one does not spit Life out of one's mouth.[3]

O'Faolain's experience at University College, Cork,
as both an undergraduate and a graduate student, was
also strongly colored by provincialism. He felt that
such surroundings, the "soft smother of the provincial
featherbed,"[4] would be dangerous for a writer if he
made no effort to escape from them. The qualities he
feared most to absorb from the Cork atmosphere were
complacency and smugness. He gained much support and
inspiration during his college years from his friendships with Daniel Corkery and Frank O'Connor. Corkery
served as a mentor to both the younger men, but in
later years they became estranged from him. O'Faolain
came to believe that Corkery had succumbed to the "provincial smother" and had stopped growing as an artist.

While in college O'Faolain was also engaged in
revolutionary activity. He joined the Irish Volunteers
soon after matriculating and remained a member for six
years, though he was seldom involved in the actual fighting. Before the Treaty he was full of idealism and
brotherhood with his fellow revolutionaries. But the
Civil War brought on what he calls a "trauma," a severe
disillusionment with the Republican cause he had supported. Very embittered, he returned in 1924 to private
life and decided to work for a Master's degree at UCC.

Re-examining and recomposing his war experiences
gave O'Faolain literary material for many years afterwards. The experience "had thrown invisible barricades
across the main road" of his life and forced him to
search for "alternative roads towards the full understanding and enjoyment of life."[5] It took him a long
time to come to terms with his angry belief that the
fight for a Republic had ended in total defeat and that
the new government, dominated by a mercenary bourgeoisie
and a church devoid of culture, smelled of moral decay.
His own evaluation of his artistic development is that
in his early stories he romanticized his anger, but in
later work moved towards humor and detachment as a
result of a "gradual process of life-acceptance." In

<u>Vive Moi!</u> he provides a particularly searching analysis of the way he views the evolution of his career.

> In being privileged to see man at his best
> I had been given an exceptional vision
> of the potential wholeness and integrity
> of human nature in a moment of intense
> awareness forced on us all, collectively,
> by a crisis in our country's history; . . .
> I had thereby been blinded to the virtues
> of ordinary, average, common life as it
> is outside such rare hours; and . . . when
> the hour passed I felt at first bewildered,
> then dismayed, and finally filled with
> a wholly unreasonable anger at my fellow
> men. . . .
>   As my anger gradually abated, but
> with my curiosity still unabated, I was,
> over the years after 1924, to become
> fascinated to understand, in sympathy,
> what flaws in the intricate machinery of
> human nature keep it from fulfilling itself
> wholly, from achieving complete integrity
> other than in moments as brief, if one
> compares them with the whole span of a
> human life, as a lighthouse blink. I
> would, then, in my late life-acceptance,
> embracing as much as I had the courage
> to embrace of all life's inherent evil
> and weakness, try to write, however tan-
> gentially, about those moments of awareness
> when we know three truths at one and the
> same moment: that life requires of each
> of us that we should grow up and out whole
> and entire, that human life of its nature
> intricately foils exactly this, and that
> the possibility of wholeness is neverthe-
> less as constant and enormous a reality
> as the manifold actuality of frustration,
> compromise, getting caught in some laby-
> rinth, getting cut short by death.[6]

O'Faolain also describes his development as a process of liberation from his public self, formed by his parents, teachers, and others, into his true or private self. Acceptance of life included religious commitment resulting from a personalized interpretation of Catholic doctrine, or as he terms it, putting "the old wine into new bottles."[7]

Escape from Irish provincialism came in the form

of a scholarship to Harvard, which O'Faolain attended from 1926-29. While he was there he sent for Eileen, and they were married in 1928. They liked the United States and for a while considered living there permanently, but they decided that its vast landscape held few memories and associations for them. They "belonged to an old, small, intimate and much-trodden country, where every field, every path, every ruin had its memories, where every last corner had its story."[8]

For financial reasons the O'Faolains took temporary teaching jobs in London instead of returning immediately to Ireland. While in London O'Faolain met Edward Garnett, who took the young writer under his wing, as he had done with O'Flaherty. After an unsuccessful attempt to obtain a teaching appointment at UCC (it went to Daniel Corkery instead), O'Faolain in 1933 followed Garnett's advice and settled in Co. Wicklow, with the intention of supporting himself entirely from his writing. This proved to be a wise choice in the long run.

O'Faolain's first book of stories, Midsummer Night Madness, was published in 1932, shortly before his return to Ireland. The book, successful in England, was promptly banned by the Irish Censorship Board. O'Faolain reacted with anger and chagrin. "Censorship was then a novelty and front-page news; so that I felt very much like a man suddenly plucked from the privacy of his study and shoved naked into the pillory to be pelted by his fellow citizens with rotten vegetables."[9] Though he received scurrilous personal attacks and anonymous letters, he stood by his decision to live in Ireland.

For many years O'Faolain was actively involved in Dublin's literary affairs. He joined Yeats's Irish Academy of Letters but, a few years later, when Yeats could no longer participate, felt that it had declined. One of his closest allies during this period was Frank O'Connor, whose volatile temperament complemented his own.

> We were complementary in many ways; his
> imagination was a ball of fire, mine was
> less combustible but steadier; his memory
> was infallible, his interests more confined;
> his brain was first-class but completely
> untrained, and discipline was a word he
> had never heard; his intuitive processes
> were something to marvel at, to distrust,
> and, if one was wise, to respect profoundly,

157

because if you were patient enough to
discard the old boots and bits of seaweed
that he would bring up from his deep diving
he was certain, sooner or later, to surface
with a piece of pure gold. I do not think
he ever reasoned out anything. He was
like a man who takes a machine gun to
a shooting gallery. Everybody falls flat
on his face, the proprietor at once takes
to the hills, and when it is all over, and
[you] cautiously peep up, you find that
he has wrecked the place but got three
perfect bull's-eyes.[10]

The two men enjoyed a friendly rivalry for many years
and felt that together they were responsible for the
future of Irish literature, but "ultimately the friendship died, to our mutual loss."

In keeping with his desire to influence the direction of Irish literature, O'Faolain established in
1940 a literary magazine called The Bell and served as
its editor until 1946. The magazine, influenced by
AE's earlier magazine, The Irish Homestead, provided
an opportunity for younger writers to publish their
work, and it also provided a forum for commentary about
contemporary issues. O'Faolain was a paternal and sympathetic editor, often substantially revising work that
was submitted to him. He tried to include a wide variety of material dealing with Irish life, particularly
its more homey, personal side. The editorial policy of
The Bell was to help raise cultural standards in Ireland, to expose bad art, and to give the country a new
image of itself. O'Faolain's editorials were strongly
didactic, and the magazine soon became identified with
his personal crusade. One of his main targets was literary censorship, but he also attacked the Gaelic
League for its provincialism and the middle class for
its materialism and complacency. He criticized the government for its neutral, isolationist position during
World War II, and urged Ireland to become more actively
involved in world affairs. Deeply discouraged by the
failure of his efforts to revitalize national literature, he resigned as editor in 1946. He felt that public inertia and apathy were too pervasive. In his farewell editorial, "Signing Off," he comments, "And when
all is said and done, what I am mainly left with is a
certain amount of regret that we were born into this
thorny time when our task has been less that of cultivating our garden than of clearing away the brambles."[11]

After his resignation, O'Faolain continued to publish some articles on Irish literature in The Bell and elsewhere, but he devoted more of his time to private life and his own writing. He travelled widely and taught at several American universities, including Princeton (1953, 1959-61), Northwestern (1958), Boston College (1964 and 1965), and Wesleyan (1966). But he has maintained his permanent residence in Dublin for many years.

O'Faolain has written so extensively about the state of Irish literature, particularly Irish prose fiction, that it is difficult to summarize his views concisely. Much of the anger and frustration that he restrains in his stories finds freer expression in his critical writings. During the thirties and forties he was especially articulate about the anti-intellectualism of Irish society and the obstacles encountered by Irish writers. A central theme that runs through his writings of this period is the ambivalent attitude of Irish writers towards their fellow countrymen. One of his earliest articles describes this "revulsion-attraction complex." "Under such circumstances it is natural that the Irish writer, ignored or misunderstood at home, should gravitate away from his own people--often in bitterness and disgust--even though he knows at the same time that all his interests and sympathies are forever anchored deeply and firmly in their lives."[12] He says that the Irish public is more hostile to realistic fiction writers than to sentimentalists or idealists, and consequently realists like Moore, Joyce, and O'Flaherty have been driven into exile.

One of O'Faolain's most significant early essays on Irish literature is "The Emancipation of Irish Writers." He discusses the difficulty Irish writers face in achieving "wholeness of vision," freedom from prejudice and distortion. They need greater detachment from politics, controversy, and public opinion. To achieve this detachment he recommends that every Irish writer of his generation go into exile for at least ten years.

> In exile, if we could only avoid sentimentality, we might infuse into our work something of that warmth and geniality, that equanimity, good humour, and love which get frozen and killed in the partisan atmosphere of home. We might even, above all, add to our literature the one thing in which it is not rich--namely, a quality of wider intellectual curiosity.[13]

Irish writers should become more aware of what is happening in the literature of other countries. O'Faolain regrets the influence of Naturalism on writers like Moore and Joyce, however, because he believes that the Irish creative genius best expresses itself when it is detached from societal norms and moves towards subjective freedom, the modes of fantasy or romance.

A much later article, "Ireland after Yeats" (1952), contains one of O'Faolain's most comprehensive and balanced evaluations of his own literary generation. He asserts that Irish literature since the Renaissance has been in a state of decline. In Yeats's time, when the government was English and non-Catholic, people hostile to the arts (the petit bourgeoisie) had no political power, but under the new government the same people have obtained the power to stifle free artistic expression.

> Now the Church could wield almost unlimited power because the native government was composed of men who respected, loved, and feared it. It is evident that the new intellectual atmosphere depended on the sophistication, cultivation, and tolerance of both the native government and the Church, the new elite. Unfortunately, centuries of oppression have bred in both not only a passionate desire for liberty but the antithesis of that natural desire. They have induced a nervy, sensitive, touchy, defensive-aggressive, on-guard mentality as a result of which patriotism becomes infected by chauvinism and true religious feeling by puritanism.[14]

Censorship is one manifestation of this attitude, but it affects many other aspects of Irish life as well. But despite his detestation of the new social forces, O'Faolain still believes that the Irish way of life is uniquely attractive, "atavistically powerful, spiritually obstinate, strongly resistant, in a great many ways appealing; it represents precious and lovable qualities, and is eminently worth preservation, provided it expresses itself in achievement and not merely in emotional declaration."[15] As in earlier essays, he exhorts younger writers not to let bitterness warp their viewpoint or to evade their problems by seeking permanent exile, but to confront contemporary Irish life with ruthless, clear-eyed detachment.

When writing about the Irish prose fiction tradition, O'Faolain does not draw a sharp distinction
between the novel and the short story, as Frank O'Connor
and some other writers do, though he does agree that the
Irish are more successful with the shorter form. His
critical writings on the short story genre almost always
place it in an international rather than a national context.

Many of O'Faolain's ideas about the genre are articulated in The Short Story (1951). He defines the two
most desirable qualities in a story as "punch" and
"poetry."

> The punch and the poetry come, I
> think, from a combination of reality, in
> the simple sense of plausibility (hard-
> won), and personal voltage. The voltage
> does something to the material. It lights
> it up; it burns it up; it makes it fume
> in the memory as an aroma or essence which
> clings to us even when we have forgotten
> the details of the yarn.16

This emphasis on the author's personality is central to
O'Faolain's theory of the short story. He believes
that the main obstacles to a writer's success are not
external but internal. The writer must accept external
conditions as part of himself and constantly struggle
to maintain an equilibrium between his temperament and
his circumstances. Instead of evading the tensions of
his life, he should welcome them as the source of his
creativity. If the writer is successful, the reader
will recognize his unique personality. "What one sear-
ches for and what one enjoys in a short story is a special distillation of personality, a unique sensibility
which has recognized and selected at once a subject
that, above all other subjects, is of value to the writer's temperament and to his alone."17

The first part of The Short Story, "The Personal
Struggle," examines the relationship between personal
conflicts and the art of Daudet, Chekhov, and Maupassant. O'Faolain admires Chekhov in particular as a master of "self-management." In the second part, "The
Technical Struggle," O'Faolain discusses four problems
of short story technique: convention, subject, construction, and language. He views the short story as a
highly compressed form which achieves its best effects
through suggestion and implication. There is no such
thing as literal "realism" in a short story; realism is

161

merely a convention. Realistic detail is boring unless
it is part of the "general revelation by suggestion."
Characters, too, are merely suggested or sketched in,
not developed in detail. "The short story . . . is an
immense confidence-trick, an immense illusion, as immense a technical achievement as the performance of an
adept magician. . . . The purpose of all these tricks or
conventions is to communicate personality while appear-
ing only to 'tell a story.'"18

In the modern short story, O'Faolain says, the
actual story or anecdote is of minor importance. The
real subject of a story is the author's reaction to a
particular situation or incident. A writer "imagines
his subject into his own likeness." The modern writer
still relies on incident and plot, but he has internalized them, placing the emphasis on psychology--the "adventure through the jungle of human nature"--rather than
on action. Throughout the chapters on technique O'Faolain continues to stress the importance of compression
and indirect suggestion in evoking the sense of a communicated personality.

O'Faolain's critical comments on Irish short story
writers are not consolidated but are scattered among
writings on broader topics. Consistent with the views
expressed in The Short Story, his commentary on his
Irish predecessors and contemporaries emphasizes their
personal struggle and the degree of success they
achieved in turning their conflicts into art. In comparison with the poetic tradition of Yeats, O'Faolain
believes, the Irish prose fiction tradition is undeveloped and lacking in suitable models for the particular
blend of realism and fantasy that characterizes the
Irish genius. He agrees with Moore and others that the
best models for Irish fiction writers have always been
Russian, especially the stories of Chekhov. The central
conflict faced by writers in both countries is between
"faith" and "morals," or easygoing accommodation and
tolerance versus individual choice and action. In Ireland, "all morality, outside the confessional, is covered by an umbrella of charity, striped by evasion, and
wide as the sky."19

O'Faolain offers some interesting speculations
about why Irish writers have preferred the short story
to the novel. Irish society, he says, is too rigid,
conventional, and complacent to provide a broad enough
scope for the novelist. There is too little opportunity
for characters to rebel against social norms. Having
solved everything to their own satisfaction, the Irish

people

> have no further to go--except to Heaven.
> Like all peoples who have accepted a rigid
> ideology they are frustrated by the com-
> pleteness of their own conventions. The
> novel elsewhere may be frustrated by the
> uncertainties of men lost; here it is
> frustrated by the certainties of men saved.[20]

The short story has flourished in post-Treaty Ireland
because "there are always small, revealing themes;
rarely large ones."

    Many of O'Faolain's generalizations about Irish
fiction are illustrated by his remarks about individual
short story writers. He regards Moore and Joyce as particularly successful at coping with the disadvantages
of their Irish identity and disciplining their tempera-
ments. Moore was "translucently clear about what he
could and could not get out of Ireland."[21] Joyce is
discussed often in O'Faolain's writings, usually with a
mixture of admiration and envy. O'Faolain regrets that
Joyce did not have a stronger influence on the younger
writers. His generation tended to ignore Joyce's work
in their idealistic teens, when they should have been
reading him carefully. He would have provided a colder,
less romantic model than Yeats to help them develop as
realists. "Here, surely, if anywhere in the course of
modern Irish literature was a writer offering at least
one coherent and liberating idea [the complete acceptance of life] to the generation emerging after Yeats,
if they really wanted intellectual and imaginative freedom from the pagan swaddling clothes of their country's
infancy and the small-clothes of its over-prolonged
Christian adolescence."[22] By the time the younger writers did read Joyce, their literary standards had been
set.

    The style of Dubliners is examined in the chapter
on language in The Short Story. O'Faolain says that the
language of the modern short story has intensified so
rapidly that the earliest Joyce stories now surprise us
by "the innocence of their style and the superficiality
(in the literal sense of surface-ness) of their English."[23] Joyce's language in the early stories now
seems painstakingly explicit rather than suggestive, and
some of the words are not well-chosen. The famous last
paragraph of "The Dead," however, reveals how skilfully
Joyce could extend and dilate language, and it anticipates what he would do in his later work.

163

O'Faolain is not so sympathetic to the work of his estranged friend Daniel Corkery. He praises Corkery's early stories and novels, but says that in later life his talent dried up because "his circumstances and his environment exhausted him."[24] He also attacks Corkery's book Synge and Anglo-Irish Literature for its narrow idealism; Corkery judges Irish literature by political rather than artistic standards, and when he attempts to apply his critical standards to earlier Irish literature, he reveals his limitations as a critic. He and others of his generation were blinded by their idealism and failed to achieve a full vision of life.

When writing about the work of his contemporaries, O'Flaherty and O'Connor, O'Faolain expresses a great deal of enthusiasm. He published an article on O'Flaherty in 1937 which compares him to Don Quixote, a man driven by a search for ideal beauty. O'Faolain especially admires the quality of wonder and awe in O'Flaherty's work, the feeling that "something vast has entered into the imagination of the author." The furious pace of the novels allows no time for character analysis; the characters act from "an insane instinct" and "show their natures in external action."[25] In characterizing O'Flaherty's realism, O'Faolain says that he is not a Naturalist or pessimist, but is "like every known Irish writer, an inverted romantic." He can neither write of reality with gusto nor ignore reality and write about his own dreams; instead he "sets out in the most self-conscious and deliberate way to attack with violence the things that hurt the inarticulate dream of his romantic soul." Only in his short stories is he at rest. "There he has found something that bears a resemblance to his ideal. Not in men, but in birds and animals; and often men are seen as cruel creatures who hunt and torment these dumb things."[26] O'Faolain looks on both Joyce and O'Flaherty as men searching for a Holy Grail. Joyce, a greater artist, has more confidence than O'Flaherty. Joyce knows that reality can never completely destroy the chalice of ideal beauty, whereas O'Flaherty tilts at windmills and falls, has courage and vigor, but little faith, vision, or wisdom.

His comments about Frank O'Connor's stories reflect the same admiration that O'Faolain felt for O'Connor as a friend. O'Connor's story "Peasants" is used as an example of the conflict between faith and morals which the Irish writer must deal with. The story is highly praised as a "perfect illustration" of the conflict. "The charm of the story lies in the complete, maddening, hopeless failure of the people to see the moral point

164

of view."27   In The Short Story, O'Faolain uses another
O'Connor story, "In the Train," to exemplify skilful
construction.   It is "one of the finest of modern Irish
short stories" and achieves its effects because the
"camera angle," or narrative point of view, is con-
cealed.28

O'Faolain's own contributions to the Irish short
story tradition are contained in eight collections which
span more than fifty years of writing: Midsummer Night
Madness (1932); A Purse of Coppers (1937); Teresa and
Other Stories (1947; published in the United States with
two additional stories as The Man Who Invented Sin,
1948); The Finest Stories (mostly reprints with several
new stories, 1957); I Remember! I Remember! (1961); The
Heat of the Sun (1966); The Talking Trees (1970);
Foreign Affairs (1975). These collections provide a
straightforward revelation of his artistic development;
unlike his colleague Frank O'Connor, he did not revise
his work after book publication (except for some minor
alterations of wording), but preferred to preserve the
original version as a record of his experience at a
given period of his life. Following the precept of
Daniel Corkery, he did revise his stories carefully
while writing them.

Both O'Faolain and Frank O'Connor differed from
O'Flaherty in that they considered themselves primarily
short story writers rather than novelists, and they gave
up writing novels relatively early in their careers.
O'Faolain's three novels were all written during the
thirties, the period of his greatest social involvement:
A Nest of Simple Folk (1933); Bird Alone (1936); Come
Back to Erin (1940). He tried to write novels again
later in his career but abandoned them or turned them
into short stories. Although the novels do have some
artistic merit, as Maurice Harmon demonstrates in his
sympathetic and detailed evaluation of them,29 they are
seriously flawed and do not match the quality of his
best stories.

John Kelleher offers some speculations about O'Faolain's preference for the short story. Kelleher sees
in O'Faolain's artistic personality a difficult reconciliation between romanticism and realistic intelligence. The romantic side of his nature made it impossible for him to live in permanent exile from Ireland;
his romanticism was "fixated upon Ireland" and it "translated itself emotionally and intellectually as patriotism, a concern for tradition, and the urge to express
the unexpressed potentialities of his own people." In

his analytical articles, essays, and biographies, O'Faolain found a healthy outlet for his anger at Ireland, but he tried to achieve a more objective point of view in his fiction. Ultimately he regarded the short story as a more congenial genre than the novel, because it permitted a freer, more balanced expression of his personality.

> He did not find the answer to his
> problems as a novelist because his chief
> dilemma was half his own. He was not
> satisfied with either of the two obvious
> solutions to conflict in an Irish novel,
> frustration or the emigrant ship. . . . In
> other words, as a novelist he was beaten
> not by lack of talent--he has always had
> talent to spare and fling away--but by his
> too great demand upon a society intimate,
> homely, compact, and too rigidly narrow.[30]

The short stories, according to Kelleher, allow O'Faolain more freedom and range, since they concentrate on depiction of individual characters instead of a narrow representative society. In some of the stories he passes sharp judgment against characters who do not accept the conditions of their lives, who "in the name of romance or purity or safety, [refuse] life and the responsibility of living and loving."

O'Faolain's stories are traditional in method. The influence of the great nineteenth-century realists is evident in his work. He has frequently acknowledged the influence of the Russians, via Corkery, and he is particularly attracted to Chekhov. Both writers describe the effects of a boring provincial society on characters drawn from many levels of society, from peasants to professionals and aristocrats, and both prefer a subtle, inconclusive plot structure. It is difficult, however, to isolate the influence of individual writers on O'Faolain, since he read and imitated widely. His literary style sometimes recalls Turgenev, sometimes Hemingway, sometimes Daudet or Maupassant. He was strongly influenced by the Irish short story writers as well; his early style has much in common with George Moore's, and Joycean techniques sometimes find their way into his writing. Corkery had a major influence on the early stories, despite O'Faolain's later rejection of him. And Frank O'Connor's influence is apparent too, as the two often stimulated each other to write stories on similar themes.

The Gaelic oral and folk tradition which is so important in the stories of O'Kelly, Corkery, and O'Flaherty is less obvious in O'Faolain's work. His stories seldom present rural life or Gaelic traditions directly, but view them instead from the perspective of sophisticated and cosmopolitan characters. The oral tradition did have some impact on his technique. Like O'Kelly and Corkery, O'Faolain often uses a narrator who speaks directly and conversationally to the reader, and acts as a mediator interpreting the events he is relating.

Virtually all O'Faolain's stories are related to Ireland in some way--at least one character is of Irish birth--but not all are set in Ireland. Several stories concern Irish men and women living or traveling abroad, usually in the United States and Europe. The milieu of stories set in Ireland varies from Dublin to Cork to country towns and villages.

Although O'Faolain's favorite subjects are often similar to those of other writers already discussed-- war, religion, family life, love and marriage--his treatment is much more internalized and psychological than that of earlier writers, and his characters are more complex. Many of them have achieved a relatively high level of education or wealth, though they may come from poor backgrounds (often a source of inner conflict). They are sensitive to the pressures of the Irish environment, but in some way live outside or beyond the conventions of Irish society. Frequently they experience conflicts between their need for personal freedom and the social conscience formed by their parents and others. They are lonely individuals, alienated from Irish society, whose values they cannot accept, from other people, and from themselves, because certain forces in their personalities have been blocked or stifled. Although O'Faolain writes as a believing Catholic, his work conveys at times an intellectual probing of Catholic doctrines about sin and damnation, and a disenchantment with the Irish Church as a temporal institution.

The struggle for personal freedom and fulfillment is probably the dominant theme in O'Faolain's work. He is consistently preoccupied with psychological factors-- the mental atmosphere, both hidden and expressed, that determines to what extent an individual experiences freedom and happiness, and to what extent he experiences defeat. The faculty of memory particularly interests O'Faolain; he believes that the things people forget are often more important to their emotional life than

the things they remember. Characters sometimes seek
escape not just from stifling external circumstances
but from themselves, from some aspect of their own
identity that is painful to confront.

O'Faolain shows considerable development in his
short stories, both thematically and technically, reflecting his personal evolution from angry frustration
to sympathetic detachment. He has experimented with a
variety of narrative techniques and has not settled on
one predominant mode, though he does make frequent use
of a conversational narrator, either first or third person. In his later work he moves away from the compact,
suggestive story form towards what he calls the "tale,"
a longer, more digressive and loosely structured form
which is not always successful. In the later stories
there is even more emphasis on individual psychology and
less on social conditions.

ii

Midsummer Night Madness, O'Faolain's first volume
of stories, occupies for several reasons a special place
in his work. It brought his first literary success, in
London, as well as humiliation and notoriety when it
was banned in Ireland. The stories, set during the
Revolution and Civil War, reflect the unique romantic
atmosphere of that period and are markedly different in
tone and style from O'Faolain's subsequent stories.
Midsummer Night Madness contains many artistic flaws,
but it also displays the potential talent and craftsmanship that its author would later refine.

Since this is an apprentice volume, it is not sur-
prising that a number of influences are discernible.
The influence of Daniel Corkery's collection The Hounds
of Banba, which also deals with the war, is particularly
apparent. Although the style of the two writers is dis-
similar, there are many parallels in plot structure,
characterization, and setting. Both authors (and also
Frank O'Connor) write about sensitive, dedicated young
rebels "on the run," moving through the mountainous
landscape or seeking shelter in friendly cottages, drea-
ding capture and imprisonment and often longing for a
woman's love. The stylistic influences of Moore, Joyce,
and some non-Irish writers like Turgenev and Daudet, are
also evident.

The stories in Midsummer Night Madness relate the

effects of war on both rebel soldiers and civilians. In two relatively long stories, "Midsummer Night Madness" and "The Small Lady," O'Faolain examines the role of the Anglo-Irish gentry. Corkery deals with the same subject in "Cowards" and "Colonel MacGillicuddy Goes Home"; both writers contrast the moral deterioration of the gentry with the dedication and energy of the Catholic nationalists. "Midsummer Night Madness" contains an intriguing portrayal of old Henn, the ancient dissolute proprietor of a "big house" which has been commandeered as headquarters by a unit of rebel soldiers. The narrator, a sensitive, intelligent rebel, recounts the follies of both Henn and Stevey Long, the Commandant, as they quarrel over a pregnant gipsy woman. Eventually Stevey forces the eighty-year-old Henn to marry the twenty-year-old girl, and in a humorously incongruous ending, they go off to Paris for their honeymoon. The story suggests the uneasy position of the Anglo-Irish, accepted neither by the Catholic Irish nor by the English, beset by economic and moral deterioration, and finally confronted by the imminent destruction of their way of life as their houses are commandeered or burned.

In addition to the stories about the gentry, O'Faolain wrote several stories about the effects of war on ordinary people, mainly in Cork. "Lilliput" describes a tinker woman's defiance of a British curfew which the more timid townspeople fearfully observe. "The Bombshop" dramatizes the tension that builds up among a group of rebels hiding in a house to make bombs. The climactic incident emphasizes the irony and absurdity of war; during an argument they accidentally shoot and kill an old woman living downstairs who has been friendly to their cause. The plot of this story connects with "The Death of Stevey Long," the character introduced in "Midsummer Night Madness"; Stevey comes to the bombshop after escaping from prison and finds the old woman's corpse, before being captured and executed. These stories represent almost the only time that O'Faolain experimented with overlapping characters and incidents in the manner of Moore or O'Kelly, though he does establish thematic unity in some of his later volumes--i.e., memory in I Remember! I Remember! and love in The Heat of the Sun.

The most successful stories in Midsummer Night Madness are "Fugue" and "The Patriot," both concerned with the relationship between love and war. Maurice Harmon sees in these stories evidence of O'Faolain's changing attitude to the war, a change from romantic involvement to disillusionment and withdrawal. "The transition from 'Fugue' to 'The Patriot' showing the growing detachment from violence, also shows a growing artistic detachment. It is part of the writer's search for objectivity."[31] "Fugue," which O'Faolain wrote in 1927 while still at Harvard, takes place before the Treaty and reflects his early idealism, whereas "The Patriot" looks back on the Civil War after it has ended, with a recognition of futility and defeat.

Many external influences are apparent in "Fugue." Its style, as Joseph Rippier has demonstrated, follows the practice of Moore and Joyce in such devices as the frequent joining of clauses with "and" or "but," and the use of repetition.[32] The idea of imitating a musical fugue may have come from Daniel Corkery, who gave his protegés an appreciation of classical music and whose war story "An Unfinished Symphony" also imitates a musical form.

"Fugue" makes use of recurring motifs and counterpointed voices. The protagonist, a young unnamed rebel fleeing with a companion from the Black and Tans, meets twice in the same day a young woman who strongly attracts him and makes him long for an end to the fighting. At the end of the story his companion, Rory, is killed and he must flee once again.

The rebel narrates the story in the first person; his poetic sensibility imposes its own structure on the hectic and chaotic experiences of the day. The "fugue" develops in his mind as he alternates between flight and repose. Natural sights and sounds, together with brief human encounters, are woven into a rhythmic pattern around the central motif, his longing for the girl. Rory, excitable and talkative, adds his humorous voice to the fugue as he chatters about the day's events.

As the story opens, at dawn, the rebels are waking up in a cottage where they have found shelter after a night of stumbling through rugged, hilly terrain in West Cork. The landscape is at the same time a source of protection and a source of danger, since a swollen river prevents them from a further retreat. Because of their fear and isolation, the young men respond to every natural sight and sound with heightened sensibility. This alternation between security and fear is one of the underlying structural features of the story.

O'Faolain's descriptions of the Irish landscape in "Fugue" and other stories in the volume are extraordinarily poetic and evocative. He romanticizes the landscape, identifying its changing moods with the characters' emotions.

> The damp of dawn was everywhere. It
> softened the lime gable of the outhouse
> beneath me, it hung over the sodden hay
> in the barn and, like the fog and mist
> last night under the blazing moon, it
> floated over the rumbling river to my right.
> I could imagine the flow taking strange
> courses in its flood, swishing in this
> neither dawn nor day nor dark through
> all the alders and the reeds and the rushes
> and, doubtless, covering the steppingstones
> that we hoped would give us an escape to
> the mountains beyond.[33]

The dampness, haziness, and strangely flowing water suggest the uncertainty that the rebels feel about their fate.

The young woman who becomes the narrator's symbol of love and security is first seen as a visitor at the cottage. Her silent smile tortures him with loneliness. This encounter is very brief, but it provides the basic theme for the fugue.

The alternation between flight and repose continues as the two men escape the bullets of English soldiers and enjoy several hours of calm in a grove. Orchestral imagery suggests their relative peacefulness after the recent danger; they listen to the "bass viol" of a stream and the "drumming" of a distant lorry. During this respite the narrator daydreams about the young woman and reflects on the significance of their meeting; he refuses to see it as casual and accidental, but compares himself to a chessman "fingered by a hesitant player."

As the rebels move towards the mountains in search of a night's lodging, the cold and windswept terrain projects a more ominous mood. For safety, the narrator leaves Rory at a roadside cottage and goes on to a separate lodging, but before he leaves he thinks again of the woman. Her memory is now receding and losing its force. As he walks deeper into the mountains, he thinks of the comfortable bed where he will lie composing his fugue, weaving the images of the day's events into a coherent scheme. The outcome of his search for shelter is his discovery that his lodging is the home of the woman he met that morning. Instead of fading away into insignificance, the earlier encounter and his daydreams now take on a sharper reality. He talks to the woman and finds that she, too, is restless and dissatisfied, but once again their intimacy is shortlived; as he embraces her, someone rushes to the door with the message that Rory has been killed and he must leave. With the reawakening of fear, the tone of the fugue changes once again. Fleeing, the narrator is "like a man who has been listening to music the livelong day and after it his mind is full of strange chords, and ill-recollected they torture him with a sense of something lost."[34] He walks for miles in the rain and finally rests in a ruin--symbol of defeat and loneliness. Resisting the feeling that he is the only man still living in the world, he recites a Gaelic poem which links his misery to that of his ancestors. The fugue concludes with a Yeatsian image as dawn arrives again and the narrator feels his life merge with the endless cycle of time, life's "ancient, ceaseless gyre."

The contrast between the security and contentment of normal domestic life and the disruption of war is also a central feature of "The Patriot." In this story the perspective on war is more disillusioned. O'Faolain uses a flashback to distance the war and view it in the context of the "normal" life that preceded and followed it. Because of his fascination with the processes of memory, O'Faolain uses the flashback device frequently.

Bernie, the protagonist, is a former Irregular. He marries his childhood sweetheart, Norah, after the Civil War and takes her to the coastal resort town of Youghal for their honeymoon, a place full of memories for both of them. They met there first as young children and then later as young adults. It was also in Youghal that Norah met Edward Bradley, a former teacher of Bernie's and an ardent nationalist. Bernie admired Bradley intensely during his idealistic years, but the relationship was complicated when Bradley, a bachelor, showed obvious admiration for Norah. The war years brought disruption and separation to the lovers, and increasing disillusionment to Bernie. By the time of his marriage he has become disenchanted with Bradley's passionate nationalism and is ready for a normal, settled life with Norah.

"The Patriot" contains several parallels with Corkery's war stories. Both "The Ember" and "On the Heights" describe relationships between young rebels and the older generation of nationalists, though without the ambivalence that O'Faolain expresses. "An

172

Unfinished Symphony" portrays a weary young soldier on the run, who, like Bernie, longs to see his girl; he risks capture to visit her, but his desire is frustrated when he is arrested and imprisoned.

The style of "The Patriot," though still highly romantic, is somewhat more objective than the style of "Fugue." The story is told in the third person from Bernie's point of view. He is sensitive and idealistic, but not so fully immersed in romantic dreams as the narrator of "Fugue." He can analyze realistically the hopelessness of the Irregular's position.

The central section of the story, after the description of Bernie's first meetings with Norah and their incipient love, covers a period of several months which he spends hiding alone in the mountains, moving aimlessly from place to place without involvement in the actual fighting. He becomes so detached and immersed in the landscape that he loses his human identity for a time and scarcely thinks even of Norah, until one day the sudden memory of her overwhelms him with misery and longing. He decides to go to the Irregulars' headquarters, a hotel on a mountain lake, to get enough money and clean clothes to return home. He hopes that Bradley, also in hiding, will be at the hotel to persuade him that their cause is not futile, "that all their humiliation of poverty and hunger was not, as he had long since begun to feel, a useless and wasted offering."[35]

The scene at the headquarters completes Bernie's disillusionment with the war. The officers are drunk, discipline is almost non-existent, and the morale of the soldiers is very low. They can neither summon the strength to fight nor agree to stop fighting. Bradley is there, urging them to fight on at all costs. He arouses Bernie's jealousy by telling him he saw Norah several times before leaving the city. When the soldiers disperse, Bernie and two others hide in a cave in the hills, too discouraged to attempt the trip home. There they are captured, and Youghal becomes prominent again in Bernie's life when he passes through it as a prisoner. A year later, when he is released, he goes there with Norah to recover from his imprisonment.

The culminating visit to Youghal, the honeymoon, takes place at Easter, when the tourists have not yet arrived and signs of renewal are strongest. The beauty and solitude of the landscape contribute to the lovers' ecstasy. Bradley is there too, to address a public meeting, but Bernie no longer reacts to him with enthusiasm. The lovers, absorbed in each other and the stillness of the evening, leave the meeting without even speaking to Bradley. Their lives have taken a different direction. Yet just as Bernie is about to make love to Norah in their hotel room, he sees Bradley's departing car through the window.

> He saw the white hair of their orator
> friend, the old bachelor, the patriot,
> driving out of the town into the country
> and the dark night. The hedges would race
> past him; the rabbits skip before his
> headlights on the road; the moths in the
> cool wind would fly around his flushed
> face and his trembling hands. But that
> wind would not for many miles cool the
> passion in him to which he had given his
> life.[36]

The old man forms an image of lonely dedication which Bernie holds in his mind as he turns toward Norah. He cannot escape Bradley's influence without some ambivalent feelings.

The story is unified in spite of the long time period it covers. Unity of place is provided by Youghal, with its changing associations for the lovers in their relationship with each other and with Bradley. The return to Youghal, by evoking both pleasant and painful memories for them, helps intensify and deepen their love. The consistent point of view and the compression of the flashback technique also help unify the narrative.

Despite their differences in tone, "Fugue" and "The Patriot" offer similar perspectives on war. In both stories, the main character feels impelled to escape from the physical and psychological dangers of war and to resume a normal life. War is viewed as a disruptive and isolating condition, in sharp contrast to the solace of nature and the comfort of ordinary domestic relationships. O'Faolain's attitude to war is similar to O'Flaherty's and O'Connor's, though not so severe in its moral outrage as theirs is; he did not write a story as strongly pacifistic as O'Connor's "Guests of the Nation." O'Faolain focuses instead on the effects of war on the rebel's psychological state. He identifies closely with the rebel and often uses him as a vehicle for his own thoughts.

The differences between O'Faolain's early style in Midsummer Night Madness and his later style are suggested by O'Faolain himself, in the 1957 Foreword to The Finest Stories. Looking back on these early stories, he observes that they are highly romantic, full of the personal thoughts of the author, "his own devouring daemon." "Fugue" is a lovely story and he wishes he could still feel as he did when he wrote it. When he conceived these stories, O'Faolain says, "I did not know from Adam what I wanted to say. I had no grasp at all of the real world, of real people. . . . I could only try to convey my astonishment and delight at the strangeness of this bewildering thing called life." The revolutionary period was "too filled with dreams and ideals and a sense of dedication to be an experience in the meaning of things perceived, understood and remembered." The early stories are "all the time trying to take off in an airplane."37

iii

Once he had completed the war stories, O'Faolain turned his attention to post-war domestic and social life. The period from the late thirties through the late fifties was his most prolific, and the three collections of stories published during this time--A Purse of Coppers, The Man Who Invented Sin (Teresa in England), and The Finest Stories--contain most of his best work. These stories emphasize the relationship between the individual and the community, and the powerful influence of the Irish milieu on character development. As this phase progresses, we can observe in O'Faolain a gradual detachment from social issues and an increasing interest in the conflicts of the individual psyche; there is also a gradual shedding of the influence of earlier European and Irish writers, as he develops a more individual style.

O'Faolain evaluates his changing attitude to Ireland during this period in the Foreword to The Finest Stories. He says that after the romanticism of the first collection, the stories in A Purse of Coppers show "a certain adjustment and detachment," but complete detachment did not occur until the writing of The Man Who Invented Sin. He realized then that Irishmen were fundamentally confused and self-contradictory, still clinging to a romantic "tea-rose" image of themselves, sentimentalizing religion and the Gaelic tradition, while at the same time practicing hard-headed

175

materialism, and dodging "more awkward social, moral and political problems than any country might, with considerable courage, hope to solve in a century of ruthless thinking." It is challenging for the writer to find the proper literary mode for such intractable material; he must find a way of reconciling romanticism and realism. O'Faolain says he has always tried to be open to growth and change, and has never been content with a single approach to story writing. "One is always searching for different forms, since otherwise one's passion would have the same form from birth to death, which would merely mean that one had got stuck, or given up, or agreed to compromise on some easy formula somewhere along the line, and that would be premature death, since not to change is to die though still apparently alive."38

The stories in A Purse of Coppers generally convey a mood of bitterness. Many of the characters suffer from frustration, as Irish society stifles their ideals. The mood in The Man Who Invented Sin is somewhat more tolerant. Maurice Harmon sums up the change. "Now he concentrates on the variable nature of man, and this attentiveness to the delightful complexity of human nature lightens the tone of his stories. Their narrators, unlike the compulsive and haunted figures in A Purse of Coppers, stand apart, in detached and understanding sympathy, from what they describe."39 The eight new stories in The Finest Stories also reflect this altered tone.

Narrative techniques undergo a corresponding change. O'Faolain's evolving theories of the short story, later systematized in The Short Story, are effectively applied to his own work. There is a marked development of objectivity and artistic maturity between Midsummer Night Madness and A Purse of Coppers, and his technical mastery and control are even more apparent in The Man Who Invented Sin. His best stories of this period make use of compression and implication; they are structured in a deceptively casual, indeterminate way that evokes a richness and depth of meaning. Always a painstaking stylist, O'Faolain in these stories refines an individual style that is sensuous and poetic, yet economical.

O'Faolain's sense of humor is evident in these collections, and many of the stories are written in the comic or satiric mode. His experiments with satire are not entirely successful, because, as he admits, he has "much too soft a corner for the old land."40 In his

176

better satires, critical judgment is usually mollified by amusement and affection.

Not surprisingly, A Purse of Coppers contains fewer humorous stories than the later collections. It includes one blatant and not particularly successful satire on Irish economic policy, "Sullivan's Trousers." More effective is the blend of caricature and pathos in "The Old Master," which ridicules Irish chauvinism. The story employs a device that many earlier Irish writers used, the illumination of Irish attitudes by contrasting them with the attitudes of visiting foreigners--in this case, a Russian ballet company performing in Cork. The "old master," John Aloysius Gonzaga O'Sullivan, is like many of O'Faolain's humorous characters, an eccentric, self-deluded bachelor. He thinks of himself as a cultured cosmopolitan, and he expresses much enthusiasm for the ballet, until the local canon leads a demonstration against it for its supposed immorality. Because he fears losing his job, O'Sullivan equivocates and hides in a lavatory to escape the problem. The narrator condemns him harshly for his pomposity and cowardice.

The satiric stories in The Man Who Invented Sin and The Finest Stories are usually lighter in tone than those in A Purse of Coppers. "The End of a Good Man" and "Vive La France" are slight comic treatments of the Irish character. "Lord and Master" describes a conflict between a retired teacher and a landowner over a drainage problem, and gives a suggestion of sadness at the loss of aristocratic traditions in Ireland. "Persecution Mania" and "An Enduring Friendship" are unexceptional satires about the antics of journalists and their adversaries. Several of O'Faolain's best satiric stories treat the interreaction of religious beliefs with other character traits. "Unholy Living and Half Dying," "One True Friend," and "Childybawn" are pointed studies of the perverse and incongruous blend in the Irish character of piety and such impious qualities as malice or petty vice.

The subject of religion is of central importance in O'Faolain's work. He probes the religious consciousness of laymen on a serious as well as a humorous level, and includes a diversified selection of priests, monks, and nuns in his stories, depicting them sometimes sympathetically, sometimes critically. Among the writers we are considering, only Frank O'Connor surpasses O'Faolain in portraying the clergy.

Several stories in A Purse of Coppers are about

177

priests. As is characteristic of this collection, the individuality of the priests is subordinate to their social role. "Sinners" introduces a theme that O'Faolain would come back to in his later work--the estrangement of a priest from the real needs and feelings of his parishioners, and from his own humanity, as a result of too literal and mechanical adherence to dogma. The occasion of weekly confession establishes a contrast between a cold, bad-tempered canon and his curate, who is so compassionate that his parishioners prefer him as their confessor. Two other stories about priests are among the best in the volume--"A Broken World" and "Discord." Both stories are pessimistic, though not despairing. The titles suggest a condition of fragmentation or disharmony in the lives of the priests and in Irish society as a whole.

In "A Broken World," the condition of Ireland is revealed through the conversation of three strangers riding on a train. The train journey, a convenient device that O'Faolain also uses in "Up the Bare Stairs," was used earlier by European story writers like Chekhov and Maupassant. It enables the writer to bring characters together in a casual way, and the interaction of their personalities generates the story.

The three characters in "A Broken World" are carefully chosen to reflect the conflicts of modern Irish life. The first person narrator is a sensitive intellectual much like the ones we have seen in other O'Faolain stories. There is also an idealistic priest, silenced for his political involvement in the land movement, and a lethargic, dull-witted farmer, representative of the agricultural class who, though vital to Ireland's economic future, are resistant to innovation and progress. The conversation turns on the priest's search for "moral unity" in Irish life. He is portrayed sympathetically, though not in depth, as a defeated idealist who has lived a cold and lonely life. The two halves of the "broken" world are symbolized by two parishes outside Dublin: a parish of poor, hilly farms where the priest formerly lived, and a neighboring lowland parish of large estates. The priest suggests that the role of the poor farmers as servants and dependents of the gentry was debilitating, and when the gentry abandoned their land they left a void in Irish life that has not been filled. The narrator and the farmer are briefly inspired and drawn together by this narrative, but then each retreats into himself and they disperse, exemplifying the condition of people in modern Ireland, isolated from each other and working at cross-purposes.

At the end of the story the narrator expresses his hope that Ireland will awaken from its dormancy and find a new vital image of itself, but he is frustrated by the apathy and ignorance of the farmer.

Landscape and setting are used metaphorically. The winter scene outside the train affects the characters' moods. As he attempts to refute in his mind the gloomy talk of the priest, the narrator thinks "that he had merely spoken out of the snowy landscape, which above all other conditions of nature is so powerful to make life seem lonely, and all work futile, and time itself a form of decay. . . . But . . . I could not deny to the wintry moment its own truth, and that under that white shroud, covering the whole of Ireland, life was lying broken and hardly breathing."[41] The suggestion that "truth" may be temporary and relative or fragmented is, as we have seen, a characteristic attitude of modern short story writers, not only in Ireland but elsewhere.

Snow used as an image of Ireland of course recalls "The Dead." Commenting on the relationship between his story and Joyce's, O'Faolain says that writers often are not fully aware of their own creative processes.

> A friend suggested to me that "A Broken World" was my unconscious reply to Joyce's wonderful story, "The Dead." I certainly did not consciously mean any such thing; but I can agree that what with the snow over Dublin, and the suggestion that Ireland is not dead but sleeping, as against Joyce's feeling that Ireland is paralyzed by its past, one could, I suppose, say that the stories contrast the attitudes of two different generations.[42]

Another story which provides an interesting comparison with "A Broken World" is Corkery's "Carrig-an-Afrinn," in which a farmer leaves his poor farm for a better one abandoned by the gentry, and rebuilds it through his extraordinary energy and will. Their portrayal of opposite types of farmers as representatives of Ireland's future emphasizes the irreconcilable differences of outlook between Corkery and his protegé. O'Faolain's ambivalence and cautious hope are in part a reaction to the excesses of Joyce's despair and Corkery's optimism.

Fr. Peter in "Discord" is portrayed less sympathetically than the priest in "A Broken World." He is not a villain, but like many of O'Faolain's priests, a

basically good man whose humanity has become somewhat
calloused in response to the unremitting demands of his
vocation, in this case the extreme neediness of his
parishioners, Dublin slumdwellers. He has developed a
cheerful, humorous manner which belies the conditions
of his life. There is no separate narrator; Fr. Peter's
viewpoint is objectively contrasted with that of a young
naive couple from his rural hometown who are honeymoo-
ning in Dublin.

As in "A Broken World," there is in this story a
significant historical dimension, an awareness of past
forces that have shaped the present. O'Faolain's view
of the past is here somewhat similar to Moore's and
Joyce's; it seems defeating rather than inspiring. The
attic room where Fr. Peter lives was once a gathering
place for Young Irelanders, and Mangan wrote poetry
there. Wolfe Tone was born in the neighborhood, and
Robert Emmet was hanged nearby. But the patriotism and
self-sacrifice of these martyrs has had little apparent
impact on present-day Dublin, since the scene is dominated by urban blight.

Spatial symbolism represents the painful experience
that Fr. Peter unwittingly inflicts on his guests. They
descend from his attic room with its wide view of the
city to the gloomy crypt of the church. On the way
they pass some parishioners whom Fr. Peter dismisses
off-handedly. In the crypt they see many further remin-
ders of human suffering: the coffin of MacNally, a
traitor, and several coffins of tenement-dwellers killed
in a gas explosion. Maurice Harmon comments that for
Fr. Peter, "custom has diminished the ugliness of his
familiar inferno but for the lovers the descent into
the underground crypt leads them uncomfortably close to
the knowledge of death and age for which they are altogether unprepared."[43] Fr. Peter afterward takes them
out on the town, but they are uncomfortable the whole
time, like "children lost in a wood," and once safely
back in their hotel room they laugh away their painful
thoughts and make love passionately. The contrast
between the older solitary man and the young lovers
absorbed in each other is similar to the ending of "The
Patriot."

"A Broken World" and "Discord" are both good examples of O'Faolain's concept of organic form at this
stage of his career. The influence of Chekhov and Joyce
is evident in the inconclusive, "slice-of-life" plots
and in the compression and poetic suggestiveness of the
style. Characters are briefly sketched, and realistic,

180

economically constructed dialogue is used to reveal character traits.

O'Faolain's treatment of clergy is generally more sympathetic in The Man Who Invented Sin than in A Purse of Coppers. "Good" or likeable clergy appear more frequently. One way to illustrate this change is to compare two stories about nuns. "Mother Matilda's Book," from A Purse of Coppers, is a bleak story of an old nun given the task of writing the history of the order, as "busy work." She devotes herself to the project, but becomes increasingly senile, an embarrassment to the convent, and she botches the book so much that the nuns are ashamed to show it to anyone. "Teresa," from The Man Who Invented Sin, is a lighter, more amusing story of a young novice, Teresa, and an older nun, Sr. Patrick, who go on a pilgrimage to St. Teresa's shrine in Lisieux to resolve Teresa's doubts about her vocation. Teresa thinks of herself as more saintly than the other nuns, but she actually proves to be shallow and inconsiderate, and eventually runs away from the order. Sr. Patrick, on the other hand, is solid and kind-hearted despite her limitations, clearly the more genuine character of the two.

Two excellent stories in The Man Who Invented Sin-- "The Silence of the Valley" and the title story--combine portraits of clergy with a lament for the waning of the Gaelic language and traditions. "The Silence of the Valley" is not primarily about religious life, though a priest is the dominant character. It describes the wake and burial of an old cobbler, last of the traditional storytellers, and shares some common features with O'Kelly's "The Weaver's Grave" and Corkery's "The Rivals," which also describes the funeral of an old storyteller. O'Faolain again employs the device of contrasting natives with outsiders--a group of tourists staying at the local hotel. The natives are deeply affected, but to the tourists, the cobbler's death is fairly meaningless, since they do not understand the significance of what has been lost. The priest, intelligent and compassionate, is also a visitor from the city, but he knows the local people well and has been completely accepted by them. He is comfortably attentive to both groups, performing the funeral Mass for the cobbler, consoling his widow, and keeping up pleasant conversation with the tourists. He comprehends more fully than anyone else the historical importance of the cobbler's death and the loss it represents for Irish culture. Like O'Faolain himself, the priest combines a cosmopolitan outlook with a veneration for Irish

tradition. His inner conflicts and attitude to his
vocation are not dealt with directly; he is carried
outside himself by a mood of pure mourning.

The occasion of "The Man Who Invented Sin" is a
summer school in the Irish language, like the one
O'Faolain attended around 1920. The story has a first
person narrator much like O'Faolain, a man looking back
on his youth many years afterwards. While attending the
school, he boarded in a farmhouse where two nuns and
two monks were also staying, because their hostels were
overcrowded. For a few weeks they all enjoyed a happy
companionship, though the local curate, nicknamed
"Lispeen" (frog), watched them disapprovingly, regarding
their innocent pleasures as sinful. At the end of the
summer the clergy returned to their orders in the city
slums and never again found the emotional freedom they
experienced that summer. The association of the country
with liberation and inspiration, and the city with
entrapment and sterility, is a pattern characteristic of
O'Faolain at this period, though his attitude to city
life is not as consistently antipathetic as O'Flaherty's
and becomes more positive later in his career.

The narrator is very sympathetic towards the nuns
and monks, and harsh in his judgment of the puritanical
curate, yet he is not deeply involved in the action; he
is compassionate but detached. He is one of several
narrators in this volume who illustrate O'Faolain's
increasing objectivity. The atmosphere of the summer
school contributes to the emotional liberation that the
characters experience. The narrator describes the special gaiety and idealism of the participants, their
spirit of national renewal. The landscape itself is
changed by their presence; normally gloomy and barren,
the hills are now teeming with life.

The inhibitions of the clergy do not break down
easily, and it takes a while for them to be at ease
with each other. Gradually a real companionship develops, based on affectionate teasing, spirited, idealistic
arguments, shared childhood memories, and singing and
dancing. They acquire a fuller, deeper sense of themselves and appreciation for each other. But their happiness is blighted by the arrival of Lispeen, to lecture
them grandiloquently for their carrying-on. The mood
of the story changes abruptly with the introduction of
Lispeen. Imagery anticipates the change as the door
bangs open: "For that second it was as if a cinema
reel stopped dead."[44] From this moment on, we feel
that something artificial and absurd has corroded the

value of their shared experience. For the nuns and monks, "sin" has been invented; they have acquired a sense of guilt which they did not previously feel, and they persist in their pleasures in a spirit of childish defiance and rebelliousness. O'Faolain reinforces this idea by associating Lispeen with Satan and the Serpent, and describing the nuns and monks as inhabitants of Eden who have been forbidden to eat the apple. O'Faolain has made the caricature of Lispeen so ridiculous that to the reader, he seems trivial and irrelevant. He is much like the ominous and melodramatic priest in O'Flaherty's "The Fairy Goose." Both caricatures suggest the coarseness and mediocrity of the people who control Irish life.

The ending of the story contains an ironic comment on the state of Irish society after the revolution. The narrator skips over a period of many years, and describes a day when he coincidentally met both Majellan, one of the monks, and Lispeen. The coincidence is a little implausible, but it does not really detract from the story, because O'Faolain has already shifted from realism to a more figurative mode of caricature and satire. Majellan, intelligent and sensitive, has deteriorated since that summer. Years of institutional religious life have suppressed his spirit, and he looks stooped and defeated. The narrator remarks that "the mountains are empty"--no one wants to learn Irish any more. The narrow, puritanical Ireland that emerged from the revolution has not lived up to his youthful dream. Religious life reflects the general social condition. Majellan replies, "'I'm not sure that I altogether approve of young people going out to these places. . . . You know the sort of thing that goes on out there.'" His memory of that summer is not happy; it is "'not good to take people out of their rut.'"[45]

When the narrator meets Lispeen, he seems thriving and content. As a priest, he has attained a position of authority in the Church that is denied to the monks and nuns, and he obviously flourishes on the attention and reverence of his parishioners. His power is incongruously out of proportion with the pettiness of his values. His memory of that summer has changed, too. He is oblivious to the destructiveness of his attitude, laughs merrily and says the nuns and monks were innocents, like children. "'Of course, I had to frighten them.'" As in many early stories, O'Faolain here depicts a close relationship between individual and communal consciousness. The fate of individual characters reflects the condition of Ireland as a whole. He

implies that in post-revolutionary Ireland, the Church
is controlled by the wrong people and has acquired too
much power. Its values have become perverted and life-
denying, so that clergy are discouraged from developing
such qualities as compassion and tolerance. In both
"The Silence of the Valley" and "The Man Who Invented
Sin," O'Faolain conveys from his more cosmopolitan perspective the mood of sadness and loss that O'Kelly,
Corkery, and O'Flaherty express in their stories, as
they record the Gaelic traditions that are dying out.

Another frequently recurring subject in O'Faolain's
work is Irish family life. He wrote many stories about
childhood or the relationships between children and
their parents. Although he sometimes tells a story
from a child's viewpoint, he is usually more successful
when describing childhood from the viewpoint of an adult
looking back; he lacks the ability of Joyce or O'Connor
to render the special consciousness of the child. Some
of his efforts at recreating a child's world include
"The Confessional," similar to O'Connor's "First Confession" in its portrayal of children's awe of the sacra-
ment; "The Trout," a story about a little girl overcoming her fears to rescue a trapped fish; "The Judas
Touch," like Joyce's "An Encounter" a story of a truant
boy's excursion to the seaside which turns into a fias-
co.

O'Faolain is particularly gifted at creating belie-
vable middle-aged characters, and he turns this to good
account in his stories of adults reliving childhood in
the present or recapturing it in memory, such as "A
Born Genius" and "Up the Bare Stairs." As in many
stories of family life by O'Flaherty and earlier writers, emigration often breaks up the family unit. Characters seek temporary or permanent escape not so much
from poverty as from the family's stifling attitudes.

"A Born Genius" is a fairly long story about a man
with a musical talent that he wastes. Pat Lenihan, a
dreamy, unworldly man, has grown up in Prout Lane, a
very poor area of Cork. He still lives with his mother
and brother, works (appropriately) as a clerk in a vinegar factory, and spends his spare time either singing in
amateur theatricals or working on handicraft projects
which he never completes. Stimulated by a chance meeting with Trixie Flynn, a former friend who has made a
successful career for herself as an opera singer and is
now married to a Cork businessman, he goes to New York
to study singing. His father has been living there
since deserting his mother twelve years previously and

has offered to pay for his lessons. But when Lenihan discovers that his father is living with an Italian woman and has had several children by her, he leaves New York indignantly and abandons his singing career. Once back in Ireland he resumes a boring and futile existence. Eventually he has to give up even his half-hearted relationship with Trixie, because people are starting to talk about them.

This story shows many of the influences that were at work in O'Faolain's early writing. Lenihan resembles some of the bored clerks and embittered artists in nineteenth-century Russian fiction. The mood of stagnation and paralysis is also derived from the stories of Moore and Joyce; in particular, Lenihan recalls the clerk and aspiring poet Little Chandler of "A Little Cloud."

The deprivation of his surroundings and the attitudes of his family and friends are partially responsible for Lenihan's failure. His mother is obsessed with religion, his brother with drinking and boasting, and neither can offer the real support or guidance he needs. The indiscriminate adulation of his family and fellow workers gives him an overinflated view of his abilities. The phrase "a born genius" is ironic, because he never disciplines and channels his inborn gifts. Instead he loses himself in daydreams as vague as the mist on the marshes he stares at through his office window.

The trip to New York elates Lenihan and renews his hope. He has dreamed of establishing a close relationship with his father and persuading him to return home, reconciled to his mother. But the dream is unrealistic, and it is shattered. His angry rejection of his father is motivated by his narrow religious upbringing and by the memory of his mother struggling alone. He does not begin to feel compassion for his father until much later, but once he does, he becomes a divided, embittered man, unable to resolve the conflict in himself. He drifts further and further into fantasy. His cynical submission to public opinion and evasive daydreaming are symptomatic of Irish society after the revolution. Lacking the capacity for hard self-analysis and decisive action, many sensitive, intelligent Irish people acquiesced in sterile conventions and lived passively, without fulfillment.

Although it is somewhat flawed by diffuseness, the story provides evidence of O'Faolain's growing technical skill. The point of view and treatment of time are more complex than in most of his other early stories.

185

The beginning and end are particularly effective. At the beginning Lenihan is standing in his doorway at evening, staring into the mist. After a digression describing his job at the vinegar factory, the author returns to the description of him standing in the doorway. On impulse he sits down at the piano, which he has not touched for a long time. The sound of his playing and singing draws Trixie Flynn to the house for the encounter that precipitates the trip to New York. At the end, Lenihan repeats the actions of staring out the door and sitting down at the piano, but this time no significant meeting takes place. "He began [the song], several times, and each time he paused, and sat listening for a noise at the door."[46]

"Up the Bare Stairs" demonstrates the technical mastery and artistic maturity that we have observed in other stories from The Man Who Invented Sin. It concerns a family situation similar to O'Faolain's own. On a train journey to Cork the narrator meets Sir Francis Nugent, a successful career soldier knighted for war services. The coincidence that both attended the same school in Cork gives them an opening for conversation. Nugent is returning to Cork to bury his mother, who has been living with him in London, and he tells the narrator the story behind his success. His parents were poor but ambitious people; they sacrificed and pushed him to succeed in school and make a respectable career for himself. Their pathetic martyrdom filled him with pity and contempt. He drove himself to do well in school, not from love of learning but as a means of escape from their solicitations. He even perpetuated an antagonism between himself and Brother Angelo, a teacher he had formerly loved, as a spur to scholastic achievement. His success has been achieved at the cost of personal wholeness.

The first person narrator, like the narrator in "The Man Who Invented Sin," remains more detached than his earlier counterparts. Joseph Rippier draws a contrast between this narrator and the one in "A Broken World."

> The narrator in "A Broken World" cannot just listen passively to the priest and country farmer he meets on the train. He has a point of view of his own which is expressed; he is part of a triangular situation. The narrator in "Up the Bare Stairs" remains disinterested.[47]

In "A Broken World," the narrator participates actively in the conversation; in "Up the Bare Stairs," he speaks only at the beginning and the end, and the rest of the story is told by Nugent without interruption. The narrator does show some emotional response, though, as he fears at first he will be bored by the story, but as he listens becomes deeply absorbed in it.

Several factors contribute to the compression and intensity of this story. The narrator meets Nugent at a significant, bittersweet moment in his life, when he has just been knighted, his mother has just died, and he is returning to the place he fled from many years earlier. The conversation on the train takes only a short time, but by talking to a stranger at that moment Nugent puts his whole life into perspective. The life story, or "story-within-a-story," is itself compressed, as Nugent concentrates on one particular incident that determined what course his life would follow.

The central incident sheds light on many destructive characteristics of Irish family and school life. Up to the point where the story begins, Nugent has enjoyed school and admired his teacher, Brother Angelo, a boyishly enthusiastic and dedicated monk. But Angelo is involved in the petty political factionalism that is rampant in Cork at the time, between the Molly Maguires and the All for Irelanders. He divides his class into two teams representing the two parties. Nugent, the star of the Molly Maguires, which is also Angelo's side, lets his team down one day by incorrectly answering a geometry problem. Out of spite Angelo keeps him late at school, knowing this punishment will get him into trouble with his parents.

The scene which Nugent's parents create when he gets home turns his love for them into pity and makes him resolve to get out at all costs. His father chides him for disgracing the Molly Maguires and his mother for not working hard enough. "'What are we slaving for, boy, day and night, and all the rest of it. . . . Nothing matters, boy, but the work! The work!'"48 Although Nugent bursts into tears and promises to work harder, inside him a major change has taken place. From then on he deliberately antagonizes Angelo. He stays up late every night to prepare his assignments perfectly and challenges Angelo to catch him in an error. But he has sacrificed his youth and tells the narrator he has not become a whole man. He worked not because he loved his parents but because he hated them. "They broke my spirit with pity. . . . Pity is the most

disintegrating of all human emotions. It's the most
disgusting of all human emotions. I know it."[49]

The ending of the story conveys the sadness and
waste underlying Nugent's apparently successful life.
The narrator watches him leave the train to meet his
poor relatives as his mother's coffin is placed in a
hearse. Shortly afterwards they all drive away into the
night. The homecoming is a tribute to the dead rather
than the living. The narrator is clearly moved by what
he has heard and his sympathy for a man he will probably
never see again heightens the pathos.

In both "A Born Genius" and "Up the Bare Stairs,"
we can see O'Faolain's preoccupation with the theme of
personal fulfillment, his interest in "what flaws in
the intricate machinery of human nature keep it from
fulfilling itself wholly." Both Lenihan and Nugent,
like many of O'Faolain's characters, encounter "road-
blocks" in the path of their growth. Their efforts at
escape do not bring genuine liberation and fulfillment,
because the psychological damage inflicted by their
early family life is too great. Since their emotional
responsiveness has been stifled, both characters suffer
from cynicism and apathy. Nugent is characterized more
positively than Lenihan, however; he has at least partially compensated for the deficiencies of his youth by
achieving success and fame.

"Up the Bare Stairs" also emphasizes another of
O'Faolain's broad underlying themes, the nature of time
and memory. Many of his stories have, to use Frank
O'Connor's phrase, a "backward look." He is acutely
conscious of both the historical forces that have shaped
modern Ireland and the childhood forces that have shaped
the individual adult psyche. This sense of the past
operating on the present, as well as the present rede-
fining the past, is apparent in almost all of the stories we have examined, and he continued to explore the
subject further in his later work.

In addition to the stories about religion, childhood, and family life, O'Faolain also wrote many stories
about love and marriage. This is the dominant subject
in his later collections, though it is less important in
the early and middle periods. In his early stories
O'Faolain does not treat love relationships in depth.
He is more preoccupied with social issues, and when he
does introduce love relationships, he uses them mainly
to illustrate the effect of external communal pressures
on individuals. The relationship between Lenihan and

188

Trixie Flynn in "A Born Genius" is a good example.
Other love stories from A Purse of Coppers and The Man
Who Invented Sin include "Kitty the Wren," about a
woman ostracized for having an illegitimate child; "A
Meeting," about a woman who was formerly a revolutionary and is now bogged down in a stagnant marriage; "The
Woman Who Married Clark Gable," a humorous account of a
woman pretending her husband is Clark Gable, so that
she will feel more passionate towards him (Frank O'Connor also uses this device in "The Holy Door"); "Lady
Lucifer," a superior story about a love relationship in
the setting of an insane asylum, a situation that O'Faolain uses again in the late story "Liberty"; "The Fur
Coat," a commentary on the distrust of material prosper-
ity ingrained in a middle-aged couple who have had to
sacrifice and work hard all their lives.

By far the best love story of O'Faolain's middle
period, and one of the best stories he ever wrote, is
"Lovers of the Lake." This masterpiece is the culmination of all his work up to this time, and in many ways
it anticipates the direction he would follow afterwards. The story dramatizes the effect of Irish religious consciousness on two middle-aged adulterous
lovers. The woman, Jenny, is married to a wealthy man
whom she does not love. For several years she has been
having an affair with Bobby Flanigan, a Dublin surgeon.
They are both Catholics; Jenny is more religious than
Bobby, but neither attends church regularly. One day
Jenny asks Bobby to drive her to Lough Derg so she can
make the penitential pilgrimage. At first Bobby cannot
understand why Jenny wants to do it; he reacts with
angry skepticism and accuses her of feeling guilty about
him. But eventually he joins her on the island and
separately they perform the acts of fasting and penance.
They transcend themselves for a short time and achieve
a new religious awareness, a sense of their relationship
to eternity. But the experience makes their love even
stronger. They cannot obey the Church's command to
renounce each other. After leaving the island they prolong the period of fasting and chastity for one more
day, but it is clear that when they return to Dublin,
they will resume their previous relationship.

The story is long and detailed. It does not have
a recognizable narrator, but is told primarily from
Jenny's point of view. The opening sections are presented dramatically. We do not see into the characters'
minds, but must infer their thoughts from their conversations and actions. We do not share Jenny's thoughts
until she is on the island, experiencing the complex

189

emotions of the pilgrim. This technique of showing
Jenny first from the outside and then from the inside
parallels the story's theme: on the island people
reveal themselves to each other in a way they cannot in
the world.

When Jenny and Bobby are first presented, neither
seems particularly susceptible to religious emotion.
Both are worldly and sophisticated. Jenny is spoiled
and attached to physical comforts, and Bobby has the
rational, skeptical mind of a surgeon. But as they are
driving to Lough Derg, Jenny tells Bobby that she has
clung to her religious belief as a solace for her unhappy and childless marriage. The pilgrimage to Lough Derg
is for her profoundly identified with Irish Catholicism
and she has always wanted to go there. She says that
although it sounds blasphemous, all she has is Bobby
and God. This paradoxical relationship between her
"sinful" love for Bobby and her religious need is the
central conflict of the story. It is not a simple conflict between desire and conscience, but something much
more complex.

Bobby's exasperation with Jenny results from his
fear that she may feel guilty about their relationship
and may be seeking the spiritual strength to give him
up. He has not practiced his religion since childhood
and has little sympathy with the self-abasing rituals
the pilgrims follow, like fasting, staying awake all
night, and walking barefoot on stony ground. But since
he loves Jenny, he is curious about her motives and
joins the pilgrimage in an effort to find out more about
her.

O'Faolain uses natural settings to enhance the
experiences of the characters. The drive to Lough Derg
has the outward appearance of a holiday trip. Part of
the route passes along the sunny and tranquil seacoast,
which suggests liberation and pleasure. But when they
turn inland to the lake, the landscape becomes more
hilly, the weather more gloomy and rainy. In his description of the lake and the island, O'Faolain uses
metaphors that contribute to the penitential atmosphere
of the pilgrimage. Lough Derg is a place remote and
essentially different from the world.

> Other pilgrims stood by the boat slip,
> waiting for the ferry, their backs hunched
> to the wind, their clothes ruffled like
> the fur of cattle. She looked out across
> the lough at the creeping worms of foam. . . .

> Confused and hairy-looking clouds combed
> themselves on the ridges of the hills.
> The lake was crumpled and gray, except
> for those yellow worms of foam blown across
> it in parallel lines.[50]

Jenny is disturbed when the island itself does not live
up to her expectations. Instead of a medieval island
containing old ruins, a romantic retreat to the past,
she sees a harsh reminder of the present, a barren place
dominated by "tall buildings like modern hotels." Her
first reaction is a sense of oppression, not inspiration.

During the pilgrimage itself, Jenny passes through
a series of conflicting emotions. At first she feels
abased and humiliated by her loss of identity. Upset
because she cannot respond as passionately as the other
pilgrims, she prays to be released from herself.

Instead of finding a new faith, Jenny finds Bobby
once more, since he has decided to join the pilgrimage.
She thinks he has come only to mock her, but he says he
wants to find out what she believes in. In a series of
encounters during the pilgrimage, they argue and discuss
their relationship more openly than they have done
before. Bobby exposes some of Jenny's motives and says
she is too attached to the world to give it up; she
goes on living with her husband because she likes the
comfort his money provides. At this point Bobby still
holds back from committing himself fully to the pilgrimage, but already he has begun to respond, as memories
of his childhood religious experiences are revived.

During the night-long vigil in the church, Jenny
experiences intense religious ecstasy. She is so exhausted and hungry that objects appear as hallucina-
tions. The crucifix in particular draws her attention
as she feels that Christ is embracing her. She achieves
a moment of complete escape from herself and union with
Christ.

> The crucifix detached itself from the wall
> and leaned towards her, and for a long
> while she saw nothing but the heavy pendent
> body, the staring eyes, so that when the
> old man at her side let his head sink over
> on her shoulder and then woke up with a
> start she felt him no more than if they
> were two fishes touching in the sea. Bit
> by bit the incantations drew her in; sounds

191

came from her mouth; prayers flowed
between her and those troubled eyes that
fixed hers. She swam into an ecstasy as
rare as one of those perfect dances of
her youth when she used to swing in a
whirl of music, a swirl of bodies, a
circling of lights, floated out of her
mortal frame, alone in the arms that
embraced her.[51]

The imagery in this passage continues a pattern that
O'Faolain introduced earlier. The use of sensual images
like dancing and embracing to describe Jenny's relationship with Christ suggests a close connection between
human and divine love. The lake has become an image
for an internal state. When Jenny first prays to be
released from herself, she feels separate from the
other pilgrims: "The waves of voices beat and rumbled
in her ears as in an empty shell." The pilgrims are
exposed to wind, rain, and darkness as they walk their
rounds barefooted, but when Jenny meets Bobby for the
first time, there is a slight break in the weather: "A
slow rift in the clouds let down a star; by its light
she saw his smile."[52] This delicate image, which is
repeated later in the story, hints at a spiritual quality in their relationship. When Jenny is submerged in
her ecstasy, the lake image is replaced by a sea image;
the reference to her and the old man as "two fishes
touching" has Biblical connotations. Metaphors related
to water--swimming, being submerged, and so on--are
thus associated with loss of identity, self-surrender,
and spiritual communion. The lake seems to be related
to human consciousness, the sea to divine knowledge.

The effect of Jenny's moment of ecstasy is not to
make her more chaste and ascetic but to arouse a need
for Bobby. After emerging from the church during a
break, she goes to find him and learns with surprise that
he has not slept. He angers her by providing a rational, scientific explanation for the ecstasy she has just
experienced. She furiously tells him she never wants to
see him again. She meets him again the next day, however, and when he tells her he is still making the pilgrimage and has not eaten, she feels a surge of affection for him.

When the lovers meet late in the afternoon of the
second day, Jenny feels ready to talk about her reasons
for coming on the pilgrimage. She was motivated both by
a fear of old age and by religious conscience. She has
reached her fortieth birthday and realizes that some day

192

she may have to give Bobby up. When she tells him that twice a year, when she goes to confession, she promises to stop seeing him, he looks at her in astonishment. She admits she lives in a perpetual state of self-contradiction, which she can control only by living for the present, one moment at a time. Bobby gains a new compassion for her predicament.

The pilgrimage brings Jenny closer not only to Bobby but to some of the other pilgrims. She exchanges confidences with a young woman who is worried because her husband keeps getting her pregnant, and with an Englishman who feels guilty for the way he has treated his wife. These conversations help Jenny to see her own problems in a larger context, as part of the human condition.

As the pilgrimage nears its end, the theme of the story is stated more explicitly. Jenny and Bobby are "separated by their identities, joined by their love." Both of them, in coming to the island, have been searching for an identity of soul rather than of body. Jenny reflects,

> She had received the island's gift:
> its sense of remoteness from the world,
> almost a sensation of the world's death.
> It is the source of the island's kind-
> ness. Nobody is just matter, poor to be
> exploited by rich, weak to be exploited
> by the strong; in mutual generosity each
> recognizes the other only as a form of
> soul; it is a brief, harsh Utopia of equal-
> ity in nakedness.[53]

This glimpse of other people's souls gives Jenny a new understanding of the concept of identity. It is not fixed and circumscribed, but open and expansive. In describing the boundaries of identity, O'Faolain uses the metaphor of a house; its solidity contrasts with the fluid metaphors of lake and sea, which suggest loss of identity and merging of self with God. Jenny is "overcome by the thought that inside ourselves we have no room without a secret door; no solid self that has not a ghost inside it trying to escape." Even in the relatively solid identity which people develop in the world, doors of escape are essential; people create illusions and alternative identities in their lives.

When Jenny and Bobby leave the island at noon of the third day, they retreat behind their "impenetrable

wall of identity." Bobby does not tell Jenny whether
or not he has gone to confession; some aspects of his
experience on the island remain hidden from her. They
have escaped from their private worlds briefly, but
their "Utopia of equality in nakedness" cannot be pro-
longed in the world. Jenny reflects that if lovers
could sacrifice everything for each other, they might
attain the kind of self-surrender she experienced on
the island, but she realizes sadly that she and Bobby
will never achieve that condition.

The awe the lovers experienced on the island does
not wear off immediately. They decide to prolong their
fast until midnight, according to the rules. They spend
a long quiet day driving around the Galway coast. Bobby
spends some time fishing while Jenny stares into a pool;
the acts recall the earlier religious imagery of fish
and water. They cook the fish but decide at the last
minute not to eat them. At midnight they arrive at a
hotel in Galway, eat and drink their fill, and then
dance together, but Jenny asks that they sleep in separate rooms. She wants to preserve her chastity for one
more night before they return home and resume their
affair. Their decision is both a tribute to the spiritual identity they have found and a recognition that
this identity cannot be maintained in the world. The
pilgrimage ironically has deepened their relationship
as lovers.

Towards the end of the story the natural imagery
reflects the lovers' contemplative mood. Though the
experience of the lake has become more distant, an
"ember," the hazy Galway landscape retains a suggestion
of the lake's power to dissolve and transform. An hour
before midnight the lovers walk along the seashore; as
on the island, a star illuminates the darkened water,
and seems to hint at the invisible presence of God. The
final sea image occurs when they have finished dancing
and are deciding whether or not to sleep together. They
embrace on the hotel porch and stand "looking long over
the brightness and blackness of the sea." The sea, like
God, is both "bright" and "black"--visible and invisible, enlightening and mysterious, accessible and hidden. Through the ironies and paradoxes of his imagery
O'Faolain hints at a spiritual presence which he does
not explicitly assert. In a mysterious way the adulterous love between Jenny and Bobby is connected with
divine love.

The subject of adultery was seldom mentioned in
stories by earlier Irish writers. That O'Faolain could

handle such a thorny subject with such objectivity and open-mindedness reveals the extent to which he had grown as an artist. This story reflects the best quali- ties of his mature years--sympathy, largeness of vision, psychological penetration. To Maurice Harmon the story "reveals much about the generous and intelligent manner in which O'Faolain approaches his work." Harmon asserts that O'Faolain's sensitivity allows him to "view his story with the widest sympathy and understanding. . . . After a lifetime of creative endeavor and technical advancement, he moves confidently through all the phases of the story, holding the balance between Bobby and Jenny at all stages in a steady and precise focus; the judgment is clear but not harsh."[54] The story evidences extraordinary technical skill as well as profound insight. The theme of identity is internalized; it becomes something much more than a set of social and religious circumstances. Genuine escape from the self and surrender to God is possible only in brief moments, but these moments, ambiguous as they are, can illuminate and deepen human relationships.

"Lovers of the Lake" provides a bridge between O'Faolain's earlier and later work. It relates the past and present on both a cultural and a personal level. It resembles earlier stories in its examination of the effect that religious institutions and attitudes have on Irish life, and anticipates the later work in its in-depth psychological study of characters who are weal- thy, sophisticated, and to some extent liberated from the mores of their society, yet still affected by them.

iv

The two collections that O'Faolain published dur- ing the sixties, I Remember! I Remember! and The Heat of the Sun, demonstrate his continuing search for new insights and new forms to express them in. The stories differ markedly in mood and style from his earlier work, yet a continuity is also apparent, and it is not diffi- cult to trace the evolution of these stories from their predecessors.

O'Faolain had become considerably more detached from Irish society by the sixties, more international in outlook. He remarked on this broadened viewpoint in an autobiographical essay published in 1976. "I have changed in one way. To me, now, Ireland is worth my attention only when it is the world. I have no least speck of local patriotism left in me."[55] Besides writing about foreigners in Ireland, he also writes more often about Irishmen abroad; many of these stories are set in the United States or Europe. Characters tend to be wealthier and more cultured than in earlier stories. Some connection with Ireland is always maintained, though, not just by including characters brought up in Ireland, but by exploring the effect of their Irish background on their personality and behavior. Despite their relative emancipation, the characters in O'Faolain's late stories are still affected in some way by Irish communal attitudes.

The stories in each of these volumes are linked by a central theme--time and memory in I Remember! I Remember! and love in The Heat of the Sun. As we have seen, these themes are not new, but have been present in O'Faolain's work since the beginning. They are both connected with his paramount interest in the individual's search for fulfillment, and the obstacles that prevent him from realizing his potential. This theme has become more internalized in the later collections; inner conflict is emphasized more than conflict with society. A passage from "Lovers of the Lake" quoted previously could serve as a thematic statement for most of O'Faolain's later work: "Inside ourselves we have no room without a secret door; no solid self that has not a ghost inside it trying to escape." Characters in these stories often explore alternate identities or possibilities for their lives. Even though it does not usually produce substantial change, this imaginative exploration can enlarge and enrich the characters' self-awareness. Feelings of loss and regret are often aroused as characters contemplate the permanently closed doors in their lives.

In keeping with his desire not to stagnate, O'Faolain experiments with a variety of storytelling techniques in these two collections, some more successful than others. During this period he worked out a distinction between the "short story," which follows the tenets he outlined in The Short Story, and the "tale," a more leisurely and discursive form. Although the stories in I Remember! I Remember! are all labelled "short stories," and the tale is not defined as a separate form until the Foreword to The Heat of the Sun, several of the stories in the former volume would clearly qualify as tales.

In the Foreword, O'Faolain uses metaphors of flight to explain the difference between the two forms. A

short story is "like a child's kite, a small wonder, a
brief, bright moment. . . . The main thing a writer of
a short story wants to do is to get it off the ground
as quickly as possible, hold it up there, taut and
tense, playing it like a fish." A tale, a form he says
he derived from Mérimée and Hemingway, has more room for
elaboration and digression. More like a small plane
than a kite, "it is much more free, carries a bit more
cargo, roves farther, has time and space for more complex characterization, more changes of mood, more incidents and scenes, even more plot."[56] The tale, though
not so difficult to write as the short story, still presents some problems of construction. The writer must
"orchestrate his Tale into a single, satisfying shape
of flight." O'Faolain's concept of the tale thus
requires greater artistry and a more unified structure
than was found in the earlier tales of Griffin, Carleton, and others. O'Faolain's own earlier experiments
with a form more expanded than the simple short story
can be seen in such stories as "The Patriot," "A Born
Genius," and "Lovers of the Lake."

There is critical disagreement about the merit of
O'Faolain's tales. Some critics believe that the larger
space enables him to present characters and situations
in more depth. Guy LeMoigne, for example, speculates
that the short story form may have limited O'Faolain too
much.

> In view of the turn taken by his evolution
> over recent years, one may wonder whether
> the more leisurely and traditional form
> of the "tale" has not been the genre that
> suited O'Faolain best. . . . There is in
> O'Faolain a suppressed novelist who needs
> a broader canvas than the one currently
> allotted to the short-story. . . . He relishes
> the part of narrator and carries it with
> gusto in the manner of the 18th century
> novelists and those writers who took the
> tradition into the following century.[57]

This view of O'Faolain as a "suppressed novelist" is
borne out by the fact that two of the tales from I Remember! I Remember!, "Love's Young Dream" and "No Country for Old Men," were originally conceived as novels.
But LeMoigne points out that O'Faolain is not always
successful with his tales, especially when he moves too
far outside his limited range of inspiration. Paul
Doyle takes a more negative view and asserts that in
general O'Faolain's tales are less successful than his

197

stories.

> In O'Faolain's handling, the longer length
> of the tale lends itself to greater dis-
> cursiveness, to a slackening of tight
> and deft control, to more obvious manipu-
> lation of the plot and, barring an excep-
> tion here and there . . . to more shallow
> characterization. Too much material is
> covered in too short a space; as a conse-
> quence the reader is often jarred by a
> deficiency in story probability and veri-
> similitude. The bones of the narrative
> protrude rather sharply and yield an
> impression of thinness and even at times
> of flimsiness.[58]

In evaluating O'Faolain's later work it is important not
to overgeneralize, since the quality is very uneven.
It does seem valid to conclude that the artistry of
I Remember! I Remember! is superior to that of The Heat
of the Sun--perhaps because the subject of memory and
the past inspired him more than the subject of love, or
perhaps because his preference for the tale in the latter volume weakened his art.

For the sake of comparison, the stories in these
two volumes can be classified into the same subject-
areas discussed earlier: religion, childhood and family
life, love and marriage. Religion is a factor in several of these stories, but only two portray a priest as
the main character--"The Younger Generation" and "The
Human Thing." Both are short stories, not tales, and
both are artistically satisfying.

"The Younger Generation" describes the visit of a
bishop to the castle of his old friend Sir Toby, a wealthy Count. The bishop has hoped for peace and quiet to
compose his pastoral letter, but instead walks into the
middle of a bitter family quarrel. Toby's wife, a para-
noid alcoholic, opposes her daughter's engagement to a
Protestant, and the husband is too meek and long-suffer-
ing to settle things. As the various family members
try to discuss their troubles with the bishop, it
becomes obvious that he lacks the humanity to be of any
real help. Like earlier O'Faolain clerics, he has sub-
stituted rules and conventions for compassion and understanding, and has become estranged from his parishioners. He seems human only when recalling distant childhood memories of his hometown and his devoted mother,
now deceased.

The story is tightly constructed, and details are carefully chosen to reveal character. There is no identifiable narrator and most of the story is told from the bishop's point of view. The setting is the room where he is writing his pastoral; through the window he can see the beautiful grounds of the castle and the sea beyond. Several times during the story he notices a yacht becalmed offshore, perhaps imaging the stagnation that has overtaken his life despite his high position in the Church and his association with wealthy aristocrats.

An ironic parallel is drawn between the bishop's pastoral letter and his conversations with the various characters who seek him out. As the story opens, Sir Toby is just leaving the room after a long confession about his family troubles, and the bishop is obviously unsympathetic and impatient to get on with his writing. The trite words of the pastoral about the "wonderful cycle of love, marriage and parenthood" are hollow in this context. Shortly afterwards the daughter, Anne, comes in. Again, small details suggest character; the bishop is irritated because she has not changed out of her riding clothes and does not kiss his ring. She talks very honestly with him, apologizing for her mother's drunken scene the night before, and questioning why he will not allow people in his diocese to marry Protestants. She points out that mixed marriages are now allowed in other dioceses. Instead of responding in kind to her honesty, the bishop utters a series of platitudes about a mother being the best guide for her children, wiser in the ways of the world. He explains his objection to mixed marriages by making a shallow and irrelevant analogy between the Church and a club where members must follow the rules, and he becomes huffy when Anne calls his rule "silly." As soon as she leaves, he starts writing fatuously about "Duties of Children to Parents and Superiors."

A more genuine side of the Bishop is revealed when he talks to the maid who brings an egg flip he has been waiting for and discovers that she is from Cootehill, his hometown. He starts to reminisce with boyish delight, but becomes distracted when he realizes there is no sugar in his egg flip--this trivial preoccupation aborts the more meaningful pleasures of reminiscence. A brief, hysterical visit from the mother confirms the daughter's description of her. When the maid comes back, she says she is leaving soon to join her boyfriend in England, presumably to escape the painful atmosphere of the castle. Disturbed by so many emotion-charged encounters, the bishop writes a sentimental letter to his dead mother, and then tears it up. His obvious adoration of her contrasts with Anne's hatred of her mother, and helps to explain his lack of sympathy for the girl.

The day's events have a depressing effect on the bishop. As he finishes his pastoral he feels "no joy or pride in it, no more than if this, too, were a letter not to the living but to the dying and the dead."[59] In tacit recognition of his failure to be of help, he and Toby agree that it would be better for him to leave that afternoon. Toby tells him that Anne has decided to take a flat in Dublin, and the bishop realizes that she is "trying a new club," evading his prohibition against mixed marriages. The world has changed, society has become more liberal even in Ireland, but the bishop has succumbed to stuffiness and arrogance, and has cut himself off from real communication and growth. O'Faolain treats the problem as an individual rather than a social one, though he implies that the extraordinary reverence with which clergymen are treated in Ireland is a contributing factor to the bishop's egotism.

The priest in "The Human Thing" is more humane. The conflict he experiences is similar--a choice between adhering literally to the rules or bending them for the sake of human kindness. The story takes place in the Basses-Alpes, where the priest, Fr. "Morphé," an Irishman, has served for many years. The first person narrator is also an Irishman, a writer named Sean visiting the priest to seek material about the region for an article. This use of a narrator identified by name and/or occupation with O'Faolain himself occurs several times in the later stories, and represents a variant on the sensitive, intellectual, nameless narrator used in earlier stories like "Midsummer Night Madness," "A Broken World," "Up the Bare Stairs," and "The Man Who Invented Sin." This subjective type of narrator is consistent with O'Faolain's emphasis on "communicated personality" in his artistic theories. In "The Human Thing" the narrator is a curious outsider who learns something very different about the Basses-Alpes from what he expected. On the day of his visit, one of Fr. Morphé's parishioners has been killed in an accident. The priest learns from the housekeeper that the man has been living with a mistress, and has a wife and four children who are living with his mother. The priest, very orthodox in his views, angrily declares that he cannot give the man a Catholic funeral. He pays a visit to the mistress to denounce her, but finds that the wife is also there, and the two women are consoling each other. Deeply moved and surprised by the wife's charity, he agrees to hold the funeral. In this case, humanity wins out over dogma. The story reflects O'Faolain's cosmopolitanism, as its connection with Ireland is tenuous, though the conflict between traditional provincial morality and compassionate compromise is one that would naturally interest an Irish writer.

The stories of childhood and family life in I Remember! I Remember! contain several variations on the theme of memory. The title story is one of the most insightful in the collection. It dramatizes the relationship between two sisters, Sarah and Mary Cotter, from the small Irish town of Ardagh. Sarah has been confined to a wheelchair since the age of eleven and lives alone in a small cottage in Ardagh. She lives vicariously, depending on information supplied by other people, and possesses an infallible memory. Mary, married to Richard Carton, an American buyer, spends her life traveling back and forth between Europe and America. Twice a year she stops off in Ireland to visit Sarah. But Sarah's inexhaustible memory for factual details disturbs Mary more and more until she can no longer endure the visits and evades the question of when she will return.

The story is told by a first person narrator somewhat different from the one in "The Human Thing." He does not appear as a character in the story, but speaks as if he has lived in Ardagh and has known the sisters since childhood. His tone is philosophical and sympathetic as he comments throughout the story on general insights and on the characters' motives and thoughts. The reflective, philosophical tone is established with the first sentence, which introduces the central theme of memory: "I believe that in every decisive moment of our lives the spur to action comes from that part of the memory where desire lies dozing, awaiting the call to arms."[60] The benevolent intrusions of this narrator detract a little from the story, since they limit the reader's freedom to interpret characters and events.

Because of her physical handicap and consequent isolation, Sarah is a unique character. Although the atmosphere of Ardagh does play a part in the story, Sarah cannot be considered a typical product of the local environment. Mary, who has lived abroad and traveled widely, is also removed from the ordinary life of the town. The story thus illustrates O'Faolain's increasing emphasis on individuals and detachment from

201

social conditions. The two sisters also represent opposite concepts of memory; Sarah's is factual and literal, and Mary's emotional and romantic.

The narrator introduces Sarah first and conveys the frustration and severe limitation of her life. Her accident "absolved her from all but the simplest decisions: there was no far-off island for her to dream of." His attitude is apparently compassionate.

> She lives in almost constant pain. She never complains of it. I have met nobody who does not admire her, nobody who has the least fault to find with her, apart from her invulnerable memory, which all Ardagh both enjoys and fears, and whose insistence can kill like the sirocco.[61]

This sympathetic portrayal of Sarah makes the reader at first critical of Mary for not visiting her sister more often. But the phrase "kill like a sirocco" also introduces a warning note, and as we learn more about the situation we see another side of Sarah's character and can accept, or at least understand, Mary's fear of returning to Ardagh.

Mary, a warm, impulsive woman, values her memories as part of her real self. She objects to Sarah's memories because, in spite of their factual accuracy, they do not adequately convey her own experience of life. At the time the story takes place, Mary has been married for twelve years. By using a flashback, O'Faolain dramatizes her husband's first and only visit to Ardagh, early in their marriage. Richard listened in fascination to Sarah's account of Mary's girlhood, in particular one day when she went fox-hunting, and laughed at Mary's desperate protest that her own exaggerated and emotional version of the day was closer to the truth. But afterwards when he saw how upset she was at the destruction of one of her happiest memories, he resolved to stay away from Ardagh.

After several years of marriage, Richard's passion for Mary has cooled considerably. The narrator comments that her "life has stopped being the flowing, straightforward river it once was,"[62] and has become complicated and uncertain. The relationship between Mary and Sarah has also grown more distant.

The incident which brings about Mary's permanent escape from Sarah is Sarah's inquiry about Nathan Cash, a man with whom Mary has had an unhappy affair. Mary talked to her sister about Nathan on her previous visit, hiding their true relationship, because she had to talk to someone about him. But six months later she cannot bear to hear Sarah mention him. She goes for a walk, and the streets and river in Ardagh remind her of her girlhood and the difference between her living memories and the "bones" in Sarah's "vaults." She wonders, "Would Nathan Cash one day join these dead bones? Had he already gone there, with all she had been through because of him? Would all her life, unless she really went away and left her past behind her?"63 She decides to leave in the morning. During her last evening with Sarah, the atmosphere of Ardagh seems lifeless and desolate, no longer capable of evoking familiar and comforting memories. It is dark and rainy, few sounds can be heard, and no ground-floor windows are lit. The appearance of the town symbolically foreshadows Mary's permanent departure and spiritual exile. Mary does not admit to Sarah that she will not return, but Sarah guesses the truth. Although Richard, Sarah, and Mary are all well-intentioned, the effects of memory and time drive them apart. The story is intriguing and thought-provoking both in its exploration of the memory theme and in its reflective, poetic technique.

O'Faolain's probing of memory somewhat resembles George Moore's view of the subject. Moore in "Home Sickness" and O'Faolain in this story associate memory with an idealized or romanticized dream-world which sustains a character through an active adult life. Both James Bryden and Mary Cotter leave Ireland abruptly, without admitting that they will not return; their subconscious life-instinct urgently compels them to get away. Mary differs from many earlier Irish emigrants in that her decision not to visit Ardagh is voluntary. Since she has wealth and access to jet travel, she is not separated permanently from her homeland by poverty and the hardships of travel, as former emigrants were. But her exile is as necessary to her psychological survival as emigration was to economic survival for other Irishmen. O'Faolain implies that we must sometimes sacrifice and escape from one part of ourselves--in this case Mary's bond with Sarah and her contact with Ardagh--so that our overall sense of freedom and fulfillment can be preserved. Mary does not sacrifice Sarah and Ardagh easily, or without a sense of loss; her decision is not reached overnight but results from a long, unconscious accumulation of experiences and insights. We are left wondering if her emancipation will be complete, since she has repressed many memories that may continue to haunt her.

Another story that considers the conflict between
romanticism and realism in the process of memory is
"Two of a Kind." It concerns a reconciliation rather
than an estrangement between two family members, an
aunt and nephew. Both ran away from County Limerick in
their youth and emigrated to the United States. A sailor on leave, Maxer Creedon finds himself alone and
slightly drunk in New York on Christmas Eve. He calls
up his mother's sister, Aunt Lily, who disgraced herself by running away to New York with an Italian almost
fifty years before and has not been in touch with the
family since.

Maxer and Lily retain Irish character traits, both
positive and negative, even though they have been away
from Ireland for a long time. When they meet, they immediately begin to make up elaborate and devious stories
to protect their pride. Maxer pretends that everyone in
the family is fine and that he visits them in Ireland
regularly. Lily says that her husband was rich and successful before he died and that her son is also happy
and successful. But when Lily takes out a photograph
of her son to show Maxer, he begins to realize that
something is wrong. She grows more and more upset and
finally throws the photograph across the room, blurting
out her fear that Maxer has been sent by the family to
spy on her. She admits that she and her baby were
deserted by the Italian soon after arriving in New York.
She wrote letters home but received no answer. Her son
ran off with a Polish woman and has not contacted her
since, and she earns a bare living cleaning out offices.
Maxer then admits that everyone in the family is dead,
that he ran away to sea when he was sixteen and has not
been back to Ireland for eight years.

The confessions serve to bring them closer and they
celebrate Christmas Eve together. Maxer consoles Lily
by telling her that his mother tried to write to her and
talked about her constantly and affectionately. They
spend hours sharing their memories of Ireland. Maxer
continues to visit Lily every time he comes to New York
and they develop a substitute mother-son relationship.
They both have lived lonely lives as exiles, and their
distant but real memories of a warm family life and the
peace of the Irish countryside dissolve the bitterness
of family conflict and estrangement, and allow them to
form a strong attachment to each other.

The descriptions of places in the story contribute

204

a poetic delicacy and suggestiveness to the mood. New York at first looks beautiful and exciting to Maxer on Christmas Eve, but when he begins to feel lonely his mind reverts to images of the Limerick plain. Memories of his mother and his childhood are inseparable from memories of the landscape. Aunt Lily's room reveals much about her life; it is large, dingy, sparsely and shabbily furnished. Outside the window a light snow is falling, and the snow becomes an image for the lives of the people inside, very different in effect from the snow in "A Broken World." When Maxer first starts telling lies to his aunt, the snowflakes are tapping at the window "like kittens' paws trying to get in"--an image of tenderness and vulnerability. When Aunt Lily throws the photo across the room just before confessing the truth, the snowflakes are mentioned again, this time as images of transience and illusion. "Maxer saw snowflakes melting as often as they touched the pane." When her confession is finished, and before he tells her everyone in the family is dead, he looks "at the snowflakes feeling the windowpane and dying there"64; the image suggests that death encroaches on people even as they reach out for warmth and life.

In "Two of a Kind" the past which Maxer and Lily share becomes a source of inner sustenance and intimacy rather than a cause of estrangement, as in "I Remember! I Remember!" The difference is that both Maxer and Lily are romantics; they both care more about the emotional associations of their memories than about their factual accuracy. Both of them originally left Ireland because their family circumstances were unhappy, but they ignore the painful aspects of their memories and preserve the pleasant aspects. They need something to compensate for the loneliness and disillusionment of exile. The story is a somewhat sentimental one, but it effectively portrays the feelings of characters in exile.

Other stories in the collection show different kinds of relationships between characters' childhood memories and their present lives. "A Shadow, Silent as a Cloud" and "A Touch of Autumn in the Air" both describe successful, well-to-do men not prone to dwell on the past. In each story, something happens to arouse long-dormant memories and to provide insight into the emotional cost of the character's success. Both men are bachelors, and remembered fragments of past happiness represent the love and warmth they have sacrificed. These characters are somewhat similar to the career soldier in "Up the Bare Stairs" who also achieved success at great emotional cost, except that his childhood memories are oppressive, not happy. Two other stories, "The Sugawn Chair" and "Love's Young Dream," also deal with lost happiness associated with youth and the Irish countryside.

A contrast between country and city is drawn in several of these stories, a contrast we have already seen in several earlier stories. In I Remember! I Remember! the country is usually the scene of happy childhood memories which are retained in the adult psyche only as blurred fragments, and which are accompanied by undefined feelings of loss and regret, of "roads not taken." In the later stories the city is not simply a place of blight and deprivation, as it is in O'Flaherty's work and in some of O'Faolain's own earlier stories. It is the appropriate setting for a stimulating adult existence; modern man is essentially urban, but still has a deep-rooted need for the beauty and peace of the countryside, and by association, for the innocence of childhood. Many of the characters in the later stories have a sense of incompleteness, are unable to put their lives into clear perspective, because they cannot fully recover their past.

The subject of childhood and family life is treated to a lesser extent in The Heat of the Sun. "Billy Billee" is an elderly man's reminiscence of his adolescent fascination with a voluptuous dancer who boarded in his house. "Dividends" describes the narrator's amusing and maddening return to his native city of Cork after many years away. A sense of the past is also interwoven into most of the other stories in the collection, but is not emphasized as strongly as in I Remember! I Remember!

The subject of love and marriage becomes increasingly dominant in O'Faolain's later work. Often, he emphasizes the absurdities and paradoxes of love; sometimes the element of absurdity is so strong that the characters lose their credibility. This is true of "One Night in Turin," a long tale from I Remember! I Remember! that illustrates some of the weaknesses of O'Faolain's tales. It describes the infatuation of a middle-aged bachelor, Walter Hunter, for an opera singer whom he knew as a boy. The plot is a highly contrived one, full of coincidences and implausibilities. Hunter's fantasies and rationalizations are described in tedious detail; he is a fastidious, self-deluded protagonist somewhat like John Marcher in Henry James's "The Beast in the Jungle," but less convincingly portrayed. George Brandon Saul has criticized "One Night in Turin" as an

206

example of "the author's characteristic effort to read significance into matter intrinsically of little import."[65] In the less successful later stories, O'Faolain's subtle, discriminating sensibility is not controlled enough, and his efforts to communicate personality become self-indulgently verbose. Another problem illustrated by "One Night in Turin" is what Vivian Mercier calls O'Faolain's "most dangerous temptation . . . , a yearning after metropolitan sophistication."[66] Other amusing but implausible characters of this type include the wealthy stockbroker Mel Meldrum in "Dividends" and the Italian Guido Rucellai in "A Sweet Colleen." Both are middle-aged, worldly men deluding themselves with fantasies about beautiful, "innocent" young women.

One of the more interesting love stories of this period is "In the Bosom of the Country," which portrays a real rather than an illusory relationship. Like "Lovers of the Lake," it examines the effects of Irish religious attitudes on a love relationship, but it lacks the intensity and psychological penetration of the earlier story, and in comparison seems a little out-of-focus. It might be considered satirical, but the tone is somewhat uncertain.

The story concerns the relationship between a Cork-woman, Anna Mohan, who like Jenny is married to a man she does not love, and Major Frank Keene, a retired English officer who has inherited a house near Cork and has settled there. At the time the story begins, they have been lovers for several years, but their relationship is not so passionate as it once was and they see each other infrequently. When Anna's husband dies, Frank is persuaded by a friend that he should marry her. He proposes, but she says she wants him to be converted to Catholicism so that they can be married properly in the church and win social acceptance from their neighbors. After a long inner struggle, he agrees to visit the Monsignor for instruction. They debate Catholic doctrines during a series of enjoyable dinners, and Frank eventually does become a sincere Catholic. But after his marriage he discovers that Anna is not really interested in religion; she wanted his conversion for reasons of superstition and social conformity rather than genuine faith. For several months he becomes even more devout and lives in a state of war with Anna, but after the Monsignor's death Frank also loses his interest in religion. He and Anna decide to travel and escape the local environment.

The characters in this story are more absurd and

superficial than the characters in "Lovers of the Lake."
Maurice Harmon compares the two sets of lovers.

> [Frank and Anna] are not saved from mockery
> by the profound spiritual and emotional
> issues that involved the adulterous lovers
> in "Lovers of the Lake." Those were gran-
> ted the dignity of real religious conflict,
> and the eternal background was never wholly
> forgotten. Their love for each other was
> mature, fully satisfying, and vibrant.
> Anna and the Major, however, are not
> spared the absurdities of their situation;
> and of the two it is the weakly-compliant,
> self-deceiving and sentimental major who
> is most keenly mocked.[67]

The story is told from Frank's point of view, but his
limitations are apparent to the reader. This represents
a more complex version of the familiar narrative device
of using an outsider to evaluate Irish attitudes.

Community attitudes play a more important part than
in many of the later stories. The provincial social
atmosphere that Frank and Anna live in seems as dreary
as the damp climate. People adhere to certain social
and religious conventions which only worsen the loneliness of their lives. Public opinion exerts considerable
pressure on individuals. Frank thinks his affair with
Anna has been kept secret, but after the death of Anna's
husband, he learns that people have been gossiping
about them. He marries her not because he loves her
deeply, but because he knows how empty her life would
be without him, and he feels a sense of duty towards
her.

The section of the story dramatizing the discussions between Frank and the Monsignor about religious
doctrines is the most overtly satirical. Frank gets
along well with the Monsignor because they are both old
soldiers, old bachelors, and connoisseurs of food and
wine. The Monsignor, an astute and tolerant man, arouses Frank's interest in religious doctrines by using
military analogies. The analogies have the opposite
effect on the reader from their effect on Frank, and
make certain Catholic doctrines seem absurd. For example, the Monsignor compares accepting Papal infallibil-
ity to obeying an order to charge a hill with three men
against a thousand. We suspect that Frank's enjoyment
of the Monsignor's company--the conversation and good
dinners--is the real basis of his conversion.

The earnestness with which Frank approaches his religious instruction contrasts with Anna's casual dismissal of doctrines she does not agree with or understand. She tells Frank that she does not believe their affair was a sin but will go to confession only as a formality. She also tells him that debates about subjects like Limbo are absurd; his "new friends" like the Monsignor make things unnecessarily complicated, "tying everything up in knots with their laws, and rules, and regulations, and definitions, and sub-definitions that nobody can make head or tail of." Her religion consists of vague sentiments: "I never think about Limbo. I never think about stupid things like that. I think only of God, and the stars, and of Heaven, and of love, and of you."[68] Again, we are not sure what attitude to Catholicism O'Faolain wants to convey. Frank's literal-minded earnestness and Anna's vague emotionalism are equally unacceptable.

Frank's loss of faith at the end of the story is the logical result of preceding circumstances. Once the wedding is over and the couple have gained respectability, Anna is content and rapidly loses all interest in going to church. Frank is very disillusioned with her, and all winter they live in estrangement. But one beautiful spring morning he looks at her and suddenly realizes that "everything she saw and he remembered came out of one eggshell."[69] The metaphor implies that everything is part of the original creation and there is no reason for Frank and Anna to quarrel. Shortly afterwards the Monsignor dies. Once Frank's personal link to the Church is gone, he loses his religion literally overnight. His faith cannot withstand the test of time and experience, and he realizes that his human love for Anna is the most important thing in his life. He and Anna both feel a strong urge to travel, to escape the stifling local climate, "the bosom of the country." Anna suggests that they go to Lausanne, where she went to school. Frank replies, "'Indeed, indeed! Anywhere! Anywhere! To get away!'" They realize there is no reason why they have to stay in Cork; no fate is holding them there.

Although we feel that Frank and Anna are right in escaping from the dreary atmosphere of Cork, we are not sure they will find fulfillment abroad. They may be merely exchanging one form of emptiness for another. We do not know whether Frank has discovered the true spirit of religion in his new attitude to Anna or whether religion has simply lost all meaning for him, and he is running away from the experience of conversion. O'Faolain seems at times to mock his characters, at other times to sympathize with them. Although his technical mastery is evident in many passages, the central conflict between worldliness and spirituality is not clearly articulated.

Several other stories in The Heat of the Sun illustrate the paradox that love can survive despite mistakes, disagreements, compromises, and neglect. "The Heat of the Sun," like "The Human Thing," describes a woman who still loves her husband and mourns his death even though they have been separated for many years. In "One Man, One Boat, One Girl," love survives in spite of the couple's quarrels over religious differences. In "£1000 for Rosebud," the heroine does not find genuine love until she leaves her flamboyant, crooked husband and marries a less spectacular but more reliable Irish customs officer, who loves her in spite of her shady past. Although the stories and tales in this collection contain many insights into the nature of love, its ironies, contradictions, follies, and transience, and they are usually entertaining to read, none of them approaches O'Faolain's achievement in "Lovers of the Lake." His detachment and amusement have become almost too complete; his imagination does not seem to be deeply engaged.

v

At a time when we might reasonably have expected O'Faolain to lay down his pen and enjoy the fruits of his secure reputation, he continued to write stories and tales, publishing two more collections in the last decade, The Talking Trees and Foreign Affairs. These stories share some of the weaknesses apparent in the two preceding collections, but they are also surprisingly inventive and varied. They demonstrate that O'Faolain in his seventies was still capable of growth, responsive to the changing world around him, and open to new possibilities of subject matter and technique. Robie Macauley, the Playboy editor who published several of these stories in his magazine, calls him "Ireland's Youngest Writer." Quoting O'Faolain's own statement about his refusal to stagnate, Macauley comments that these stories "are an exemplary demonstration of an intelligence that has not got stuck, not given up, not agreed to compromise on a formula. Each is different from the others not only in subject but in that individual heartbeat that makes a good story live a life of

its own."70   O'Faolain's method of storytelling is still
essentially traditional, but he has incorporated some
contemporary features.

The stories in The Talking Trees are loosely connected by the concept of personal growth and those in
Foreign Affairs by the concept of exploring foreign or
unfamiliar territory in love. The Talking Trees is the
better of the two collections; it is much grimmer in
mood than The Heat of the Sun, and probes further into
areas of sexual and psychological stress, treating such
subjects as impotence, sexual temptations of priests,
obsessive dreams, alcoholism, and insanity. Some of
these subjects are also explored in Foreign Affairs,
though on the whole it is a more light-hearted, optimistic volume, as if O'Faolain were surveying human existence with a kind of mellow, genial amusement.

The four stories about clergy confront some issues
that O'Faolain did not previously raise, at least not
in so direct a manner. The psychological devastation
that can be wrought by institutional religious life is
exposed in "Brainsy" and "Of Sanctity and Whiskey,"
both very bleak and pessimistic stories. In "Brainsy,"
an order of teaching monks suppress and eventually drive
insane one of their members, a gifted teacher, because
he is too free-thinking and unconventional in the class-
room. "Of Sanctity and Whiskey" is the story of an
alcoholic artist commissioned to paint a portrait of a
former teacher, a priest now Headmaster of the school.
As he works on the portrait, long-repressed memories
surface of the priest's sadism and his favoritism
towards the artist as a boy, and the consequent misery
and humiliation he suffered. He gets carried away and
paints a portrait so true to life that the townspeople
destroy it, and he drinks himself to death.

A priest's temptation to violate his celibacy is
treated on a serious level in "Feed My Lambs" and more
humorously in "Falling Rocks, Narrowing Road, Cul-de-
Sac, Stop." "Feed My Lambs" contains one of O'Faolain's
most sympathetic portrayals of a priest. Fr. Tom Tim-
lin, a young curate, meets Rita, a teacher, in a cable
car near Lourdes. They are attracted to each other
immediately. Another passenger in the car is Jerry
Lamb, a farmer and butcher from Kildare, whom Rita also
finds attractive and eventually marries. Fr. Tom visits
Rita occasionally after her marriage, when he passes
her house on his way to Dublin, but one day he admits
that he loves her, and she says they must never see
each other again. If they did, they would only torment

211

and frustrate each other. He agrees not to return.

"Feed My Lambs" is tautly constructed and relatively short. It begins on the day that Fr. Tom and Rita see each other for the last time, and the rest is told through flashbacks. The point of view throughout the story is Rita's, though much of the story consists of dialogue and O'Faolain conveys Rita's thoughts only in brief, suggestive phrases. The description of Rita's house at the beginning captures all the loneliness, monotony, and frustrated aspiration of her married life.

> The unfrequented road that crosses the
> level bogland from skyline to skyline
> passes on its way a few beech trees,
> a white cottage fronted by a small garden
> still bright with roses and snapdragons,
> a cobbled path and a small wooden gate
> bearing, in white celluloid letters,
> the name Pic du Jer. In the vast empti-
> ness of the bog these unexpected and
> inexplicable beech trees, the pretty
> cottage, the tiny garden, the cobbled
> path suggest only a dream in the mind
> of somebody who, a long time back, thought
> better of it, or died, or gave up the
> struggle with the bog.[71]

O'Faolain's use of the present tense in this passage contributes to the feeling of dreary monotony. There are many ironic parallels between Rita's present life and the scene at Lourdes. For example, the name Pic du Jer is Rita's way of commemorating her meeting with Jerry on the mountain near Lourdes. The contrast between mountain and bog suggests what has happened to her hopes. One subject of conversation at Lourdes concerned the number of children she would like to have, but her marriage has been childless.

O'Faolain does not describe Fr. Tom's life in his remote Galway parish, but we sense that his life is even lonelier than Rita's. They are both intelligent and articulate, and they look forward to their occasional meetings when they can enjoy some stimulating conversation. For years they probe each other's feelings without openly revealing them.

O'Faolain carefully portrays the qualities that attract Rita and Tom to each other, but in spite of his skill, the scene in which Rita says they must not see each other again is unconvincing. In an almost perverse way she pushes Fr. Tom into confessing that he loves her, she deliberately tempts him to kiss her, and when he does, she says abruptly, "'You can never come here again.'" From this point the tone of the story becomes melodramatic, as they part emotionally and then passively accept their fate. We can sympathize with the characters and understand their decision, but nevertheless we feel that something in the characterizations is missing, that there should have been a more intense inner struggle to escape such a barren, futile existence.

A happier solution is found in "Falling Rocks. . . ." Fr. Tim Buckley, a priest with an inordinate passion for Freudian analysis, is one of three eccentric bachelors in a provincial Irish town. The other two are Morgan Myles, a librarian and aspiring writer with a mother complex, and Dr. Frank Breen, a misanthropist who hates medicine and has never had a patient. These are among O'Faolain's funniest bachelor characters, as Robie Macauley remarks. "The lonely bachelor, the celibate, the man who will not or cannot marry, who grows a little more cracked as each year goes by--a familiar figure of pathos or sympathy in modern Irish writing. Putting him in three different shapes, O'Faolain explodes him into high comedy, with thoroughly refreshing results."[72] The arrival of a German family throws the lives of all three men into turmoil. Fr. Buckley becomes involved with the sensual and strong-willed daughter, and when he is banished to a remote parish for his indiscretion, he instead goes off to Stockholm with her. The story is a pleasant antidote to the many stories we have examined of clergy warped or defeated by their vocations.

The stories of childhood and family life also explore some new territory. "The Talking Trees" and "Thieves" are relatively slight stories about children's adventures, but "The Planets of the Years," "The Kitchen," and "How to Write a Short Story" are all intriguing portrayals of adults looking back on childhood. In "The Planets of the Years," O'Faolain uses for the first time a first person woman narrator, the wife of an Irish professor on sabbatical at Harvard. "How to Write a Short Story" uses a contemporary technique, the presentation of a story as raw material, in the process of being written. It is O'Faolain's first explicit treatment of homosexuality. Two of the characters from "Falling Rocks . . . ," Morgan Myles and Dr. Frank Breen, are engaged in a conversation about Frank's childhood. Morgan wants to write a short story in the manner of Maupassant, and as he listens to the doctor he is mentally recomposing the material. The story concerns a homosexual relationship the doctor experienced as a young schoolboy with an older student. It was a very painful, traumatic experience for him, and it took him many years to get over his repulsion. O'Faolain mocks Myles's artistic detachment, which is almost flippant, and contrasts it with the human reality and sadness of the Doctor's experience.

"The Kitchen" is one of the best of O'Faolain's late stories. It is autobiographical and deals with a psychological conflict that results in unpleasant recurring dreams. The narrator is an adult looking back on his family life in Cork and expressing his ambivalent feelings towards his parents. The family situation very closely resembles O'Faolain's own: the narrator's parents are transplanted peasants; his father is a policeman; his family lives upstairs in a rented house, and his mother ekes out their income by taking in lodgers. The plot concerns his mother's long struggle with her landlord to keep possession of her kitchen, which the landlord needs to cook lunch for the employees in his bootmaker's shop downstairs. After her husband's death, when she is living alone, the landlord offers to install a new kitchen for her on the third floor, but she cannot be dislodged from her old kitchen until her death. The narrator analyzes the complex attitudes, surviving from the days of the Land War, which account for his mother's stubbornness and his own need to escape from home.

The use of dream sequences gives the story a haunting atmosphere. The narrator begins by telling us that disturbed memories of his childhood and his mother's kitchen sometimes enter his dreams. He has escaped the city physically but he cannot push it from his mind. He keeps recalling the words of the landlord's son, when he first saw the shabby kitchen after the old woman's death: "'So this is what all that was about?'" The bootmaker's son's casual dismissal of the struggle for the kitchen exasperates and obsesses the narrator.

The narrator's parents' peasant background made them hunger for land ownership, and although they could afford only to rent the house, they clung to it as possessively as owners. When the bootmaker bought the house from the former owner and indicated that he might take over some of their rooms, they lost all traces of the urban refinement they had acquired during long years in the city and reverted to their peasant heritage. "They might at that moment have been two peasants from Limerick or Kerry peering timidly through the rain from

214

the door of a thatched hovel at a landlord, or his
agent, or some villainous land-grabber driving up their
brambled boreen to throw them out on the side of the
road to die of cold and starvation."[73]

The narrator tells us that he left home shortly
after this event and learned about later stages of the
battle from his parents' letters; he does not explain at
this point why he left or what his own feelings about
the battle were. His parents did give up one room and
access to the bathroom, and after his father's death
his mother protestingly gave up a second room. But
when the landlord requested the kitchen, she held firm.
The landlord thought the request reasonable but "what
he completely failed to reckon with, was that there is
not a peasant widow woman from the mountains of west
Cork to the wilds of Calabria who does not feel her
kitchen as the pulse and center of her being as a wife
and mother."[74] She had four centuries of ancestral
land-pride behind her, and was fighting for her ancestors as well as herself. The bootmaker never realized
what "nerve of time" he had touched. The kitchen is
thus a symbol for the woman herself, and her identification with the traditions that gave her life wholeness
and value.

The story ends with the narrator's description of
his own feelings after his mother's death. These feelings are presented through dream images instead of
rational discourse, and the reader must interpret them
for himself. When the narrator was cleaning out his
mother's possessions after her death and heard the
remark of the bootmaker's son, he tells us "a shock of
weakness flowed up through me like defeat until my head
began to reel and my eyes were swimming." He realized
that all his previous interpretations of his parents'
attitudes were inaccurate. The kitchen symbolized not
merely the power of time but "something beyond reason
and time," something irrational which had the potential
to defeat him. When he left Cork he swore he would not
return, but since then his memories keep ambushing him
and he has returned there many times unwillingly in his
dreams. Each time he wakes up in the night recalling
the words of the landlord's son. He uses the peculiar
image of a "scratching mole," burrowing in the dark,
perhaps to represent the forces that undermine the freedom of an individual. His mother refused to listen to
the mole's whisperings in her own time. The narrator
has also refused to listen, but for him the mole is
identified with his mother, whose memory he must thrust
away if he is to be free. Ironically she is now the

landlord and he the tenant. "When I switch on the bulb over my head I do it only to banish her, to evict her, to push her out of my kitchen, and I often lie back to sleep under its bright light lest I should again hear her whispering to me in the dark."[75] The implication is that he has chosen his own battles, within a rational, modern style of life, and they are different from his mother's. Although he respects and admires her spirit, he is unwilling to be enslaved emotionally by the past.

The story is especially interesting for its evocation of the power of historical memory in the Irish character. Even in the most intelligent and emancipated of Irishmen, like the narrator, buried memories of ancestral struggles against oppression can rise to the surface and renew an emotional conflict that has centuries of tradition behind it. For him these national memories are closely linked with memories of his parents, and he must constantly struggle to assert his freedom from them.

Most of the stories in The Talking Trees and Foreign Affairs are tales about love and marriage. As in The Heat of the Sun, O'Faolain approaches the subject in a variety of ways, and his tone ranges from comedy to pathos. In general these tales are too long and diffuse. When writing about love, O'Faolain often has a tendency to describe in detail his characters' delusions and fantasies, so that the love affairs seem shallow and insubstantial, and the style is excessively verbose. In a few of the love stories he avoids these problems.

Among the lighter, more entertaining love stories are "The Time of Their Lives," a lengthy account of a holiday love affair between an Irish spinster and an aging Italian count, and "Murder at Cobbler's Hulk," a mock-mystery story about a fatal passion and an unsolved murder. Several stories deal with the difficulties and compensations of married life. "A Dead Cert" and "The Faithless Wife" suffer from the faults described above, and are relatively tedious stories about restless married women who want lovers but will not leave their husbands. "Hymeneal," though quite lengthy, is a much better story about an insensitive, egocentric husband who does not realize how much he has hurt his wife until they are both elderly, and he experiences a chastening revelation. "Liberty" is a somewhat implausible but cheerful story of a rejuvenating and therapeutic marriage between a doctor and a patient in a mental hospital.

The hidden sources of suffering in marriage are probed in the excellent story "'Our Fearful Innocence.'" It is narrated in the first person by Jerry Doyle, a bachelor engineer in a small Irish seacoast town. He describes his friends, Jill and Jack Jennings, an unhappily married couple who eventually separate. Jill takes a small house outside of town and lives there alone until she dies of leukemia. Jerry is in love with Jill and visits her often before her death, but the love is one-sided and never consummated. Afterwards he moves into the lower flat in Jack's house, and the two provide companionship for each other in a stagnant existence. Many years later, Jerry learns from his secretary that Jill left her husband because he was impotent. She did not try to have the marriage annulled because she did not want to disgrace him before the whole town.

Jerry is different from most other O'Faolain narrators we have discussed, since he is treated ironically. As a resident of the town closely involved with the people he is describing, his point of view is biased and limited, and he cannot be identified with the author. The use of Jerry as narrator gives compression and unity to an otherwise diffuse plot. Jerry describes the Jennings' relationship over a period of several years. For the most part he summarizes and generalizes about their lives, emphasizing feelings and attitudes rather than specific events. He is more intelligent and open-minded than most of the town's residents, yet he is very much affected by local attitudes and has not freed himself from them. Instead he has settled like the other townspeople for a life of narrow and stultifying routine. For example, although he has lost his faith in God, he still goes to church to keep up appearances. His feeling for Jill Jennings is much like Walter Hunter's love in "One Night in Turin": although he does bring himself to declare his love for her openly, he prefers to cherish a distanced, romanticized dream image of her. Like Walter and many other bachelors, he does not want the pain of a genuine relationship. The time at which Jerry narrates the story is fifteen years after Jill's death. He has continued to think of her all that time as his beloved.

Jill is an intelligent, well-educated woman stifled by the atmosphere of the town. Her family is "a dynasty famous for long-tailed families," and they expect her to perform her conventional function of producing children. Since her husband is not well-read, Jerry is the only person she can talk to about her intellectual interests--philosophy, religion, and literature. One dismal, snowy night while Jerry is visiting her and Jack, Jack feels left out of the conversation and suddenly goes off to his club. When Jerry suggests that they are boring Jack, Jill replies that she and Jack should both escape from the town before it chokes them. But as the conversation continues, Jill realizes that happiness is not dependent merely on physical location. Using Chekhov's Three Sisters as an example, she says that the sisters might have been just as unhappy in Moscow as in the country. "'There is no such place as Moscow. If I went to Moscow I would hear nothing there but the same stupid, empty chitter-chatter that I hear day after day in this bloody town--and nothing at all going on inside me.'"76 Jill does not tell Jerry about Jack's impotence, but says she is going to leave him and escape to a place where she can live a full inner life and be "born all over again." Jerry tries to kiss her but she says he is not in love with the real her, and that he should leave the town too, before it knocks "the truth and the honesty and the guts" out of him. It is clear from his narrative that the town eventually does just this.

Jerry learns soon after this conversation that Jill has bought an isolated lockhouse nearby where she can be close to nature. The town gossips about her and regards her as odd, and her family tells her it is her duty to return to her husband. When Jerry visits her, however, she tells him she is content and has no intention of returning. She loves to observe nature, work on her house, and sit and think. She lives in solitude and exile without actually leaving home.

Jerry wonders what Jill is really thinking about. For fifteen years after her death, he continues to speculate about her. Her image keeps "ambushing" him at odd moments. He moves into Jack's house, where he is surrounded by Jill's books and antiques. His intimacy with Jack strikes us as peculiar; it may represent his desire to share vicariously in Jack's memories of his marriage. One night close to the time he is narrating the story, Jerry finds a journal that Jill kept at the lockhouse. He is surprised to see that it merely records almost childlike descriptions of nature, quotations from books she has been reading, and financial accounts. Jill's inner life remains a mystery. When he shows the diary to his secretary, she tells him about Jack's impotence and Jill's decision to leave rather than seek an annulment and disgrace him. From the secretary's point of view, Jill's love of nature was merely a compensation for sexual frustration, but through Jerry

218

O'Faolain raises more complex issues.

The end of the story describes Jerry's thoughts as a series of questions about life which continue to disturb him. He questions why life is so frustrating, why people cannot do the things they set out to do. He also continues to think about Jill and longs to see her image floating in again before she "turns for home"; he has internalized the sterility of the town in his preference for a dead woman's image over the real world. By using an ending which is poetic and meditative, O'Faolain avoids drawing clearcut judgments about Jill's escape to solitude. Instead he raises questions about the mysterious nature of life and invites the reader to speculate in his own way about the relationship between sexual and intellectual needs.

Another story about a failed marriage, not as thought-provoking as "'Our Fearful Innocence'" but interesting for its technical ingenuity, is "An Inside-Outside Complex." It concerns another of O'Faolain's uncommitted bachelors--Bertie Bolger, dealer in fake antiques--who takes the plunge into marriage only to find out he has made a mistake. O'Faolain portrays Bertie's evasive and perpetually dissatisfied character by using spatial symbolism of "inside" and "outside." Bertie first meets his future wife, a widowed seamstress, when he is walking in Bray on a desolate autumn day and sees the warmth and cosiness of her living room through a window. Once inside the house, however, he finds it less appealing and longs to be in one of the other cosy houses he can see outside through the same window. In the same way, he longs for marriage until he is actually married and then he longs to escape it, and eventually he does move out.

Mirror imagery is also incorporated into the symbolic pattern. Bertie and his wife both own mirrors. Hers is associated with the genuine, happy memories of her first marriage, and she will not give it up even though Bertie has offered to buy it from her. His mirror is very large, like his self-image. He promises it to his wife as a gift, but keeps procrastinating the delivery until long after they have separated. In the final scene of the story he finally brings it to her, but it is too large to go through the door. A final reversal turns defeat to triumph, as he and his wife look out at the mirror leaning against the hedge and see an image of themselves looking in. To Bertie it makes everything look more real, and completes their incomplete love. Reality is not bearable to him without an imaginary escape route. The symbolism perhaps implies that Bertie has at last found a way of making a real commitment, and will stay with his wife.

Uncommitted, elusive bachelors like Bertie and Jerry are portrayed frequently in O'Faolain's stories. He shows that sexual repression contributes to evasiveness and inhibition in the Irish character and encourages the substitution of fantasy for reality. The naiveté of these characters is seen as a kind of arrested development, a failure to accept the sometimes painful adult role. They are trapped in a sterile society by their own evasions. These characters are often placed in contrast with mature, vital characters who are able to work out their own solutions to the disappointments and inadequacies of their lives, and whose psychological growth continues even in an uncongenial environment.

O'Faolain's capacity for balanced intellectual analysis has brought new and valuable insights to the Irish short story tradition. He has articulated fully and convincingly the deep ambivalence that Irish writers have experienced toward their homeland, the burden of the Irish historical consciousness, and the frustration of post-Revolutionary Irish writers who saw their hopes and ideals defeated. His preoccupations as an artist are often similar to those of his predecessors and contemporaries, but he has probed more deeply than other writers into the psychology of the Irish character, and he has experimented with new possibilities of form and technique. His acceptance of the contradictions inherent in his Irish identity, reached after a long inner struggle and several periods of exile and exposure to other cultures, has affected both his successes and his failures as an artist. His best stories derive depth and authority from his personal confrontation of the emotional and psychological tensions in Irish life. In some of his less successful stories, we feel that his hard-won acceptance of his material has given way to over-tolerance and indulgence.

The relationship between the individual and the community in Ireland preoccupied O'Faolain throughout his career. The persistent focus on Irish social conditions in the early stories broadens to a more detached and international perspective in the later work, but communal attitudes still have a significant impact on the psychological development of individuals, and can create "road-blocks" to their development. Many of the late stories portray intelligent, well-educated characters who live in a dreary, stagnant provincial environ-

ment that limits their opportunity for self-realization--
"In the Bosom of the Country," "Feed My Lambs," "'Our
Fearful Innocence,'" and many others. Even some of his
characters who have escaped physically have been so
thoroughly conditioned by rigid social and religious
attitudes that they cannot free themselves emotionally
from them.

O'Faolain's concept of short story form changed
with his changing artistic vision. From the sensuous
and romantic early war stories, to the taut, compressed,
understated stories of his middle period, to the increasingly elaborate and stylistically refined later tales,
he constantly sought to test and expand the potentialities of short story form. His concept of the short
story as a vehicle for communicating personality led
him to choose narrative methods that allowed full expression of his subjective moods and observations; many
of his narrators are thinly disguised projections of
himself, and many of his stories are overtly autobiographical. This view of storytelling sometimes leads to
excessive indulgence of his own voice at the expense of
character or situation, but at his best O'Faolain offers
an intelligence, richness and subtlety of perception not
found in other Irish short story writers. His experiments with novels and tales suggest that although the
short story was the form in which he could express his
view of Irish life most effectively, he often found it
too confining. Because of the gap between his articulate intelligence and fecund imagination and the thin-
ness and intractability of his material, he found it
difficult to achieve the equilibrium between temperament
and circumstances which he believed was essential to a
writer's success. The Irish environment to some extent
thwarted his artistic expression as it did O'Flaherty's.

Notes

[1] Sean O'Faolain, *Vive Moi!* (Boston: Little, Brown, 1964), pp. 43-44.

[2] Ibid., p. 60.

[3] Ibid., p. 156.

[4] Ibid., p. 170.

[5] Ibid., p. 220.

[6] Ibid., pp. 225-26.

[7] Sean O'Faolain, "A Portrait of the Artist as an Old Man," *Irish University Review*, 6, no. 1 (1976), 13.

[8] *Vive Moi!*, p. 311.

[9] Ibid., p. 342.

[10] Ibid., pp. 368-69.

[11] Sean O'Faolain, "Signing Off," *The Bell*, 12, no. 1 (1946), 1.

[12] Sean O'Faolain, "Literary Provincialism," *Commonweal*, 17 (Dec. 21, 1932), 215.

[13] Sean O'Faolain, "The Emancipation of Irish Writers," *Yale Review*, NS 23 (1934), 498.

[14] Sean O'Faolain, "Ireland After Yeats," *The Bell*, 18 (1953), 38-39.

[15] Ibid., pp. 40-41.

[16] Sean O'Faolain, *The Short Story* (New York: Devin-Adair, 1951), p. ix.

[17] Ibid., p. 30.

[18] Ibid., p. 169.

[19] Sean O'Faolain, "Ah, Wisha! The Irish Novel," *Virginia Quarterly Review*, 17 (1941), 268.

[20] "Ireland After Yeats," p. 45.

21 The Short Story, p. 13.

22 Sean O'Faolain, The Irish, rev. ed. (Harmondsworth: Penguin, 1969), p. 140.

23 The Short Story, p. 225.

24 Vive Moi!, p. 168.

25 Sean O'Faolain, "Don Quixote O'Flaherty," London Mercury, 37 (Dec., 1937), 171.

26 Ibid., pp. 173-74.

27 "Ah, Wisha! The Irish Novel," p. 270.

28 The Short Story, p. 205.

29 See Maurice Harmon, Sean O'Faolain: A Critical Introduction (Notre Dame: University of Notre Dame Press, 1966), pp. 139-86.

30 John V. Kelleher, "Sean O'Faolain," Atlantic, 199 (May, 1957), 68-69.

31 Harmon, p. 68.

32 See Joseph Storey Rippier, The Short Stories of Sean O'Faolain: A Study in Descriptive Techniques (Gerrards Cross, Buckinghamshire: Colin Smythe, 1976), pp. 33-48.

33 Sean O'Faolain, The Finest Stories of Sean O'Faolain (New York: Bantam, 1959), p. 35.

34 Ibid., p. 48.

35 Ibid., p. 56.

36 Ibid., p. 69.

37 Ibid., pp. vii-viii.

38 Ibid., pp. ix-xi.

39 Harmon, p. 62.

40 The Finest Stories, p. xi.

41 Ibid., p. 81.

[42] Ibid., p. ix.

[43] Harmon, p. 85.

[44] The Finest Stories, p. 176.

[45] Ibid., p. 181.

[46] Ibid., p. 137.

[47] Rippier, p. 93.

[48] The Finest Stories, p. 217.

[49] Ibid., pp. 219-20.

[50] Ibid., pp. 315-16.

[51] Ibid., p. 322.

[52] Ibid., pp. 319-20.

[53] Ibid., p. 328.

[54] Harmon, pp. 127-28.

[55] "A Portrait of the Artist as an Old Man," p. 18.

[56] Sean O'Faolain, The Heat of the Sun: Stories and Tales (Boston: Little, Brown, 1966), pp. vii-viii.

[57] Guy Le Moigne, "Sean O'Faolain's Short-Stories and Tales," The Irish Short Story, ed. Patrick Rafroidi and Terence Brown (Gerrards Cross, Buckinghamshire: Colin Smythe, 1979), p. 215.

[58] Paul A. Doyle, Sean O'Faolain (New York: Twayne, 1968), p. 121.

[59] Sean O'Faolain, I Remember! I Remember! (Boston: Little, Brown, 1961), p. 81.

[60] Ibid., p. 3.

[61] Ibid.

[62] Ibid., p. 11.

[63] Ibid., pp. 17-18.

[64] Ibid., pp. 128, 132, 133.

[65] George Brandon Saul, "The Brief Fiction of Sean O'Faolain," _Colby Library Quarterly_, Ser. 7 (1964), p. 73.

[66] Vivian Mercier, "The Professionalism of Sean O'Faolain," _Irish University Review_, 6, no. 1 (1976), 52.

[67] Harmon, p. 187.

[68] _The Heat of the Sun_, p. 26.

[69] Ibid., p. 33.

[70] Robie Macauley, "Sean O'Faolain, Ireland's Youngest Writer," _Irish University Review_, 6, no. 1 (1976), 111.

[71] Sean O'Faolain, _The Talking Trees and Other Stories_ (Boston: Little, Brown, 1970), p. 147.

[72] Macauley, p. 117.

[73] _The Talking Trees_, pp. 270-71.

[74] Ibid., pp. 273-74.

[75] Ibid., p. 279.

[76] Ibid., pp. 174-75.

Chapter Nine

FRANK O'CONNOR

It is appropriate to end with a consideration of Frank O'Connor's stories, because he described more fully than any previous writer the evolution and characteristics of the Irish short story tradition, and because he contributed more masterpieces of the genre than any Irish writer before or since. Though strongly indebted to earlier Irish writers, especially through his friendship with Daniel Corkery and Sean O'Faolain, he developed a concept of the short story that was distinctive and original. His stories are more sociable and humane than O'Flaherty's, more objective and dramatic than O'Faolain's. His struggles with the genre were focused on his attempt to recreate the effect of a human speaking voice in the narrative. In addition to his numerous collections of short stories and his two novels, he wrote autobiographies, a biography, some poetry, several volumes of translations from Irish poetry, several plays, and many books and articles on history, literary criticism, and commentary about Irish life. Like O'Faolain, he spent some time in exile but was dedicated to improving Irish culture, and despite considerable persecution and hostility he kept returning to live in Ireland. By the time of his death in 1966 he had become somewhat reconciled with his countrymen and had won their admiration and respect.

The story of O'Connor's early years and his efforts to rise above almost intolerable circumstances is told very movingly in his first autobiography, An Only Child (1961). Childhood had a profound impact on his creative imagination and he drew on it much more directly and frequently in his writing than did O'Flaherty or O'Faolain.

O'Connor was born Michael O'Donovan, the only child of Minnie and Michael O'Donovan, in Cork in 1903. His father, a navvy, was a violent, unstable man; he indulged in periodic drinking bouts during which he terrorized his family and drove them into destitution. During his sober periods he was a melancholy, solitary, home-loving man, demanding and irritating to live with, and exhibiting a streak of paranoia. O'Connor's hatred of his father led to a mistrust of all forms of authority. His hatred extended to his father's family, because of their "drunkenness, dirt, and violence."

It was natural under such circumstances that O'Connor should develop into "the classic example of the Mother's Boy." His mother, a gentle and refined person, was the single greatest influence on his life. She gave him companionship, encouragement, and dedication to high standards, and he remained devoted to her until her death in 1952. She was an orphan, raised by nuns, and her stories of orphanage life deeply impressed her son, making him sensitive to the human need for a secure home. "For me, there has always been in imagination a stage beyond death--a stage where one says 'I have no home now.'"[1] Besides the orphan's fear of homelessness, his mother also had the orphan's instinct for survival. Her gaiety and belief in appearances were ways of coping with the harshness of reality. She stayed with her husband through even his worst bouts, sympathizing with him in some way which O'Connor found impossible to comprehend.

With his mother's support, O'Connor began at an early age to seek an escape from the Cork slums. For him education represented the only possible means of escape, but his ideas about what constituted an education were vague. School was a source of more misery than enlightenment. He disliked his teachers, many of whom were coarse and sadistic, did poorly on examinations, and finally left school at fourteen. Ill-at-ease with neighborhood children, he constructed alternative identities for himself and imagined that he belonged to a high social class. He studied carefully any books or pieces of information he could get hold of, and imitated the behavior of people he admired. Day-dreaming provided him with an escape, but it also brought loneliness and fear of the unknown. Human companionship was essential to him.

After leaving school, O'Connor took a job as a messenger boy at the railway. This was the low point of his adolescence; the contrast between the awkwardness and drudgery of his everyday life and the freedom of his imaginary world was painfully acute. He clung to a belief in words and conceived the ambition of becoming a translator. He memorized poetry, both good and bad, and learned to write in different languages, especially Irish. Ironically, the day he was fired from his job was the same day he read publicly his first paper in Irish, an essay on Goethe. The day was a crucial turning point in his life.

> While I was speaking, it was suddenly
> borne in on me that I no longer had a

> job or a penny in the world, or even
> a home I could go back to without humili-
> ation, and that the neighbours would say,
> as they had so often said before, that
> I was mad and a good-for-nothing. . . .
> All that did matter was the act of faith,
> the hope that somehow, somewhere I would
> be able to prove that I was neither mad
> nor a good-for-nothing; because now I
> realized that whatever it might cost me,
> there was no turning back.[2]

Underlying the somewhat desperate tone of this passage
is the determination and strength of character that
enabled O'Connor to succeed in his ambition.

During his teens O'Connor formed some friendships
with people who shared his intellectual interests and
gave him some encouragement and direction. The most
important of these friendships was with Daniel Corkery.
Corkery had been his teacher for several months in elementary school and had given him his first instruction
in Irish, at that time an almost unknown subject. Corkery's circle of friends included Sean O'Faolain, who
excited O'Connor's envy. O'Faolain was "three years
older than I and all the things I should have wished to
be--handsome, brilliant, and, above all, industrious.
For Corkery, who loved application, kept on rubbing it
in that I didn't work as O'Faolain did."[3] Corkery
introduced his protegés to classical music and to Russian fiction, and taught them habits of careful composition and painstaking revision. O'Connor, like O'Faolain, eventually became estranged from Corkery because
of his increasingly rigid and fanatical political views.

The political activity preceding the Revolution
provided a convenient outlet for O'Connor's emotional
conflicts. Identification with Irish problems provided
a "safety valve" for his own anger. He and Ireland
were both engaged in an "elaborate process of improvisation." He joined the Volunteers in 1918, but was too
young to become actively involved in the fighting.

The Truce of 1922 was a brief triumph for O'Connor,
but the outbreak of the Civil War marked the beginning
of a severe disillusionment with Ireland. "What neither
group saw was that every word we said, every act we committed, was a destruction of the improvisation and what
we were bringing about was a new Establishment of Church
and State in which imagination would play no part, and
young men and women would emigrate to the ends of the

earth, not because the country was poor, but because it was mediocre."⁴ He fought on the Republican side because of Corkery, but at first had no clear idea of what war was like. His involvement in the war became more and more painful, however, as he gained a stronger sense of the reality of danger and death. In the spring of 1923 he was captured by Free State soldiers and interned at Gormanstown. Ironically, the year he spent in prison was a relatively happy and profitable time for him. It relieved him from responsibility, allowed him to meet men of high caliber, and gave him an opportunity to further his education.

O'Connor's new maturity brought grave doubts about the political ideals he had formerly accepted without question. He thought that idealism carried to extremes was inhuman, that life was more important than death, and that martyrdom was a pretense. When he returned to Cork after his release, he was no longer at ease with his neighbors, their "introverted religion and introverted patriotism." He does not describe the change in his religious views in any detail, but in the final paragraph of An Only Child there is a suggestion that he did not completely lose his faith. He reveals his sense of unworthiness, but regards short story writing almost as an act of atonement inspired by his love for other people. "I knew that there were souls that were immortal, that even God, if He wished to, could not diminish or destroy, and perhaps it was the thought of these that turned me finally from poetry to story-telling, to the celebration of those who for me represented all I should ever know of God."⁵ O'Connor found an emotional sustenance in his relationships with other people that he could not find within himself alone.

O'Connor's ambivalent attitude to Cork and Ireland in general is discussed more fully in his other autobiography My Father's Son, which covers the period from his release from prison to the death of Yeats in 1939. With the assistance of Lennox Robinson, whom he met through Corkery, he trained to become a librarian, and after a period of apprenticeship in Sligo and Wicklow, he returned to Cork to accept a position as county librarian. It took him only a short time to realize that he would always be uncomfortable there. He encountered constant frustration in his attempts to side-step the ignorance and prejudice of the Cork County Council. "At last I was beginning to get a picture of Ireland, the real Ireland, lonely and dotty. This was no longer the romantic Ireland of the little cottages and the hunted men, but an Ireland where everyone was searching

frantically for a pension or a job."[6] Yet he loved
Cork, and even when he applied for a job in Dublin in
1928, he thought he would eventually make Cork his permanent home. "Nothing could cure me of the notion that
Cork needed me and that I needed Cork. Nothing but
death can, I fear, ever cure me of it."[7] His persistent
attachment to a place where he no longer felt comfortable follows a pattern we have already observed in
O'Flaherty and O'Faolain.

In Dublin O'Connor formed friendships with AE,
Yeats, and their associates. He had begun to write
poems and short stories, some of which AE published in
The Irish Statesman. Through Yeats O'Connor became
actively involved with the Abbey Theater, which was then
in decline, and in 1935 he joined the Board of Direc-
tors. Although he quarreled constantly with Yeats
about the type of plays that should be presented and
the style of acting that should be used (O'Connor preferred poetic realism), they were united in their commitment to high artistic standards. O'Connor married
an Abbey actress, Evelyn Speaight, in 1938, and they
had two children. The marriage ended in separation in
1948 and later was annulled.

O'Connor's involvement with the theater and with
public life in Dublin was very closely tied to his
friendship with Yeats. The death of Yeats in 1939
brought not only the end of an era but a significant
change in O'Connor's relationship to Irish affairs. The
tendencies in Irish society which had irritated and disillusioned him before Yeats's death now seemed insuper-
able.

> When a great man dies, not only does
> a legend spring up, but a phase of rea-
> lity ends. . . . The things that happen
> after the death of a man like that have
> already been happening before he dies,
> but because he is alive they seem of no
> great importance. . . . With Yeats perma-
> nently gone, I began now to realize that
> mediocrity was in control, and against
> mediocrity there is no challenge or appeal.[8]

O'Connor mistrusted the people who surrounded him in
Dublin and felt that he could not stand up to them by
himself; he could not be a man of action and a good writer at the same time. In 1938 he had resigned his job
as librarian, and at the suggestion of his publisher,
Harold Macmillan, he eventually resigned from the Abbey

and from every other organization he belonged to, and devoted himself to his writing.

The period from Yeats's death to the early fifties was a very troubled one for O'Connor. During the war he found it difficult to earn a living. He survived by publishing articles in the Dublin Sunday Independent under the name Ben Mayo. The government regarded him as a public enemy, and when he cycled around Ireland to examine ruins for his book on Irish architecture, he was trailed by detectives. Beginning in 1941 he went regularly to London to work for the Ministry of Information and the BBC, but resided mainly in Ireland despite his difficulties there. By 1950 his marriage had broken up, he was having serious financial problems, and much of his work was suppressed in Ireland. He accepted positions as Visiting Professor at Northwestern and Harvard in 1951, stayed in America for several years, and began to publish his stories mainly in American magazines like the New Yorker. In 1953 he married an American, Harriet Rich. When they finally returned to Ireland a few years later, he had established an international reputation and was ready to enter confidently upon the extraordinarily productive last phase of his career.

The last years of O'Connor's life brought not only international acclaim but greater acceptance and recognition within Ireland. His stories were published widely in the United States and England, and many were translated into foreign languages. He also acquired a reputation as an outstanding Irish scholar and translator of Irish poetry. In 1961 he taught for a year at Stanford, and in 1962 received an honorary D.Litt. from Trinity College and an invitation to become a guest lecturer there. This achievement was especially gratifying to him. By the time of his death he had overcome much of the bitterness and anger of his middle years, since he had won the respect of his countrymen as well as the love and reverence of many younger writers and students.

O'Connor's withdrawal in the thirties from public involvement to private life exemplified a trend he felt was common among Irish writers of his generation. When he writes about the place he and his contemporaries occupy in Irish literary history, his tone usually reflects his bitterness over the devastating impact of censorship and anti-intellectualism. In "The Future of Irish Literature" (1942), he discusses the changes that have taken place in Irish society since the Treaty and speculates about whether Ireland will continue to produce worthwhile literature. His words echo similar commentaries by O'Flaherty and O'Faolain. After the Revolution, he says,

> Irish society began to revert to type. All the forces that had made for national dignity, that had united Catholic and Protestant, aristocrats like Constance Marcievicz, Labour revolutionalists like Connolly and writers like AE, began to disintegrate rapidly, and Ireland became more than ever sectarian, utilitarian . . . , vulgar and provincial.[9]

Since De Valera's rise to power, the situation has grown even worse, as every year has "strengthened the grip of the gombeen man, of the religious secret societies like the Knights of Columbanus; of the illiterate censorships." Young people are leaving the country in thousands because they cannot stand the moral atmosphere in Ireland. In such an atmosphere, writers can no longer take a romantic view of Ireland. If there is any hope for Irish literature, he says, it must take the direction of satire rather than romanticism. O'Connor's own stories of this period are often harshly satirical.

One incident in particular brought home to O'Connor the extremes to which the Censorship Board would go. In My Father's Son he recalls his friendship with Tim Buckley, "The Tailor," a delightful old storyteller who knew an abundance of traditional Irish tales. When a book of his stories was published in 1942, with an introduction by O'Connor, the government immediately banned it for its alleged obscenities. The Tailor and Ansty, his wife, were deeply shocked. Their neighbors boycotted them and three priests made the Tailor burn his copy of the book. O'Connor's tone in describing this incident is disgusted and sarcastic. He says that the Appeal Board lifted the ban on the book several years later, "but by that time the book was out of print and the Tailor and Ansty were dead, so it was all quite proper and perfectly safe."[10] O'Connor describes the Senate debate over the banning of the book as "a long slow swim through a sewage bed."[11] Another similar incident was the controversial banning in 1945 of O'Connor's own translation from Irish of Bryan Merryman's The Midnight Court.

O'Connor's battle against censorship and cultural apathy continued throughout his life. In a speech given to the Trinity College Historical Society in 1962, he

asserts that even though the Censorship Act is applied
much more selectively than it used to be and the members
of the Censorship Board are more sympathetic to Irish
writers, censorship is still "insulting to the Irish
intelligence." Irish censorship has not constituted a
serious attempt to define evil literature, but is rather
a "censorship of opinion and a censorship exercised on
behalf of one creed." The effect of censorship on contemporary Irish literature and education has been devastating.

> The most awful thing about the censorship
> is the way it perpetuates the negative
> attitude we oppose to every manifestation
> of intellect and scholarship. . . . We have
> a Censorship Board and a Censorship Appeals
> Board, but we have no such thing as a
> Society for the Encouragement of Irish
> Literature. . . . We have a Censorship
> Board, but we have no publishers. We have
> a great literature, published by Englishmen
> and Americans, and, thanks to our censors,
> ninety-nine per cent of it is out of print
> and unobtainable, so that, as I have said
> before, we have brought up a generation
> which knows nothing of its own country,
> or its own literature.[12]

Even though he is less bitter than in his earlier years,
O'Connor's anger against the social attitudes that permit censorship is still evident.

It is difficult to assess the effect that O'Connor's battles with Irish society had on his creative
work. Sometimes uncontrolled anger detracted from his
stories, but to a certain extent he required antagonism
and confrontation to stimulate his imagination; he once
remarked that "All the literature that matters to me
was written by people who had to dodge the censor."[13]
In her reminiscence of O'Connor, Shevawn Lynam comments
on his need for contact with Ireland.

> Apart from writing, I think that throughout
> his life Ireland was his deepest passion
> and that his criticisms belonged more to
> the scoldings that take place within a
> family than anything else. . . . It was on
> his country and his people that he nourished
> his brilliant imagination. . . . His crea-
> tivity needed the constant contact with
> the world in which he had grown up.[14]

234

As in the case of Sean O'Faolain, O'Connor's frequent trips abroad relieved the pressures of his involvement with Ireland, gave him greater personal freedom, and restored his balance, but he could not leave Ireland for permanent exile.

O'Connor has written extensive literary criticism on the short story and other genres, and his critical insights often illuminate his own concept of storytelling. His commentary on the Irish literary tradition and especially on the Irish short story helps to define his position within that tradition. The theory of the short story outlined in the Introduction to The Lonely Voice (1962), a study of several major short story writers, is essential to an understanding of his work. The theory is somewhat cryptic and argumentative, but it accounts for the mood of many good stories, including O'Connor's own, and it has had an influence on modern short story criticism.

In the Introduction O'Connor describes the short story as a private art form like the novel, intended for "the individual, solitary, critical reader." Though it grew out of the public art of oral storytelling, the short story has become a distinctively modern art form, which expresses better than poetry or drama the modern attitude to life. He believes that there are distinct "ideological" differences between the short story and the novel; these result from contrasting attitudes to the reader and to society in the two genres. In the novel the reader can identify with the main character, and the main character functions within a "normal" society, but characters in short stories are "Little Men," mock-heroic figures with whom we cannot identify, and there is no normal society to which they can relate. "The short story remains by its very nature remote from the community--romantic, individualistic, and intransigent."

To replace the hero in a novel the short story has what O'Connor calls a "submerged population group," different for each writer and each generation, and consisting of a dissatisfied segment of society "always dreaming of escape." Using Sherwood Anderson as an example, O'Connor says that the submerged population wants to escape not merely from "material squalor," but also from "defeat inflicted by a society that has no sign posts, a society that offers no goals and no answers." The reason Ireland has produced so many good short story writers but so few good novelists is that Ireland does not have a normal, civilized society, and Irish writers

235

are treated with "incomprehension, ridicule, and injustice." Because the short story deals with "outlawed figures wandering about the fringes of society," its mood differs from the predominant mood of novels. The short story conveys an "intense awareness of human loneliness." This mood is best expressed for him by Pascal's saying, "Le silence éternel de ces espaces infinis m'effraie."[15]

Although many objections have been raised to O'Connor's theory of the short story, it has proved remarkably fruitful in interpreting short stories from many countries. As might be expected, it applies particularly well to the Irish short story.[16] O'Connor points out that the Irish writer is more severely outcast than are writers from Russian, American, or English society. But to understand fully O'Connor's theory and its application to his own stories, we must realize that he has stated his views polemically, as part of his ongoing quarrel with Irish society. The Irish short story writer in particular is highly conscious of the community and his need for it. Although many Irish short stories deal with outlawed, lonely characters and submerged population groups, there is usually also in these stories an impulse toward reconciliation, an attachment to the Irish physical and social environment that persists in spite of the most severe disillusionment and alienation. Characters keep turning to the community for support even when they know the support will be inadequate or entirely lacking. This ambivalent attitude probably results from the strength of traditional community ties in Ireland, and the intense psychological effect that ostracism has on an individual.

In The Lonely Voice, O'Connor discusses formal as well as ideological differences between the short story and the novel. In this section of the Introduction, his own biases and preferences are even more apparent than in the previous section. His analysis of form concentrates primarily on the treatment of time in the two genres. He believes that the structure of the novel is heavily dependent on chronological time, and that the extensive use of devices like flashbacks tends to weaken the form. Chronological development is "essential form as we see it in life, and the novelist flouts it at his own peril." O'Connor usually prefers traditional, chronologically structured novels to modern ones that experiment with time sequences.

The short story, O'Connor believes, has no "essential form." It has instead what he calls "organic form"; the story is organized around a significant moment in time when a major change or revelation takes place in a character's life. Referring to Browning's dramatic lyrics for illustration, he says, "Since a whole lifetime must be crowded into a few minutes, those minutes must be carefully chosen indeed and lit by an unearthly glow, one that enables us to distinguish present, past, and future as though they were all contemporaneous."[17] Because it is so condensed and open a form, the short story demands from a writer a high degree of artistic and dramatic skill.

One danger of the short story form is that the story may become too artistically pure, too abstract and detached from the material of daily life. O'Connor dislikes stories of writers like Hemingway which give the reader too little information. He makes a distinction between the conte and nouvelle, similar to O'Faolain's distinction between the short story and the tale. There is no convention of length to tell the short story writer how much information to include; he must rely on his own judgment. The short story should have, like the novel, a "physical body." It should be rooted in a recognizable place and the characters' motives should originate from animal instincts as well as from intellect. In his own work he tries to achieve the sense of a human voice telling the story. "I once tried to describe my own struggle with the form by saying that 'Generations of skilful stylists from Chekhov to Katherine Mansfield and James Joyce had so fashioned the short story that it no longer rang with the tone of a man's voice speaking.'"[18] For O'Connor, this human narrator is essential if the author wants to communicate directly with the reader. "The lonely voice" is an apt phrase for his own approach to writing the short story.

The concepts of the submerged population and organic form underlie much of O'Connor's criticism on other short story writers. The Lonely Voice primarily discusses non-Irish writers (Gogol, Turgenev, Maupassant, Chekhov, Kipling, Mansfield, Lawrence, Hemingway, Coppard, Babel, Salinger, and Anderson), but he has written at length elsewhere about the Irish short story tradition and about his predecessors and contemporaries in the genre. In his Introduction to Modern Irish Short Stories, an anthology which he edited, he asserts that there is a recognizable Irish short story tradition. "I believe that the Irish short story is a distinct art form: that is, by shedding the limitations of its popular origin it has become susceptible to development in the same way as German song, and in its attitudes it can be distinguished from Russian and American stories which have developed in the same way."[19] He illustrates this thesis by making a rapid survey of major Irish short story writers, and suggesting some connections among them.

Like many other critics, O'Connor regards George Moore's The Untilled Field as the beginning of the Irish short story tradition, a realistic tradition which diverged from Yeats's romantic school. Moore introduced the "art" story that supplanted slapstick tales such as those of Somerville and Ross, and the short story writers who followed Moore, including Joyce and minor writers like O'Kelly and Corkery, wrote "art" stories rather than tales. On several occasions O'Connor uses Moore's "Home Sickness" as an example of perfected organic form and as a model for comparison with stories by other writers. In The Lonely Voice he compares this story to the tales of Somerville and Ross. After quoting the last paragraph of "Home Sickness," he says:

> Here there is no contrivance, not so much as a single coincidence. The narrative line is merely a pattern: the pattern of human life as we have all experienced it--nostalgia and disillusionment and a fresh nostalgia sharpened by experience. It has the absolute purity of the short story as opposed to the tale.[20]

James Joyce's Dubliners, in O'Connor's view, was heavily influenced by Moore, and both The Untilled Field and Dubliners owe much to Russian and French models. The main difference between Moore's stories and Joyce's is that Joyce's follow "not so much the patterns of life itself as the patterns formed in a man's mind by reading and reflection and which he imposes on reality."[21] The later stories of Moore and Joyce took different directions: "Whereas Moore's stories develop a disillusionment that turns into polemic, Joyce's stories, though equally disillusioned, become formally more and more intricate."[22] Both writers regarded emigration as the most practical solution for those who could not stand the restrictiveness of Irish life. Comparing "Home Sickness" to "Eveline," O'Connor remarks that while Moore concentrates mainly on the Irish countryside, Joyce is an exclusively urban writer. As a result Eveline is "more trapped" than James Bryden. Joyce's exile represents an alternative which O'Connor himself rejected, and his antipathy to Joyce seems natural in view of the different choices they made and their different conceptions of short story technique. O'Connor also frequently seems envious of Joyce's achievement.

In spite of this antipathy, O'Connor writes at greater length about Joyce than about any other Irish short story writer. He had a reluctant fascination with Joyce and was influenced by him more than is commonly recognized. In his discussion of Dubliners in The Lonely Voice, O'Connor raises the question of why Joyce gave up short story writing after completing "The Dead." He believes that Dubliners illustrates several stages in the development of a short story writer. The first three stories are "sketches" interesting mainly for their style.

> It is a highly pictorial style; one intended to exclude the reader from the action and instead to present him with a series of images of the events described, which he may accept or reject but cannot modify to suit his own mood or environment. Understanding, indignation, or compassion, which involve us in the action and make us see it in terms of our own character and experience, are not called for.

The passage reflects O'Connor's preoccupation with the author-reader relationship, which was of central importance in his own work.

The middle group of stories in Dubliners are harsh and naturalistic. O'Connor admires these middle stories ("Two Gallants," "Clay," "Counterparts," and "A Little Cloud" are mentioned specifically) more than Joyce's earlier stories, because in their re-creation of a submerged population, they approach more closely to his own idea of what a short story should be. These stories contain further development of the stylistic devices discussed in relation to the first stories, such as the repetition of certain words for hypnotic effect. "Ivy Day in the Committee Room" and "Grace" are written in the mock-heroic manner with even more elaboration of style. These stories show Joyce moving away from the stance of a genuine storyteller, since he has "deprived his submerged population of autonomy." By this O'Connor means that the characters have no "skill and wisdom of their own"; Joyce's heavy irony has made them farcical caricatures. "The Dead," the most elaborate story of all, shows why Joyce gave up story writing. "One of his main passions--the elaboration of style and form--had taken control, and the short story is too tightly knit to permit expansion like this."[23] He had lost sight of his submerged population group.

In his discussions of Daniel Corkery, O'Connor's personal relationship with the man colors the commentary on his writing. O'Connor wrote an essay on Synge (1939) in which he sarcastically denounces Corkery's book Synge and Anglo-Irish Literature, objecting to the puritan narrowness of Corkery's thesis and his exclusion of Yeats from truly "Irish" literature. O'Connor disagrees with many of Corkery's comments on individual plays. But at the end of the essay, O'Connor remarks that he still regards Corkery as "the greatest artist of his generation,"[24] indicating that he has retained some of his admiration for his former teacher.

O'Connor does not discuss Corkery's short stories in any detail, except for one passage from An Only Child in which he uses "The Ploughing of the Leaca" to illustrate the personal conflict that was drawing Corkery away from art. Referring to the ending, in which the farmhand ploughing the leaca plunges with the horses over the cliff, he says, "It describes the suicidal destruction of the creative faculty as an act of revolt against the worldliness of everyday life. . . . It is as though the imaginative improvisation of the community had begun to dominate the imaginative improvisation of the artist and make its fires seem dim by comparison." There are other stories, like "The Wager," which contain the same "symbolic equation," and "even in the stories where there is no symbolism there is a celebration of imaginary heroes and an attack on imaginary enemies who are not far removed from windmills."[25] Corkery came to believe more in the authority of men of action than in his own authority as an artist.

When writing about Liam O'Flaherty's stories, O'Connor shows considerable enthusiasm. O'Flaherty's only faults in O'Connor's eyes are that "his English lacks the distinction and beauty of his Gaelic, and his form is occasionally very dull indeed."[26] O'Flaherty, as a member of O'Connor's own generation of writers, demonstrates the turning from the public to the private realm which was described in My Father's Son. Once again O'Connor uses Moore as a reference point in illustrating this tendency. He compares "Home Sickness" to O'Flaherty's "Going into Exile." O'Flaherty's stories do not reflect political and social controversies, as Moore's do, and therefore they have a more basic and universal appeal. "Moore, writing when he did, cannot

240

ignore the fact that emigration is largely caused by the sheer boredom of religious authoritarianism; O'Flaherty ignores everything but the nature of exile itself: a state of things like love and death that all men must in some way endure."27 O'Flaherty can "fling himself on a theme with the abandonment and innocence of a child," without reflection, and he is at his best when writing about the instinctual lives of animals or characters who resemble animals. Comparing him to D. H. Lawrence, O'Connor says,

> He has all Lawrence's power of conveying
> the enchantment of the senses which is part
> of the instinctual life and, unlike Lawrence,
> does not romanticize or rationalize it.
> He begins to go false only when he has
> to deal with people who are compelled to
> live by their judgment rather than their
> instincts, and this, and not any theologi-
> cal dispute, seems to me the real basis
> of his quarrel with Catholicism in Ireland.28

The reference to the conflict between "instinct" and "judgment" indicates a major preoccupation in his own stories. His concern with the repression of instinctual life in Irish society and his hatred of inhuman abstrac- tions makes him respond with particular enthusiasm to O'Flaherty's work.

   O'Connor's published commentary on Sean O'Faolain's stories shows the same reticence that he shows when wri- ting of Corkery's; perhaps because the two men were his friends and rivals at the same time, and because he dis- liked certain qualities in their writing, he preferred not to analyze them critically. (A more revealing and personal account of his attitude towards O'Faolain can be found in his correspondence.) O'Connor regards O'Faolain as "first and foremost a man of letters," whose "stories and novels are a commentary on his bio- graphies, histories, and essays." Whereas O'Flaherty's work remains at a consistent level of performance, O'Faolain's is constantly changing according to his intellectual development. Commenting on A Purse of Coppers, one of O'Faolain's early collections, O'Connor says "the stories . . . are full of a sort of wry resig- nation to the emotional and intellectual limitations of Irish life."29 A later volume, Teresa, shows the effect of the destructive pressures exerted by the government and the Church during the forties and suggests "contempt for the newer [Ireland] with its intellectual dishon- esty, its vague words and vaguer ideas."30 Beyond

241

scattered remarks like these, O'Connor says little about O'Faolain as a short story writer.

In his article "The Future of Irish Literature," O'Connor discusses perceptively O'Faolain's inability to write good novels. He says that Catholic writers like O'Faolain are more dominated by their material than Protestants like Yeats and Synge were. Irish Catholic writers have difficulty writing successful novels because their material is too restricted. In O'Faolain's novel Bird Alone, "the characters have begun to be articulate: to demand a fuller, richer life for themselves, but as their aspiration grows, the sense of the dead weight of his material hangs more and more heavily on the author's mind, and the book is almost choked by the feeling of anguish and claustrophobia."31 O'Faolain has outgrown his material and cannot translate what he has learned in America and elsewhere back into an Irish idiom.

It should be clear that O'Connor felt himself very much a part of an Irish short story tradition. He reacted to the work of his predecessors and contemporaries in ways which suggest his own literary preoccupations and his deep commitment to Irish culture. In his own stories we can see some of the same conflicts and ambivalent attitudes that are present in his autogiographies and his critical writings. The impulse to attack and to escape from the restrictions of Irish life coexists with a strong need for reconciliation and identification with Ireland.

O'Connor has published ten major collections of stories: Guests of the Nation (1931); Bones of Contention (1936); Crab Apple Jelly (1944); The Common Chord (1947); Traveller's Samples (1951); The Stories of Frank O'Connor (1952); More Stories (1954); Domestic Relations (1957); Collection Two (the revised English version of More Stories, 1964); A Set of Variations (published in England with slightly different contents as Collection Three, 1969). Many of the stories in Stories and later collections are revised versions of stories published earlier. There are also several selected editions.

Early in his career, after experimenting with poetry and novels, O'Connor realized that he could express his attitudes towards Irish life most effectively in the short story. His two novels, The Saint and Mary Kate (1932) and Dutch Interior (1940) are both unsuccessful, lacking in consistency and unity. James

Matthews has suggested why O'Connor was a better short story writer than a novelist.

> A novel traces human life on a sustained
> line in time and space; a story locates
> a singular, irreducible point. The formal
> demands of the one, extension and duration,
> are distinct from those of the other,
> immediacy and clarity. The sense of con-
> tainment, of closed energy, that charac-
> terizes O'Connor's stories is precisely
> what hinders the progressive and differen-
> tiating strategy of the novel.32

As his remarks about the art of short story writing indicate, O'Connor was attracted by the combination of
freedom and discipline that the genre offers. His view
of Irish society as abnormal also helps to account for
his choice of the short story. The subject matter which
aroused his deepest interest and sympathy was the lonely, thwarted, submerged population of Ireland.

The short story writers who had the greatest influence on O'Connor were those who emphasized the oral
aspect of storytelling without sacrificing artistry,
like Turgenev and George Moore; he resisted the heavily
symbolic and intellectual approach of writers like
Joyce, though he did occasionally imitate Joycean techniques with remarkable success. His discussions of
major short story writers in The Lonely Voice give a
clear idea of what qualities he liked or disliked in
each writer. He admired Chekhov but said it was dangerous for a writer to imitate him. He preferred writers who valued innocence and instinct, like Lawrence,
Coppard, and O'Flaherty. The more immediate influences
of Corkery and O'Faolain are also evident, especially
in his early stories.

In the composition of his stories O'Connor was a
meticulous craftsman. He revised his stories carefully,
even after publication. Several of his early stories
were rewritten at a considerably later date and in a
few cases there are three or more published versions of
the same story. O'Connor humorously defends this practice against the criticisms of Sean O'Faolain and others
in the Preface to Collection Two. "'Forgery' is how an
eminent Irish writer [O'Faolain] has described this
method of editing one's own work, but 'forgery' is not
a term of literary criticism, and is, I think, an unnecessarily harsh one to describe what at worst is a harmless eccentricity. Literature is not an aspect of

243

banking."33 He seemed to know intuitively when a story
was "finished," and then he would stop revising it.
Some were never finished to his satisfaction.

O'Connor's method of composition emphasized the
design or structure of the story. He often told students in his creative writing classes to condense the
essence of their stories into four lines before they
began to write, to free them from particular circumstances or characters. Once the design was established,
the story could be rewritten repeatedly until the style
was satisfactory. Another very important aspect of the
story for O'Connor was its oral quality, its re-creation
of the human voice. Physical description and sense
impressions were of secondary importance.

> I begin the story in the man's head and
> it never gets out of the man's head. . . .
> If you're the sort of person that meets
> a girl in the street and instantly notices
> the color of her eyes and of her hair and
> the sort of dress she's wearing, then you're
> not in the least like me. I just notice
> a feeling from people. I notice particular-
> ly the cadence of their voices, the sort
> of phrases they'll use, and that's what
> I'm all the time trying to hear in my head,
> how people word things--because everybody
> speaks an entirely different language,
> that's really what it amounts to.

His interest in the Irish oral tradition was connected
with his own sensitivity to voices, his preference for
the immediacy of oral communication. This method of
storytelling places heavy demands on the reader and
engages his imagination to complete the portrait of the
character suggested by the speaking voice. "It's trans-
ferring to the reader the responsibility for acting
those scenes. I've given him all the information I
have and put it into his own life."34 The act of storytelling is incomplete without the imaginative participation of the reader.

Some other underlying preoccupations characterize
O'Connor's stories. Virtually all of them are about
Irish people. Most of them are set in Ireland and treat
conflicts and crises generated by Irish social and religious attitudes. Most of the stories are set in Cork
or in small Irish towns, though some take place in Dublin or in the country, and a few in England. The characters are usually poor or have known poverty at some

stage of their lives, and most are not highly educated.
Many of his characters are children or have childlike
natures. At least in his writing, O'Connor seldom
shared O'Faolain's attraction to wealthy and sophisticated characters. The classifications of subject matter
we have applied to other writers apply equally well to
O'Connor: religion and the clergy, childhood, family
life, love and marriage, and old age. Early in his
career he also wrote about war and peasant life.

The characterizations in O'Connor's stories often
involve a conflict between what he terms "instinct" and
"judgment." He dislikes abstractions and is particularly concerned with the efforts of characters to liberate
their instincts from the excessively rigid judgments of
Irish society. This antithesis corresponds roughly but
not exactly to O'Faolain's distinction between "romanticism" and "realism" in the Irish character. O'Connor
views the conflict between instinct and judgment within
the limits of relatively normal behavior, and he usually
avoids treating extremely violent or pathological material.

The most universal of O'Connor's themes is human
loneliness, as was suggested by its prominence in his
theory of the short story. On the metaphysical level,
which is seldom treated explicitly in his stories, loneliness originates in a sense of alienation from God.
More typically O'Connor examines the sources of loneliness in the Irish family, social, and religious structure. In a society so overburdened with taboos,
restrictions, and abstractions, in which even the security of home is often threatened by public censure or
family conflict, warm human contact between individuals
is the only meaningful source of fulfillment. In order
to achieve a fulfilling individual relationship it is
often necessary for a character to escape either temporarily or permanently from his home town or from Ireland
itself. But despite his insistence on the short story's
remoteness from the community, there is usually in
O'Connor's work a strong impulse toward reconciliation
with it. Few of his characters live in permanent exile;
many return after a brief period of rebellion and find
social acceptance through marriage or some other means.

ii

O'Connor's war experiences provided much of the
material for his first collection, <u>Guests</u> <u>of</u> <u>the</u> <u>Nation</u>.

A comparison with O'Faolain's Midsummer Night Madness is appropriate, since the collections were published at about the same time and since they both reflect the writers' transition from romantic idealism to disillusionment with the war. Both writers seem uncomfortable depicting violence, but O'Connor presents it more directly than O'Faolain does. O'Connor's treatment of war is more varied than O'Faolain's. In general his style is less subjective and lyrical, more impersonal and dramatic. Natural settings are much less detailed. Another difference between the two collections is that Guests of the Nation contains several stories that are not about the war and therefore the volume appears less unified than Midsummer Night Madness. Although he does use recurring characters in later stories, none of O'Connor's collections has the kind of thematic unity found in some of O'Faolain's collections and, to a much greater extent, in The Untilled Field and Dubliners. As James Matthews remarks, "What unity Guests of the Nation possessed was more of tone than of theme, . . . for inevitably O'Connor's mind gravitated from idea to situation, from theme to character. For a storyteller like O'Connor, life is a highly fragile and personal affair unified not by grand abstractions but by the inconvenient, elusive, and diverse patterns etched by common humanity across the surface of events."[35]

Besides Corkery and O'Faolain, the writer who had the greatest influence on O'Connor's war stories was the Russian Isaac Babel. Some stories in Babel's Red Cavalry (1926) describe a bookish young cossack's efforts to resolve his inner conflict between a need to prove his manhood through violence and his instinctive repulsion towards it. O'Connor discusses this conflict in his chapter on Babel in The Lonely Voice and acknowledges that Babel's book profoundly affected him.

O'Connor's tone in Guests of the Nation ranges from a kind of hysterical humor and enjoyment to a pervasive sadness and repulsion. There are several stories about the effects of war on civilians, constructed with a variety of narrative techniques. "Nightpiece with Figures" is a lyrical sketch about two idealistic nuns who give shelter to a group of rebels. "Soirée chez une Belle Jeune Fille" describes the war from a feminine point of view, as it recounts a girl's first experience as a courier for the Republicans. Her discovery of the banality of war and the reality of death unsettles and disillusions her. "Jumbo's Wife" is a sordid, naturalistic story about a wife who betrays her crude and violent-tempered husband to the Republicans when she

246

learns that he is a government informer. Though she
immediately regrets her action, the Republicans hunt him
down and shoot him, and she is ostracized by her neighbors. The naturalistic mode was not compatible with
O'Connor's temperament, and "Jumbo's Wife" represents
an experiment that he did not repeat. The story may
have been inspired by O'Flaherty's novel The Informer.

Several other stories in Guests of the Nation focus
on the reactions of rebel soldiers to their war experiences. Most of these are narrated in the first person
with varying degrees of detachment. One important
exception is "September Dawn," narrated in the third
person but in a comparatively subjective and lyrical
mode. "September Dawn" has several features in common
with "Fugue" and may have been influenced by it, as
O'Faolain's story was written in 1927 and O'Connor's in
1929. Their correspondence indicates that at this period the two writers were still close and read each
other's work with much interest. Both stories portray
two rebels of opposite personalities, who are pursued
by enemy soldiers and seek shelter in a friendly cottage. The more sensitive of the pair is attracted by a
beautiful young woman staying at the cottage, and he
longs for an end to the fighting. Both stories end
with a symbolic dawn. The stylistic differences between
them provide an excellent illustration of the tempera-
mental differences between the two writers. O'Faolain's
writing is richly sensuous and meditative, and he identifies closely with his narrator. O'Connor's style is
also poetic, but more compact and understated, and his
characters are more objicified.

In "September Dawn," two young Republican officers,
Keown and Hickey, are forced to disband their column
after several days of dodging Free State soldiers.
Together the two men flee through the countryside, frequently encountering rifle and machine-gun fire, and
finally after reaching safety they decide to spend the
night with an old aunt and uncle of Hickey's. Hickey
and Keown are both attracted by Sheela, a girl who
helps the old couple with their chores. During the
night a strong wind makes both men restless and apprehensive, and Hickey experiences a sense of the futility
and loneliness of his life as a soldier. At dawn he
sees Sheela working in the yard; he goes downstairs and
silently kisses her in an "ache of longing" for the
loving domestic life she represents.

O'Connor was just beginning to learn his craft when
he wrote this story, but the characterizations and point

of view are handled skillfully. The point of view is objective during the first section, which describes the disbanding of the column. After Keown and Hickey are left alone, the point of view shifts to Hickey and the rest of the story is told as he sees it. This shift from an external to an internal perspective allows the author to emphasize the contrast between Hickey as a capable, dedicated soldier, and as a lonely disillusioned man.

Keown and Hickey are characterized as opposite types of men. Keown is "unscrupulous, good-natured, and unreliable, and [has] a bad reputation for his ways with women," whereas Hickey is described as conscientious, a little fanatical, lacking in humor and imagination, but "a good soldier and cautious where men's lives were concerned."36 When they are running from enemy bullets, Keown keeps up a bantering commentary; Hickey speaks more tersely and matter-of-factly.

The dangers Hickey and Keown undergo while fleeing the enemy arouse in both men an intense desire to return home, as the members of their disbanded column have done. The unfamiliarity of the countryside heightens their fear. The night spent with Hickey's aunt and uncle is a step on the journey homeward, and the description of their arrival at nightfall reflects their increasing security. "A sombre maternal peace enveloped the whole countryside." The house is "simple and old-fashioned . . . but comfortable, with a peculiar warmth."37 The old couple have only a vague awareness of the realities that the young men are facing. They still live in the past, in the time of Parnell, "spending their last days in childless, childish innocence, without much hope or fear."38 The cottage, remote from the turmoil of danger and flight, is an appropriate setting for the emotion that Hickey experiences.

During the evening Keown drinks too much whiskey and says he will fall in love with Sheela. His jealousy aroused, Hickey quarrels with him and finally makes him go to bed. In the night the rising wind is an alarming externalization of the fear and restlessness the two men feel. Hickey, lying awake and listening to the wind, has a sudden revelation of the futility of his life. "It became clear to him that his life was a melancholy, aimless life, and that all this endless struggle and concealment was but so much out of an existence that would mean little anyhow."39 Since he has dropped out of college, he will probably have to go to America to earn a living if his side loses. The idea of leaving

248

home seems intolerable to him, especially since he has fought so hard for the national cause. Even in this early story we can see O'Connor's desire to keep his characters in Ireland and his recognition of their need for a secure home.

Hickey's feeling for Sheela is expressed through gestures rather than words; after seeing her in the yard he goes downstairs, almost silently helps her start the fire, and then kisses her. The gesture expresses his overwhelming emotions, which, as the story ends, seem to be released and merged with the natural setting. "And for him in that melancholy kiss an ache of longing was kindled, and he buried his face in the warm flesh of her throat as the kitchen filled with the acrid smell of turf; while the blue smoke drifting through the narrow doorway was caught and whirled headlong through grey fields and dark masses of trees upon which an autumn sun was rising."[40] Sheela embodies Hickey's longing to escape from war; she is associated with the warmth of fire and the light of dawn, evoking hope after the fears of the windy night. His attraction to her is an expression of his need for human contact. Although his future remains uncertain, he has taken the first step in replacing the cold idealism of war with humanistic values.

In the first person narratives of rebel experiences, we can see O'Connor's earliest efforts at recreating the human speaking voice and establishing the right distance between the narrator and the story he tells. These first person narrators are more involved in the plot than most of O'Connor's later narrators. The most humorous of these stories is "Machine Gun Corps in Action," a rebel's account of his meeting with a quixotic character who wanders around the countryside with a machine gun, doing his part for the Revolution, until his wife arrives to take him home. "Laughter," which describes a rebel's emotional state as he participates in an ambush, has a grotesquely humorous, almost nightmarish quality. In "Jo" and "Alec," the narrator describes fellow rebels who are more wild and reckless than he is, and whom he regards with ambivalence.

The first person method is used with extraordinary impact in the masterpiece "Guests of the Nation," the only story in the volume that O'Connor felt was good enough to revise for later collections. It concerns two young Irish soldiers, Noble and Bonaparte, who are forced to participate in a reprisal execution of two English hostages, Hawkins and Belcher, with whom they

249

have become friends. The point of view is Bonaparte's. This story has greater universality than any of his other war stories. Men are seen as helpless agents in a relentless chain of events. The conflict between instinct and judgment is evident; by stripping war of its abstractions and viewing it in strictly personal terms, O'Connor achieves an insight into human realities which makes national differences seem absurd and tragic.

The four men have been living together in a cottage belonging to an old woman who keeps house for them. The atmosphere at the beginning is friendly and domestic. The two Englishmen do not really need guarding, since they feel at home in Ireland and make no effort to escape from the cottage. They lack the nationalistic prejudices of the Irish. Ignoring the fact that they are officially enemies, the men develop a friendship based on shared experience that includes both trivial and lofty matters. They play cards together every evening and argue about religion and the afterlife. The tone of Bonaparte's narrative is casual and humorous.

One evening Jeremiah Donovan, the liaison with the local brigade, tells Bonaparte that the Englishmen may have to be shot as an act of reprisal. Bonaparte is stunned to realize that his duty as a soldier conflicts violently with his human feelings. He and Noble spend the next day sickened and dazed, hoping for another alternative. The responsibilities they have undertaken lightly, in their youthful enthusiasm, have grown intolerable.

As the story moves relentlessly to its conclusion, all possible escape routes are closed. When the orders for execution arrive, the Englishmen plead for mercy and say they would never shoot a pal, but the Irishmen, knowing they will be shot themselves if they refuse to obey orders, have grown numb and helpless. Right up until the end Bonaparte keeps hoping for a way out; he tells us that if the Englishmen tried to run away, he would not fire at them. But the Englishmen are too bewildered by the betrayal to think of flight.

In a horrified trance, Noble and Bonaparte watch while Jeremiah shoots their friends. Just before he dies, Belcher, usually reticent about himself, heightens the pathos by revealing that he is a lonely, homeless man; the cottage has provided companionship and domestic surroundings that were missing in his life. The shock sensitizes the perceptions of Noble and Bonaparte, and all around them they see a vast, menacing desolation that is usually hidden from people. The setting, a bogland made eerie and lonely in the darkness of night, reinforces the feeling of impotence and desolation. "It was all mad lonely with nothing but a patch of lantern-light between ourselves and the dark, and birds hooting and screeching all round, disturbed by the guns."41

O'Connor refuses to pass judgment on the Irish soldiers for their participation in an inhuman act. He presents them sympathetically, as men caught up in a situation that has gone beyond their control. Their tragedy is that they must continue to live with themselves. As the story ends, Bonaparte tells us that the emotional shock has changed him permanently. "I was somehow very small and very lost and lonely like a child astray in the snow. And anything that happened to me afterwards, I never felt the same about again."42 This personal, individual response to the horror of war has greater impact than any abstract theorizing could have. Just as the Englishmen cannot escape actual death, Bonaparte cannot ever escape the emotional death that his betrayal has caused.

The story embodies almost perfectly the concept of "organic form" that O'Connor presents in The Lonely Voice. Each detail of plot, character, and setting converges towards the climactic moment when the characters are changed permanently. The events are condensed into two successive evenings, but the story extends much further into the past and future. O'Connor makes effective use of dramatic foreshadowing. As the story develops, details introduced casually in the first section become charged with irony. For example, Hawkins and Noble are arguing about religion and the afterlife when Jeremiah Donovan goes for a walk with Bonaparte and reveals that the Englishmen may have to be shot. When Bonaparte returns to the cottage, the argument is still going on but has acquired new depth and immediacy for him.

The organic structure is also enhanced by the careful balancing and interplay of characters. The two Englishmen are opposite types of men; Hawkins is talkative and excitable, Belcher quiet and contemplative. Jeremiah Donovan, the man who actually does the shooting, is callous and repressed. He lacks the good-natured friendliness of Noble and Bonaparte. The housekeeper, the only person not subject to the laws of war, acts as a kind of oracle whose judgments are made on purely human terms. The Englishmen win her affection and she is appalled at the Irishmen for shooting them.

The setting is an unnamed, almost metaphorical place. There is only an isolated cottage with a warm hearth inside and a desolate bog outside. Images of light and dark, warmth and coldness, contribute to the symbolic pattern that enlarges the theme. Most of the action takes place at dusk or in the dark, when everything takes on a greater sense of mystery and obscurity.

The strongest unifying device in the story is the use of Bonaparte as narrator. He is the human mediator between the situation and the reader. It was on this aspect of the story that O'Connor concentrated when he revised it for publication in More Stories and Collection Two. He makes it more readable by eliminating the phonetic spelling of Bonaparte's dialect and of the Englishmen's cockney speech. For example, "'Mary Brigid Ho 'Connell was arskin abaout you and said 'ow you'd a pair of socks belonging to 'er younger brother'"[43] is changed to "'Mary Brigid O'Connell told me to ask what you'd done with the pair of her brother's socks you borrowed.'"[44] Much of the narrator's Irish idiom is retained but many awkward or peculiar expressions are eliminated. Several other changes improve the subtlety and suggestiveness of the story.

Bonaparte is unusual among O'Connor's narrators because he is fully involved in the experience he is describing. Usually it is only the child narrators who bring catastrophe on themselves, and they are young and innocent enough to recover. In stories about adults O'Connor prefers to have characters other than the narrator bear the weight of events. Artistically, a position of detachment gives him a better perspective and tighter control over his emotions. Potentially destructive guilt is transferred to other characters and observed primarily from the outside. Even in "Guests of the Nation," it is Jeremiah Donovan rather than Bonaparte who does the actual shooting.

An enlightening comparison between some of Joyce's stories and "Guests of the Nation" has been presented by M. G. Cooke. He says that Joyce, in breaking away from traditional short story form, introduced the "metamorphic" story. (The metamorphic stories in Dubliners include "Clay," "Araby," "Two Gallants," "An Encounter," and "The Dead.") This type of story begins

> on a plane of assurance and centrality,
> in an atmosphere combining elements of

252

> adventure and energy and dexterity, gaiety
> and benignity, giving every indication
> that life is at least negotiable, and
> may be enjoyable. That is what is given.
> Yet each of them, imperceptibly but inexor-
> ably, in a wholly intelligible but stunning-
> ly unpredictable way like a swan resuming
> the ugly duckling, undergoes a transfor-
> mation toward a universe of impotence,
> vulnerability, malice, tawdry egotism,
> and omnipresent death. . . . The world
> of pain, in the new short story mode I
> am examining, has need of the world of
> joy, and in a poignant way, depends on
> it. The credibility of joy establishes
> the definition of pain.[45]

"Guests of the Nation," like several other O'Connor
stories, has a metamorphic structure because it begins
in the realm of comedy and ends in the realm of terror.
The comedy is an essential part of the story's meaning.

> The total scene suggests a kind of beauty
> and a kind of gentle, luminous, transmu-
> ting tragedy in the everyday earth. . . .
> [Bonaparte's] terror in part consists
> of the knowledge of good, and in knowing
> it lost.[46]

The experience of terror reaffirms the human values of
compassion, tolerance, and courage. Cooke's perceptive
essay suggests one of the many unacknowledged debts that
O'Connor owes to Joyce.

Some of O'Connor's lifelong preoccupations begin
to emerge in these early stories--his concern with human
contact and domestic security, for example, and his
interest in oral narrative style--but the war stories
are essentially different from his subsequent work. It
is obvious from these stories as well as from comments
in An Only Child that O'Connor was deeply troubled by
violence. In most of his later work he avoids episodes
of physical violence, though he does depict emotional
violence. He wrote a few more war stories after Guests
of the Nation, but most of these do not contain violent
scenes, and some are comic stories. Even within Guests
of the Nation, we can see O'Connor moving away from the
subject of war towards a consideration of Irish domestic
and social life. Two stories, "Attack" and "The Patri-
arch," use the war as a setting for stories that are
really about domestic life. Several stories in the

253

volume do not refer to war at all. The best of these, "The Procession of Life," is the earliest of many stories about the growing pains of childhood and adolescence.

iii

O'Connor's second and third collections, Bones of Contention and Crab Apple Jelly, show him experimenting with narrative methods and working out his concept of the short story as the recreation of a lonely human voice. The volumes contain a large proportion of masterpieces, but not all of them are representative of his most typical methods. Some of his most uncharacteristic stories, such as "Guests of the Nation" and "In the Train," are extraordinarily successful. Like O'Faolain's stories of the same period, O'Connor's reflect his anger and disappointment with Irish society. At times these negative emotions are detrimental to his art, but he usually achieves enough detachment and control so that his personal feelings are transformed into either lyrical melancholy or humor. O'Connor's special humor is one of his trademarks as a writer. Among earlier short story writers, only O'Kelly possessed humor anything like it. Both O'Kelly and O'Connor have the gift of rendering their characters' amusing foibles and eccentricities without depriving them of dignity. At times O'Connor's caricatures become much harsher than O'Kelly's, as when he portrays narrow, bigoted people who inflict harm on others. Often O'Connor's humor has undertones of sadness, anger, or outrage.

The stories in Bones of Contention and Crab Apple Jelly have an atmosphere of entrapment. Characters may struggle briefly to escape and find warmth and love, but they are usually defeated and remain enclosed within the constricted moral and emotional boundaries of their community. In terms of the conflict between instinct and judgment, their instincts are atrophied or perverted by the excessively rigid judgments of their society. In later stories O'Connor would allow his characters more freedom to fulfill themselves. Fulfillment for O'Connor is defined not in terms of heroic courage and endurance, as in O'Flaherty's work, or personal wholeness, as in O'Faolain's, but in terms of human contact, the establishment of lasting, satisfactory relationships with other people, preferably including reconciliation with the community. He believes that to overcome loneliness, excursions into fantasy or romanticism should be

254

balanced by a return to a relatively normal, socially acceptable way of life, through marriage, reaffirmation of family ties, or some other means.

One type of story that O'Connor wrote early in his career but seldom later is the peasant story, dramatizing the conflict between traditional and modern cultures. Bones of Contention contains a small but important group of stories that examine the peasants' attitude towards criminal behavior--a subject treated frequently by earlier Irish writers, especially Griffin, Carleton, and Synge. O'Connor's stories depict the traditional Irish mistrust of legal institutions and the clash between tribal and institutional (traditional and modern) concepts of justice, also analogous to the conflict between instinct and judgment. The community supports the individual in efforts to escape legal punishment for a crime, but imposes the more psychologically damaging punishment of ostracism. O'Connor's attitude to this conflict is ambivalent. The traditional ways are full of poetry; they have evolved over hundreds of years into timeless rituals. They survive from an earlier, more innocent time which provides a refuge from the complexities of the present. At the same time, tribal customs can be barbaric and permit behavior that is cruel and unjust. Obstinate clinging to the old ways in a time of change can result in sterility, vacancy, and spiritual death.

"Tears-Idle-Tears" is a humorous treatment of the subject, a mock-detective story in which the police fail to solve a murder because of a conspiracy of silence among the local people. The three more serious crime stories are all masterpieces: "Peasants," "The Majesty of the Law," and "In the Train."

"Peasants" focuses on a clash between a priest, Father Crowley, and his parish, a community of peasants. One of the parishioners, a worthless young man named Michael John Cronin, has stolen the funds of a local club and the priest insists that he should be prosecuted. The peasants prefer the traditional solution of sending the young man to America without involving the police. When the priest stubbornly insists on going through with the trial, an ironic reversal of justice takes place: the priest is ostracized, and finally, broken-hearted, has to leave the parish. When Michael John is released from jail, he is welcomed back into the community and is even given money to open a shop. The irony is a double-edged one, however, since Michael John marries a rich girl and becomes a usurer who

255

torments his neighbors. The peasants perversely blame Father Crowley for not letting them send Michael John to America.

The story suggests the deep-rooted strength of traditional attitudes and the relative impotence of modern institutions in the face of communal resistance. Even the authority of the priest, which normally would not be questioned, cannot overcome the peasants' determination. The parish provides the boundary for their emotional lives. They are intensely concerned with everything that happens inside it, and indifferent to everything that happens outside. If Michael John went to America, he would virtually cease to exist for them. They support him not because of his character but because the Cronin family has lived in their parish for generations. The fact that the Cronins have a long history of drunkenness and immoral behavior makes no difference. The peasants do not want Michael John to be punished, because the punishment would disgrace not only members of his family who are innocent of the crime, but also the parish as a whole. Compared to Michael John, Father Crowley is a "foreigner" whose native territory is fifteen miles away. Father Crowley, also from peasant stock, is not motivated just by abstract considerations of duty and justice. He is also fighting against the power of the old "long-tailed" families.

The narrative technique in "Peasants" exemplifies O'Connor's concept of "the tone of a man's voice, speaking." Although the narrative is in the third person and the narrator does not identify himself explicitly, he clearly speaks as a member of the peasant community, thoroughly familiar with its ways. His idiomatic language captures both the humor and the self-destructive perversity of the peasants' attitudes. For example, when he describes the peasants' reaction to Michael John's crime, his language implies that he takes their response for granted. "There was only one thing for them to do with Michael John; that was to send him to America and let the thing blow over, and that, no doubt, is what they would have done but for a certain unpleasant and extraordinary incident."[47]

The narrator speaks for the peasants, but the author and the reader sympathize with Father Crowley, as the injustice of punishing the virtuous man and tolerating the guilty one is made obvious. The voice of the author is clearly discernible behind the voice of the narrator in the closing paragraphs.

As for Father Crowley, till he was
shifted twelve months later, he never
did a day's good in the parish. The dues
went down and the presents went down,
and people with money to spend on Masses
took it fifty miles away sooner than leave
it to him. They said it broke his heart.
He has left unpleasant memories behind
him. Only for him, people say, Michael
John would be in America now. Only for
him he would never have married a girl
with money, or had it to lend to poor
people in the hard times, or ever sucked
the blood of Christians, For, as an old
man said to me of him: "A robber he is
and was, and a grabber like his grandfather
before him, and an enemy of the people
like his uncle, the policeman; and though
some say he'll dip his hand where he
dipped it before, for myself I have no
hope unless the mercy of God would send
us another Moses or Brian Boru to cast
him down and hammer him in the dust."[48]

The implication that Father Crowley is a rejected Moses
or Brian Boru enlarges the theme and suggests, beneath
the casual humor of the surface narrative, the author's
recognition of the unfairness and perversity of the
peasants' form of justice. O'Connor exposes a closed,
sterile society which expels the agent of constructive
change and embraces the agent of corruption. The story
provides an excellent example of O'Connor's adept sha-
ping of the narrative voice to function on two levels
at once. Often in his stories the casual humor is
deceptive, as the implied meaning contradicts the stated one and provokes the reader to thoughtful reflection.

The antithesis of "Peasants" is "The Majesty of the
Law," in which O'Connor gives free rein to his instinctive love for the traditional ways and celebrates their
poetry and grace. The story dramatizes time-sanctioned
rituals of hospitality that humanize and mitigate a
potentially painful situation, the arrest and jailing
of an old man for assault. Because Dan Bride, the
"criminal," has not violated the community's mores his
jail sentence is a kind of triumph; his victim will be
ostracized for turning him in to the police. Even in
this story there is ambivalence, though, as the aims of
modern justice are thwarted, the roles of punisher and
punished, innocent and guilty, are reversed.

257

The absence of a narrative voice and the substitution of an elaborate symbolic framework make "In the Train" unique among O'Connor's stories. It depicts the reaction of a peasant community to the murder of a local man by his wife, Helena McGuire. She has escaped prosecution because her neighbors lied for her in court, but ironically, she faces a desolate life as an outcast among the same people who have saved her from the law. O'Connor condenses and dramatizes the action by having the entire story take place after the trial is over, on the train that is carrying Helena and the villagers who appeared as witnesses back to Farranchreesht, their home. The train serves a very different function from the accidental meeting of strangers in O'Faolain's "A Broken World" and "Up the Bare Stairs." Its motion through the countryside isolates and arrests the pattern of village life, and the web of relationships is fixed vividly in our minds. The compartments of the train are representative of the hierarchical social pattern of village life. The sergeant and his wife sit in one compartment, the policemen in another, the peasants in the third, and Helena alone in a fourth. Periodically they pay visits to each other's compartments. A drunken stranger who has taken a liking to Helena provides a symbolic link between compartments as he goes from one to another in search of her.

The story is highly dramatic in form (it was adapted for the stage in collaboration with Hugh Hunt and produced at the Abbey). The narrative viewpoint is impersonal and undefined; we learn about the characters and events gradually, through the conversations of the policemen and peasants on the train. The subjects of conversation are the same in each compartment, but the attitudes of each group are different and each sheds new light on the central situation. We see Helena through the eyes of the other characters before we meet her in person. The final section of the story, narrated from Helena's point of view, gains considerable impact from the conversations leading up to it.

Much of the conversation centers on the advantages and disadvantages of village life compared with life in a large city like Dublin. Each person has his own dream of the ideal life. The snobbish sergeant's wife finds the village primitive and boring; her husband is content with his routine of newspaper, pipe, and pint; a young policeman thinks it would be exciting to work in Dublin, but the others feel safer and more at home in Farranchreesht. The peasants are deeply attached to their home and have been shy and ill-at-ease the whole

time they have been away. Everyone is intent on pleasure and companionship. In their anxiety to get back to
normal, they fail to appreciate that an event of the
highest human significance has taken place in their village. They have been lightly touched by the experience
and do not realize that they have contributed both to
Helena's desperate act and to her subsequent suffering.

Gradually it becomes clear that the peasants have
lied to have Helena acquitted. As in the case of
Michael John Cronin, they would not allow the police to
punish a neighbor. But she will be ostracized, not
because she murdered, but because she murdered her can-
tankerous and miserly husband for love of a younger man
whom her parents would not allow her to marry. In the
eyes of the peasants, murder for land or money is a jus-
tifiable part of the hard struggle for existence, but
romantic love, Helena's dream of happiness, is something
they do not acknowledge. It was really the inflexible,
sterile, malicious village environment that caused the
crime, by stifling her natural emotions until they
turned destructive.

Helena herself has gone nearly insane from the long
ordeal. As in "Guests of the Nation," the act of killing has brought a kind of inner death. She has murdered to escape her oppressive married life, and has
escaped the consequences of the law, only to find herself trapped in a worse situation. Her love for the
young man is gone, and she is left in complete isolation, staring dully at her own image in the glass.

The narrative technique bears a strong resemblance
to the incantatory, repetitive technique of Joyce's
which O'Connor analyzed in The Lonely Voice. A passage
from The Mirror in the Roadway further suggests O'Connor's reluctant fascination with this technique.

> It can best be described as "mechanical
> prose," for certain key words are repeated
> deliberately and mechanically to produce
> a feeling of hypnosis in the reader. . . .
> I have an impression that Joyce wrote with
> a list of a couple of hundred words before
> him, each representing some association,
> and that at intervals the words were dropped
> in, like currants in a cake and a handful
> at a time, so their presence would be felt
> rather than identified. I suspect that
> a number of these words . . . are of sen-
> sory significance, and are intended to

> maintain in our subconscious minds the
> metaphor of Aristotelian psychology, while
> others . . . seem to have a general sig-
> nificance in relation to the movement
> of an individual through time and space.[49]

This technique creates distance between author and reader, and eliminates the sense of a human voice speaking.

Although O'Connor asserts that after analysis he
found Joyce's technique useless for his own purposes,
his experimentation with it in "In the Train" produced
one of his most technically elaborate stories. We can
see the technique at work in the opening paragraphs of
the story. The underlined words are those which contribute to the metaphorical pattern.

> "There!" said the sergeant's wife.
> "You would hurry me."
> "I always like being in time for a
> train," replied the sergeant, with the
> equability of one who has many times
> before explained the guiding principle of
> his existence.
> "I'd have had heaps of time to buy
> the hat," added his wife.
> The sergeant sighed and opened his
> evening paper. His wife looked out on
> the dark platform, pitted with pale lights
> under which faces and faces passed, lit up
> and dimmed again. . . .
> "I have no life," sighed the sergeant's
> wife. "No life at all. There isn't a
> soul to speak to; nothing to look at all
> day but bogs and mountains and rain--
> always rain!"[50]

The metaphorical patterns are continued in both
conversational and descriptive passages. One motif
includes words related to light and darkness, beginning
with the description of the station platform, continuing
with the repeated mention of flames and lights--match-
lights, sparks, candle-flames, lighted windows, the
description of Farranchreesht as "lit up" in the peasants' minds like a "flame-blackened ruin of some mighty
city," and culminating in the "spark of life" that is
dying in Helena. There are also images of rapid motion
and flux which contrast with the larger sense of stasis
achieved by the setting and structure. The use of setting to create a spatial vastness within which the conversation and the train's motion are suspended is

260

particularly effective in passages like this one: "And while they talked the train dragged across a dark plain, the heart of Ireland, and in the moonless night tiny cottage windows blew past like sparks from a fire, and a pale simulacrum of the lighted carriages leaped and frolicked over hedges and fields."[51] There are words related to the nightmarish, almost hallucinatory atmosphere of Helena's mind, and words suggesting fear, insanity, and superstition. The word "pale" is repeated in many different contexts and contributes a ghostlike effect. Some words relate to time and its divisions, and others to philosophical and religious concepts. The analysis could continue almost indefinitely with words identifying sensations, cold and warmth, and so on.

The effect of these "submerged metaphors," in combination with the symbolic train journey, is to place the train and its passengers in an awesome universal context. The conversation, trivial on the surface, reverberates in the depths of the reader's mind, and Helena's fate is given a metaphysical significance. Farranchreesht is a spiritual as well as a physical home, where security is achieved at the cost of sterility. The village has formed in its inhabitants a mental atmosphere of traditional prejudice and blindness which results in destructive acts of hatred and violence instead of spiritual freedom and growth. Helena has been so strongly affected by this atmosphere that she cannot escape through emigration or some other means, but has become murderous instead.

After the stories published in Bones of Contention, O'Connor seldom wrote about crime except in a humorous vein. In his middle years he turned away from violent or extraordinary subjects and concentrated more on ordinary domestic and social situations. He also used rural settings less often and placed most of his stories in towns or villages, with a minimum of physical description.

Religious life is treated in a few of O'Connor's early stories, though it did not become a major subject for him until later. Fr. Crowley in "Peasants" is one of his earliest characterizations of a priest. Two other stories introduce priests who would reappear in later work (several of O'Connor's priests appear in more than one story): Fr. Whelan and Fr. Devine in "'The Star That Bids the Shepherd Fold'" and the foxy Kerryman Fr. Ring in "The Miser."

The clergy in "Song Without Words" are not priests

261

but monks in a monastery where the vow of silence is observed. One day Brother Arnold surprises Brother Michael hiding in the stable and finds out through gestures and sign language that Brother Michael was a jockey before he entered the monastery and has been reading racing papers that are smuggled in to him. The two men become friends, read the papers, drink beer together, and begin to wager "Hail Marys" on the daily races. Their self-indulgence brings back memories of their former life and its lost possibilities; it is like "a window let into [their] loneliness." Temptation grows on them until they include a game of cards in their gambling. Both simultaneously realize that things have gone too far and they must confess to the Prior and give up their "crimes" completely. Underlying the gentle humor is a suggestion of the terrible isolation to which the men have condemned themselves.

The resolution of the story is somewhat unsatisfactory and suggests a reticence that would recur in some of O'Connor's later stories about the clergy. The "sins" of the monks are harmless and innocent, but the demands of the order are so stringent that even small sins produce guilt. There is no indication in the story of what religious life can offer to compensate for the terrible loss of human warmth and involvement. The need of the monks to escape from their isolation is so obvious that we wonder why their rebellion is not more intense. By concentrating on the human emotions of the monks and excluding the religious motivation that might justify their sacrifice, O'Connor presents an incomplete, fragmented picture of their lives.

The type of story for which O'Connor is probably most famous, the story of childhood, also occurs infrequently in the early work. Occasionally a story is told from a child's point of view, as in "Old Fellows" and "Bones of Contention," but O'Connor's characteristic child persona is not fully developed until later. These early collections do contain several stories about relationships among family members, including some children and some old people.

O'Connor's old people often have much in common with characterizations of feisty or dynamic old people by earlier writers, like Moore's Biddy M'Hale, O'Kelly's Nan Hogan and the old men in "The Weaver's Grave," and Old Tom in O'Flaherty's "Galway Bay"--they are beset by physical ills and weakness, but their spirits remain vital and assertive. They are the last of a dying race that surpasses the younger generation in energy and vision. "Bones of Contention" and "The Long Road to Ummera" both portray old women close to death, whose spirited defiance of mortality profoundly affects other family members. "The Long Road to Ummera" is one of O'Connor's most moving stories of peasant traditions. It illustrates his ability to transform material that was personally painful to him, since the old woman is based on the grandmother described in An Only Child, whom he hated for her coarseness and ignorance. As in "The Majesty of the Law," O'Connor here celebrates the poetry of peasant traditions.

"The Long Road to Ummera" concerns the old woman's desire to be buried next to her husband, in the mountain village that she and her son left forty years earlier to seek a living in Cork. She believes that the proximity of the graves will ensure that she will rejoin her husband and her old neighbors after death. She wants not heavenly perfection but a return to a past life that was happier than the present, even though they were poor in Ummera. She is physically feeble, and all her remaining energy and passion are directed to this end. Her son, mediocre and materialistic, will not promise to take her back, and she arranges to make the journey without him. One night she sees a vision of her husband and knows it is time to go. An old jarvey drives her, but on the way she falls ill and has to be taken to the hospital, where an Irish-speaking priest promises her that her wishes will be carried out. After her death her son does follow the ritual she has prescribed, and says when he arrives in Ummera, "'Neighbors, this is Abby, Batty Heige's daughter, that kept her promise to ye at the end of all.'"52

In this story the longing for home, a dominant motivation throughout O'Connor's work, is treated as an instinct deeply imbedded in the racial memory, and is related to the importance of a proper burial in Irish tradition. The return of a corpse to the family grave provides the situation for many earlier stories, including "The Weaver's Grave," several of Corkery's stories, and O'Faolain's "The Silence of the Valley" and "Up the Bare Stairs," as well as many other Irish literary works. "The Long Road to Ummera" may also have borrowed some features from a work that is not Irish but American--Faulkner's As I Lay Dying, which O'Connor said he admired "enormously."53 Both works describe a family's obedience to a dying mother's wish to be buried in her home graveyard, despite the long difficult journey to the gravesite, a distance of forty miles in both cases. This archetypal pattern is one source of the

263

haunting transcendence of O'Connor's story.

Two other early stories of family relationships among rural peasants also incorporate patterns of exile and homecoming: "Michael's Wife" and "Uprooted." These stories belong within the long tradition of stories about the effects of exile on Irish family life. In both stories the homecoming is the catalyst for an intense, almost visionary awakening. These two stories contain some of O'Connor's most detailed and colorful landscapes.

"Uprooted," the better of the two, has a pattern similar to Moore's "Home Sickness." Ned Keating, the protagonist, has left his country village to become a teacher in Dublin. He and his brother Tom, a priest in Wicklow, drive home together for a visit over the long Easter weekend. The visit awakens a strong nostalgia and regret in both of them, and they realize that they can neither return to the innocent simplicity of home and childhood, nor find complete fulfillment in their present rootless lives.

"Uprooted" is elaborately structured and, like "In the Train," probably owes much to Joyce. The story is told in the third person from Ned's point of view and is divided into five sections linked by structural correspondences and parallels and by symbolic motifs. The first section contains a characterization of Ned and a description of his present and future existence. For Ned, Dublin is a kind of realistic middle ground between his memories of home and his daydreams about breaking away and going to Glasgow or New York to work as a laborer, to "find out what all his ideals and emotions meant." Because of his gentle passivity and caution, it is unlikely that he will ever leave Dublin, though he is weary and bored with city life. He has a girl whom he sees once a week and will probably marry eventually, when he has saved enough money to buy a small house. O'Connor leaves little doubt about the impossibility of Ned's escaping from the trap he is in. "His nature would continue to contract about him, every ideal, every generous impulse another mesh to draw his head down tighter to his knees till in ten years time it would tie him hand and foot."[54]

By disposing of Ned's whole present and future life in the introductory section, O'Connor intensifies the attraction of the past as represented by the journey home. The visit is described in a highly structured and stylized manner; the spontaneous confusion of real life is transformed through Ned's sensitive eyes into a dramatic pageant of his past. The setting is a picturesque village on a high, rocky coastline. The description of Ned's and Tom's arrival at nightfall at their parents' house establishes an image pattern of light and darkness that continues throughout the story; the lamp inside the house illuminates the area "as far as the whitewashed gateposts."

The family and village life are described as a familiar, unchanging, timeless drama. The sea provides a pervasive background against which the drama takes place. The gestures and conversation of the characters are described in theatrical terms. Ned's father gazes out the door "in the pose of an orator." His conversation is full of innocent excitement: "Like an old actor he turned everything to drama." His unpleasant qualities, the over-cautiousness and silent calculation that Ned suffered from as a child, are only mentioned in passing, since Ned no longer has to contend with them. He is free to appreciate his father as a colorful, dynamic figure. Everyone carries on an endless conversation about the people who pass along the road, forming a "pantomime." The people are securely rooted in their surroundings. Although this life is familiar to Ned, the theatrical images suggest that his perspective has become that of an outsider, an audience for something he can no longer wholly participate in.

The third and fourth sections continue the journey motif with an account of a visit paid by Ned, Tom, and their father to some maternal relatives across the bay. Ned's father borrows a boat for the occasion and the rapid sail across the bay fills him with childish delight. Light imagery becomes associated with him, as the water reflects on his face. As Ned watches his father posing in the bow, the old man is transformed into a symbolic figure: "His flesh seemed to dissolve, to become transparent, while his blue eyes shone with extraordinary brilliance."[55]

Their relatives, the O'Donnells, are a land-owning family who have preserved the patriarchal solidity and continuity that Ned and Tom have given up. Several generations of O'Donnells live together in two adjacent houses, a modern and an old. Again, Ned views the scene with unusual acuteness. His father sets off immediately to pay a series of calls as an excuse to have a drinking spree.

After dinner Ned, Tom, and some of the younger

O'Donnells make a visit of their own, to see Cait
Deignan, a girl whom Tom had once been fond of. This
progression from filial ties to possible courtship and
love provides the climax of the story, and appropriately
O'Connor places the Deignan house high on a hill over-
looking the countryside for miles; he implies that the
perspective of love is more far-reaching than any other.
When Ned meets Cait he is immediately attracted by her
and tempted by the idea of marrying her and settling
down at home. Like his father, she seems transformed
by a special light. "Her complexion had a transparency
as though her whole nature were shining through it."[56]

Cait and her sisters walk back down the hill with
the others. Since it is raining, Cait shares her shawl
with Ned, and once again Ned is overcome by a sense of
timelessness, as if he has "dropped out of time's pocket." As they wait in a cottage near the shore for his
father's return, the scene becomes even more formal,
stylized, and distant. To Ned it has the static beauty
of an artistic masterpiece. The light is now a "dim
blue light" which illuminates the cottage "with the delicacy of light on old china, picking out surfaces one
rarely saw." One of Cait's sisters looks out the door,
a "watcher as in a Greek play," while Cait and another
sister sit against the wall like a "composition in
black and white."[57]

They sail home with their father in a highly intoxicated state. The rain has stopped, night has fallen,
and under the starry sky Ned's perspective undergoes
still another change. The little boat seems "lost
beyond measure" in the "waste of water," a vast universe
mysterious to man. The experiences of the whole day are
crystallized in their father's cheerful, tipsy song.

The final section describes a conversation between
Ned and Tom when they wake up early the next morning,
shortly before leaving for the city. The realities of
their lives have begun to descend on them once again.
Roused by the preceding day's events they share a new
intimacy, and Tom confides to Ned the loneliness of his
life as a priest. He is a warm-hearted, emotional man
"hunted down by his own nature," living in a perpetual
state of suspicion and fear. When he asks Ned why he
does not marry Cait, Ned replies that they both have
made their choices and cannot go back to the simpler way
of life. Its very simplicity implies a narrowness and
intellectual dullness that Ned and Tom would now find
intolerable. Underneath the excitement and drama remain
the same conditions of meanness and poverty that caused

them to leave home in the first place. Ned's final perspective is a view of his home transfigured by a "magical light," "something he had outgrown and could never return to, while the world he aspired to was as remote and intangible as it had seemed even in the despair of youth."[58] It seems to him that he has realized for the first time what it means to leave home.

Ned's escape is incomplete but irrevocable. He cannot find the fulfillment in Dublin that Moore's James Bryden found in America, and the childhood he cannot return to holds more appeal for him than anything in his future. The title of the story suggests the cause of Ned's dilemma. His peasant background has instilled in him a love for innocent, passionate life and a need for close contact with nature. When his intellect cannot be satisfied by this life, he uproots himself and seeks a more modern existence, but he discovers that without the sustenance of his native environment his emotions and mind are withering. His judgment has triumphed over his instincts, but at great cost. Murray Prosky sees Ned as a man who has sacrificed his human needs for abstract ideals. He and Tom suffer because "they lead lives that contradict the laws of their own being. Unlike the peasants . . . they no longer live in a world that is an extension of their own natures."[59] Because contact with home gives Ned and Tom a spiritual anchor, they cannot leave it without feeling that they have lost an essential part of themselves. O'Connor's characters frequently find themselves in dilemmas similar to Ned's; exile in his stories is often accompanied by a disintegration of identity. This attitude is not consistent, however; in other stories, characters disintegrate because they stay at home in a stagnant, repressive environment.

"Uprooted" is one of O'Connor's finest achievements, and it epitomizes his nostalgia for traditional Irish life. In contrast to O'Faolain's rendering of country life in terms of elusive memory fragments, O'Connor's rendering has the measured proportion, wholeness, and stasis of a work of art. His rural landscape is an arena full of motion, contrast, and color, where an emotional liberation can take place which brings about more precise and profound self-definition. His use of image patterns taken from dramatic and visual arts suggests both the distance between his modern, urban perspective and the peasant ways, and his desire to fix the vanishing culture in permanent, memorable form, illuminated by the transcendent light of imagination.

267

Within Crab Apple Jelly, we can observe a major shift in O'Connor's perspective. A group of stories set in small Irish towns and emphasizing the stifling, "fish-bowl" quality of life there marks a new phase of his career. He comments on this change in the Foreword to a later selected edition of his work. Stories like "The Luceys" and "The Mad Lomasneys" "describe for the first time the Irish middleclass Catholic way of life with its virtues and faults without any of the picturesqueness of earlier Irish writing which concentrated on colour and extravagance."[60] The "picturesqueness" of "Uprooted" and other rural stories is replaced by a storytelling mode that concentrates on characters and voices. There is a spareness of physical description in these stories, just enough to create a visual impression of the characters and a recognizable setting. The sense of entrapment is worse than in the peasant stories, because there is no inspiring landscape for the characters to identify with.

This change in O'Connor's viewpoint is illustrated by "The Luceys," a powerful story about family relationships. It describes a bitter feud between two brothers, Tom and Ben Lucey, in a small town where everything occurs under public scrutiny. Tom and Ben have very different personalities. Tom, a shopkeeper, is dry, formal, irascible, and proud. Ben, a member of the County Council, is more humorous and personable, well-liked in the town, but he also has some of his brother's cautious shrewdness. Tom adopts a self-important tone because as the elder he has inherited the family business and is wealthier than Ben. Both men are intelligent and educated. They have been at odds with each other for years, each denigrating the other in public.

The story is told mostly from the viewpoint of Charlie, Ben's son. He is good-natured and sensitive, and is disturbed by the family quarreling. We meet him first when he is still a boy, and has a close friendship with Tom's only son Peter. The main events of the story occur after the boys have grown up. Peter, a high-living solicitor, is caught embezzling money and runs away. His father desperately hopes that Ben will pull a few strings to get Peter off, but Ben refuses to become involved and criticizes Tom and Peter openly in the town. Tom stops speaking to Ben, and the situation is aggravated when Peter dies in a plane crash soon afterward. Tom vows never to speak to Ben again, and he keeps his word even when Ben is on his deathbed and asks to see him. The town is shocked at Tom's behavior and Charlie, who has been trying to make peace between them, is deeply grieved.

O'Connor carefully depicts the circumstances and character traits that produce such a tragic situation. Public opinion is an important factor, since both men have occupations that give them considerable public exposure, and their awareness that an audience is watching their every move makes it harder for them to back down. But ultimately responsibility falls on the characters themselves, particularly on Tom, whose rigid idealism and adherence to old-fashioned "principles," reinforced by guilt over his harsh treatment of his son, have stifled his instinctive love for his brother. As time goes by he becomes more and more withered and eccentric. In one of O'Connor's most pitiful scenes, when Charlie comes to plead with his uncle to visit his dying father, Tom admits that he loves Ben, has forgiven him, and knows he will regret his action later, but he will not go back on his vow. He is one of O'Connor's most irrevocably trapped characters, trapped mainly by his obstinate denial of his nature.

"The Luceys" underwent considerable revision for its re-publication in Stories. The revisions provide much enlightenment about O'Connor's concept of his art. Several other stories of this period were revised in a similar way. The first version is highly dramatic, and like "In the Train" consists mostly of dialogue. It lacks the symbolic framework that unifies "In the Train," however, and is too episodic. There are few descriptive passages and almost no commentary and interpretation.

The revised version is much better, as are most of O'Connor's revisions. The story is given more focus and coherence by the addition of a generalized narrator of the type found in "Peasants" and "The Majesty of the Law"--an unidentified voice that speaks with intimate knowledge of the community, but preserves a degree of detachment. The narrator offers comments and generalizations at the beginning and end of the story, and at a few crucial points in between. Much of the original dialogue is retained though it is streamlined in places. The main flaw in this narrative technique is that sometimes it becomes over-explicit. O'Connor sometimes gives in to an impulse to interpret the story for the reader. "The Luceys" is such a powerful story that this does not detract from it, but over-explicitness becomes an increasingly serious weakness in O'Connor's later work.

The stories of love and marriage in Bones of Contention and Crab Apple Jelly overlap with the stories of family life, since O'Connor almost always takes into account the effect of family attitudes on love relationships. He differs in this way from O'Faolain, many of whose lovers are portrayed with minimal reference to their families, and who therefore seem more independent of circumstances. O'Connor's love stories are like his other stories of this period in their depiction of relationships that fail because the characters are too trapped by the materialistic and puritanical Irish milieu.

One of O'Connor's most poignant love stories, "The Bridal Night," belongs to the "peasant" category. The protagonist is Denis, a slow-witted young man who lives with his mother in an unfrequented coastal village. He falls in love with the local schoolteacher and follows her silently from place to place. At first she encourages him, but when she realizes how intense his feelings are, she tries to avoid him. In his loneliness he begins to show increasingly violent signs of insanity and sleepwalks through the rough countryside.

The night before Denis is to go to the asylum, as he lies strapped to his bed, he calls the teacher's name. When she is summoned, he asks her to lie in bed with him and she agrees, in spite of the mother's protests. Denis falls peacefully asleep in her arms. The momentary contact and the teacher's unfulfilled promise that she will come again the next night create an expectancy that reaches beyond time. Deeply moved, the mother says, "'I declare for the time being I felt 'twas worth it all, all the troubles of his birth and rearing and all the lonesome years ahead.'"[61] The teacher's act is so inherently generous and innocent that no one ever maligns her for it. The plot and atmosphere of this story are reminiscent of Corkery's "Storm-Struck," the story about a blind boy crossed in love who wanders through rough terrain and has moments of near-visionary longing.

"The Bridal Night" is remarkable for its simplicity and lyricism. The story exemplifies perfectly O'Connor's theory of organic form. It is told by the boy's mother to an unidentified traveller twelve years afterwards, and its significance extends forward and backward in time from the single resonant moment of contact between Denis and the teacher.

Each detail of the story contributes to its mood.

Local color is used sparingly and metaphorically. The traveller comes upon the old woman's cottage at sunset, an appropriately melancholy and serene time of day. Characters are not described realistically, but are idealized and closely identified with the natural environment. Images of birds, in particular, are used to suggest that here human words and actions spring directly from natural instincts, and the characters' speech has the lyrical, spontaneous quality of a bird's song. The end of the story is marked by another image appropriate to the mood, the falling of darkness over the vast sea, "blank grey to its farthest reaches."

The narrative has the quality of a legend. The guise that O'Connor assumes, that of a man listening to another person's story about long-past events and recording the storyteller's exact words, links the story to oral tradition. This type of design was used several times by Moore and Corkery, and occasionally by O'Faolain. In other stories, such as "Orpheus and His Lute," O'Connor uses this technique in the original version but eliminates the listener in revision, telling the story directly to the reader instead.

The idealism of "The Bridal Night" is found in several other early treatments of love, including "September Dawn," "The Long Road to Ummera," and "Uprooted." Lovers are separated by death or other circumstances, contact is fleeting and at times brings something approaching mystical or visionary insight. Usually the past dominates the present; relationships fixed in the memory are preserved from the corroding flux of time. The shift from rural to town settings already described was accompanied by a more realistic treatment of the day-to-day, long-term problems of courtship and marriage. O'Connor examines the inhibitions, misunderstandings, and failures of communication that bring unhappiness in love. Several of these stories are about bachelors in small towns who are too inhibited and cautious to court a woman normally, and who, like O'Flaherty's Bartley Delaney in "The Caress," work themselves into such a state of desperation that they break out in absurd ways. In "The New Teacher" ("The Cheapjack") a bachelor teacher loses out to a more aggressive rival and then reads the other man's diary, containing details of the love affair, aloud to his class. He has to leave town in disgrace. Ned Lowry of "The Mad Lomasneys" loses his girl to another man because he is too successful at hiding his true feelings in order to appear self-assured and "cool." He ends up precipitously marrying another woman with whom he has little in common.

271

One of O'Connor's best characterizations of an
inhibited bachelor is Johnny Desmond of "The House that
Johnny Built." Johnny, a middle-aged shopkeeper, has
spent his life establishing his business and making
money. He falls in love with the new lady doctor, and
without any preliminaries, proposes to her. Raised with
the traditional concept of matchmaking, he assumes that
his wealth will guarantee his success and is shocked
when she refuses him. The modern idea of wooing her
never even penetrates his mind. His need for love has
been awakened and he tries again, but he still substi-
tutes materialism for romance. He builds a new chem-
ists' shop and brings a young woman from Dublin to take
care of it, with the idea that he will eventually marry
her. He plans an elaborate dinner to welcome her, but
when she finds out that he is not married and that he
expects her to live in his house, she runs out in hys-
terics. Since he is so naive about sex he misses the
obvious implications of the situation, and when he
finally does see his mistake and apologetically proposes to her, she also refuses him. Mystified by his
failures, he dies a year later, probably of a broken
heart.

"The House That Johnny Built" is an entirely different type of love story from "The Bridal Night."
Physical surroundings are barely suggested. Characterization and humor replace poetic effect. The tone is
not lyrical but conversational and ironic. The narrator, though not specifically identified, is clearly a
neighbor or fellow-villager, someone who often observes
Johnny and regards him as a local "character." The
point of view is sometimes projected into Johnny's mind,
but usually we see him from the outside. The use of the
speaker contributes to the organic form as it allows
large periods of time to be compressed through indirect
narration and at the same time provides a consistency
of viewpoint and tone.

The description of Johnny at the beginning borders
on caricature. The incongruous combination of images
makes him appear a peculiar figure.

> He was like an old cat stretching himself
> after a nap. . . . He had a red face,
> an apoplectic face which looked like a
> plum pudding you'd squeezed up and down
> till it bulged sideways, so that the fea-
> tures were all flattened and spread out
> and the two eyes narrowed into slits. As
> if that was not enough he looked at you

> from under the peak of his cap as though
> you were the headlights of a car, his
> right eye cocked, his left screwed up,
> till his whole face was as wrinkled as
> a roasted apple.[62]

Johnny's two botched marriage proposals reinforce his
comical image. The doctor, in particular, finds him
absurd and likes to tease and ridicule him. But at the
same time, there are depths of pathos in the story that
build up force as it approaches its end. As in "Peasants," we must distinguish between the narrator's voice
and the author's. Johnny has some worthwhile traits
which are not appreciated by anyone in the town; he has
imagination, curiosity, and persistence, as well as a
stock of unique personal observations on life, but he
has not found an appropriate outlet for his energies.
His elaborate scheme to build a house and shop represents his dream of love, distorted by the materialism
and sexual naiveté he has absorbed from his culture.

By the time Johnny apologizes to the chemist, he
has become a pathetic as well as a comic figure. His
persistent need for love dignifies him and saves him
from caricature, and we can sense O'Connor's underlying
compassion. Caricature is a way of making a character
speak for his environment; the side of Johnny that is
caricatured belongs to a type, the naive bachelors living in small Irish towns. O'Connor's caricatures are
not belittling; they are almost always deflations of
false attitudes in order to get at what is genuine
underneath. Beneath the surface he creates an individual, an autonomous character who commands our sympathy
and respect. Johnny has much in common with the eccentric bachelors of O'Flaherty and O'Faolain, but O'Connor's special combination of humor and pathos, absurdity
and dignity, and stereotyped and individualized traits,
sets his characters apart from those of other writers.

                                 iv

O'Connor's severely antagonistic relationship with
Ireland during the forties, when he was the object of
much public hostility and suspicion, is reflected in his
next two collections, The Common Chord and Traveller's
Samples. But his departure for America in 1951 and the
publication of Stories in 1952 marked a turning point in
his career. Stories, which contains a few new stories
but mostly stories culled from earlier collections, some

                                273

heavily revised, established his reputation on a solid
international footing. His perspective on Ireland after
that time was more mellow and tolerant, and his later
stories, like O'Faolain's, are more detached from social
problems.

The alterations in subject matter and narrative
method that were apparent in Crab Apple Jelly are further developed in The Common Chord, Traveller's Samples,
and Stories. O'Connor stops writing about peasant life
almost completely, and writes more frequently about
religious life, childhood, and sexual relations. He
treats the conflict between sex and religion more explicitly, particularly the ruthless intolerance of Irish
society towards unwed mothers and their children. Characters are given more freedom to pursue their dreams,
and many succeed in creating a satisfying life either
in their home towns or elsewhere. Settings are expanded
to include England; some characters escape there temporarily, and some stay permanently and find greater happiness than would be possible in Ireland.

These collections contain more stories about religious life and the clergy than earlier volumes, but the
subject is still not as prominent as it would be in the
last phase of O'Connor's career. Often the religious
stories deal with a conflict between a priest and his
parishioners. "News for the Church," like O'Faolain's
"Sinners," portrays an unsympathetic priest hearing the
confession of a wayward young woman. In O'Connor's
story, the confession is a romanticized version of the
woman's first sexual experience, and the priest sourly
questions her about the details until the affair seems
sordid. "The Miracle," one of the Fr. Ring stories,
describes a conflict between Ring and the local doctor,
who triumphs over the priest by importing a Jesuit to
perform a "miracle," the conversion of an old reprobate
whom Ring has failed to reach. Another humorous story
is "The Sentry," in which a conflict between a lonely
Irish priest stationed in England and a soldier caught
stealing onions from his garden brings about the
priest's social integration with the military camp.

A more painful conflict is explored in "The Frying
Pan," a priest's inner conflict over his love for a mar-
ried woman. The story introduces Fr. Fogarty (called
"Fr. Foley" in the original version), a warm-hearted
and thoroughly likeable priest who reappears in several
later stories. The character of Fogarty is based on
O'Connor's friend Fr. Tim Traynor, described in My
Father's Son. "He gave me an understanding of and

274

sympathy with the Irish priesthood which even the antics of its silliest members have not been able to affect."[63] Despite his attacks against the Irish Church, O'Connor formed close personal friendships with several priests, and his portrayals of such humane and intelligent priests as Fr. Fogarty and Fr. Devine balance the more satiric portrayals like Fr. Ring and Fr. Whelan. In the sympathetic characterizations, O'Connor always emphasizes the priest's human needs and emotions, his struggles against the loneliness of his vocation.

In "The Frying Pan," Fr. Fogarty is in love with Una Whitton, whose husband is a spoiled priest--a prudish, ascetic ex-seminarian, better suited to celibate life than Fogarty is. Fogarty and the Whittons live in a dull provincial town and depend on each other for companionship. One evening while Fogarty is having dinner at the Whittons, he realizes they have been quarreling. When Tom Whitton rudely leaves after dinner to attend a meeting, Una breaks down and reveals that her marriage has been unhappy because her husband is still drawn to the priesthood and feels guilty about making love to her. Fogarty innocently reveals that he is in love with her. But he realizes that all three of them must continue to live unfulfilled, frustrated lives.

The story is condensed into two successive episodes, a dinner at Fogarty's house, followed a few days later by one at the Whittons'. O'Connor skillfully designs these two compressed episodes to reveal the whole past and future history of the triangular relationship. The story is told from Fogarty's point of view and we are made aware of his attraction to Una long before he confesses it.

The first episode introduces us to the characters and gives us some information about their relationship. Fogarty admires Una and enjoys the intellectual companionship of Whitton, whom he has known since they were in the seminary together. He feels that Whitton does not really like him and disapproves of his minor vices, such as betting on horses. The contents of Fogarty's house evidence his many attempts to escape from his loneliness. He collects things and pursues numerous hobbies for a short time. The conversation during the evening reveals that the parish priest, whom Fogarty assists as curate, is an ignorant, narrow-minded, miserly old man with little understanding of men like Fogarty. After dinner Fogarty shows movies of a day he and the Whittons spent at the races; his reaction to the pictures of Una on the film betrays his feeling for her.

After she has left, his house seems desolate and inert. The countryside seems to possess "supernatural animation--bogs, hills and fields, full of ghosts and shadows."[64] He indulges in thoughts about what life with Una and her children would have been like.

The central crisis occurs after the dinner at the Whittons. Una goes upstairs to cry after her husband's abrupt departure for the meeting, and Fogarty with his natural warmth of heart goes up to find her. The situation puts them on intimate, confidential terms for the first time. In describing Fogarty's love for Una, O'Connor emphasizes its innocence. It exists without violating the religious beliefs of either Fogarty or Una. Fogarty suddenly realizes that he has admitted his love and she has acknowledged it, "without an indelicate word on either side. Clearly these things sometimes happened more innocently than he had ever imagined."[65] As Una explains her husband's jealousy of Fogarty's vocation and his sexual coldness towards her, Fogarty realizes that his loneliness is shared by both the Whittons, and that the frustrating triangular relationship will continue as long as they are living in the same town. They have chosen to live within the limits of their religious beliefs and have avoided mortal sin, but at a great emotional cost.

The situation in "The Frying Pan" closely resembles the one in O'Faolain's story "Feed My Lambs," though O'Connor's story was published two decades earlier. The ending of "The Frying Pan" seems more realistic and consistent than the ending of "Feed My Lambs" (in which Rita provokes Fr. Tom to kiss her and when he does, declares melodramatically that they can never see each other again) but both stories leave the reader unsatisfied. The characters accept their fates too passively, without intense inner conflict, and they seem too vital and imaginative for such a ready acquiescence to orthodoxy. The underlying problem may be that because of their religious views both O'Faolain and O'Connor are reluctant to challenge the concept of celibacy directly, as Moore did in The Lake.

O'Connor's growing preoccupation with the subject of childhood manifests itself often in these collections, particularly in Traveller's Samples. The childhood stories are of two types, those told in the third person or in the first by a narrator who is not the protagonist, and the first person "Larry Delaney" stories in which the narrator describes his own painful experiences of growth and is fairly closely identified with O'Connor himself; often the story is a transformation of

276

an autobiographical incident. In the first group are "The Babes in the Wood," "The Stepmother," and "My Da," in the second a large number including "First Confession," "The Man of the House," "The Idealist," "The Drunkard," "The Thief" ("Christmas Morning"), and "My Oedipus Complex."

Many of O'Connor's child characters are orphans, illegitimate children, or victims of broken homes. He felt deep outrage and compassion for the suffering of children, and was especially angry about the treatment of illegitimate children. Irish society was so harsh towards unwed mothers that they usually had to flee to England or give up their children to foster homes. Some women became so desperate that they murdered their babies. Referring to the World War II years, O'Connor says, "I was living in County Wicklow at the time and became aware that all round me there were farmed-out illegitimate children, many of whom were cruelly ill-treated."66 "The Babes in the Wood," one of his most poignant stories, concerns two "farmed-out" illegitimate children, Terry and Florrie, each of whom lives with an old woman near a country village. Terry's mother, who calls herself his "auntie," visits him periodically and brings him presents. One day she tells him she may marry an Englishman, Mr. Walker, who will take them both to England. A few months later she brings Mr. Walker to visit him and they take a trip to the seaside. Terry is overjoyed at the prospect of having parents and a real home. But although he waits expectantly for weeks afterward, neither his mother nor Mr. Walker returns. Eventually he learns from Florrie, his only friend, that his mother could not marry Mr. Walker because he was already married, and she has instead married a "respectable" Irish Catholic who will not let Terry live with them.

By telling the story in the third person from the point of view of Terry, a five-year-old boy, O'Connor achieves a darker pathos than if he had used satire or polemic against society. The child's inarticulate feeling of desertion is touchingly rendered. At the same time the reader is given a clear picture of the social intolerance and adult irresponsibility that Terry only dimly understands.

The setting helps to reinforce the sense of isolation. The cottage where Terry lives with an unpleasant old woman and her son is a mile outside the village, in the wood, which becomes an image of Terry's confusion and loss. The only child who comes from the village to

277

play with him is Florrie. England, as described by his
mother, represents a magical dream world containing
everything lacking in his present life; it would provide
both material comfort and emotional security.

O'Connor characterizes Terry's mother so that the
reader can understand aspects of the situation that are
mystifying to Terry. She is an impulsive, high-spiri-
ted, but irresponsible woman who thoughtlessly builds
up Terry's hopes about living in England before any
definite decision has been made. She likes to bring
Terry presents and tell him stories but does not face
the real necessities of his life.

Florrie, who hears village gossip, is Terry's only
source of information. Everyone else treats him like a
baby. Because she is also deprived of a real home,
Florrie is very possessive of Terry and jealous of anything he has that she does not have. She is a strange
child, too knowing for her nine years, almost a prophe-
tic voice. When Terry boasts about going to England,
she gets mad and tells him that his "Auntie" is really
his mother. She pretends to feel sorry for him as she
torments him, telling him the whole village knows about
the deception.

Mr. Walker is the embodiment of Terry's dream. He
is a well-mannered, affectionate man, drives a big car,
and dresses like a gentleman. During the trip to the
seaside he asks Terry if he would like him for a father.
When Terry reveals that his mother has already told him
about the marriage, Mr. Walker angrily accuses her of
giving him false hopes. Mr. Walker tells Terry more
about England, and on the way home carries him in his
arms. The physical contact makes Terry realize even
more keenly what has been lacking in his life, and when
Mr. Walker is about to leave, he screams hysterically
that he wants to stay with him. Even after one day,
Terry trusts Mr. Walker more than his mother, because
she has lied to him and has failed to acknowledge that
he is her child.

After this scene Terry's loneliness is overwhelming. The description of him waiting for Mr. Walker and
his mother every Sunday captures the terrible sadness
of the situation. Each week, regardless of the weather,
he walks down to the main road.

> In case there might be any danger of having
> to leave them behind, Terry brought his
> bucket and spade as well. You never knew

> when you'd need things like those. . . .
> Sometimes a gray car like Mr. Walker's
> appeared from round the corner and he
> waddled up the road towards it, but the
> driver's face was always a disappointment.[67]

In this passage the point of view is Terry's, but the
underlying perspective is much more comprehensive.

Once again Florrie is the vehicle of truth and
tells him his mother and Mr. Walker are not coming back.
Since she understands what the loss means to him, she
is more sympathetic than she was before. At the end
there is an effective broadening of viewpoint; it
shifts first to Florrie and then to the adult narrator,
who draws away from his characters. His brief revelation of himself as a solitary, compassionate observer,
watching the children fall asleep, extends the mood of
helpless desolation.

> She put her arms about him and he
> fell asleep, but she remained solemnly
> holding him, looking at him with detached
> and curious eyes. He was hers at last.
> There were no more rivals. She fell
> asleep too and did not notice the evening
> train go up the valley. It was all lit
> up. The evenings were drawing in.[68]

The distant, lighted train seems to carry the children's
hopes away with it, as they remain alone in the oppressive darkness.

O'Connor's first person child narrator has several
characteristics that distinguish him from other O'Connor
narrators. He is not a cautious observer, like most of
the adult narrators, but an enthusiastic, imaginative
adventurer. In most of these stories, he forms some
ideal scheme of life, which he tests by attempting to
impose it on the real world, usually a dismal, impoverished environment. The imaginative improvisation provides a possible escape from confining circumstances,
but usually reality reasserts itself at the end. The
clash between imagination and reality often helps the
child to mature.

Many writers have used a sensitive first person
narrator who describes his own childhood experiences,
but O'Connor's child narrator is probably most directly
influenced by Joyce. In Dubliners, Joyce uses a sensitive, self-conscious first person narrator in the

stories of childhood, and then shifts to third person
for his stories of adolescents and adults, as O'Connor
does. Joyce's child narrators also follow the pattern
of testing an ideal scheme of life against a dismal reality.

O'Connor's child narrator allows him to deal with
personal conflicts that are too threatening on an adult
level, such as guilt over betrayal of a trust. Some of
the stories are more humorous than others, but all of
them have an undertone of pain. Distance and objectivity are achieved by using a kind of double perspective,
that of an adult recreating a child's point of view,
telling of long-past events. Painful incidents from
O'Connor's past are transformed through the lively,
spontaneous, and innocent vision of the child. The narrator has a good dramatic sense and knows how to make
himself attractive to his audience. Through the child
O'Connor appears to be seeking a kind of exorcism and
renewal, a relationship with his readers based on innocent delight in life and spontaneous intimacy.

The child narrator first came into being during the
writing of O'Connor's much-anthologized story "First
Confession." (He is called Jackie in this story, not
Larry as in subsequent ones.) The first version, published in a magazine in 1935, was written in the third
person and covered a time period of several months.
O'Connor said in a radio lecture that he felt dissatisfied with the story, even after revising it and compres-
sing the time element. It was not until he changed the
narrative from third to first person that he felt it
was right. He asserted that the choice between first
and third person is "one of the most dangerous choices"
a writer has to make. "By using the first person, you
can get effects of depth that cannot be got by any
other means, but in doing so, you sacrifice any objective treatment of any character other than that of the
narrator's, you sacrifice a mass of incident which may
be of great significance."[69] Though O'Connor usually
prefers a more objective approach, stories like "First
Confession" must be in the first person because their
real subject is a subjective one--the reaction of a creative and impressionable mind to the external world,
reduced to the microcosm of childhood.

Some of the first person childhood stories end with
a painful discovery or recognition--"The Thief" and "The
Pretender," for example. The pattern in many others is
the restoration of a potentially abnormal and damaging
situation to normalcy through humor, natural affection,

and common sense. In "First Confession," Jackie's guilt
over his fantasy of murdering his grandmother and his
terror of the confessional, instilled by his religious
training, are relieved by a kind and sensible priest.
In "The Idealist," Larry retreats from his attempt to
live up to the high, idealized ethical standards he has
absorbed from reading English school stories, and he
accepts his classmates' more realistic values of evasion
and accommodation.

One of the best-known stories about a restoration
to normalcy is "My Oedipus Complex," from Stories. Larry is younger, more precocious and imaginative than in
the earlier Larry Delaney stories. Ironically, his
life is very peaceful while his father is away in the
war. He adores his mother, and every morning climbs
into bed with her and contentedly tells her his plans
for the day. But his father's return home brings turmoil into his serene world. The man, who until now has
been an imaginary, almost mythical "Santa Claus" figure,
seems as huge, remote, and invulnerable as a mountain.
Larry is disturbed but does not recognize the full
extent of his danger until the next morning, when he
climbs into bed with his parents and his mother tells
him to be quiet. The first time he reacts with surprised indignation, but the second morning he wakes his
father out of spite and creates an uproar in a desperate
attempt to preserve his intimacy with his mother. He
and his father scream at each other, and the scene
serves to bring the father down to Larry's level, making
him seem more real and familiar. Gradually Larry realizes that his father has some hold over his mother that
he lacks, and that it has something to do with "sleeping
together." The arrival of his baby brother Sonny produces a new crisis, because the baby claims most of his
mother's attention. One morning Larry wakes up and discovers that his father has climbed into bed with him to
escape the baby's crying. They are brought together by
their mutual feeling of neglect; this new intimacy
restores to normal proportions Larry's former intimacy
with his mother, his "Oedipus complex."

The adult's point of view underlies the child's.
We know from the beginning that he is speaking long
after the events. The gap between the child's and the
adult's perspective provides detachment and humor. The
tone recaptures the spontaneity of the child's vision.
His emotions do not become mechanical or jaded, and his
engaging optimism renews itself each morning. "I always
woke with the first light and, with all the responsibilities of the previous day melted, feeling myself rather

like the sun, ready to illumine and rejoice."[70] He is
intensely curious and observant, and nothing is lost on
him. Even after his father's return, when he is experiencing anger and jealousy for the first time, he
retains his innocent and creative response to life.

The resolution of this story is characteristic of
O'Connor's artistic vision in the middle phase of his
career. The psychological abnormality implied in the
title is reduced to a normal process of growth, delayed
somewhat by the father's long absence. The abnormal
personal experience from which the story is drawn is
also normalized; instead of describing an only child who
worships his mother and hates his alcoholic and unreliable father, as was the case in O'Connor's own childhood, he describes a boy who gains a baby brother and
establishes a loving, balanced relationship with both
his parents. O'Connor at this period is interested
mainly in ordinary human experience, domestic and
social, and the characters' efforts to develop healthy
vital instincts within the bounds of sensible and decent
social and familial relationships. Excessive indulgence
of instinct and excessive social repression are both
regarded as detrimental. His "happy" endings usually
involve affectionate reconciliation, a harmonious reintegration into the family or social group; his "unhappy"
endings often involve the painful loneliness and remorse
that follow an act of betrayal or rejection.

O'Connor's love stories of this period are also
concerned with the characters' efforts to establish normal, fulfilling relationships. Many of the stories
satirize Irish social and religious attitudes that stifle or pervert the expression of love. The instinctive,
physical side of love--sex and childbirth--is treated
more explicitly. Characters are given more freedom.
Many indulge in irresponsible sexual escapades but with
a few exceptions, as in "Don Juan (Retired)" and "Don
Juan's Temptation," O'Connor prefers to have his characters establish lasting relationships and be reconciled
with the community through marriage; the escapade is a
temporary means of liberation from excessively inhibi-
ting circumstances. Sometimes the couple cannot achieve
reconciliation with the community, because of a previous
divorce or some other reason, and they must escape to
England.

During this period O'Connor's attacks on Irish
Catholicism become more caustic and direct. Two of the
best satiric stories emphasizing the conflict between
sexual needs and religion are "The Custom of the

Country" and "The Holy Door." Both describe love relationships that end happily after a long ordeal of conflicts and misunderstandings. (It should be noted that during the period of his severest attacks on the Irish Church, O'Connor also wrote several stories about characters who find happiness by conversion or reconversion to Catholicism--"The Miracle," "This Mortal Coil," and "My First Protestant." These stories are probably attempts to restore balance, and they express his need for reconciliation with the religion that he never completely denied.)

In "The Custom of the Country," Anna Martin, daughter of a widow who keeps a small shop in an Irish town, falls in love with Ernest Thompson, an Englishman working in her town. They decide to marry, but Anna's mother, who is snobbish, pious, and malicious, will not allow the marriage to take place unless Ernest becomes a Catholic. After a catastrophic encounter with the local nuns, he does become converted, but as he and Anna are crossing on the boat to England, he tells her he is married already and has two children. She returns home indignantly, but discovers she is pregnant. Her mother and the neighbors adopt a gloomy, unforgiving moral tone and make her life so unbearable that she decides to reject her upbringing and goes to live with Ernest in England. O'Connor's humor takes on the sharpness of satire as he exposes the narrowness and meanness of small Irish towns. The device of the objective outsider is used effectively; Ernest's liberal English attitudes imply a judgment on Irish attitudes.

The story was considerably revised for publication in Collection Two. One change is a strengthening of the narrative voice, similar to the revision in several earlier stories. The opening paragraph in the second version is a kind of homely philosophic commentary suggesting a general thematic context for the story. "It is remarkable the difference that even one foreigner can make in a community when he is not yet accustomed to its ways, the way he can isolate its customs and hold them up for your inspection."71 As the plot unfolds we are caught up in events and become less aware of the narrator as a separate entity, but he intrudes his wisdom again in the final paragraph, thus completing the narrative frame. He approves of Anna's decision to go to England, saying, "Once those foreign notions have found their way into your mind, it is impossible ever to expel them entirely afterwards." As we have seen elsewhere, this type of narrator provides O'Connor with a spokesman who is both inside and outside

283

the story. He is the "lonely human voice" who speaks
for the submerged population, articulating perceptions
that they cannot articulate for themselves. The caution
and restraint of his tone, and the limitations of his
outlook, also provide an objective control for the
author's emotions.

The other revisions are mostly stylistic ones,
improving the clarity and humor of the narrative. One
good example is a passage characterizing Mrs. Martin,
Anna's mother. The early version reads: "She was a
nice, well-preserved, well-spoken little roly-poly of a
woman who sat for the greater part of the day in the
kitchen behind the shop, very erect in her high-backed
chair, her hands joined in her lap, while she thought
of the past glories of her family."[72] The second version retains most of the content of the first while
expanding and improving the satiric touches: "She was
a nice, well-preserved, well-spoken little roly-poly of
a woman with bad feet which gave her a waddle, and
piles, which made her sit on a high hard chair, and she
sat for the greater part of the day in the kitchen
behind the shop with her hands joined in her lap and an
air of regret for putting the world to the trouble of
knowing her, though all the time she was thinking com-
placently of the past glories of her family, the
Henebry-Hayeses of Coolnaleama."[73] This method of characterization is typical of O'Connor's satiric stories.
Mrs. Martin is described as she appears in a habitual
pose, sitting in her chair thinking of her family's
superiority. The revisions bring out her deviousness
and make her physical appearance more concrete. She is
basically a peasant woman trying to live above herself.
The caricature is harsher than in "The House That Johnny
Built," but still not severe enough to obliterate the
realistic human quality. O'Connor allows his readers
to respond to his characters on their own terms.

Mr. Martin and her neighbors represent the oppressive community standards that Anna must escape from.
Mrs. Martin is in a perpetual competition with the Maho-
neys, two spinster sisters who are also snobbish about
their family's superiority. Either family's disgrace
is regarded with glee by its rivals. Mrs. Martin's
snobbery also extends to her religious views, and she
will not have anything to do with Protestants. She
accepts Ernest because he is not Irish, but she takes
it for granted that he must be converted if he is going
to marry Anna.

Anna's decision to leave home is an act of emotional

liberation resulting from desperation. She has absorbed most of her mother's values; she is a pious, innocent girl and tells Ernest it would be a sin to have sexual relations before marriage. His more liberal values deeply shock her at first. But gradually his attitudes give her a larger perspective from which to view her upbringing. She is able to see through her mother's snobbishness, and realizes that she is being victimized by the competition between her mother and the neighbors. Her pregnancy resulted not from an irresponsible affair but from genuine love. Her instincts overcome her judgment, and she knows she must live with Ernest. In this story escape to England is a more obvious and clear-cut solution than in many O'Connor stories.

"The Holy Door" is one of O'Connor's longest stories, a masterpiece of the nouvelle form. It consists mostly of dramatized scenes, with O'Connor's typically colorful and lively dialogue, connected by brief descriptive and explanatory passages. His nouvelles are more compressed, economical, and dramatic than O'Faolain's tales.

"The Holy Door" belongs to a group of interconnected stories set in the same Irish country town, where Fr. Ring is the parish priest. The stories were not published in a single volume, like Dubliners or Anderson's Winesburg, Ohio, but were scattered among three collections ("The Miser," "The New Teacher," and "The House That Johnny Built" in Crab Apple Jelly, "The Miracle," "The Holy Door," and "A Thing of Nothing" in The Common Chord, and "The Masculine Principle" in Traveller's Samples.) Other characters besides Fr. Ring are referred to in more than one story, like Johnny Desmond and Frank Carmady. This group of stories, together with the group of Larry Delaney stories and the group about Fr. Fogarty and Fr. Devine, suggest that O'Connor may have been searching for a broader scope than a single story could provide. Some of his characters and settings were such rich mines of material that he could not exhaust all their possibilities in one story, yet he did not develop them into a novel or even into a unified collection of stories. His vision remained essentially fragmented and diversified. Even the same character is not always consistent from one story to another. Fr. Ring is a shrewd and greedy materialist in "The Miser" and "The Masculine Principle," but in "The Holy Door" he plays a more constructive role.

The complex plot of "The Holy Door" touches on almost every aspect of the conflict between sex and religion in Ireland--inhibition, frigidity, superstition, public gossip, infidelity, and illegitimacy. Nora Lawlor and Polly Donegan are two friends who have lived in the same town all their lives. Both are fastidious, naive, and pious, but Nora has a natural liveliness and curiosity, particularly about the facts of life, which Polly lacks. Charlie Cashman, owner of the hardware store, falls in love with Nora, but she will not encourage him because his hairyness repels her. Charlie is a romantic, looking for something "larger than life"; his ideal of love is formed from Romeo and Juliet. He marries Polly when Nora rejects him, but the marriage is unhappy from the beginning. Polly, cold and strong-willed, feels no sexual attraction to her husband and instead, aided by his malicious mother, uses her piety as a weapon to dominate him. Nora is still unconsciously attracted to Charlie and interferes continually between him and his wife.

Disturbed by their failure to have children, Polly and Charlie decide, at Nora's suggestion, to make a pilgrimage to the Holy Door in Rome, which is supposed to promote fertility. Polly still fails to conceive, however, and (again at Nora's instigation) she asks Fr. Ring if it is all right to pretend that when Charlie is making love to her, he is really Mr. Carmady, a teacher who she thinks is more attractive. When Charlie finds out what has happened and that Nora has gossiped about it in public, he feels like the laughing-stock of the town. To prove his virility he has an affair with the maid and gets her pregnant, but this makes his position even more painful and absurd. Fr. Ring prevents Polly from walking out on Charlie, but she insists on having a separate bedroom with a huge bolt on the door. They both go into a decline and eventually Polly contracts a serious illness and dies. After some more doubts and misunderstandings, and with some prompting from Fr. Ring, Charlie's romantic love for Nora surfaces, and his passion makes her realize finally that she loves him too.

The original version of the story contains some lapses of style and tone, but the revised version in Stories is a masterful and mature rendering of O'Connor's satiric method. The dry, humorous, casual narrative voice functions as it does in other stories, giving compression and coherence to the elaborate plot and acting as a restraint on the characters' emotional conflicts. The point of view changes several times, but it becomes centered on Charlie as he undergoes his difficult process of growth and self-discovery.

Throughout the story, O'Connor stresses the conflict between human needs and social and religious conventions. The satire is directed at the attitudes and
customs which obstruct the characters' search for fulfilling love. Characters who substitute orthodoxy for
human feeling, like Polly and Mrs. Cashman, are sharply
caricatured. For example, when Nora questions Polly
about her wedding night, Polly's sexual prudery makes
her appear wrinkled and prematurely aged. Mrs. Cashman,
a spiteful and malicious old woman, is portrayed even
more harshly, and towards the end, as the love between
Nora and Charlie strengthens, Charlie's mother becomes
more like an incongruous caricature or apparition. The
marvelous scene in which she tries to frighten Charlie
away from courting Nora by placing Polly's photograph
between two candles in a darkened room shows how Charlie
has matured, as he is able to confront her angrily and
banish the superstition she invokes.

Settings are sketched in with a minimum of detail,
but the details are carefully chosen to enhance the
satiric effect. The image of the "holy door" is played
on in several ways--literally, in the pilgrimage, figur-
atively in the bolted door to Polly's bedroom and in
the sexual rejection and barrenness which the closed
door implies. The large number of holy pictures Polly
has on her walls, the holy statues, and the Lourdes
clock on the mantelpiece also image her excessive and
prudish piety. Her habit of sitting alone in a dark
room suggests the emptiness of her life.

The affirmative and joyous mood with which the
story ends results from the triumph of Charlie's and
Nora's romantic dream over the many formidable obstacles
that threatened to destroy it. The dream is not an
aberrant fantasy, but an expression of a genuine need,
and as Fr. Ring's approval suggests, it is grounded in
reality and common sense. Instinct and judgment are
balanced. Charlie's marriage with Nora does not require
him to escape from the town, but enables him to be reconciled with it, to keep his hardware business and
restore his position as a respected citizen. Because
of O'Connor's concern with the human need for a secure
home and supportive relationships with the family and
community, there is usually a greater sense of affirma-
tion in the stories about couples who find happiness in
Ireland than in those about couples forced into exile.

Other love stories of this period usually present
variations on the themes we have analysed in "The Custom
of the Country" and "The Holy Door." In some of them

O'Connor's emotions are not controlled sufficiently, and the result is excessive anger or melodrama. "A Thing of Nothing," "Friends of the Family," and "The Lady of the Sagas" are relatively unsuccessful stories about sexual attitudes in Irish towns. In some stories, like "Jerome" and "Darcy in the Land of Youth," O'Connor describes working-class Irishmen living in England, and contrasts Irish sexual inhibition with more liberal English standards, as he does in "The Custom of the Country."

Two of the better love stories in Traveller's Samples, "Legal Aid" and "The Masculine Principle," explore the relationship between love and materialism in Irish culture. This subject was treated in earlier stories like "The House That Johnny Built," but here the emphasis is changed somewhat. Instead of regarding materialism as an inadequate substitute for passion, O'Connor seems to regard it as a healthy counterbalance to promiscuity or excessive romanticism. "Legal Aid," a funny satire on traditional Irish marriage customs, describes the collusion of two lawyers to bring about the marriage of a young couple who have had an illegitimate baby. The boy's family opposes the marriage because the girl belongs to a lower social class, but when she receives a large sum in an out-of-court settlement, the boy's parents agree to the marriage to keep the money in the family. In "The Masculine Principle," a young man refuses to marry his girl until he has saved enough money for a down payment on a house. One day after a quarrel she steals his money and absconds to England, where she gets involved in a sordid love affair. When she returns home she and her former beau resume their relationship, but even after they have a child he refuses to marry her until he has enough savings. Finally after several years, while the baby has been in a foster home in the country and the girl has despaired of marrying anyone, her beau reaches his goal and triumphantly announces that they can marry, bring the child home, and regain their respectability in the town. The story is an atypical one, since it runs counter to O'Connor's usual preference for instinct over judgment, and since his apparent approval of the young man's "masculine" behavior seems inconsistent with his concern for the plight of illegitimate children separated from their parents.

O'Connor wrote prolifically during the last period of his life, producing several volumes of stories as well as major critical works, autobiographies, and other writings. It is difficult to trace chronological development clearly in the late stories, because of his habit of revising earlier work extensively and also because of his premature death, which left a large number of stories that had been published in magazines but not arranged into book collections. More Stories (1954), containing about half new stories and half taken from earlier collections, was published in the United States but not in England, because O'Connor was dissatisfied with it. Collection Two (1964) is the revised version of More Stories, published only in England. It contains many of the same stories, but some of the poorer ones have been dropped and some new ones added. Domestic Relations (1957) contains all new stories. Previously uncollected stories, mostly from the fifties and sixties, were collected posthumously in 1969 by O'Connor's wife and editors in A Set of Variations (United States) and Collection Three (England). The contents and arrangement of the two volumes are somewhat different.

The two volumes that are the most successful as collected editions are Stories and Collection Two. In these volumes O'Connor achieves what he calls an "ideal ambience" in the arrangement of stories.[74] His concept of a mosaic-like unity is less coherent and definite than the unity of theme and setting found in The Untilled Field, Dubliners, and Hillsiders, the unity of subject and situation in The Hounds of Banba and Midsummer Night Madness, or even the more general thematic unity of I Remember! I Remember! or The Heat of the Sun. Nevertheless, the fact that O'Connor did try to achieve at least an atmospheric unity in his collections is additional evidence that he, like O'Faolain and some earlier writers, sometimes found the short story form too confining and limited in scope.

In general the late stories do not measure up to the quality of O'Connor's earlier work, but they do reveal continuing growth and exploration of new subject matter, and a few of them can be included among his best achievements. There are several parallels with O'Faolain's late stories. O'Connor's stories become increasingly detached from the circumstances of Irish life, more personal and individualized. The perspective becomes more international as more stories are set in England, though he does not use the European settings that O'Faolain uses. O'Connor probes areas of abnormal psychology that he previously avoided--insanity and even suicide among the clergy, sexual aberration, neurotic morbidity and escapism. A larger proportion of stories are about death. Another parallel with O'Faolain is that some of the lighter stories contain a wise, serene humor that is not satirical but conveys tolerant amusement at the foibles and vanities of the human race. O'Connor's late stories are considerably shorter and more economical than O'Faolain's, however.

The weaknesses in these stories include some awkward, unconvincing plots, excessive or maudlin sentimentality, and a compulsion to explain and justify points which the reader could infer for himself. Some stories represent enervated variations on character types or situations that O'Connor had used earlier with greater intensity and impact. Richard Thompson comments that the later stories "begin to grow formulaic. . . . These stories often retreat from the horror and absurdity of life that one finds in his most mature stories and substitute instead puckish charm, mannered humor, quaint local color, predictable warmth, and general blandness."[75] Although Thompson's sweeping dismissal of all O'Connor's stories after The Common Chord is unjustified, his remarks can be justly applied to at least some of the stories.

In the stories of religious life, the clergy are usually presented more compassionately than they were earlier. Fr. Fogarty replaces Fr. Ring as the most frequently portrayed priest. There is a considerable variety of clergymen in situations ranging from comic to bleakly pathetic. The most light-hearted clerical stories are the three about Dr. Gallogly, the elderly Bishop of Moyle. The refreshing charm and humor of these stories has its source in the Bishop's spirited, inquisitive, and childlike character, and his outbreaks of irrational, unepiscopal behavior. "The Old Faith" describes a dinner party at the bishop's home attended by several priests familiar to us from other stories. After a conversation about the old ways, especially the people's belief in fairies and spells, the priests drink some poteen confiscated from a parishioner that afternoon. Their collapse into various undignified postures on the Bishop's lawn is one of O'Connor's funniest slapstick scenes. In "Vanity," the Bishop breaks some bones in a fall while visiting Dublin. He stays in the hospital under an assumed name, has some eye-opening adventures, and cures himself in record time despite the doctor's gloomy prognosis, because he fears that word of his accident will leak out and he will be forced into retirement. A conflict between the Bishop and his housekeeper, Nellie, is the subject of "Achilles Heel." Because Nellie has made the Bishop so dependent on her cooking, she has considerable power in the diocese, and he finds it impossible to cope with her when he learns she has been running a smuggling operation from the episcopal palace for years.

At the opposite pole from the Bishop of Moyle stories are the stories about insanity and death among the clergy. Insanity is a subject which O'Connor prefers not to probe subjectively. He deals with it instead through indirection, with objectivity and restraint. Mentally disturbed characters are almost always viewed through the eyes of someone who is relatively sane and normal--either the narrator or another character in the story. In "The Corkerys," a young woman enters a convent for the wrong reasons, and after suffering a nervous breakdown realizes that she is better suited to marriage than to a religious vocation. "An Act of Charity" is one of O'Connor's bleakest stories. It describes the grimly efficient "cover-up" that takes place after the suicide of a young priest, to prevent the distressful scandal that would follow an action so unthinkable in Irish society. Fr. Galvin, the suicide, is the second curate in a parish where Fr. Fogarty is the first curate and Fr. Maginnis the parish priest. Maginnis, an urbane "old pro," persecutes the socially inept and painfully self-conscious Galvin. Before the suicide Fogarty admires Maginnis and enjoys "the feeling Maginnis gave him of belonging to a group, and that of the best kind--well balanced, humane, and necessary."[76] But the "group" can be very cruel to those who do not fit in. When Maginnis responds hardly at all to the human tragedy of the suicide and instead skillfully engineers a campaign of secrecy, Fogarty begins to have doubts. To spare Galvin's family and to protect the Church's image, Maginnis has denied his curate's human worth and has obliterated his last desperate act of communication. His denial of faith goes almost unheard. Fogarty's sense of belonging to a group is voided and he is left pondering the awful loneliness of the priest's life.

Insanity in the clergy is also treated in the intriguing story "Lost Fatherlands." It portrays a monk who is leaving his monastery after fifteen years because he has periodic bouts of insanity and cannot stand the rigors of monastic life. He is introduced not in the monastic setting, through the eyes of the other monks, but through the eyes of some townspeople as he is leaving to catch a train on his way to Canada. Spike Ward, a local taxi driver, picks him up at the monastery and leaves him at the railroad station after a stop at a pub. The local people do not even know who he is at first, since all kinds of people enter and leave the monastery--drunks needing a cure, novices who change their minds, and other temporary visitors. Through this choice of time and place, O'Connor lets us see the monk as an ordinary, vulnerable man in a moment of transition, when the religious context of his life has been left behind.

After a day or so Spike finds out from the station-master that the man did not take the train. Spike and two other men, Hanagan the publican and Linehan the policeman, drive up to the monastery, which is located on a mountainside. It is ironic that the monks are singing about resurrection and eternal life when one of their members is in a state of despair. Spike and the others find out that the man is a former monk, subject to mental lapses, and has been seen wandering around in the hills near the monastery, staring at the monks as they work. They also find out that he is going to Canada because it would create too much scandal if he settled down at his home in Kilkenny, where he would like to return. The personal tragedy is thus heightened by Irish intolerance. Spike and his friends find the monk on the mountain in a state of shock and take him to a hotel in town. Although they try to persuade him to rest for a couple of days, he insists on leaving town on the next train. The landscape--the bare mountain, the misty rain, the darkening night--creates a setting more overtly symbolic than most of O'Connor's settings. The description of the monk's exposure to the weather implies his inner desolation and bewilderment: "The rain seemed to have caught him somewhere on top of a peak, and he was running, looking for shelter, from rock to rock."[77]

Hanagan, the publican, is a counterpart to the monk. The theme of "lost fatherlands" is developed in relation to both men. Hanagan spent eighteen years in Boston earning the money to return and open a pub in Ireland, but since his return he has constantly com-plained about Ireland and praised America. During the first conversation in the pub, when the monk, as yet unidentified, is waiting for his train, Spike talks about the hardships of life in the monastery, and Hana-gan argues that his life is harder. He criticizes the monks for living in a way that no one asked them to, instead of doing something socially useful, and the monk retorts, "Are people to sit down and wait for someone to ask them to love God?" The remark suggests to the reader that the monk's vocation originated in a strong faith which has since weakened or grown confused.

When the men are searching for the monk on the mountainside, it is Hanagan who shows the most sympathy for him. As they are drying him off in the pub, the monk says he must get away quickly so that he will not be tempted to return to the monastery again. Hanagan sees a parallel in his own longing to return to Ireland during his years in America. Both men are torn by their persistent attachment to a place and way of life that has disillusioned them.

The final resolution is brought about by an effective shift in narrative viewpoint. Most of the story has been told from the viewpoint of Spike, who takes things at surface value and has little perception of the characters' inner feelings. But in the final paragraph, describing the departure, O'Connor speaks as an omniscient narrator who can understand the deeper relationship between Hanagan and the monk.

> Spike could see that [Hanagan] was deeply
> moved, but what it was all about was beyond
> him. Spike had never stood on the deck
> of a liner and watched his fatherland
> drop away behind him. He didn't know the
> sort of hurt it can leave in a boy's mind,
> a hurt that doesn't heal even when you try
> to conjure away the pain by returning.
> Nor did he realize, as Hanagan did at
> that moment, that there are other father-
> lands, whose loss can hurt even more deeply.[78]

The narrator in this passage speaks not only for Hanagan and the monk but also for the author. "Lost Father-lands" contains a typical dilemma of O'Connor's characters, the dilemma that has already been examined in "Uprooted": finding their "fatherland"--the set of physical, psychological, and spiritual conditions that supported them from birth--in some way inadequate, they attempt to escape to a freer, more fulfilling life. But the sense of loss and alienation which they experience in breaking away puts them in a perpetual limbo. Experience and maturity do not compensate for lost innocence, and neither a return to the old life nor an acceptance of the new can provide fulfillment. In stories like

"Uprooted" and "Lost Fatherlands" O'Connor articulates
in his own way the Irish dilemma that was first expressed in short story form by George Moore in "Home
Sickness."

The subject of death recurs in several late stories
about clergy, and Fr. Fogarty appears in all of these.
It is tempting to speculate about the personal significance of these stories for O'Connor and his attraction
to the character of Fogarty; perhaps through Fogarty
O'Connor expressed his need for reconciliation with the
Church, as his own death approached. Fogarty possesses
the instinctive qualities O'Connor admired--warmth, compassion, impulsiveness--while remaining within the
limits set by the Church. His actions never violate
his religious faith. Fogarty interests O'Connor also
because his large humanity makes him even more vulnerable to loneliness than most clergy, and he is acutely
aware of what he is missing. "The Teacher's Mass" portrays Fogarty's difficult relationship with his acolyte,
a retired teacher, who dies during Mass. "The Wreath,"
which describes the funeral of Fr. Devine, is a
restrained and tactful treatment of the temptations of
celibacy. Fogarty attends the funeral and burial with
an acquaintance, Fr. Jackson. A wreath of red roses
sent by an unknown woman causes much gossip and agitation among Devine's mourners. Fogarty does not like
Jackson at first, but as they work together to prevent
the removal of the wreath, they become friends. During
the long drive from the church to the cemetery, they
speculate about Devine's involvement with a woman and
trade confessions about their own temptations. By the
end of the story the wreath has become a symbol not
only of "the essential mystery of a priest's life," but
also of human love, "between son and mother, man and
sweetheart, friend and friend."[79] The wreath seems not
to violate Devine's priestly role but to enlarge its
meaning. O'Connor's final tribute to Fogarty is his
rendering of the priest's own romantic and unconventional funeral in "The Mass Island."

The stories of childhood in O'Connor's late work
are mostly Larry Delaney stories, all in Domestic Relations. (A different child persona, Denis Halligan,
appears in three stories--"Masculine Protest," "Pity,"
and "A Minority.") These stories represent Larry at
different ages, from early childhood through adolescence. Their plots are based on his curiosity about
sex or his daydreams about girls. "The Genius" and "The
Study of History" describe his interest as a small boy
in the facts of life and his own conception. In "The

Man of the World," a friend's invitation to spy on a married couple through their bedroom window results in Larry's ashamed recognition that he has violated something sacred and private. "The Duke's Children" and "Daydreams" both portray Larry's adolescent fantasies about adopting a new, more exalted identity that will attract women to him. The treatment seems more autobiographical than in the earlier Larry Delaney stories; Larry is even more imaginative and precocious than he was earlier, and is also more aware of being different from the people around him. He is an only child and in other ways bears a very close resemblance to the author. The narrative is more self-conscious and at times a note of self-pity intrudes. This emphasis on the child's acceptance of his differences from others rather than on the restoration of healthy normalcy, as in "First Confession" and "My Oedipus Complex," is consistent with much of O'Connor's late work.

These stories lack the intensity and drama of O'Connor's best stories, but they are interesting because they deal so directly with autobiographical material and personal conflicts. By reducing these conflicts to the level of a child O'Connor makes them more manageable and less threatening. A good example of his scaling down of subjective conflicts found in the adult sensibility is "The Study of History." Larry in this story loves to indulge in theoretical speculation, especially about sex and heredity, and wonders what his life would have been like if his parents had married different people. His speculations provide an escape into an imaginary life of wealth and status. He goes to visit one of his father's former sweethearts, Mrs. O'Brien, and imagines himself as a member of her noisy and common family, but when he returns home he sees that his mother is jealous and hurt by what he has done. That night he speculates further about life in the O'Brien family. He is alone with the infinite possibilities he has uncovered, and becomes panicky when he tries and fails to regain his former sense of identity. He does not calm down until his mother comes into his room and holds his hand. The physical contact soothes him and restores his sense of security.

The story is a symbolic exploration of the problem of identity. The child's development as a genius depends on the continual imaginative exploration of new possibilities, but this is accompanied by fear of the unknown. From the beginning it is clear that he is exploring an interior, mental world. His discovery of how babies get born gives him a different view of his parents.

> Up to this, they had been principles,
> not characters, like a chain of mountains
> guarding a green horizon. Suddenly a
> little shaft of light, emerging from behind
> a cloud, struck them, and the whole mass
> broke up into peaks, valleys, and foot-
> hills; you could even see whitewashed farm-
> houses and fields where people worked
> in the evening light, a whole world of
> interior perspective.[80]

The landscape metaphor is odd, but appropriate in this
context. It relates Larry's feeling for his parents to
the feeling he gets from contemplating a hilly landscape. Both the parents and the landscape provide
security and protection, but the "little shaft of light"
reveals that the parents and mountains are more complex
and less formidable than Larry has supposed.

After he has completed his exploration of alternative identities, Larry finds that he has ventured too
far into the unknown. He tries to soothe himself by
reciting known facts about himself, but even these
familiar facts seem distant and unreal to him. "It was
as though my own identity was a sort of sack I had to
live in, and I had deliberately worked my way out of it,
and now I couldn't get back again because I had grown
too big for it. . . . I was away in the middle of empty
space, divorced from mother and home and everything permanent and familiar."[81] When his mother holds his hand
he regains his sense of self and leaves "infinity and
all its anguish behind." He tells his mother he never
wanted anyone but her.

In "The Study of History," O'Connor is describing
the power of his imagination to carry him too far out
of himself. His identity depends on maintaining close
relationships with the people he loves. The mood of the
story is similar to the mood of Pascal's saying, already
quoted: "The eternal silence of those infinite spaces
terrifies me." For O'Connor the universe often seems
vast, alien, and empty, and the only security and peace
possible for man results from close emotional and physical contact with other people. Only through people can
man have any knowledge of God. Too persistent efforts
at escape from the familiar may result in terror and
disintegration. In particular, this story reflects
O'Connor's dread of hurting or displeasing his mother.
His relationship with her provided one of the main

sources of continuity in his life. He makes an analogy between his feeling for her and his need for an external anchor for his imagination. Many earlier stories also reflect his special relationship with his mother and his dread of betraying her--"Judas," "The Man of the House," "The Drunkard," "The Thief"--but none of these has the metaphysical dimension found in "The Study of History."

Several other late stories deal with family life and parent-child relationships from an adult's view-point. These, too, are more personal and detached from social circumstances than earlier stories of family life. Some are set in England and the connections with Ireland are of secondary importance. There are several stories about the loneliness of widowed elderly people and their relationships with their adult children--"A Sense of Responsibility," "Lonely Rock," and "The Party." Several others concern fathers' difficulties with their role of fatherhood--"Fish for Friday," a comic treatment about a father's boredom with child-birth, "Father and Son," about a father's efforts to cope with his son's unhappiness over the father's divorce and remarriage, "The Weeping Children," about a husband's reaction to the discovery that his wife has an illegitimate child living in a foster home, and "An Out-and-Out Free Gift," about a father's confrontation of his rebellious and insolent son.

A very unusual family is the subject of "A Set of Variations," one of the best late stories. It is a nouvelle set in Cork. Kate Mahoney, a sixty-year-old woman who has already raised two daughters, takes in a foster child, Jimmy, after her husband's death so that she will not have to give up her house. Later she takes in a second foster son, coincidentally and inconven-iently named James. Her daughters, respectable middle-class Irish Catholics, oppose their mother's action, but she is fiercely independent, and her daughters and the neighbors tolerate the children for her sake. The boys have opposite temperaments--Jimmy is wild and demonstrative, James quiet and reserved. As Jimmy grows up he wants to know more about his background, but after spending time with both his natural parents realizes he is happier with Kate. She raises both boys well; she is honest and open with them, and teaches them to respect themselves. On her deathbed she reveals that she loved her second family even more than her first, probably because of the obstacles she had to overcome to raise them and because the foster children allowed her to assert her independence in old age.

In "A Set of Variations," O'Connor has taken several of the ingredients characteristic of his middle period--social intolerance of illegitimacy, illegitimate children farmed out to foster homes, children pursuing dreams of normal family life--and has combined them into a celebration of the power of imagination and love to transform an unpromising reality. As in many late stories the unconventional, socially misunderstood solution proves more satisfactory than the conventional one. The narrator tells us that at Kate's wake, everyone wonders enviously, "How could a woman who was already old take the things the world had thrown away and out of them fashion a new family, dearer to her than the old and finer than any she had known."[82] She is one of the dreamy romantics who make up the submerged population of Ireland. James Matthews comments, "Kate and the boys are outcasts, lonely people forced to live at the fringe of society and to adopt radically creative measures to cope with existence. . . . What is real, in the end, is not the normal, the logical, or the predictable, but the imaginative improvisation."[83]

The "imaginative improvisation" is prominent also in the largest group of late stories, the stories of love and marriage. Characters who cannot or will not follow the normal pattern of courtship and marriage seek alternate routes to the fulfillment of their dreams. Their success or failure is often determined more by inner psychological factors than by social pressures and obstructions. There are a few comic or lightly satiric studies of love, such as "Counsel for Oedipus" and "A Salesman's Romance." The cautious or inhibited lover reappears in various forms. In "The Sorcerer's Apprentice," a woman chooses a divorced Englishman who is comfortable with sex over her long-time Irish beau, who feels guilty about it. In "A Bachelor's Story," a cautious bachelor falls in love for the first time, but loses the girl because he takes offense too easily.

Several stories describe unusual or "improvised" love relationships that succeed beyond expectation. Family circumstances are a factor in all of these. "Orphans" depicts a woman who must choose between a sensible marriage and a more improbable one with the brother of her former fiance, a soldier killed in the war. She chooses the brother because he has no family or home of his own and needs her more than her other suitor does. The lovers in "The Impossible Marriage" both live with possessive widowed mothers and feel they cannot marry until their mothers die. Eventually they do marry but continue living apart, since their mothers would not be compatible. The husband dies prematurely, cheating them of their future, but in the strange marriage they have achieved a kind of inner happiness that other people do not understand.

Heavy family responsibilities also affect a love relationship in "The Little Mother." It is a long, much-revised story about Joan Twomey, a girl in a Cork family who takes over the role of mother to her two younger sisters after her mother's death. She is not ready for such a heavy responsibility, and her own personality and sexual development are adversely affected. Her sisters become rebellious and wild. After several years of perpetual family crisis and scandal, the younger sisters are safely married in a double wedding, and Joan is free to marry Chris Dwyer, a young man who has also been burdened with family responsibilities. The night after her sisters' wedding she tells her father that she is pregnant; she has not been able to live up to her own prudish standards, and she and Chris have decided to live in Dublin to avoid disgrace.

In this story the conflict between instinct and judgment takes the form of conflict between Joan's feminine needs and her desire to preserve family respectability, as defined by local Catholic morality. O'Connor characterizes Joan as a humorous, dashing, and somewhat wild girl. She loses much of her girlish spontaneity, however, when she assumes her mother's role. She makes several serious mistakes in judgment, is alienated from and partly reconciled with her sisters, before eventually finding happiness with Chris. Because of the circumstances of her mother's death, she regards her new role almost as a mission or a religious dedication. Her father, a kind, emotional man with little sense of discipline, transfers part of his own responsibility to her. Her family role is closely associated with her religious conscience. Since she feels responsible for her sisters, she regards any sign of flighty behavior with disapproval. She treats them with a maddening, self-righteous politeness that makes them resentful and rebellious.

Joan's new responsibilities also cause her to break off with Dick Gordon, her steady beau for several years, because he is an atheist and does not believe in Catholic sins and virtues. But when Dick starts seeing Kitty, one of her sisters, she is deeply hurt. Her tender feminine instincts have been submerged by her censoriousness but have not disappeared. Her father

finally has to interfere and ask Dick to stop seeing
Kitty. Kitty is hurt in turn, and Dick loses both
girls because he has not adequately understood the family situation. Kitty gets a job in Dublin and leaves
home.

Joan has to rescue both her sisters from scrapes
they have gotten into because of their rebelliousness
against her. May, the youngest, has become involved
with Timmy McGovern, a married man. Joan confronts him
and threatens to expose him unless he leaves May alone.
When he reacts in a weak and cowardly way, however,
Joan is very upset. Her woman's instincts, in opposi-
tion to her conscience, expect Timmy to declare his
love for May in spite of all the obstacles. Later Kitty
meets a young student, Con Rahilly, in Dublin, and gets
pregnant. Joan insists that Con marry Kitty, even
though it means his mother will cut off his income and
he will have to leave school and get a job. This turns
out to be the best solution, since Con is too passive
to make the decision on his own.

During all the troubles with her sisters, Joan's
relationship with Chris Dwyer has been steadily developing. She confides all her worries to him, and he
responds by giving her advice and telling her about his
problems with his own family. They both realize that
their personalities and roles have been strongly affected by other members of the family. In a perfectly
natural way their intimacy leads to a sexual relationship which gives both of them a feeling of delighted
release. But when she too gets pregnant and tells her
father, Joan is overcome by shame and guilt at her own
hypocrisy. She wishes she and Chris could live in Cork
and take care of her father, but she realizes that the
local scandal would be too great. Like Kitty, she has
made a choice that requires her to leave home.

In "The Little Mother," the family situation is
complicated by the unusual circumstances of the mother's
death and the father's weakness of character. Joan's
concern with respectability and social acceptance is
more extreme than it would have been if she were not
forced prematurely into the mother's role. If their
mother had not died, all three girls would probably
have found husbands in a more conventional way, without
creating scandal. They could have settled down in Cork
near their parents. But the special circumstances make
the conventional way impossible, and they must improvise
their happiness.

Several other love stories portray neurotic, dissatisfied, self-lacerating women, of the type seen earlier in Rita of "The Mad Lomasneys" and Evelyn of "The
Masculine Principle." Their tendency to indulge in
idealized fantasy is unhealthy, as it prevents them
from living in the present and forming genuine, sensible
relationships. The idealism of these stories is not
innocent but morbid and escapist. The narrator's attitude to these characters is often ambiguous. In "Expectation of Life," a woman refuses to marry her steady
beau and marries an older man in poor health instead.
She keeps in touch with her former suitor and worries
about what she will do when her husband dies. He
thrives on the marriage but she cannot live in the present, and her fantasies make her more and more unhappy.
Ironically, it is she who dies first. The American
woman in "The American Wife" marries an Irishman but
cannot settle down in Ireland contentedly. She returns
to America to give birth to each of her children, and
eventually stays there. A more obviously pathological
situation occurs in "A Life of Your Own." A single
woman, the pharmacist in a small Irish town, lives
alone in a small cottage on the edge of town to preserve
her independence and privacy. She has had relationships
with men who are wrong for her, but has not committed
herself to marriage. This life style is regarded as
somewhat daring and unconventional by the townspeople.
Her home is invaded in her absence by an unknown, mentally disturbed man who is sexually attracted to her;
he steals her underwear and writes "I love you" with
lipstick on her wall. Her compassionate recognition of
his deep, twisted loneliness and need jolts her out of
herself, and she realizes that "she no longer had a
place of refuge from the outside world. She would never
be able to live alone again; never again would she have
a life of her own."84 In the twisted intruder she sees
her own neurotic isolation magnified, and must admit
her interdependence with other people. In some ways
the story is similar to "The Bridal Night," but it
lacks the innocent simplicity of the earlier story.
O'Connor is more willing to probe the subject of sexual
aberration realistically, instead of romanticizing it.

A woman who fears commitment to marriage is also
characterized in "The Ugly Duckling." This story
describes an unusual love relationship between two people who grew up together in Cork, Nan Ryan and Mick
Courtney. Nan is the "ugly duckling," an unattractive
tomboy transformed into a beautiful woman. She dates
several men before deciding to marry Mick. She persuades him to get a job in Dublin so they can both

301

escape the boredom and narrowness of Cork, but before
the wedding she tells him she is going to marry someone
else. Mick goes to Dublin anyway, marries and settles
down there. Many years later he learns that Nan has
gone into a convent instead of marrying the other man.
When he finally returns to Cork he goes to visit her
and realizes that she has found a kind of inner fulfillment she probably could not have found in marriage.
She still loves him, but the love affair is carried on
in her imagination, where it is safe from the painful
effects of sexual involvement and the passing of time.

In his characterization of Nan, O'Connor stresses
the effects of the "inferiority complex" she develops
as a result of her adolescent unattractiveness. She is
a sensitive girl who suffers from "night-panics," and
the unusual piety she exhibits in early adolescence is
in part a compensation for her fears. Her mother, a
beautiful woman to whom physical appearance is important, intensifies Nan's feeling of inferiority by criti-
cizing her clothes and behavior. Nan retaliates defen-
sively by saying that she wants to be a nun and develops
an obstinate, masculine personality. She avoids friendships with her peers and spends time instead with old
or sick people.

Nan develops into a sensual woman as well as a
beautiful one. O'Connor implies that she may be afraid
of the strength of her instincts. When one of her admi-
rers persuades her to make love with him, she reacts
with disillusionment; it is after this incident that
she suggests to Mick that they get married and move to
Dublin. But even after she is engaged she continues to
go out with other men. Finally she tells Mick she cannot marry him because she is afraid, not just of him
but also of herself. She does not think Mick can control her sufficiently if she decides to "kick over the
traces." The "night-panics" of her childhood have
grown into a fear of commitment to sex and marriage.

Since the story is told from Mick Courtney's point
of view, the development of Nan's character is seen primarily through his eyes. His outlook has been shaped by
the same environment that shaped Nan's, and his mental
limitations keep him from understanding her fully until
many years later. He is a creature of habit, unambi-
tious, intelligent in a narrow way, deeply attached to
his immediate surroundings and not too aware of anything
beyond them. He has tended to take Nan for granted;
the discovery that she has become beautiful is a major
shock to him. He constantly analyzes the motives and

302

feelings behind Nan's actions, but he does not reach his conclusions until it is too late. Nan tries to push him beyond himself, but her criticisms have a destructive tone, and he reacts by emotionally retreating from her. He tolerates her minor infidelities because he is "almost devoid of jealousy," and does not see the real danger. Nan is "unknown territory" for Mick; he is both fascinated and bewildered by her. When he moves to Dublin and marries, he becomes absorbed in his immediate life and seldom thinks of Cork, but from time to time Nan crosses his mind and he tries to understand her decision. He gradually pieces together a solution, but it is not complete until his meeting with Nan in the convent.

In this final scene the author's voice can be clearly heard. It becomes identified with Mick's thoughts, which acquire a more universal context. Everything O'Connor has been implying about Nan is explicitly stated.

> Because of some inadequacy in themselves--
> poverty or physical weakness in men,
> poverty or ugliness in women--those with
> the gift of creation built for themselves
> a rich interior world; and when the inade-
> quacy disappeared and the real world
> was spread before them with all its wealth
> and beauty, they could not give their
> whole heart to it. Uncertain of their
> choice, they wavered between goals--were
> lonely in crowds, dissatisfied amid noise
> and laughter, unhappy even with those
> they loved best. The interior world called
> them back, and for some it was a case of
> having to return there or die.[85]

This explanation is superfluous, since O'Connor has already conveyed Nan's hidden motivation. As in other late stories, excessive analysis flaws the narrative. It is as if O'Connor distrusts his powers of indirect suggestion and relies instead on explicit statements only slightly masked as Mick's thoughts. The tone is indulgent and benevolent. Mick is not judged harshly for his caution and slowness of perception, and Nan seems to be regarded as an admirable idealist in spite of the neurotic, escapist tendencies clearly evident in her actions. O'Connor's ambivalent attitude toward her is not satisfactorily resolved.

As we have seen in the stories about insanity in

the clergy, O'Connor's treatment of abnormal or neurotic love relationships is always controlled by perspectives of normality and sanity. The fantasies and delusions that lead to abnormal behavior are not presented directly, but are implied. The technique is consistent with O'Connor's views about the essential loneliness of individuals. As he asks at the end of "The Ugly Duckling," "Which of us can feel, let alone describe, another's interior world?"

Although O'Connor sometimes chafed at the limitations of the short story, he was extraordinarily successful at adapting its unique potentialities to express the contradictory and discordant realities of Irish life. He tried to compensate for his materially and emotionally deprived childhood through an idealistic identification with Ireland's future, but was disappointed. Like his contemporaries O'Flaherty and O'Faolain, he developed a "revulsion-attraction complex" to Ireland as a result of his early idealism and subsequent disillusionment. His resolution of the conflicts inherent in his Irish identity was not clear-cut or consistent, but deeply ambivalent. He remained committed to Ireland but attacked the country's failings relentlessly, and he required frequent restorative periods of exile. At times his anger adversely affected his art, but his imagination was vigorous and resilient, and he was more consistently successful than either O'Flaherty or O'Faolain at transforming his frustrations into superb stories. As he became more mellow and reconciled in his later years, the quality of his work declined somewhat, though he still produced some fine stories.

The concept of the "submerged population" reflects O'Connor's preoccupation with the relationship between the individual and the community in Ireland. His submerged population consists of people with strong instinctive needs, often warm, impulsive, and imaginative people. In a universe that can appear vast and desolate, they seek to anchor themselves in loving relationships with other people and in a secure home. But they cannot satisfy their needs in a society pervaded by rigid principles and conventions. They are often torn between their need for love and personal fulfillment and their need for belonging, for membership in the community, and must choose one at the expense of the other. O'Connor's characters are also affected by social disruption, the transition from traditional to modern life. The attraction of the traditional ways is very powerful, and some of the stories offer a moving tribute to the dying culture, but other stories convey the sterility and stagnation that attachment to outmoded customs can produce. The aspect of Irish Catholic middle-class society that O'Connor most frequently attacks is its regressiveness and immaturity, its refusal to undertake the risks of spiritual growth. Members of the submerged population must often "improvise," or find a creative and unorthodox approach to overcoming the external or internal obstacles to happiness that they encounter, but they usually do this within the bounds of decency and common sense; instinct and judgment are balanced. The relationship of the submerged population to the larger community changes many times during O'Connor's career. The early stories tend to romanticize or idealize some aspects of Irish community life; the middle stories examine the choice between accommodation with a restrictive community or exile; and the later stories explore either unconventional, improvised solutions or the psychological deviation and neurotic escapism produced in the submerged population by unhealthy family or community pressures that have become internalized.

O'Connor's concept of "organic form" occupies a middle ground between O'Flaherty's objectivity and O'Faolain's subjectivity. Although like O'Faolain he draws heavily on autobiographical material, he is more self-effacing and objectifies his experiences more than O'Faolain does. Probably because his temperament is so volatile, self-doubting and fearful of imaginative excess, he uses the discipline of the short story form to scale down and control his material. He prefers to project his inner conflicts and perceptions into child characters or adults who are simpler and more ordinary than he is, and to concentrate on significant moments or incidents rather than on extended chronological development. The narrative voice is of central importance to his art, but he does not identify as closely with his narrators as O'Faolain does, nor, except for the child narrators and a few others, does he describe their emotional responses to the story. They are lonely human voices, but only occasionally does the author speak directly through them. Instead his narrators provide a static frame around the dramatic rendering of the story, and they serve as devices for achieving distance and control, as mediators between the author, his material, and the reader. O'Connor has evolved a concept of the short story that is ideally suited both to his own temperament and to the Irish material he portrays in his art.

305

Notes

[1] Frank O'Connor, An Only Child (New York: Alfred A. Knopf, 1961), p. 47.

[2] Ibid., pp. 179-80.

[3] Ibid., pp. 193-94.

[4] Ibid., p. 210.

[5] Ibid., p. 276.

[6] Frank O'Connor, My Father's Son (New York: Alfred A. Knopf, 1969), p. 50.

[7] Ibid., p. 61.

[8] Ibid., pp. 230-31.

[9] Frank O'Connor, "The Future of Irish Literature," Horizon, 5, no. 25 (1942), 56.

[10] My Father's Son, p. 160.

[11] Frank O'Connor, The Backward Look: A Survey of Irish Literature (London: Macmillan, 1967), p. 225.

[12] Frank O'Connor, "Censorship," Dublin Magazine, 1, no. 2 (1962), 43.

[13] Frank O'Connor, "Should Provincial Writers Stay at Home?" The Listener (March 16, 1938), 591.

[14] Shevawn Lynam, "A Sparring Partner," Michael/Frank: Studies on Frank O'Connor, ed. Maurice Sheehy (New York: Alfred A. Knopf, 1969), p. 93.

[15] Frank O'Connor, The Lonely Voice: A Study of the Short Story (London: Macmillan, 1965), pp. 14-21.

[16] See Brendan Kennelly, "George Moore's Lonely Voices: A Study of his Short Stories," in George Moore's Mind and Art, ed. Graham Owens (Edinburgh: Oliver and Boyd, 1968), p. 144; Eamon Grennan, "Introduction," in A Land of Loneliness and Other Stories, Seumas O'Kelly (Dublin: Gill and Macmillan, 1969), p. 9; and John Zneimer, The Literary Vision of Liam O'Flaherty (Syracuse: Syracuse University Press, 1970), p. 177.

[17] *The Lonely Voice*, pp. 21-22.

[18] Ibid., p. 29.

[19] Frank O'Connor, ed., *Modern Irish Short Stories* (London: Oxford University Press, 1957), p. ix.

[20] *The Lonely Voice*, p. 37.

[21] Frank O'Connor, "A Good Short Story Must Be News," *New York Times Book Review*, 61, no. 24 (June 10, 1956), I.

[22] *Modern Irish Short Stories*, p. x.

[23] *The Lonely Voice*, pp. 113-25.

[24] Frank O'Connor, "Synge," *The Irish Theatre*, ed. Lennox Robinson (London: Macmillan, 1939), p. 52.

[25] *An Only Child*, pp. 203-4.

[26] "A Good Short Story Must Be News," p. 20.

[27] *Modern Irish Short Stories*, p. xii.

[28] "A Good Short Story Must Be News," pp. 1, 20.

[29] *Modern Irish Short Stories*, pp. xii-xiii.

[30] *The Backward Look*, p. 227.

[31] "The Future of Irish Literature," p. 59.

[32] James H. Matthews, *Frank O'Connor* (Lewisburg: Bucknell University Press, 1976), p. 48.

[33] Frank O'Connor, *Collection Two* (London: Macmillan, 1964), p. v.

[34] Frank O'Connor, "Frank O'Connor," Anthony Whittier, interviewer, *Paris Review*, 5, no. 17 (1957), 49-50.

[35] James H. Matthews, "Women, War and Words: Frank O'Connor's First Confessions," *Irish Renaissance Annual*, 1, no. 1 (1980), 75-76.

[36] Frank O'Connor, *Guests of the Nation* (New York: Macmillan, 1931), p. 74.

[37] Ibid., pp. 86-87.

[38] Ibid., p. 90.

[39] Ibid., p. 92.

[40] Ibid., p. 98.

[41] Collection Two, p. 11.

[42] Ibid., p. 12.

[43] Guests of the Nation, p. 2.

[44] Collection Two, pp. 1-2.

[45] M. G. Cooke, "From Comedy to Terror: On Dubliners and the Development of Tone and Structure in the Modern Short Story," Massachusetts Review, 9 (1968), 334-35.

[46] Ibid., p. 343.

[47] Frank O'Connor, The Stories of Frank O'Connor (New York: Alfred A. Knopf, 1952), p. 155.

[48] Ibid., pp. 162-63.

[49] Frank O'Connor, The Mirror in the Roadway: A Study of the Modern Novel (London: Hamish Hamilton, 1957), pp. 302-3.

[50] Stories, pp. 163-64.

[51] Ibid., p. 167.

[52] Ibid., p. 137.

[53] "Frank O'Connor," Paris Review, p. 46.

[54] Stories, p. 197.

[55] Ibid., p. 203.

[56] Ibid., p. 208.

[57] Ibid., pp. 210-11.

[58] Ibid., pp. 214-15.

[59] Murray Prosky, "The Pattern of Diminishing

Certitude in the Stories of Frank O'Connor," *Colby Library Quarterly*, 9 (1970), 318.

[60] Frank O'Connor, *Stories by Frank O'Connor* (New York: Vintage, 1956), pp. vii-viii.

[61] *Stories*, p. 144.

[62] Ibid., p. 246.

[63] *My Father's Son*, p. 147.

[64] *Collection Two*, p. 99.

[65] Ibid., pp. 101-2.

[66] *The Backward Look*, p. 227.

[67] *Stories*, pp. 226-27.

[68] Ibid., p. 229.

[69] Frank O'Connor, "Across St. George's Channel," *The Journal of Irish Literature*, 4, no. 1 (1975), 155.

[70] *Stories*, p. 3.

[71] *Collection Two*, p. 56.

[72] Frank O'Connor, *The Common Chord: Stories and Tales* (New York: Alfred A. Knopf, 1948), pp. 18-19.

[73] *Collection Two*, p. 57.

[74] See Frank O'Connor, *A Set of Variations* (New York: Alfred A. Knopf, 1969), p. v.

[75] Richard J. Thompson, "A Kingdom of Commoners: The Moral Art of Frank O'Connor," *Eire-Ireland*, 13, no. 4 (1978), 67.

[76] *A Set of Variations*, p. 315.

[77] Ibid., p. 269.

[78] Ibid., p. 271.

[79] *Collection Two*, p. 325.

[80] Frank O'Connor, *Domestic Relations* (New York: Alfred A. Knopf, 1957), p. 20.

81 Ibid., p. 34.

82 A _Set_ _of_ _Variations_, p. 31.

83 Matthews, _Frank_ _O'Connor_, pp. 85-86.

84 A _Set_ _of_ _Variations_, p. 162.

85 _Domestic_ _Relations_, p. 168.

BIBLIOGRAPHY

I. GENERAL SOURCES

Bates, H. E. The Modern Short Story: A Critical
    Survey. London: Thomas Nelson and Sons, 1941.

Beachcroft, T. O. The Modest Art: A Survey of the
    Short Story in English. London: Oxford Univ.
    Press, 1968.

Beckett, J. C. The Making of Modern Ireland, 1603-1923.
    London: Faber and Faber, 1966.

Carleton, William. Traits and Stories of the Irish
    Peasantry. 10th ed., Vol. 1. London: William
    Tegg, n.d.

Coogan, Timothy Patrick. Ireland Since the Rising.
    New York: Frederick A. Praeger, 1966.

Cowley, Malcolm. Exile's Return: A Literary Odyssey
    of the 1920's. New York: Viking, 1951/62.

Edwards, R. Dudley. A New History of Ireland. Toronto:
    Univ. of Toronto Press, 1972.

Fallis, Richard. The Irish Renaissance. Syracuse:
    Syracuse Univ. Press, 1977.

Flanagan, Thomas. The Irish Novelists, 1800-1850. New
    York: Columbia Univ. Press, 1959.

Kelleher, John V. "Irish Literature Today." Atlantic
    Monthly, 175 (1945), 70-76.

Kiely, Benedict. Modern Irish Fiction: A Critique.
    Dublin: Golden Eagle Books, 1950.

May, Charles E., ed. Short Story Theories. Ohio Univ.
    Press, 1976.

Mercier, Vivian, ed. Great Irish Short Stories. New
    York: Dell, 1964.

_____. "The Irish Short Story and Oral Tradition."
    The Celtic Cross: Studies in Irish Culture and
    Literature. Eds. Ray B. Browne, William John

311

Roscelli, and Richard Loftus. Purdue: Purdue Univ. Press, 1964, pp. 98-116.

Rafroidi, Patrick, and Terence Brown, eds. The Irish Short Story. Gerrards Cross, Buckinghamshire: Colin Smythe, 1979.

Saul, George Brandon. Rushlight Heritage: Reflections on Selected Irish Short-Story Writers of the Yeatsian Era. Philadelphia: The Walton Press, 1969.

Turgenev, Ivan. The Hunting Sketches. Tr. Bernard Guilbert Guerney. New York: New American Library, 1962.

II. GEORGE MOORE

Primary Sources

George Moore in Transition: Letters to T. Fisher Unwin and Lena Milman, 1894-1910. Ed. Helmut E. Gerber. Detroit: Wayne State Univ. Press, 1968.

Hail and Farewell: Ave. Vol. 1. New York: D. Appleton, 1920.

The Untilled Field. Macmillan of Canada: Maclean-Hunter Press, 1931/76.

Secondary Sources

Hone, Joseph. The Life of George Moore. New York: Macmillan, 1936.

Kennedy, Eileen. "Turgenev and George Moore's The Untilled Field." English Literature in Transition, 18 (1975), 145-59.

Newell, Kenneth B. "The 'Artist' Stories in The Untilled Field." English Literature in Transition, 14 (1971), 123-36.

Owens, Graham, ed. George Moore's Mind and Art. Edinburgh: Oliver and Boyd, 1968.

III. JAMES JOYCE

Primary Sources

Dubliners: Text, Criticism, Notes. Eds. Robert Scholes
    and A. Walton Litz. New York: Viking, 1969.

Letters of James Joyce. Ed. Richard Ellmann. Vol. 2.
    London: Faber and Faber, 1966.

A Portrait of the Artist as a Young Man. New York:
    Viking, 1971.

Secondary Sources

Baker, James R., and Thomas F. Staley, eds. James
    Joyce's Dubliners: A Critical Handbook. Belmont,
    Cal.: Wadsworth, 1969.

Beckson, Karl. "Moore's The Untilled Field and Joyce's
    Dubliners: The Short Story's Intricate Maze."
    English Literature in Transition, 15 (1972),
    291-304.

Brown, Homer Obed. James Joyce's Early Fiction: The
    Biography of a Form. Cleveland and London: Press
    of Case Western Reserve Univ., 1972.

Cooke, M. G. "From Comedy to Terror: On Dubliners and
    the Development of Tone and Structure in the Modern
    Short Story." Massachusetts Review, 9 (1968),
    331-43.

Ellmann, Richard. James Joyce. New York: Oxford Univ.
    Press, 1959.

Garrett, Peter K., ed. Twentieth Century Interpreta-
    tions of Dubliners: A Collection of Critical
    Essays. Englewood Cliffs, N.J.: Prentice-Hall,
    1968.

Hart, John Raymond. "Moore on Joyce: The Influence of
    The Untilled Field on Dubliners." Dublin Magazine,
    10, no. 2 (1973), 61-76.

Kennedy, Eileen. "Moore's Untilled Field and Joyce's
    Dubliners." Eire-Ireland, 5, no. 3 (1970), 81-89.

Magalaner, Marvin. Time of Apprenticeship: The Fiction

of Young James Joyce. London: Abelard-Schuman, 1959.

Scott, B. K. "Joyce's Schooling in the Field of George Moore." Eire-Ireland, 9, no. 4 (1974), 117-41.

Solomon, Albert J. "The Backgrounds of 'Eveline.'" Eire-Ireland, 6, no. 3 (1971), 23-38.

Walzl, Florence L. "Pattern of Paralysis in Joyce's Dubliners: A Study of the Original Framework." College English, 22 (1960-61), 221-28.

IV. SEUMAS O'KELLY

Primary Sources

The Golden Barque and the Weaver's Grave. Dublin: Talbot Press, 1919.

Hillsiders. Dublin: Talbot Press, 1921.

A Land of Loneliness and Other Stories. Ed. Eamon Grennan. Dublin: Gill and Macmillan, 1969.

Waysiders: Stories of Connacht. Dublin: Talbot Press, 1924.

Secondary Source

Saul, George Brandon. Seumas O'Kelly. Lewisburg: Bucknell Univ. Press, 1971.

V. DANIEL CORKERY

Primary Sources

Earth Out of Earth. Dublin: Talbot Press, 1939.

The Hounds of Banba. New York: Huebsch, 1922.

A Munster Twilight. New York: Frederick A. Stokes, n.d.

The Stormy Hills. Dublin: Talbot Press, 1929.

Synge and Anglo-Irish Literature. Cork: The Mercier Press, 1931/66.

The Wager and Other Stories. New York: Devin-Adair, 1950.

Secondary Source

Saul, George Brandon. Daniel Corkery. Lewisburg: Bucknell Univ. Press, 1973.

VI. LIAM O'FLAHERTY

Primary Sources

"The Irish Censorship." The American Spectator Year-book. Eds. G. Jean Nathan, Theodore Dreiser, et al. New York: Frederick Stokes, 1934, pp. 131-34.

"Literary Criticism in Ireland." The Irish Statesman, 6 (September 4, 1926), 711.

The Mountain Tavern and Other Stories. New York: Harcourt, Brace, 1929.

"National Energy." The Irish Statesman, 3 (October 18, 1924), 171.

The Pedlar's Revenge and Other Stories. Ed. A. A. Kelly. Dublin: Wolfhound Press, 1976.

Shame the Devil. London: Grayson and Grayson, 1934.

Spring Sowing. London: Jonathan Cape, 1924.

The Stories of Liam O'Flaherty. Ed. Vivian Mercier. New York: Devin-Adair, 1956.

The Tent. London: Jonathan Cape, 1926.

A Tourist's Guide to Ireland. London: Mandrake Press, 1929.

Two Lovely Beasts and Other Stories. New York: Devin-Adair, 1950.

Two Years. London: Jonathan Cape, 1930.

"A View of Irish Culture." The Irish Statesman, 4 (June 20, 1925), 460-61.

Secondary Sources

Doyle, Paul A. Liam O'Flaherty. New York: Twayne, 1971.

_____. Liam O'Flaherty: An Annotated Bibliography. Troy, N.Y.: Whitston, 1972.

Kelly, A. A. Liam O'Flaherty the Storyteller. New York: Barnes and Noble, 1976.

Murphy, Maureen O'Rourke. "The Double Vision of Liam O'Flaherty." Eire-Ireland, 8, no. 3 (1973), 20-25.

Murray, Michael H. "Liam O'Flaherty and the Speaking Voice." Studies in Short Fiction, 5 (1967-68), 154-62.

O'Brien, James H. Liam O'Flaherty. Lewisburg: Bucknell Univ. Press, 1973.

O'Connor, Helene. "Liam O'Flaherty: Literary Ecologist." Eire-Ireland, 7, no. 2 (1972), 47-54.

Sheeran, Patrick F. The Novels of Liam O'Flaherty: A Study in Romantic Realism. Atlantic Highlands, N.J.: Humanities Press, 1976.

Zneimer, John. The Literary Vision of Liam O'Flaherty. Syracuse: Syracuse Univ. Press, 1970.

VII. SEAN O'FAOLAIN

Primary Sources

"Ah, Wisha! The Irish Novel." Virginia Quarterly Review, 17 (Spring, 1941), 265-74.

"Don Quixote O'Flaherty." London Mercury, 37 (Dec., 1937), 170-75.

"The Emancipation of Irish Writers." Yale Review, NS 23 (March, 1934), 485-503.

The Finest Stories of Sean O'Faolain. New York: Bantam, 1959.

Foreign Affairs and Other Stories. Boston: Little, Brown, 1975.

The Heat of the Sun: Stories and Tales. Boston: Little, Brown, 1966.

I Remember! I Remember! Boston: Little, Brown, 1961.

"Ireland After Yeats." The Bell, 18 (Summer, 1953), 37-48.

The Irish. Rev. ed. Harmondsworth: Penguin, 1969.

"Literary Provincialism." Commonweal, 17 (Dec. 21, 1932), 214-15.

The Man Who Invented Sin and Other Stories. New York: Devin-Adair, 1958.

Midsummer Night Madness and Other Stories. London: Jonathan Cape, 1932.

"A Portrait of the Artist as an Old Man." Irish University Review, 6, no. 1 (1976), 10-18.

A Purse of Coppers. New York: Viking, 1938.

Short Stories: A Study in Pleasure. Ed. Sean O'Faolain. Boston: Little, Brown, 1961.

The Short Story. New York: Devin-Adair, 1951.

"Signing Off." The Bell, 12, no. 1 (1946), 1.

The Talking Trees and Other Stories. Boston: Little, Brown, 1970.

Vive Moi! Boston: Little, Brown, 1964.

Secondary Sources

Doyle, Paul A. Sean O'Faolain. New York: Twayne, 1968.

Hanley, Katherine. "The Short Stories of Sean O'Faolain: Theory and Practice." Eire-Ireland, 6, no. 3 (1971), 3-11.

Harmon, Maurice. *Sean O'Faolain: A Critical Introduction*. Notre Dame: Univ. of Notre Dame Press, 1966.

Kelleher, John V. "Sean O'Faolain." *Atlantic*, 199 (May, 1957), 67-69.

McCartney, Donal. "Sean O'Faolain: 'A Nationalist Right Enough.'" *Irish University Review*, 6, no. 1 (1976), 73-86.

Macauley, Robie. "Sean O'Faolain, Ireland's Youngest Writer." *Irish University Review*, 6, no. 1 (1976), 110-17.

Mercier, Vivian. "The Professionalism of Sean O'Faolain." *Irish University Review*, 6, no. 1 (1976), 45-53.

Rippier, Joseph Storey. *The Short Stories of Sean O'Faolain: A Study in Descriptive Techniques*. Gerrards Cross, Buckinghamshire: Colin Smythe, 1976.

Saul, George Brandon. "The Brief Fiction of Sean O'Faolain." *Colby Library Quarterly*, Ser. 7 (1964), 69-74.

VIII.   FRANK O'CONNOR

Primary Sources

"Across St. George's Channel." *The Journal of Irish Literature*, 4, no. 1 (1975), 146-51.

The Backward Look: A Survey of Irish Literature. London: Macmillan, 1967.

Bones of Contention and Other Stories. New York: Macmillan, 1936.

"Censorship." *Dublin Magazine*, 1, no. 2 (1962), 39-44.

Collection Three. London: Macmillan, 1969.

Collection Two. London: Macmillan, 1964.

The Common Chord: Stories and Tales. New York: Alfred A. Knopf, 1948.

Crab Apple Jelly: Stories and Tales. New York: Alfred
A. Knopf, 1944.

Domestic Relations. New York: Alfred A. Knopf, 1957.

"Frank O'Connor." Anthony Whittier, interviewer.
Paris Review, 5, no. 17 (1957), 43-64.

"The Future of Irish Literature." Horizon, 5, no. 25
(1942), 55-63.

"A Good Short Story Must Be News." New York Times Book
Review, 61, no. 24 (June 10, 1956), 1, 20.

Guests of the Nation. New York: Macmillan, 1931.

The Lonely Voice: A Study of the Short Story. London:
Macmillan, 1965.

The Mirror in the Roadway: A Study of the Modern Novel.
London: Hamish Hamilton, 1957.

Modern Irish Short Stories. Ed. Frank O'Connor. London: Oxford Univ. Press, 1957.

More Stories. New York: Alfred A. Knopf, 1954.

My Father's Son. New York: Alfred A. Knopf, 1969.

An Only Child. New York: Alfred A. Knopf, 1961.

A Set of Variations. New York: Alfred A. Knopf, 1969.

"Should Provincial Writers Stay at Home?" The Listener,
March 16, 1938, 591-92.

Stories by Frank O'Connor. New York: Vintage, 1956.

The Stories of Frank O'Connor. New York: Alfred A.
Knopf, 1952.

"Synge." The Irish Theatre. Ed. Lennox Robinson.
London: Macmillan, 1939, pp. 29-52.

Traveller's Samples: Stories and Tales. New York:
Alfred A. Knopf, 1951.

Secondary Sources

Brenner, Gerry. "Frank O'Connor's Imprudent Hero."
Texas Studies in Literature and Language, 10
(1968), 457-69.

Cooke, Michael G. "Frank O'Connor and the Fiction of
Artlessness." University Review (Dublin), 5
(1968), 87-102.

Matthews, James H. Frank O'Connor. Lewisburg: Bucknell
Univ. Press, 1976.

_____. "Women, War and Words: Frank O'Connor's
First Confessions." Irish Renaissance Annual, 1,
no. 1 (1980), 73-112.

Prosky, Murray. "The Pattern of Diminishing Certitude
in the Stories of Frank O'Connor." Colby Library
Quarterly, 9 (1970), 311-21.

Sheehy, Maurice, ed. Michael/Frank: Studies on Frank
O'Connor. Dublin: Gill and Macmillan, 1969.

Thompson, Richard J. "A Kingdom of Commoners: The
Moral Art of Frank O'Connor." Eire-Ireland, 13,
no. 4 (1978), 65-80.

Wohlgelernter, Maurice. Frank O'Connor: An Introduction. New York: Columbia Univ. Press, 1977.

325

Conger Eel," 130; "The Cow's Death," 130; "Desire," 143; "The Ditch," 135; Duil, 117; "The Eviction," 143; "The Fairy Goose," 134-35, 183; Famine, 117; "The Fight," 122; "Galway Bay," 147-48, 262; "Going Into Exile," 122-24, 125, 128, 240; "Grey Seagull," 143; "The Hawk," 143; "His First Flight," 130; "The Hook," 130; The House of Gold, 121; The Informer, 121, 247; "The Inquisition," 121, 143; Insurrection, 121; "The Lament," 145; "The Landing," 126-28, 129, 132, 133, 143; "The Letter," 136, 139; "Life," 147; "The Lost Thrush," 130; "Mackerel for Sale," 135, 145; The Martyr, 121; "Milking Time," 125; The Mountain Tavern, 117, 132, 133, 135, 136, 139, 143; "The Mountain Tavern," 132; "The New Suit," 143; "The Oar," 132-33; "Offerings," 121, 134; "The Old Woman," 147; "The Outcast," 121, 134; "The Painted Woman," 135; "The Parting," 143; The Pedlar's Revenge, 117; "Poor People," 125; "The Post Office," 143; "A Pot of Gold," 122; "Prey," 133; "Red Barbara," 135; "A Red Petticoat," 122; "The Rockfish," 130; "Selling Pigs," 122; Shame the Devil, 112, 114, 116, 117, 139; "A Shilling," 122; Skerrett, 121; "The Sniper," 121; "Sport: The Kill," 130;

Spring Sowing, 20, 117, 121; "Spring Sowing," 125-26, 128, 143; "The Stolen Ass," 122; "The Stone," 135; "Stoney Batter," 122; The Stories of Liam O'Flaherty, 117, 142; "The Strange Disease," 135; "The Stream," 135; "The Struggle," 122; The Tent, 117, 121; "The Tent," 122; "Three Lambs," 130; Thy Neighbour's Wife, 118, 121; "The Touch," 145; "The Tramp," 121; "Trapped," 128-29; Two Lovely Beasts, 117, 142; "Two Lovely Beasts," 144-45; Two Years, 113; "The Wedding," 145-47; "The Wild Goat's Kid," 130-31; "The Wild Sow," 130; "The Wounded Cormorant," 130; "The Wren's Nest," 130

O'Grady, Standish, History of Ireland's Heroic Period, 13

O'Kelly, Seumas, 15, 20, 21, 22, 24, 69-81, 83, 86, 87, 88, 94, 96-97, 120, 149, 167, 169, 184, 238, 254, 262; "The Apparitions of Oul' Darmody," 72; "Both Sides of the Pond," 76-77, 87, 124, 136; "The Building," 76; By the Stream of Killmeen, 70, 71; "The Can with the Diamond Notch," 75, 122; "The Derelict," 78; "The Elks," 72; The Golden Barque and the Weaver's Grave, 70, 77; "Hannah," 72; "Hike and Calcutta," 78; Hillsiders, 70, 72, 75, 79, 289; The Lady of Deerpark, 70; "The Land of Loneliness," 71; The Leprechaun of Killmeen, 70, "Michael and Mary," 78; "The Miracle of the Tea," 72; "Nan Hogan's House,"

72-75, 128; "The Prodi-
gal Daughter," 72; "The
Rector," 75-76; "The
Shoemaker," 87; "The
Sick Call," 135; "A Way-
side Burial," 75, 78;
Waysiders, 70, 75, 76;
"The Weaver's Grave,"
69, 78-81, 94, 148, 181,
262, 263; Wet Clay, 70;
"The White Goat," 75
O'Shea, Captain William,
12

Parnell, Charles Stuart,
12, 13
Pearse, Patrick, 14
Playboy, 210
Plunkett, James, 25
Poe, E. A., 15
Poems and Ballads of Young
Ireland, 13
Power, Arthur, 47
Prosky, Murray, 267

Rippier, Joseph, 170, 186
Robinson, Lennox, 230;
Patriots, 154
Richards, Grant, 48, 49,
50, 64
Russell, George (AE), 13,
46, 114, 158, 231, 233

Salinger, J. D., 237
Saul, George Brandon, 70,
92, 206
Scott, Sir Walter, 4, 6,
7
Shaw, G. B., John Bull's
Other Island, 84
Sheeran, Patrick, 112, 142
Sigerson, George, 13
Somerville and Ross (Edith
Somerville and Violet
Martin), 14-15, 22, 25,
238; Further Experiences
of an Irish R. M., 15;
In Mr. Knox's Country,
15; Some Experiences of
an Irish R. M., 15
Speaight, Evelyn, 231

Stephens, James, 15, 25
Stuart, Francis, 106, 107
Sunday Independent, 232
Swift, Jonathan, 115
Synge, J. M., 242, 255; The
Playboy of the Western
World, 14

Thompson, Richard, 290
Tolstoy, Leo, 47
To-morrow, 114
Turgenev, Ivan, 15, 16, 30,
31, 41, 47, 69, 71, 166,
168, 237, 243; "Bezhin
Meadow," 91; The Hunting
Sketches, 15-16, 30-31,
47-48, 72; "Living Relics,"
38; "The Singers," 40-41,
77; Virgin Soil, 31

Walzl, Florence, 50, 62-63
Whelan, Denis, 153

Yeats, W. B., 13, 14, 15,
25, 29, 46, 114, 120, 157,
160, 162, 163, 230, 231,
232, 238, 240, 242

Zneimer, John, 118, 138
Zola, Emile, 30

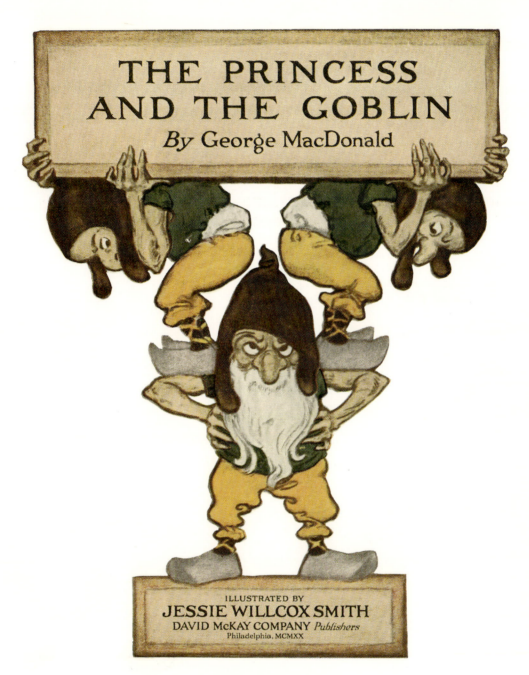

THE PRINCESS
AND THE GOBLIN

By George MacDonald

ILLUSTRATED BY
JESSIE WILLCOX SMITH
DAVID McKAY COMPANY *Publishers*
Philadelphia, MCMXX

BOOKS OF WONDER
WILLIAM MORROW & COMPANY, INC.
NEW YORK

THE PRINCESS AND
THE GOBLIN

Library of Congress Cataloging-in-Publication Data
MacDonald, George, 1824–1905.
The princess and the goblin.
Summary: A little princess is protected by her friend
Curdie from the goblin miners who live beneath the castle.
[1. Fairy tales]   I. Smith, Jessie Willcox, 1863–1935, ill.   II. Title.
PZ8.M1754Pr   1986   [Fic]   86-2532
ISBN 0-688-06604-6

ILLUSTRATIONS

CONTENTS

THE PRINCESS AND
THE GOBLIN

CHAPTER I

WHY THE PRINCESS HAS A STORY ABOUT HER

THERE was once a little princess who—

"But, Mr. Author, why do you always write about princesses?"

"Because every little girl is a princess."

"You will make them vain if you tell them that."

"Not if they understand what I mean."

"Then what do you mean?"

"What do you mean by a princess?"

"The daughter of a king."

"Very well, then every little girl is a princess, and there would be no need to say anything about it, except that she is always in danger of forgetting her rank, and behaving as if she had grown out of the mud. I have seen little princesses behave like the children of thieves and lying beggars, and that is why they need to be told they are princesses. And that is why, when I tell a story of this kind, I like to tell it about a princess. Then I can say better what I mean, because I can then give her every beautiful thing I want her to have."

"Please go on."

There was once a little princess whose father was king over a great country full of mountains and valleys. His palace was built upon one of the mountains, and was very grand and beautiful. The princess, whose name was Irene, was born there, but she was sent soon after her birth, because her mother was not very strong, to be brought up by country people in a large house, half castle, half farm-house, on the side of another mountain, about halfway between its base and its peak.

The princess was a sweet little creature, and at the time my story begins was about eight years old, I think, but she got older very fast. Her face was fair and pretty, with eyes like two bits of night-sky, each with a star dissolved in the blue. Those eyes you would have thought must have known they came from there, so often were they turned up in that direction. The ceiling of her nursery was blue, with stars in it, as like the sky as they could make it. But I doubt if ever she saw the real sky with the stars in it, for a reason which I had better mention at once.

These mountains were full of hollow places underneath; huge caverns, and winding ways, some with water running through them, and some shining with all colors of the rainbow when a light was taken in. There would not have been much known about them, had there not been mines there, great deep pits, with long galleries and passages running off from them, which had been dug to get at the ore of which the mountains were full. In the course of digging, the miners came upon many of these natural caverns. A few of them had far-off openings out on the side of a mountain, or into a ravine.

Now in these subterranean caverns lived a strange race of beings, called by some gnomes, by some kobolds, by some goblins. There was a legend current in the country that at one time they lived above ground, and were very like other people. But for some reason or other, concerning which there were different legendary theories, the king had laid what they thought too severe taxes upon them, or had required observances of them they did not like, or had begun to treat them with more severity in some way or other, and impose stricter laws; and the consequence was that they had all disappeared from the face of the country. According to the legend, however, instead of going to some other country, they had all taken refuge in the subterranean caverns, whence they never came out but at night, and then seldom showed themselves in any numbers, and never to many people at once. It was only in the least frequented and most difficult parts of the mountains that they were said to gather even at night in the open air. Those who had caught sight of any of them said that they had greatly altered in the course of generations; and no wonder, seeing they lived away from the sun, in cold and wet and dark places. They were now, not ordinarily ugly, but either absolutely hideous, or ludicrously grotesque both in face and form. There was no invention, they said, of the most lawless imagination expressed by pen or pencil, that could surpass the extravagance of their appearance. And as they grew mis-shapen in body, they had grown in knowledge and clevernesss, and now were able to do things no mortal could see the possibility of. But as they grew in cunning, they grew in mischief, and their great delight was in every way they could think of to annoy the people who lived in the open-air-story above them. They had enough of affection left for each other, to preserve them from being absolutely cruel for cruelty's sake to those that came in their way; but still they so heartily cherished the ancestral grudge against those who occupied their former possession, and especially against the descendants of the king who had caused their expulsion, that they sought every opportunity of tormenting them in ways that were as odd as their inventors; and although dwarfed and mis-shapen, they had strength equal to their cunning. In the process of time they had got a king, and a government of their own, whose chief business, beyond their own simple affairs, was to devise trouble for their neighbors. It will now be pretty evident why the little princess had never seen the sky at night. They were much too afraid of the goblins to let her out of the house then, even in company with ever so many attendants; and they had good reason, as we shall see by-and-by.

CHAPTER II

THE PRINCESS LOSES HERSELF

I HAVE said the Princess Irene was about eight years old when my story begins. And this is how it begins.

One very wet day, when the mountain was covered with mist which was constantly gathering itself together into rain-drops, and pouring down on the roofs of the great old house, whence it fell in a fringe of water from the eaves all round about it, the princess could not of course go out. She got very tired, so tired that even her toys could no longer amuse her. You would wonder at that if I had time to describe to you one half of the toys she had. But then you wouldn't have the toys themselves, and that makes all the difference: you can't get tired of a thing before you have it. It was a picture, though, worth seeing—the princess sitting in the nursery with the sky-ceiling over her head, at a great table covered with her toys. If the artist would like to draw this, I should advise him not to meddle with the toys. I am afraid of attempting to describe them, and I think he had better not try to draw them. He had better not. He can do a thousand things I can't, but I don't think he could draw those toys. No man could better make the princess herself than he could, though—leaning with her back bowed into the back of the chair, her head hanging down, and her hands in her lap, very miserable as she would say herself, not even knowing what she would like, except to go out and get very wet, catch a particularly nice cold, and have to go to bed and take gruel. The next moment after you see her sitting there, her nurse goes out of the room.

Even that is a change, and the princess wakes up a little, and looks about her. Then she tumbles off her chair, and runs out of the door, not the same door the nurse went out of, but one which opened at the foot of a curious old stair of worm-eaten oak, which looked as if never any one had set foot upon it. She had once before been up six steps, and that was sufficient reason, in such a day, for trying to find out what was at the top of it.

Up and up she ran—such a long way it seemed to her! until she came to the top of the third flight. There she found the landing was the end of a long passage. Into this she ran. It was full of doors on each side. There were so many that she did not care to open any, but ran on to the end, where she turned into another passage, also full of doors. When she had turned twice more, and still saw doors and only doors about her, she began to get frightened. It was so silent! And all those doors must hide rooms with nobody in them! That was dreadful. Also the rain made a great trampling noise on the roof. She turned and started at full speed, her little foot-steps echoing through the sounds of the rain—back for the stairs and her safe nursery. So she thought, but she had lost herself long ago. It doesn't follow that she *was* lost, because she had lost herself though.

She ran for some distance, turned several times, and then began to be afraid. Very soon she was sure that she had lost the way back. Rooms everywhere, and no stair! Her little

[14]

heart beat as fast as her little feet ran, and a lump of tears was growing in her throat. But she was too eager and perhaps too frightened to cry for some time. At last her hope failed her. Nothing but passages and doors everywhere! She threw herself on the floor, and began to wail and cry.

She did not cry long, however, for she was as brave as could be expected of a princess of her age. After a good cry, she got up, and brushed the dust from her frock. Oh what old dust it was! Then she wiped her eyes with her hands, for princesses don't always have their handkerchiefs in their pockets any more than some other little girls I know of. Next, like a true princess, she resolved on going wisely to work to find her way back: she would walk through the passages, and look in every direction for the stair. This she did, but without success. She went over the same ground again and again without knowing it, for the passages and doors were all alike. At last, in a corner, through a half-open door, she did see a stair. But alas! it went the wrong way: instead of going down, it went up. Frightened as she was, however, she could not help wishing to see where yet further the stair could lead. It was very narrow, and so steep that she went up like a four-legged creature on her hands and feet.

CHAPTER III

THE PRINCESS AND—WE SHALL SEE WHO

WHEN she came to the top, she found herself in a little square place, with three doors, two opposite each other, and one opposite the top of the stair. She stood for a moment, without an idea in her little head what to do next. But as she stood, she began to hear a curious humming sound. Could it be the rain? No. It was much more gentle, and even monotonous than the sound of the rain, which now she scarcely heard. The low sweet humming sound went on, sometimes stopping for a little while and then beginning again. It was more like the hum of a very happy bee that had found a rich well of honey in some globular flower, than anything else I can think of at this moment. Where could it come from? She laid her ear first to one of the doors to hearken if it was there—then to another. When she laid her ear against the third door, there could be no doubt where it came from: it must be from something in that room. What could it be? She was rather afraid, but her curiosity was stronger than her fear, and she opened the door very gently and peeped in. What do you think she saw? A very old lady who sat spinning.

"Oh, Mr. Editor! I know the story you are going to tell: it's The Sleeping Beauty; only you're spinning too, and making it longer."

[16]

She ran for some distance, turned several times, and then
began to be afraid.

THE PRINCESS AND—WHO?

"No, indeed, it is not that story. Why should I tell one that every properly educated child knows already? More old ladies than one have sat spinning in a garret. Besides, the old lady in that story was only spinning with a spindle, and this one was spinning with a spinning wheel, else how could the princess have heard the sweet noise through the door? Do you know the difference? Did you ever see a spindle or a spinning wheel? I daresay you never did. Well, ask your mamma to explain to you the difference. Between ourselves, however, I shouldn't wonder if she didn't know much better than you. Another thing is, that this is not a fairy story; but a goblin story. And one thing more, this old lady spinning was not an old nurse—but—you shall see who. I think I have now made it quite plain that this is not that lovely story of The Sleeping Beauty. It is quite a new one, I assure you, and I will try to tell it as prettily as I can."

Perhaps you will wonder how the princess could tell that the old lady was an old lady, when I inform you that not only was she beautiful, but her skin was smooth and white. I will tell you more. Her hair was combed back from her forehead and face, and hung loose far down and all over her back. That is not much like an old lady—is it? Ah! but it was white almost as snow. And although her face was so smooth, her eyes looked so wise that you could not have helped seeing she must be old. The princess, though she could not have told you why, did think her very old indeed—quite fifty—she said to herself. But she was rather older than that, as you shall hear.

While the princess stared bewildered, with her head just inside the door, the old lady lifted hers, and said in a sweet, but old and rather shaky voice, which mingled very pleasantly with the continued hum of her wheel:

"Come in, my dear; come in. I am glad to see you."

That the princess was a real princess, you might see now quite plainly; for she didn't hang on to the handle of the door, and stare without moving, as I have known some do who ought to have been princesses, but were only rather vulgar little girls. She did as she was told, stepped inside the door at once, and shut it gently behind her.

"Come to me, my dear," said the old lady.

And again the princess did as she was told. She approached the old lady—rather slowly, I confess, but did not stop until she stood by her side, and looked up in her face with her blue eyes and the two melted stars in them.

"Why, what have you been doing with your eyes, child?" asked the old lady.

"Crying," answered the princess.

"Why, child?"

"Because I couldn't find my way down again."

"But you could find your way up."

"Not at first—not for a long time."

"But your face is streaked like the back of a zebra. Hadn't you a handkerchief to wipe your eyes with?"

"No."

"Then why didn't you come to me to wipe them for you?"

"Please I didn't know you were here. I will next time."

"There's a good child!" said the old lady.

Then she stopped her wheel, and rose, and, going out of the room, returned with a little silver basin and a soft white towel, with which she washed and wiped the bright little face. And the princess thought her hands were so smooth and nice!

When she carried away the basin and towel, the little princess wondered to see how straight and tall she was, for, although she was so old, she didn't stoop a bit. She was dressed in black velvet with thick white heavy-looking lace about it; and on the black dress her hair shone like silver. There was hardly any more furniture in the room than there might have been in that of the poorest old woman who made her bread by her spinning. There was no carpet on the floor—no table anywhere—nothing but the spinning-wheel and the chair beside it. When she came back, she sat down again, and without a word began her spinning once more, while Irene, who had never seen a spinning-wheel, stood by her side and looked on. When the old lady had succeeded in getting her thread fairly in operation again, she said to the princess, but without looking at her:

"Do you know my name, child?"

"No, I don't know it," answered the princess.

"My name is Irene,"

"That's *my* name!" cried the princess.

"I know that. I let you have mine. I haven't got your name. You've got mine."

"How can that be?" asked the princess, bewildered. "I've always had my name."

"Your papa, the king, asked me if I had any objection to your having it; and of course I hadn't. I let you have it with pleasure."

[19]

"It was very kind of you to give me your name—and such a pretty one," said the princess.

"Oh, not so *very* kind!" said the old lady. "A name is one of those things one can give away and keep all the same. I have a good many such things. Wouldn't you like to know who I am, child?"

"Yes, that I should—very much."

"I'm your great-great-grandmother," said the lady.

"What's that?" asked the princess.

"I'm your father's mother's father's mother."

"Oh, dear! I can't understand that," said the princess.

"I daresay not. I didn't expect you would. But that's no reason why I shouldn't say it."

"Oh no!" answered the princess.

"I will explain it all to you when you are older," the lady went on. "But you will be able to understand this much now: I came here to take care of you."

"Is it long since you came? Was it yesterday? Or was it to-day, because it was so wet that I couldn't get out?"

"I've been here ever since you came yourself."

"What a long time!" said the princess. "I don't remember it at all."

"No. I suppose not."

"But I never saw you before."

"No. But you shall see me again."

"Do you live in this room always?"

"I don't sleep in it. I sleep on the opposite side of the landing. I sit here most of the day."

"I shouldn't like it. My nursery is much prettier. You

[20]

must be a queen too, if you are my great big grand-mother."

"Yes, I am a queen."

"Where is your crown then?"

"In my bedroom."

"I *should* like to see it."

"You shall some day—not to-day."

"I wonder why nursie never told me."

"Nursie doesn't know. She never saw me."

"But somebody knows that you are in the house?"

"No; nobody."

"How do you get your dinner then?"

"I keep poultry—of a sort."

"Where do you keep them?"

"I will show you."

"And who makes the chicken broth for you?"

"I never kill any of my chickens."

"Then I can't understand."

"What did you have for breakfast this morning?"

"Oh! I had bread and milk, and an egg.—I daresay you eat their eggs."

"Yes, that's it. I eat their eggs."

"Is that what makes your hair so white?"

"No, my dear. It's old age. I am very old."

"I thought so. Are you fifty?"

"Yes—more than that."

"Are you a hundred?"

"Yes—more than that. I am too old for you to guess. Come and see my chickens."

Again she stopped her spinning. She rose, took the princess by the hand, led her out of the room, and opened the door opposite the stair. The princess expected to see a lot of hens and chickens, but instead of that, she saw the blue sky first, and then the roofs of the house, with a multitude of the loveliest pigeons, mostly white, but of all colors, walking about, making bows to each other, and talking a language she could not understand. She clapped her hands with delight, and up rose such a flapping of wings, that she in her turn was startled.

"You've frightened my poultry," said the old lady, smiling.

"And they've frightened me," said the princess, smiling too. "But what very nice poultry! Are the eggs nice?"

"Yes, very nice."

"What a small egg-spoon you must have! Wouldn't it be better to keep hens, and get bigger eggs?"

"How should I feed them, though?"

"I see," said the princess. "The pigeons feed themselves. They've got wings."

"Just so. If they couldn't fly, I couldn't eat their eggs."

"But how do you get at the eggs? Where are their nests?"

The lady took hold of a little loop of string in the wall at the side of the door, and lifting a shutter showed a great many pigeon-holes with nests, some with young ones and some with eggs in them. The birds came in at the other side, and she took out the eggs on this side. She closed it again quickly, lest the young ones should be frightened.

"Oh what a nice way!" cried the princess. "Will you give me an egg to eat? I'm rather hungry."

[22]

"I will some day, but now you must go back, or nursie will be miserable about you. I daresay she's looking for you everywhere."

"Except here," answered the princess. "Oh how surprised she *will* be when I tell her about my great big grand-grand-mother!"

"Yes, that she will!" said the old lady with a curious smile. "Mind you tell her all about it exactly."

"That I will. Please will you take me back to her?"

"I can't go all the way, but I will take you to the top of the stair, and then you must run down quite fast into your own room."

The little princess put her hand in the old lady's, who, looking this way and that, brought her to the top of the first stair, and thence to the bottom of the second, and did not leave her till she saw her half way down the third. When she heard the cry of her nurse's pleasure at finding her, she turned and walked up the stairs again, very fast indeed for such a very great grandmother, and sat down to her spinning with another strange smile on her sweet old face.

About this spinning of hers I will tell you more next time.

Guess what she was spinning.

CHAPTER IV

WHAT THE NURSE THOUGHT OF IT

"WHY, where can you have been, princess?" asked the nurse, taking her in her arms. "It's very unkind of you to hide away so long. I began to be afraid—" Here she checked herself.

"What were you afraid of, nursie?" asked the princess.

"Never mind," she answered. "Perhaps I will tell you another day. Now tell me where you have been?"

"I've been up a long way to see my very great, huge, old grandmother," said the princess.

"What do you mean by that?" asked the nurse, who thought she was making fun.

"I mean that I've been a long way up and up to see my GREAT grandmother. Ah, nursie, you don't know what a beautiful mother of grandmothers I've got upstairs. She is *such* an old lady! with such lovely white hair!—as white as my silver cup. Now, when I think of it, I think her hair must be silver."

"What nonsense you are talking, princess!" said the nurse.

"I'm not talking nonsense," returned Irene, rather offended. "I will tell you all about her. She's much taller than you, and much prettier."

"Oh, I daresay!" remarked the nurse.

"And she lives upon pigeon's eggs."

"Most likely," said the nurse.

"And she sits in an empty room, spin-spinning all day long."

"Not a doubt of it," said the nurse.

"And she keeps her crown in her bedroom."

"Of course—quite the proper place to keep her crown in. She wears it in bed, I'll be bound."

"She didn't say that. And I don't think she does. That wouldn't be comfortable—would it? I don't think my papa wears his crown for a night-cap. Does he, nursie?"

"I never asked him. I daresay he does."

"And she's been there ever since I came here—ever so many years."

"Anybody could have told you that," said the nurse, who did not believe a word Irene was saying.

"Why didn't you tell me then?"

"There was no necessity. You could make it all up for yourself."

"You don't believe me then!" exclaimed the princess, astonished and angry, as well she might be.

"Did you expect me to believe you, princess?" asked the nurse coldly. "I know princesses are in the habit of telling make-believes, but you are the first I ever heard of who expected to have them believed," she added, seeing that the child was strangely in earnest.

The princess burst into tears.

"Well, I must say," remarked the nurse, now thoroughly vexed with her for crying, "it is not at all becoming in a princess to tell stories *and* expect to be believed just because she is a princess."

"But it's quite true, I tell you, nursie."

"You've dreamt it, then, child."

"No, I didn't dream it. I went up-stairs, and I lost myself, and if I hadn't found the beautiful lady, I should never have found myself."

"Oh, I daresay!"

"Well, you just come up with me, and see if I'm not telling the truth."

"Indeed I have other work to do. It's your dinner-time, and I won't have any more such nonsense,"

The princess wiped her eyes, and her face grew so hot that they were soon quite dry. She sat down to her dinner, but ate next to nothing. Not to be believed does not at all agree with princesses; for a real princess cannot tell a lie. So all the afternoon she did not speak a word. Only when the nurse spoke to her, she answered her, for a real princess is never rude— even when she does well to be offended.

Of course the nurse was not comfortable in her mind—not that she suspected the least truth in Irene's story, but that she loved her dearly, and was vexed with herself for having been cross to her. She thought her crossness was the cause of the princess' unhappiness, and had no idea that she was really and deeply hurt at not being believed. But, as it became more and more plain during the evening in every motion and look, that, although she tried to amuse herself with her toys, her heart was too vexed and troubled to enjoy them, her nurse's discomfort grew and grew. When bedtime came, she undressed and laid her down, but the child, instead of holding up her little mouth to be kissed, turned away from her and lay still. Then nursie's heart gave way altogether, and she began to cry. At the sound of her first sob, the princess turned again, and held her face to kiss her as usual. But the nurse had her handkerchief to her eyes, and did not see the movement.

"Nursie," said the princess, "why won't you believe me?"

"Because I can't believe you," said the nurse, getting angry again.

"Ah! then you can't help it," said Irene, "and I will not be vexed with you any more. I will give you a kiss and go to sleep."

"You little angel!" cried the nurse, and caught her out of bed, and walked about the room with her in her arms, kissing and hugging her.

"You *will* let me take you to see my dear old great big grandmother, won't you?" said the princess, as she laid her down again.

"And *you* won't say I'm ugly, any more—will you, princess?"

"Nursie! I never said you were ugly. What can you mean?"

"Well, if you didn't say it, you meant it."

"Indeed, I never did."

"You said I wasn't so pretty as that—"

"As my beautiful grandmother—yes, I did say that; and I say it again, for it's quite true."

"Then I *do* think you *are* unkind!" said the nurse, and put her handkerchief to her eyes again.

"Nursie, dear, everybody can't be as beautiful as every other body, you know. You are *very* nice-looking, but if you had been as beautiful as my grandmother—"

"Bother your grandmother!" said the nurse.

"Nurse, that's very rude. You are not fit to be spoken to— till you can behave better."

The princess turned away once more, and again the nurse was ashamed of herself.

"I'm sure I beg your pardon, princess," she said, though still in an offended tone. But the princess let the tone pass, and heeded only the words.

"You won't say it again, I am sure," she answered, once more turning toward her nurse. "I was only going to say that if you had been twice as nice-looking as you are, some king or other would have married you, and then what would have become of me?"

"You are an angel!" repeated the nurse, again embracing her.

"Now," insisted Irene, "you *will* come and see my grand-mother—won't you?"

"I will go with you anywhere you like, my cherub," she answered; and in two minutes the weary little princess was fast asleep.

CHAPTER V

THE PRINCESS LETS WELL ALONE

WHEN she woke the next morning, the first thing she heard was the rain still falling. Indeed, this day was so like the last, that it would have been difficult to tell where was the use of it. The first thing she thought of, however, was not the rain, but the lady in the tower; and the first question that occupied her thoughts was whether she should not ask the nurse to fufill her promise this very morning, and go with her to find her grandmother as soon as she had had her breakfast. But she came to the conclusion that perhaps the lady would not be pleased if she took anyone to see her without first asking leave; especially as it was pretty evident, seeing she lived on pigeons' eggs, and cooked them herself, that she did not want the household to know she was there. So the princess resolved to take the first opportunity of running up alone and asking whether she might bring her nurse. She believed the fact that she could not otherwise convince her she was telling the truth, would have much weight with her grandmother.

The princess and her nurse were the best of friends all dressing time, and the princess in consequence ate an enormous little breakfast.

"I wonder, Lootie"—that was her pet-name for her nurse —"what pigeons' eggs taste like?" she said, as she was eating her egg—not quite a common one, for they always picked out the pinky ones for her.

"We'll get you a pigeon's egg, and you shall judge for yourself," said the nurse.

"Oh, no, no!" returned Irene, suddenly reflecting they might disturb the old lady in getting it, and that even if they did not, she would have one less in consequence.

"What a strange creature you are," said the nurse—"first to want a thing and then to refuse it!"

But she did not say it crossly, and the princess never minded any remarks that were not unfriendly.

"Well, you see, Lootie, there are reasons," she returned, and said no more, for she did not want to bring up the subject of their former strife, lest her nurse should offer to go before she had had her grandmother's permission to bring her. Of course she could refuse to take her, but then she would believe her less than ever.

Now the nurse, as she said herself afterward, could not be every moment in the room, and as never before yesterday had the princess given her the smallest reason for anxiety, it had not yet come into her head to watch her more closely. So she soon gave her a chance, and the very first that offered, Irene was off and up the stairs again.

This day's adventure, however, did not turn out like yesterday's, although it began like it; and indeed to-day is very seldom like yesterday, if people would note the differences—even when it rains. The princess ran through passage after passage, and could not find the stair of the tower. My own suspicion is that she had not gone up high enough, and was searching on the second instead of the third floor. When she turned to go back, she failed equally in her search after the stair. She was lost once more.

Something made it even worse to bear this time, and it was no wonder that she cried again. Suddenly it occurred to her that it was after having cried before that she had found her grandmother's stair. She got up at once, wiped her eyes, and started upon a fresh quest. This time, although she did not find what she hoped, she found what was next best: she did not come on a stair that went up, but she came upon one that went down. It was evidently not the stair she had come up, yet it was a good deal better than none; so down she went, and was singing merrily before she reached the bottom. There, to her surprise, she found herself in the kitchen. Although she was not allowed to go there alone, her nurse had often taken her, and she was a great favorite with the servants. So there was a general rush at her the moment she appeared, for every one wanted to have her; and the report of where she was soon reached the nurse's ears. She came at once to fetch her; but she never suspected how she had got there, and the princess kept her own counsel.

Her failure to find the old lady not only disappointed her, but made her very thoughtful. Sometimes she came almost to the nurse's opinion that she had dreamed all about her; but that fancy never lasted very long. She wondered much whether she should ever see her again, and thought it very sad not to have been able to find her when she particularly wanted her. She resolved to say nothing more to her nurse on the subject, seeing it was so little in her power to prove her words.

CHAPTER VI

THE LITTLE MINER

THE next day the great cloud still hung over the mountain, and the rain poured like water from a full sponge. The princess was very fond of being out of doors, and she nearly cried when she saw that the weather was no better. But the mist was not of such a dark dingy gray; there was light in it; and as the hours went on, it grew brighter and brighter, until it was almost too brilliant to look at; and late in the afternoon, the sun broke out so gloriously that Irene clapped her hands, crying,

"See, see, Lootie! The sun has had his face washed. Look how bright he is! Do get my hat, and let us go out for a walk. Oh dear! oh dear! how happy I am!"

Lootie was very glad to please the princess. She got her hat and cloak, and they set out together for a walk up the mountain; for the road was so hard and steep that the water could not rest upon it, and it was always dry enough for walking a few minutes after the rain ceased. The clouds were rolling away in broken pieces, like great, overwoolly sheep, whose wool the sun had bleached till it was almost too white for the eyes to bear. Between them the sky shone with a deeper and purer blue, because of the rain. The trees on the road-side were hung all over with drops, which sparkled in the sun like jewels. The only things that were no brighter for the rain, were the brooks that ran down the mountain; they had

She clapped her hands with delight, and up rose
such a flapping of wings.

changed from the clearness of crystal to a muddy brown; but what they lost in color they gained in sound—or at least in noise, for a brook when it is swollen is not so musical as before. But Irene was in raptures with the great brown streams tumbling down everywhere; and Lootie shared in her delight, for she too had been confined to the house for three days. At length she observed that the sun was getting low, and said it was time to be going back. She made the remark again and again, but, every time, the princess begged her to go on just a little farther and a little farther; reminding her that it was much easier to go down hill, and saying that when they did turn, they would be at home in a moment. So on and on they did go, now to look at a group of ferns over whose tops a stream was pouring in a watery arch, now to pick a shining stone from a rock by the wayside, now to watch the flight of some bird. Suddenly the shadow of a great mountain peak came up from behind, and shot in front of them. When the nurse saw it, she started and shook, and tremulously grasping the hand of the princess turned and began to run down the hill.

"What's all the haste, nursie?" asked Irene, running alongside of her.

"We must not be out a moment longer."

"But we can't help being out a good many moments longer."

It was too true. The nurse almost cried. They were much too far from home. It was against express orders to be out with the princess one moment after the sun was down; and they were nearly a mile up the mountain! If his Majesty,

Irene's papa, were to hear of it, Lootie would certainly be dismissed; and to leave the princess would break her heart. It was no wonder she ran. But Irene was not in the least frightened, not knowing anything to be frightened at. She kept on chattering as well as she could, but it was not easy.

"Lootie! Lootie! why do you run so fast? It shakes my teeth when I talk."

"Then don't talk," said Lootie.

But the princess went on talking. She was always saying, "Look, look, Lootie," but Lootie paid no more heed to anything she said, only ran on.

"Look, look, Lootie! Don't you see that funny man peeping over the rock?"

Lootie only ran the faster. They had to pass the rock and when they came nearer, the princess clearly saw that it was only a large fragment of the rock itself that she had mistaken for a man.

"Look, look, Lootie! There's *such* a curious creature at the foot of that old tree. Look at it, Lootie! It's making faces at us, I do think."

Lootie gave a stifled cry, and ran faster still—so fast, that Irene's little legs could not keep up with her, and she fell with a clash. It was a hard down-hill road, and she had been running very fast—so it was no wonder she began to cry. This put the nurse nearly beside herself; but all she could do was to run on, the moment she got the princess on her feet again.

"Who's that laughing at me?" said the princess, trying to keep in her sobs, and running too fast for her grazed knees.

"Nobody, child," said the nurse, almost angrily.

But that instant there came a burst of coarse tittering from somewhere near, and a hoarse indistinct voice that seemed to say, "Lies! lies! lies!"

"Oh!" cried the nurse with a sigh that was almost a scream, and ran on faster than ever.

"Nursie! Lootie! I can't run any more. Do let us walk a bit."

"What *am* I to do?" said the nurse. "Here, I will carry you."

She caught her up; but found her much too heavy to run with, and had to set her down again. Then she looked wildly about her, gave a great cry, and said—

"We've taken the wrong turning somewhere, and I don't know where we are. We are lost, lost!"

The terror she was in had quite bewildered her. It was true enough they had lost the way. They had been running down into a little valley in which there was no house to be seen.

Now Irene did not know what good reason there was for her nurse's terror, for the servants had all strict orders never to mention the goblins to her, but it was very discomposing to see her nurse in such a fright. Before, however, she had time to grow thoroughly alarmed like her, she heard the sound of whistling, and that revived her. Presently she saw a boy coming up the road from the valley to meet them. He was the whistler; but before they met, his whistling changed to singing. And this is something like what he sang:

"Ring! dod! bang!
Go the hammers' clang!
Hit and turn and bore!
Whizz and puff and roar!

Thus we rive the rocks,
Force the goblin locks.
See the shining ore!
One, two, three—
Bright as gold can be!
Four, five, six—
Shovels, mattocks, picks!
Seven, eight, nine—
Light your lamp at mine.
Ten, eleven, twelve—
Loosely hold the helve.
We're the merry miner-boys,
Make the goblins hold their noise."

"I wish you would hold *your* noise," said the nurse rudely, **for** the very word goblin at such a time and in such a place made her tremble. It would bring the goblins upon them to a certainty, she thought, to defy them in that way. But whether the boy heard her or not, he did not stop his singing.

"Thirteen, fourteen, fifteen—
This is worth the siftin';
Sixteen, seventeen, eighteen—
There's the match, and lay't in.
Nineteen, twenty—
Goblins in a plenty."

"Do be quiet," cried the nurse, in a whispered shriek. But the boy, who was now close at hand, still went on.

"Hush! scush! scurry!
There you go in a hurry!
Gobble! gobble! gobblin!
There you go a wobblin';
Hobble, hobble, hobblin'!
Cobble! cobble! cobblin'!
Hob-bob-goblin—Huuuuuh!"

[36]

THE LITTLE MINER

"There!" said the boy, as he stood still opposite them. "There! that'll do for them. They can't bear singing, and they can't stand that song. They can't sing themselves, for they have no more voice than a crow; and they don't like other people to sing."

The boy was dressed in a miner's dress, with a curious cap on his head. He was a very nice-looking boy, with eyes as dark as the mines in which he worked, and as sparkling as the crystals in their rocks. He was about twelve years old. His face was almost too pale for beauty, which came of his being so little in the open air and the sunlight—for even vegetables grown in the dark are white; but he looked happy, merry indeed—perhaps at the thought of having routed the goblins; and his bearing as he stood before them had nothing clownish or rude about it.

"I saw them," he went on, "as I came up; and I'm very glad I did. I knew they were after somebody, but I couldn't see who it was. They won't touch you so long as I'm with you."

"Why, who are you?" asked the nurse, offended at the freedom with which he spoke to them.

"I'm Peter's son."

"Who's Peter?"

"Peter the miner."

"I don't know him."

"I'm his son, though."

"And why should the goblins mind *you*, pray?"

"Because I don't mind them. I'm used to them."

"What difference does that make?"

"If you're not afraid of them, they're afraid of you. I'm

not afraid of them. That's all. But it's all that's wanted—up here, that is. It's a different thing down there. They won't always mind that song even, down there. And if anyone sings it, they stand grinning at him awfully; and if he gets frightened, and misses a word, or says a wrong one, they— oh! don't they give it him!"

"What do they do to him?" asked Irene, with a trembling voice.

"Don't go frightening the princess," said the nurse.

"The princess!" repeated the little miner, taking off his curious cap. "I beg your pardon; but you oughtn't to be out so late. Everybody knows that's against the law."

"Yes, indeed it is!" said the nurse, beginning to cry again. "And I shall have to suffer for it."

"What does that matter?" said the boy. "It must be your fault. It is the princess who will suffer for it. I hope they didn't hear you call her the princess. If they did, they're sure to know her again: they're awfully sharp."

"Lootie! Lootie!" cried the princess. "Take me home."

"Don't go on like that," said the nurse to the boy, almost fiercely. "How could I help it? I lost my way."

"You shouldn't have been out so late. You wouldn't have lost your way if you hadn't been frightened," said the boy. "Come along. I'll soon set you right again. Shall I carry your little Highness?"

"Impertinence!" murmured the nurse, but she did not say it aloud, for she thought if she made him angry, he might take his revenge by telling some one belonging to the house, and then it would be sure to come to the king's ears.

"No, thank you," said Irene. "I can walk very well, though 1 can't run so fast as nursie. If you will give me one hand, Lootie will give me another, and then I shall get on famously."

They soon had her between them, holding a hand of each.

"Now let's run," said the nurse.

"No, no," said the little miner. "That's the worst thing you can do. If you hadn't run before, you would not have lost your way. And if you run now, they will be after you in a moment."

"I don't want to run," said Irene.

"You don't think of *me*," said the nurse.

"Yes, I do, Lootie. The boy says they won't touch us if we don't run."

"Yes; but if they know at the house that I've kept you out so late, I shall be turned away, and that would break my heart."

"Turned away, Lootie. Who would turn you away?"

"Your papa, child."

"But I'll tell him it was all my fault. And you know it was, Lootie."

"He won't mind that. I'm sure he won't."

"Then I'll cry, and go down on my knees to him, and beg him not to take away my own dear Lootie."

The nurse was comforted at hearing this, and said no more. They went on, walking pretty fast, but taking care not to run a step.

"I want to talk to you," said Irene to the little miner; "but it's so awkward! I don't know your name."

"My name's Curdie, little princess."

"What a funny name! Curdie! What more?"

"Curdie Peterson. What's your name, please?"

"Irene."

"What more?"

"I don't know what more.—What more is my name, Lootie?"

"Princesses haven't got more than one name. They don't want it."

"Oh then, Curdie, you must call me just Irene, and no more."

"No, indeed," said the nurse indignantly. "He shall do no such thing."

"What shall he call me, then, Lootie?"

"Your royal Highness."

"My royal Highness! What's that? No, no, Lootie, I will not be called names. I don't like them. You said to me once yourself that it's only rude children that call names; and I'm sure Curdie wouldn't be rude.—Curdie, my name's Irene."

"Well, Irene," said Curdie, with a glance at the nurse which showed he enjoyed teasing her, "it's very kind of you to let me call you anything. I like your name very much."

He expected the nurse to interfere again; but he soon saw that she was too frightened to speak. She was staring at something a few yards before them, in the middle of the path, where it narrowed between rocks so that only one could pass at a time.

"It's very much kinder of you to go out of your way to take us home," said Irene.

"I'm not going out of my way yet," said Curdie. "It's on the other side those rocks the path turns off to my father's."

"You wouldn't think of leaving us till we're safe home, I'm sure," gasped the nurse.

"Of course not," said Curdie.

"You dear, good, kind Curdie! I'll give you a kiss when we get home," said the princess.

The nurse gave her a great pull by the hand she held. But at that instant the something in the middle of the way, which had looked like a great lump of earth brought down by the rain, began to move. One after another it shot out four long things, like two arms and two legs, but it was now too dark to tell what they were. The nurse began to tremble from head to foot. Irene clasped Curdie's hand yet faster, and Curdie began to sing again.

> "One, two—
> Hit and hew!
> Three, four—
> Blast and bore!
> Five, six—
> There's a fix!
> Seven, eight—
> Hold it straight.
> Nine, ten—
> Hit again!
> Hurry! scurry!
> Bother! smother!
> There's a toad
> In the road!
> Smash it!
> Squash it!
> Fry it!
> Dry it!
> You're another!
> Up and off!
> There's enough!—Huuuuuh!"

As he uttered the last words, Curdie let go his hold of his companion, and rushed at the thing in the road, as if he would

trample it under his feet. It gave a great spring, and ran straight
up one of the rocks like a huge spider. Curdie turned back
laughing, and took Irene's hand again. She grasped his very
tight, but said nothing till they had passed the rocks. A few
yards more and she found herself on a part of the road she knew,
and was able to speak again.

"Do you know, Curdie, I don't quite like your song; it
sounds to me rather rude," she said.

"Well, perhaps it is," answered Curdie. "I never thought
of that; it's a way we have. We do it because they don't like it."

"Who don't like it?"

"The cobs, as we call them."

"Don't!" said the nurse.

"Why not?" said Curdie.

"I beg you won't. Please don't."

"Oh, if you ask me that way, of course I won't; though I
don't a bit know why. Look! there are the lights of your great
house down below. You'll be at home in five minutes now."

Nothing more happened. They reached home in safety.
Nobody had missed them, or even known they had gone out;
and they arrived at the door belonging to their part of the
house without anyone seeing them. The nurse was rushing
in with a hurried and not over-gracious good-night to Curdie;
but the princess pulled her hand from hers, and was just throwing her arms around Curdie's neck, when she caught her again
and dragged her away.

"Lootie, Lootie, I promised Curdie a kiss," cried Irene.

"A princess mustn't give kisses. It's not at all proper,"
said Lootie.

"But I promised," said the princess.

"There's no occasion; he's only a miner-boy."

"He is a good boy, and a brave boy, and he has been very kind to us. Lootie! Lootie! I *promised*."

"Then you shouldn't have promised."

"Lootie, I promised him a kiss."

"Your royal Highness," said Lootie, suddenly growing very respectful, "must come in directly."

"Nurse, a princess must *not* break her word," said Irene, drawing herself up and standing stockstill.

Lootie did not know which the king might count the worst —to let the princess be out after sunset, or to let her kiss a miner-boy. She did not know that, being a gentleman, as many kings have been, he would have counted neither of them the worse. However much he might have disliked his daughter to kiss the miner-boy, he would not have had her break her word for all the goblins in creation. But, as I say, the nurse was not lady enough to understand this, and so she was in a great difficulty, for, if she insisted, some one might hear the princess cry and run to see, and then all would come out. But here Curdie came again to the rescue.

"Never mind, Princess Irene," he said. "You mustn't kiss me tonight. But you sha'n't break your word. I will come another time. You may be sure I will."

"Oh, thank you, Curdie!" said the princess, and stopped crying.

"Good night, Irene; good night, Lootie," said Curdie, and turned and was out of sight in a moment.

[43]

"I should like to see him!" muttered the nurse, as she carried the princess to the nursery.

"You *will* see him," said Irene. "You may be sure Curdie will keep his word. He's *sure* to come again."

"I should like to see him!" repeated the nurse, and said no more. She did not want to open a new cause of strife with the princess by saying more plainly what she meant. Glad enough that she had succeeded both in getting home unseen, and in keeping the princess from kissing the miner's boy, she resolved to watch her far better in future. Her carelessness had already doubled the danger she was in. Formerly the goblins were her only fear; now she had to protect her charge from Curdie as well.

CHAPTER VII

THE MINES

CURDIE went home whistling. He resolved to say nothing about the princess for fear of getting the nurse into trouble, for while he enjoyed teasing her because of her absurdity, he was careful not to do her any harm. He saw no more of the goblins, and was soon fast asleep in his bed.

He woke in the middle of the night, and thought he heard curious noises outside. He sat up and listened; then got up, and, opening the door very quietly, went out. When he peeped round the corner, he saw, under his own window, a group of stumpy creatures, whom he at once recognized by their shape. Hardly, however, had he begun his "One, two, three!" when they broke asunder, scurried away, and were out of sight. He returned laughing, got into bed again, and was fast asleep in a moment.

Reflecting a little over the matter in the morning, he came to the conclusion that, as nothing of the kind had ever happened before, they must be annoyed with him for interfering to protect the princess. By the time he was dressed, however, he was thinking of something quite different, for he did not value the enmity of the goblins in the least.

As soon as they had had breakfast, he set off with his father for the mine.

They entered the hill by a natural opening under a huge rock, where a little stream rushed out. They followed its course for a few yards, when the passage took a turn, and sloped steeply into the heart of the hill. With many angles and windings and branchings off, and sometimes with steps where it came upon a natural gulf, it led them deep into the hill before they arrived at the place where they were at present digging out the precious ore. This was of various kinds, for the mountain was very rich with the better sorts of metals. With flint and steel, and tinder box, they lighted their lamps, then fixed them on their heads, and were soon hard at work with their pickaxes and shovels and hammers. Father and son were at work near each other, but not in the same *gang*— the passages out of which the ore was dug, they called *gangs*— for when the *lode*, or vein of ore, was small, one miner would have to dig away alone in a passage no bigger than gave him just room to work—sometimes in uncomfortable cramped positions. If they stopped for a moment they could hear everywhere around them, some nearer, some farther off, the sounds of their companions burrowing away in all directions in the inside of the great mountain—some boring holes in the rock in order to blow it up with gunpowder, others shoveling the broken ore into baskets to be carried to the mouth of the mine, others hitting away with their pickaxes. Sometimes, if the miner was in a very lonely part, he would hear only a tap-tapping, no louder than that of a woodpecker, for the sound would come from a great distance off through the solid mountain rock.

The work was hard at best, for it is very warm underground; but it was not particularly unpleasant, and some of the miners, when they wanted to earn a little more money for a particular

[46]

purpose, would stop behind the rest, and work all night. But you could not tell night from day down there, except from feeling tired and sleepy; for no light of the sun ever came into those gloomy regions. Some who had thus remained behind during the night, although certain there were none of their companions at work, would declare the next morning that they heard, every time they halted for a moment to take breath, a tap-tapping all about them, as if the mountain were then more full of miners than ever it was during the day; and some in consequence would never stay over night, for all knew those were the sounds of the goblins. They worked only at night, for the miners' night was the goblins' day. Indeed, the greater number of the miners were afraid of the goblins: for there were strange stories well known amongst them of the treatment some had received whom the goblins had surprised at their work during the night. The more courageous of them, however, amongst them Peter Peterson and Curdie, who in this took after his father, had stayed in the mine all night again and again, and although they had several times encountered a few stray goblins, had never yet failed in driving them away. As I have indicated already, the chief defence against them was verse, for they hated verse of every kind, and some kinds they could not endure at all. I suspect they could not make any themselves, and that was why they disliked it so much. At all events, those who were most afraid of them were those who could neither make verses themselves, nor remember the verses that other people made for them; while those who were never afraid were those who could make verses for themselves; for although there were certain old rhymes which were very effectual, yet it was well known that a new rhyme, if of the right sort, was even more distasteful to them, and therefore more effectual in putting them to flight.

Perhaps my readers may be wondering what the goblins could be about, working all night long, seeing they never carried up the ore and sold it; but when I have informed them concerning what Curdie learned the very next night, they will be able to understand.

For Curdie had determined, if his father would permit him, to remain there alone this night—and that for two reasons: first, he wanted to get extra wages in order that he might buy a very warm red petticoat for his mother, who had begun to complain of the cold of the mountain air sooner than usual this autumn; and second, he had just a faint glimmering of hope of finding out what the goblins were about under his window the night before.

When he told his father, he made no objection, for he had great confidence in his boy's courage and resources.

"I'm sorry I can't stay with you," said Peter; "but I want to go and pay the parson a visit this evening, and besides I've had a bit of a headache all day."

"I'm sorry for that, father," said Curdie.

"Oh! it's not much. You'll be sure to take care of yourself, won't you?"

"Yes, father; I will. I'll keep a sharp lookout, I promise you."

Curdie was the only one who remained in the mine. About six o'clock the rest went away, every one bidding him good

"Never mind, Princess Irene," he said. "You mustn't kiss me tonight. But you sha'n't break your word. I will come another time."

night, and telling him to take care of himself; for he was a great favorite with them all.

"Don't forget your rhymes," said one.

"No, no," answered Curdie.

"It's no matter if he does," said another, "for he'll only have to make a new one."

"Yes, but he mightn't be able to make it fast enough," said another; "and while it was cooking in his head, they might take a mean advantage and set upon him."

"I'll do my best," said Curdie. "I'm not afraid."

"We all know that," they returned, and left him.

CHAPTER VIII

THE GOBLINS

FOR some time Curdie worked away briskly, throwing all the ore he had disengaged on one side behind him, to be ready for carrying out in the morning. He heard a good deal of goblin-tapping, but it all sounded far away in the hill, and he paid it little heed. Toward midnight he began to feel rather hungry; so he dropped his pickaxe, got a lump of bread which in the morning he had laid in a damp hole in the rock, sat down on a heap of ore and ate his supper. Then he leaned back for five minutes' rest before beginning his work again, and laid his head against the rock. He had not kept the position for one minute before he heard something which made him sharpen his ears. It sounded like a voice inside the rock. After a while he heard it again. It was a goblin-voice —there could be no doubt about that—and this time he could make out the words.

"Hadn't we better be moving?" it said.

A rougher and deeper voice replied:

"There's no hurry. That wretched little mole won't be through to-night, if he work ever so hard. He's by no means at the thinnest place."

"But you still think the lode does come through into our house?" said the first voice.

"Yes, but a good bit farther on than he has got to yet. If he had struck a stroke more to the side just here," said the

[50]

goblin, tapping the very stone, as it seemed to Curdie, against which his head lay, "he would have been through; but he's a couple of yards past it now, and if he follow the lode it will be a week before it leads him in. You see it back there—a long way. Still, perhaps, in case of accident, it would be as well to be getting out of this. Helfer, you'll take the great chest. That's your business, you know."

"Yes, dad," said a third voice. "But you must help me to get it on my back. It's awfully heavy, you know."

"Well, it isn't just a bag of smoke, I admit. But you're as strong as a mountain, Helfer."

"You say so, dad. I think myself I'm all right. But I could carry ten times as much if it wasn't for my feet."

"That *is* your weak point, I confess, my boy."

"Ain't it yours, too, father?"

"Well, to be honest, it is a goblin-weakness. Why *they* come so soft, I declare I haven't an idea."

"Specially when your head's so hard, you know, father."

"Yes, my boy. The goblin's glory is his head. To think how the fellows up above there have to put on helmets and things when they go fighting. Ha! ha!"

"But why don't we wear shoes like them, father? I should like it—specially when I've got a chest like that on my head."

"Well, you see, it's not the fashion. The king never wears shoes."

"The queen does."

"Yes; but that's for distinction. The first queen, you see —I mean the king's first wife—wore shoes of course, because she came from upstairs; and so, when she died, the next queen

[51]

would not be inferior to her as she called it, and would wear shoes too. It was all pride. She is the hardest in forbidding them to the rest of the women."

"I'm sure I wouldn't wear them—no, not for—that I wouldn't!" said the first voice, which was evidently that of the mother of the family. "I can't think why either of them should."

"Didn't I tell you the first was from upstairs?" said the other. "That was the only silly thing I ever knew his Majesty guilty of. Why should he marry an outlandish woman like that—one of our natural enemies too?"

"I suppose he fell in love with her."

"Pooh! pooh! He's just as happy now with one of his own people."

"Did she die *very* soon? They didn't tease her to death, did they?"

"Oh dear no! The king worshipped her very footmarks."

"What made her die, then? Didn't the air agree with her?"

"She died when the young prince was born."

"How silly of her! *We* never do that. It must have been because she wore shoes."

"I don't know that."

"Why do they wear shoes up there?"

"Ah! now that's a sensible question, and I will answer it. But in order to do so, I must first tell you a secret. I once saw the queen's feet."

"Without her shoes?"

"Yes—without her shoes."

"No! Did you? How was it?"

"Never you mind how it was. *She* didn't know I saw them. And what do you think!—they had *toes!*"

"Toes! What's that?"

"You may well ask! I should never have known if I had not seen the queen's feet. Just imagine! the ends of her feet were split up into five or six thin pieces!"

"Oh, horrid! How *could* the king have fallen in love with her?"

"You forget that she wore shoes. That is just why she wore them. That is why all the men, and women too, upstairs wear shoes. They can't bear the sight of their own feet without them."

"Ah! now I understand. If ever you wish for shoes again, Helfer, I'll hit your feet—I will."

"No, no, mother; pray don't."

"Then don't you."

"But with such a big box on my head—"

A horrid scream followed, which Curdie interpreted as in reply to a blow from his mother upon the feet of her eldest goblin.

"Well, I never knew so much before!" remarked a fourth voice.

"Your knowledge is not universal quite yet," said the father. "You were only fifty last month. Mind you see to the bed and bedding. As soon as we've finished our supper, we'll be up and going. Ha! ha! ha!"

"What are you laughing at, husband?"

"I'm laughing to think what a mess the miners will find themselves in—somewhere before this day ten years."

"Why, what do you mean?"

"Oh, nothing."

"Oh yes, you do mean something. You always do mean something."

"It's more than you do, then, wife."

"That may be; but it's not more than I find out, you know."

"Ha! ha! You're a sharp one. What a mother you've got, Helfer!"

"Yes, father,"

"Well, I suppose I must tell you. They're all at the palace consulting about it to-night; and as soon as we've got away from this thin place, I'm going there to hear what night they fix upon. I should like to see that young ruffian there on the other side, struggling in the agonies of—"

He dropped his voice so low that Curdie could hear only a growl. The growl went on in a low bass for a good while, as inarticulate as if the goblin's tongue had been a sausage; and it was not until his wife spoke again that it rose to its former pitch.

"But what shall we do when you are at the palace?" she asked.

"I will see you safe in the new house I've been digging for you for the last two months. Podge, you mind the table and chairs. I commit them to your care. The table has seven legs—each chair three. I shall require them all at your hands."

After this arose a confused conversation about the various household goods and their transport; and Curdie heard nothing more that was of any importance.

He now knew at least one of the reasons for the constant

sound of the goblin hammers and pickaxes at night. They were making new houses for themselves, to which they might retreat when the miners should threaten to break into their dwellings. But he had learned two things of far greater importance. The first was, that some grievous calamity was preparing, and almost ready to fall upon the heads of the miners; the second was—the one weak point of a goblin's body: he had not known that their feet were so tender as he had now reason to suspect. He had heard it said that they had no toes: he had never had opportunity of inspecting them closely enough in the dusk in which they always appeared, to satisfy himself whether it was a correct report. Indeed, he had not been able even to satisfy himself as to whether they had no fingers, although that also was commonly said to be the fact. One of the miners, indeed, who had had more schooling than the rest, was wont to argue that such must have been the primordial condition of humanity, and that education and handicraft had developed both toes and fingers—with which proposition Curdie had once heard his father sarcastically agree, alleging in support of it the probability that babies' gloves were a traditional remnant of the old state of things; while the stockings of all ages, no regard being paid in them to the toes, pointed in the same direction. But what was of importance was the fact concerning the softness of the goblin-feet, which he foresaw might be useful to all miners. What he had to do in the mean time, however, was to discover, if possible, the special evil design the goblins had now in their heads.

Although he knew all the gangs and all the natural galleries with which they communicated in the mined part of the mountain, he had not the least idea where the palace of the king of the gnomes was; otherwise he would have set out at once on the enterprise of discovering what the said design was. He judged, and rightly, that it must lie in a farther part of the mountain, between which and the mine there was as yet no communication. There must be one nearly completed, however; for it could be but a thin partition which now separated them. If only he could get through in time to follow the goblins as they retreated! A few blows would doubtless be sufficient—just where his ear now lay; but if he attempted to strike there with his pickaxe, he would only hasten the departure of the family, put them on their guard, and perhaps lose their involuntary guidance. He therefore began to feel the wall with his hands, and soon found that some of the stones were loose enough to be drawn out with little noise.

Laying hold of a large one with both his hands, he drew it gently out, and let it down softly.

"What was that noise?" said the goblin father.

Curdie blew out his light, lest it should shine through.

"It must be that one miner that stayed behind the rest," said the mother.

"No; he's been gone a good while. I haven't heard a blow for an hour. Besides, it wasn't like that."

"Then I suppose it must have been a stone carried down the brook inside."

"Perhaps. It will have more room by and by."

Curdie kept quite still. After a little while, hearing nothing but the sounds of their preparations for departure, mingled with an occasional word of direction, and anxious to know whether the removal of the stone had made an opening into the goblins' house, he put in his hand to feel. It went in a good way, and then came in contact with something soft. He had but a moment to feel it over, it was so quickly withdrawn: it was one of the toeless goblin-feet. The owner of it gave a cry of fright.

"What's the matter, Helfer?" asked his mother.

"A beast came out of the wall, and licked my foot."

"Nonsense! There are no wild beasts in our country," said his father.

"But it was, father. I felt it."

"Nonsense, I say. Will you malign your native realms and reduce them to a level with the country up-stairs? That is swarming with wild beasts of every description."

"But I did feel it, father."

"I tell you to hold your tongue. You are no patriot."

Curdie suppressed his laughter, and lay still as a mouse— but no stiller, for every moment he kept nibbling away with his fingers at the edges of the hole. He was slowly making it bigger, for here the rock had been very much shattered with the blasting.

There seemed to be a good many in the family, to judge from the mass of confused talk which now and then came through the hole; but when all were speaking together, and just as if they had bottle-brushes—each at least one—in their throats, it was not easy to make out much that was said. At length he heard once more what the father-goblin was saying.

"Now then," he said, "get your bundles on your backs. Here, Helfer, I'll help you up with your chest."

[57]

"I wish it *was* my chest, father."

"Your turn will come in good time enough! Make haste. I *must* go to the meeting at the palace to-night. When that's over, we can come back and clear out the last of the things before our enemies return in the morning. Now light your torches, and come along. What a distinction it is to provide our own light, instead of being dependent on a thing hung up in the air—a most disagreeable contrivance—intended no doubt to blind us when we venture out under its baleful influence! Quite glaring and vulgar, I call it, though no doubt useful to poor creatures who haven't the wit to make light for themselves!"

Curdie could hardly keep himself from calling through to know whether they made the fire to light their torches by. But a moment's reflection showed him that they would have said they did, inasmuch as they struck two stones together, and the fire came.

CHAPTER IX

THE HALL OF THE GOBLIN PALACE

ASOUND of many soft feet followed, but soon ceased. Then Curdie flew at the hole like a tiger, and tore and pulled. The sides gave way, and it was soon large enough for him to crawl through. He would not betray himself by rekindling his lamp, but the torches of the retreating company, departing in a straight line up a long avenue from the door of their cave, threw back light enough to afford him a glance round the deserted home of the goblins. To his surprise, he could discover nothing to distinguish it from an ordinary cave in the rock, upon many of which he had come with the rest of the miners in the progress of their excavations. The goblins had talked of coming back for the rest of their household gear: he saw nothing that would have made him suspect a family had taken shelter there for a single night. The floor was rough and stony; the walls full of projecting corners; the roof in one place twenty feet high, in another endangering his forehead; while on one side a stream, no thicker than a needle, it is true, but still sufficient to spread a wide dampness over the wall, flowed down the face of the rock. But the troop in front of him was toiling under heavy burdens. He could distinguish Helfer now and then, in the flickering light and shade, with his heavy chest on his bending shoulders; while the second brother was almost buried in what looked like a great feather-bed. "Where do they get the feathers?" thought Curdie; but in a moment the troop disappeared at a turn of the way, and it was now both safe and necessary for Curdie to follow them, lest they should be round the next turning before he saw them again, for so he might lose them altogether. He darted after them like a grayhound. When he reached the corner and looked cautiously round, he saw them again at some distance down another long passage. None of the galleries he saw that night bore signs of the work of man—or of goblin either. Stalactites far older than the mines hung from their roofs; and their floors were rough with boulders and large round stones, showing that there water must have once run. He waited again at this corner till they had disappeared round the next, and so followed them a long way through one passage after another. The passages grew more and more lofty, and were more and more covered in the roof with shining stalactites.

It was a strange enough procession which he followed. But the strangest part of it was the household animals which crowded amongst the feet of the goblins. It was true they had no wild animals down there—at least they did not know of any; but they had a wonderful number of tame ones. I must, however, reserve any contributions toward the natural history of these for a later position in my story.

At length, turning a corner too abruptly, he had almost rushed into the middle of the goblin family; for there they had already set down all their burdens on the floor of a cave considerably larger than that which they had left. They were as yet too breathless to speak, else he would have had warning of their arrest. He started back, however, before any one saw him, and retreating a good way, stood watching till the father should come out to go to the palace. Before very long, both he and his son Helfer appeared and kept on in the same direction as before, while Curdie followed them again with renewed precaution. For a long time he heard no sound except something like the rush of a river inside the rock; but at length what seemed the far-off noise of a great shouting reached his ears, which however presently ceased. After advancing a good way farther, he thought he heard a single voice. It sounded clearer and clearer as he went on, until at last he could almost distinguish the words. In a moment or two, keeping after the goblins round another corner, he once more started back—this time in amazement.

He was at the entrance of a magnificent cavern, of an oval shape, once probably a huge natural reservoir of water, now the great palace hall of the goblins. It rose to a tremendous height, but the roof was composed of such shining materials, and the multitude of torches carried by the goblins who crowded the floor lighted up the place so brilliantly, that Curdie could see to the top quite well. But he had no idea how immense the place was, until his eyes had got accustomed to it, which was not for a good many minutes. The rough projections on the walls, and the shadows thrown upward from them by the torches, made the sides of the chamber look as if they were crowded with statues upon brackets and pedestals, reaching in irregular tiers from floor to roof. The walls themselves were, in many parts, of gloriously shining substances, some of them gorgeously colored besides, which powerfully contrasted with the shadows. Curdie could not help wondering whether his rhymes would be of any use against such a multitude of goblins as filled the floor of the hall, and indeed felt considerably tempted to begin his shout of *One, two, three!* but as there was no reason for routing them, and much for endeavoring to discover their designs, he kept himself perfectly quiet, and peeping round the edge of the doorway, listened with both his sharp ears.

At the other end of the hall, high above the heads of the multitude, was a terrace-like ledge of considerable height, caused by the receding of the upper part of the cavern wall. Upon this sat the king and his court, the king on a throne hollowed out of a huge block of green copper ore, and his court upon lower seats around it. The king had been making them a speech, and the applause which followed it was what Curdie had heard. One of the court was now addressing the multitude. What he heard him say was to the following effect:

"Hence it appears that two plans have been for some time together working in the strong head of his Majesty for the deliverance of his people. Regardless of the fact that we were the first possessors of the regions they now inhabit, regardless equally of the fact that we abandoned that region from the loftiest motives; regardless also of the self-evident fact that we excel them as far in mental ability as they excel us in stature, they look upon us as a degraded race, and make a mockery of all our finer feelings. But the time has almost arrived when—thanks to his Majesty's inventive genius— it will be in our power to take a thorough revenge upon them once for all, in respect of their unfriendly behavior."

"May it please your Majesty—" cried a voice close by the door, which Curdie recognized as that of the goblin he had followed.

"Who is he that interrupts the Chancellor?" cried another from near the throne.

"Glump," answered several voices.

"He is our trusty subject," said the king himself, in a slow and stately voice: "let him come forward and speak."

A lane was parted through the crowd, and Glump having ascended the platform and bowed to the king, spoke as follows:

"Sire, I would have held my peace, had I not known that I only knew how near was the moment to which the Chancellor had just referred. In all probability, before another day is past, the enemy will have broken through into my house— the partition between being even now not more than a foot in thickness."

"Not quite so much," thought Curdie to himself.

"This very evening I have had to remove my household effects; therefore the sooner we are ready to carry out the plan, for the execution of which his Majesty has been making such magnificent preparations, the better. I may just add, that within the last few days I have perceived a small out- break in my dining-room, which combined with observations upon the course of the river escaping where the evil men enter, has convinced me that close to the spot must lie a deep gulf in its channel. This discovery will, I trust, add considerably to the otherwise immense forces at his Majesty's disposal."

He ceased, and the king graciously acknowledged his speech with a bend of his head; whereupon Glump, after a bow to his Majesty, slid down amongst the rest of the undistinguished multitude. Then the Chancellor rose and resumed.

"The information which the worthy Glump has given us," he said, "might have been of considerable import at the present moment, but for that other design already referred to, which naturally takes precedence. His Majesty, unwilling to proceed to extremities, and well aware that such measures sooner or later result in violent reactions, has excogitated a more fundamental and comprehensive measure, of which I need say no more. Should his Majesty be successful—as who dares to doubt?—then a peace, all to the advantage of the goblin kingdom, will be established for a generation at least, rendered absolutely secure by the pledge which his royal Highness the prince will have and hold for the good behavior of his relatives. Should his Majesty fail—which who shall dare even to imagine in his most secret thoughts?—then will be the time for carrying out with rigor the design to which Glump referred, and for which our preparations are even now all but completed. The failure of the former will render the latter imperative."

Curdie perceiving that the assembly was drawing to a close, and that there was little chance of either plan being more fully discovered, now thought it prudent to make his escape before the goblins began to disperse, and slipped quietly away.

There was not much danger of meeting any goblins, for all the men at least were left behind him in the palace; but there was considerable danger of his taking a wrong turning, for he had now no light, and had therefore to depend upon his memory and his hands. After he had left behind him the glow that issued from the door of Glump's new abode, he was utterly without guide, so far as his eyes were concerned.

He was most anxious to get back through the hole before the goblins should return to fetch the remains of their furniture. It was not that he was in the least afraid of them, but, as it was of the utmost importance that he should thoroughly discover what the plans they were cherishing were, he must not occasion the slightest suspicion that they were watched by a miner.

He hurried on, feeling his way along the walls of rock. Had he not been very courageous, he must have been very anxious, for he could not but know that if he lost his way it would be the most difficult thing in the world to find it again. Morning would bring no light into these regions; and toward him least of all, who was known as a special rhymster and persecutor, could goblins be expected to exercise courtesy? Well might he wish that he had brought his lamp and tinder-box with him, of which he had not thought when he crept so eagerly after the goblins! He wished it all the more when, after a while, he found his way blocked up, and could get no farther. It was of no use to turn back, for he had not the least idea where he had begun to go wrong. Mechanically, however, he kept feeling about the walls that hemmed him in. His hand came upon a place where a tiny stream of water was running down the face of the rock. "What a stupid I am!" he said to himself. "I am actually at the end of my journey! —and there are the goblins coming back to fetch their things!" he added, as the red glimmer of their torches appeared at the end of the long avenue that led up to the cave. In a moment he had thrown himself on the floor, and wriggled backward through the hole. The floor on the other side was several feet lower, which made it easier to get back. It was all he could do to lift the largest stone he had taken out of the hole, but he did manage to shove it in again. He sat down on the ore-heap and thought.

He was pretty sure that the latter plan of the goblins was to inundate the mine by breaking outlets for the water accumulated in the natural reservoirs of the mountain, as well as running through portions of it. While the part hollowed by the miners remained shut off from that inhabited by the goblins, they had had no opportunity of injuring them thus; but now that a passage was broken through, and the goblins' part proved the higher in the mountain, it was clear to Curdie that the mine could be destroyed in an hour. Water was always the chief danger to which the miners were exposed. They met with a little choke-damp sometimes, but never with the explosive fire-damp so common in coal mines. Hence they were careful as soon as they saw any appearance of water.

As the result of his reflections while the goblins were busy in their old home, it seemed to Curdie that it would be best to build up the whole of this gang, filling it with stone, and clay or lime, so that there should be no smallest channel for the water to get into. There was not, however, any immediate danger, for the execution of the goblins' plan was contingent upon the failure of that unknown design which was to take precedence of it; and he was most anxious to keep the door of communication open, that he might if possible discover what that former plan was. At the same time they could not then resume their intermitted labors for the inundation without his finding it out; when by putting all hands to the work, the one existing outlet might in a single night be rendered impenetrable to any weight of water; for by filling the gang entirely up, their embankment would be buttressed by the sides of the mountain itself.

As soon as he found that the goblins had again retired, he lighted his lamp, and proceeded to fill the hole he had made with such stones as he could withdraw when he pleased. He then thought it better, as he might have occasion to be up a good many nights after this, to go home and have some sleep.

How pleasant the night-air felt upon the outside of the mountain after what he had gone through in the inside of it! He hurried up the hill, without meeting a single goblin on the way, and called and tapped at the window until he woke his father, who soon rose and let him in. He told him the whole story, and, just as he had expected, his father thought it best to work that lode no farther, but at the same time to pretend occasionally to be at work there still, in order that the goblins might have no suspicions. Both father and son then went to bed, and slept soundly until the morning.

CHAPTER X

THE PRINCESS'S KING-PAPA

THE weather continued fine for weeks, and the little princess went out every day. So long a period of fine weather had indeed never been known upon that mountain. The only uncomfortable thing was that her nurse was so nervous and particular about being in before the sun was down, that often she would take to her heels when nothing worse than a fleecy cloud crossing the sun threw a shadow on the hillside; and many an evening they were home a full hour before the sunlight had left the weathercock on the stables. If it had not been for such behavior, Irene would by this time have almost forgotten the goblins. She never forgot Curdie, but him she remembered for his own sake, and indeed would have remembered him if only because a princess never forgets her debts until they are paid.

One splendid sunshiny day, about an hour after noon, Irene, who was playing on a lawn in the garden, heard the distant blast of a bugle. She jumped up with a cry of joy, for she knew by that particular blast that her father was on his way to see her. This part of the garden lay on the slope of the hill, and allowed a full view of the country below. So she shaded her eyes with her hand, and looked far away to catch the first glimpse of shining armor. In a few moments a little troop came glittering round the shoulder of a hill. Spears and helmets were sparkling and gleamimg, banners were flying, horses prancing, and again came the bugle-blast, which was to her like the voice of her father calling across the distance, "Irene, I'm coming." On and on they came, until she could clearly distinguish the king. He rode a white horse, and was taller than any of the men with him. He wore a narrow circle of gold set with jewels around his helmet, and as he came still nearer, Irene could discern the flashing of the stones in the sun. It was a long time since he had been to see her, and her little heart beat faster and faster as the shining troop approached, for she loved her king-papa very dearly, and was nowhere so happy as in his arms. When they reached a certain point, after which she could see them no more from the garden, she ran to the gate, and there stood till up they came clanging and stamping, with one more bright bugle-blast which said, "Irene, I am come."

By this time the people of the house were all gathered at the gate, but Irene stood alone in front of them. When the horseman pulled up, she ran to the side of the white horse, and held up her arms. The king stooped, and took her hands. In an instant she was on the saddle, and clasped in his great strong arms. I wish I could describe the king, so that you could see him in your mind. He had gentle blue eyes, but a nose that made him look like an eagle. A long dark beard, streaked with silvery lines, flowed from his mouth almost to his waist, and as Irene sat on the saddle and hid her glad face upon his bosom, it mingled with the golden hair which her mother had given her, and the two together were like a cloud with streaks of the sun woven through it. After he had held her to his heart for a minute, he spoke to his white horse, and the great

beautiful creature, which had been prancing so proudly a little while before, walked as gently as a lady—for he knew he
had a little lady on his back—through the gate and up to the
door of the house. Then the king set her on the ground, and,
dismounting, took her hand and walked with her into the
great hall, which was hardly ever entered except when he came
to see his little princess. There he sat down with two of his
councillors who had accompanied him, to have some refresh-
ment, and Irene bestowed herself on his right hand, and drank
her milk out of a wooden bowl curiously carved.

After the king had eaten and drunk, he turned to the princess and said, stroking her hair—

"Now, my child, what shall we do next?"

This was the question he almost always put to her first
after their meal together; and Irene had been waiting for it
with some impatience, for now, she thought, she should be
able to settle a question which constantly perplexed her.

"I should like you to take me to see my great old grandmother."

The king looked grave, and said—

"What does my little daughter mean?"

"I mean the Queen Irene that lives up in the tower—the
very old lady, you know, with the long hair of silver."

The king only gazed at his little princess with a look which
she could not understand.

"She's got her crown in her bedroom," she went on; "but
I've not been in there yet. You know she's here, don't you?"

"No," said the king very quietly.

"Then it must be all a dream," said Irene. "I half thought

it was; but I couldn't be sure. Now I *am* sure of it. Besides, I couldn't find her the next time I went up."

At that moment a snow-white pigeon flew in at an open window and, with a flutter, settled upon Irene's head. She broke into a merry laugh, cowered a little and put up her hands to her head, saying—

"Dear dovey, don't peck me. You'll pull out my hair with your long claws, if you don't have a care."

The king stretched out his hand to take the pigeon, but it spread its wings and flew again through the open window, when its whiteness made one flash in the sun and vanished. The king laid his hand on the princess's head, held it back a little, gazed in her face, smiled half a smile and sighed half a sigh.

"Come, my child; we'll have a walk in the garden together," he said.

"You won't come up and see my huge, great, beautiful grandmother, then, king-papa?" said the princess.

"Not this time," said the king very gently. "She has not invited me, you know, and great old ladies like her do not choose to be visited without leave asked and given."

The garden was a very lovely place. Being upon a mountain side, there were parts in it where the rocks came through in great masses, and all immediately about them remained quite wild. Tufts of heather grew upon them, and other hardy mountain plants and flowers, while near them would be lovely roses and lilies, and all pleasant garden flowers. This mingling of the wild mountain with the civilized garden was very quaint, and it was impossible for any number of gardeners to make such a garden look formal and stiff.

Against one of these rocks was a garden-seat, shadowed. from the afternoon sun by the overhanging of the rock itself. There was a little winding path up to the top of the rock, and on the top another seat; but they sat on the seat at its foot, because the sun was hot; and there they talked together of many things. At length the king said:

"You were out late one evening, Irene."

"Yes, papa. It was my fault; and Lootie was very sorry."

"I must talk to Lootie about it," said the king.

"Don't speak loud to her, please, papa," said Irene. "She's been so afraid of being late ever since! Indeed she has not been naughty. It was only a mistake for once."

"Once might be too often," murmured the king to himself, as he stroked his child's head.

I cannot tell you how he had come to know. I am sure Curdie had not told him. Some one about the palace must have seen them, after all. He sat for a good while thinking. There was no sound to be heard except that of a little stream which ran merrily out of an opening in the rock by where they sat, and sped away down the hill through the garden. Then he rose, and leaving Irene where she was, went into the house and sent for Lootie, with whom he had a talk that made her cry.

When in the evening he rode away upon his great white horse, he left six of his attendants behind him, with orders that three of them should watch outside the house every night, walking round and round it from sunset to sunrise. It was clear he was not quite comfortable about the princess.

CHAPTER XI

THE OLD LADY'S BEDROOM

NOTHING more happened worth telling for some time. The autumn came and went by. There were no more flowers in the garden. The winds blew strong, and howled among the rocks. The rain fell, and drenched the few yellow and red leaves that could not get off the bare branches. Again and again there would be a glorious morning followed by a pouring afternoon, and sometimes, for a week together, there would be rain, nothing but rain, all day, and then the most lovely cloudless night, with the sky all out in full-blown stars—not one missing. But the princess could not see much of them, for she went to bed early. The winter drew on, and she found things growing dreary. When it was too stormy to go out, and she had got tired of her toys, Lootie would take her about the house, sometimes to the housekeeper's room, where the housekeeper, who was a good, kind old woman, made much of her—sometimes to the servants' hall or the kitchen, where she was not princess merely, but absolute queen, and ran a great risk of being spoiled. Sometimes she would run of herself to the room where the men-at-arms whom the king had left, sat, and they showed her their arms and accoutrements, and did what they could to amuse her. Still at times she found it very dreary, and often and often wished that her huge great grandmother had not been a dream.

One morning the nurse left her with the housekeeper for a

while. To amuse her, she turned out the contents of an old cabinet upon the table. The little princess found her treasures, queer ancient ornaments and many things the uses of which she could not imagine, far more interesting than her own toys, and sat playing with them for two hours or more. But at length, in handling a curious old-fashioned brooch, she ran the pin of it into her thumb, and gave a little scream with the sharpness of the pain, but would have thought little more of it, had not the pain increased and her thumb begun to swell. This alarmed the housekeeper greatly. The nurse was fetched; the doctor was sent for; her hand was poulticed, and long before her usual time she was put to bed. The pain still continued, and although she fell asleep and dreamed a good many dreams, there was the pain always in every dream. At last it woke her up.

The moon was shining brightly into the room. The poultice had fallen off her hand, and it was burning hot. She fancied if she could hold it into the moonlight, that would cool it. So she got out of bed, without waking the nurse who lay at the other end of the room, and went to the window. When she looked out, she saw one of the men-at-arms walking in the garden, with the moonlight glancing on his armor. She was just going to tap on the window and call him, for she wanted to tell him all about it, when she bethought herself that that might wake Lootie, and she would put her into bed again. So she resolved to go to the window of another room, and call him from there. It was so much nicer to have somebody to talk to than to lie awake in bed with the burning pain in her hand. She opened the door very gently and went through the nursery, which did not look into the garden, to go to the other window. But when she came to the foot of the old staircase, there was the moon shining down from some window high up, and making the worm-eaten oak look very strange and delicate and lovely. In a moment she was putting her little feet one after the other in the silvery path up the stair, looking behind as she went, to see the shadow they made in the middle of the silver. Some little girls would have been afraid to find themselves thus alone in the middle of the night, but Irene was a princess.

As she went slowly up the stairs, not quite sure that she was not dreaming, suddenly a great longing woke up in her heart to try once more whether she could not find the old, old lady with the silvery hair.

"If she is a dream," she said to herself, "then I am the likelier to find her, if I am dreaming."

So up and up she went, stair after stair, until she came to the many rooms—all just as she had seen them before. Through passage after passage she softly sped, comforting herself that if she should lose her way it would not matter much, because when she woke she would find herself in her own bed, with Lootie not far off. But as if she had known every step of the way, she walked straight to the door at the foot of the narrow stair that led to the tower.

"What if I should realliality-really find my beautiful old grandmother up there!" she said to herself, as she crept up the steep steps.

When she reached the top, she stood a moment listening in the dark, for there was no moon there. Yes! it was! it was the hum of the spinning-wheel! What a diligent grandmother to work both day and night!

She tapped gently at the door.

"Come in, Irene," said the sweet voice.

The princess opened the door, and entered. There was the moonlight streaming in at the window, and in the middle of the moonlight sat the old lady in her black dress with the white lace, and her silvery hair mingling with the moonlight, so that you could not have distinguished one from the other.

"Come in, Irene," she said again. "Can you tell me what I am spinning?"

"She speaks," thought Irene, "just as if she had seen me five minutes ago, or yesterday at the farthest.—No," she answered; "I don't know what you are spinning. Please, I thought you were a dream. Why couldn't I find you before, great-great-grandmother?"

"That you are hardly old enough to understand. But you would have found me sooner if you hadn't come to think I was a dream. I will give you one reason, though, why you couldn't find me. I didn't want you to find me."

"Why, please?"

"Because I did not want Lootie to know I was here."

"But you told me to tell Lootie."

"Yes. But I knew Lootie would not believe you. If she were to see me sitting spinning here, she wouldn't believe me either."

"Why."

"Because she couldn't. She would rub her eyes, and go away and say she felt queer, and forget half of it and more, and then say it had been all a dream."

[76]

"Just like me," said Irene, feeling very much ashamed of herself.

"Yes, a good deal like you, but not just like you; for you've come again; and Lootie would'nt have come again. She would have said, No, no—she had had enough of such nonsense."

"Is it naughty of Lootie then?"

"It would be naughty of you. I've never done anything for Lootie."

"And you did wash my face and hands for me," said Irene, beginning to cry.

The old lady smiled a sweet smile and said—

"I'm not vexed with you, my child—nor with Lootie either. But I don't want you to say anything more to Lootie about me. If she should ask you, you must just be silent. But I do not think she will ask you."

All the time they talked, the old lady kept on spinning.

"You haven't told me yet what I am spinning," she said.

"Because I don't know. It's very pretty stuff."

It was indeed very pretty stuff. There was a good bunch of it on the distaff attached to the spinning-wheel, and in the moonlight it shone like—what shall I say it was like? It was not white enough for silver—yes, it was like silver, but shone gray rather than white, and glittered only a little. And the thread the old lady drew out from it was so fine that Irene could hardly see it.

"I am spinning this for you, my child."

"For me! What am I to do with it, please?"

"I will tell you by and by. But first I will tell you what it is. It is spider-webs—of a particular kind. My pigeons bring it me from over the great sea. There is only one forest where the spiders live who make this particular kind—the finest and strongest of any. I have nearly finished my present job. What is on the rock now will be quite sufficient. I have a week's work there yet, though," she added, looking at the bunch.

"Do you work all day and night too, great-great-great-great grandmother?" said the princess, thinking to be very polite with so many *greats*.

"I am not quite so great as all that," she answered, smiling almost merrily. "If you call me grandmother, that will do.— No, I don't work every night—only moonlit nights, and then no longer than the moon shines upon my wheel. I sha'n't work much longer to-night."

"And what will you do next, grandmother?"

"Go to bed. Would you like to see my bedroom?"

"Yes, that I should."

"Then I think I won't work any longer to-night. I shall be in good time."

The old lady rose, and left her wheel standing just as it was. You see there was no good in putting it away, for where there was not any furniture, there was no danger of being untidy.

Then she took Irene by the hand, but it was her bad hand, and Irene gave a little cry of pain.

"My child!" said her grandmother, "what is the matter?"

Irene held her hand into the moonlight, that the old lady might see it, and told her all about it, at which she looked grave. But she only said—"Give me your other hand"; and, having led her out upon the little dark landing, opened the door on the opposite side of it. What was Irene's surprise to see the loveliest room she had ever seen in her life! It was large and lofty, and dome-shaped. From the centre hung a lamp as round as a ball, shining as if with the brightest moonlight, which made everything visible in the room, though not so clearly that the princess could tell what many of the things were. A large oval bed stood in the middle, with a coverlid of rose-color, and velvet curtains all round it of a lovely pale blue. The walls were also blue—spangled all over with what looked like stars of silver.

The old lady left her, and going to a strange-looking cabinet, opened it and took out a curious silver casket. Then she sat down on a low chair, and calling Irene, made her kneel before her, while she looked at her hand. Having examined it, she opened the casket, and took from it a little ointment. The sweetest odor filled the room—like that of roses and lilies— as she rubbed the ointment gently all over the hot swollen hand. Her touch was so pleasant and cool, that it seemed to drive away the pain and heat wherever it came.

"Oh, grandmother! it is *so* nice!" said Irene. "Thank you; thank you."

Then the old lady went to a chest of drawers, and took out a large handkerchief of gossamer-like cambric, which she tied around her hand.

"I don't think that I can let you go away to-night," she said. "Do you think you would like to sleep with me?"

"Oh, yes, yes, dear grandmother!" said Irene, and would have clapped her hands, forgetting that she could not.

"You won't be afraid then to go to bed with such an old woman?"

[79]

"No. You are so beautiful, grandmother."

"But I am *very* old."

"And I suppose I am very young. You won't mind sleeping with such a *very* young woman, grandmother?"

"You sweet little pertness!" said the old lady, and drew her toward her, and kissed her on the forehead and the cheek and the mouth.

Then she got a large silver basin, and having poured some water into it, made Irene sit on the chair, and washed her feet. This done, she was ready for bed. And oh, what a delicious bed it was into which her grandmother laid her! She hardly could have told she was lying upon anything: she felt nothing but the softness. The old lady having undressed herself, lay down beside her.

"Why don't you put out your moon?" asked the princess.

"That never goes out, night or day," she answered. "In the darkest night, if any of my pigeons are out on a message, they always see my moon, and know where to fly to."

"But if somebody besides the pigeons were to see it—somebody about the house, I mean—they would come to look what it was, and find you."

"The better for them then," said the old lady. "But it does not happen above five times in a hundred years that any one does see it. The greater part of those who do, take it for a meteor, wink their eyes, and forget it again. Besides, nobody could find the room except I pleased. Besides again—I will tell you a secret—if that light were to go out, you would fancy yourself lying in a bare garret, on a heap of old straw, and would not see one of the pleasant things round about you all the time."

"I hope it will never go out," said the princess.

In an instant she was on the saddle, and clasped in
his great strong arms.

"I hope not. But it is time we both went to sleep. Shall I take you in my arms?"

The little princess nestled close up to the old lady, who took her in both her arms, and held her close to her bosom.

"Oh dear! this is so nice!" said the princess. "I didn't know anything in the whole world could be so comfortable. I should like to lie here for ever."

"You may if you will," said the old lady. "But I must put you to one trial—not a very hard one, I hope.—This night week you must come back to me. If you don't, I do not know when you may find me again, and you will soon want me very much."

"Oh! please, don't let me forget."

"You shall not forget. The only question is whether you will believe I am anywhere—whether you will believe I am anything but a dream. You may be sure I will do all I can to help you to come. But it will rest with yourself after all. On the night of next Friday, you must come to me. Mind now."

"I will try," said the princess.

"Then good night," said the old lady, and kissed the forehead which lay in her bosom.

In a moment more the little princess was dreaming in the midst of the loveliest dreams—of summer seas and moonlight and mossy springs and great murmuring trees, and beds of wild flowers with such odors as she had never smelled before. But after all, no dream could be more lovely than what she had left behind when she fell asleep.

In the morning she found herself in her own bed. There was no handkerchief or anything else on her hand, only a sweet odor lingering about it. The swelling had all gone down; the prick of the brooch had vanished:—in fact her hand was perfectly well.

[81]

CHAPTER XII

A SHORT CHAPTER ABOUT CURDIE

CURDIE spent many nights in the mine. His father and he had taken Mrs. Peterson into the secret, for they knew mother could hold her tongue, which was more than could be said of all the miners' wives. But Curdie did not tell her that every night he spent in the mine, part of it went in earning a new red petticoat for her.

Mrs. Peterson was such a nice good mother! All mothers are more or less, but Mrs. Peterson was nice and good all *more* and no *less*. She made a little heaven in that poor cottage on the hillside—for her husband and son to go home to out of the dreary earth in which they worked. I doubt if the princess was very much happier even in the arms of her huge great-grandmother than Peter and Curdie were in the arms of Mrs. Peterson. True, her hands were hard, and chapped, and large, but it was with work for them; and therefore in the sight of the angels, her hands were so much the more beautiful. And if Curdie worked hard to get her a petticoat, she worked hard every day to get him comforts which he would have missed much more than she would a new petticoat even in winter. Not that she and Curdie ever thought of how much they worked for each other: that would have spoiled everything.

When left alone in the mine, Curdie always worked on for an hour or two first, following the lode which, according to

Glump, would lead at last into the deserted habitation. After that, he would set out on a reconnoitering expedition. In order to manage this, or rather the return from it, better than the first time, he had bought a huge ball of fine string, having learned the trick from Hop-o'-my-Thumb, whose history his mother had often told him. Not that Hop-o'-my-Thumb had ever used a ball of string—I should be sorry to be supposed so far out in my classics—but the principle was the same as that of the pebbles. The end of this string he fastened to his pickaxe, which figured no bad anchor, and then, with the ball in his hand, unrolling as he went, set out in the dark through the natural gangs of the goblins' territory. The first night or two he came upon nothing worth remembering; saw only a little of the home-life of the *cobs* in the various caves they called houses; failed in coming upon anything to cast light upon the foregoing design which kept the inundation for the present in the background. But at length, I think on the third or fourth night, he found, partly guided by the noise of their implements, a company of evidently the best sappers and miners amongst them, hard at work. What were they about? It could not well be the inundation, seeing that had in the meantime been postponed to something else. Then what was it? He lurked and watched, every now and then in the greatest risk of being detected, but without success. He had again and again to retreat in haste, a proceeding rendered the more difficult that he had to gather up his string as he returned upon its course. It was not that he was afraid of the goblins, but that he was afraid of their finding out that they were watched, which might have prevented the discovery at which he aimed. Some-

[83]

times his haste had to be such that, when he reached home toward morning, his string for lack of time to wind it up as he "dodged the cobs," would be in what seemed the most hopeless entanglement; but after a good sleep though a short one, he always found his mother had got it right again. There it was, wound in a most respectable ball, ready for use the moment he should want it!

"I can't think how you do it, mother," he would say.

"I follow the thread," she would answer—"just as you do in the mine."

She never had more to say about it; but the less clever she was with her words, the more clever she was with her hands; and the less his mother said, the more, Curdie believed, she had to say.

But still he had made no discovery as to what the goblin miners were about.

CHAPTER XIII

THE COBS' CREATURES

ABOUT this time, the gentlemen whom the king had left behind him to watch over the princess, had each occasion to doubt the testimony of his own eyes, for more than strange were the objects to which they would bear witness. They were of one sort—creatures—but so grotesque and misshapen as to be more like a child's drawings upon his slate than anything natural. They saw them only at night, while on guard about the house. The testimony of the man who first reported having seen one of them was that, as he was walking slowly round the house, while yet in the shadow, he caught sight of a creature standing on its hind legs in the moonlight, with its fore feet upon a window-ledge, staring in at the window. Its body might have been that of a dog or wolf— he thought, but he declared on his honor that its head was twice the size it ought to have been for the size of its body, and as round as a ball, while the face, which it turned upon him as it fled, was more like one carved by a boy upon the turnip inside which he is going to put a candle, than anything else he could think of. It rushed into the garden. He sent an arrow after it, and thought he must have struck it; for it gave an unearthly howl, and he could not find his arrow any more than the beast, although he searched all about the place where it vanished. They laughed at him until he was driven to hold his tongue; and said he must have taken too long a pull at the ale-jug. But before two nights were over, he had one to side with him; for he too had seen something strange, only quite different from that reported by the other. The description the second man gave of the creature he had seen was yet more grotesque and unlikely. They were both laughed at by the rest; but night after night another came over to their side, until at last there was only one left to laugh at all his companions. Two nights more passed, and he saw nothing; but on the third, he came rushing from the garden to the other two before the house, in such an agitation that they declared—for it was their turn now—that the band of his helmet was cracking under his chin with the rising of his hair inside it. Running with him into that part of the garden which I have already described, they saw a score of creatures, to not one of which they could give a name, and not one of which was like another, hideous and ludicrous at once, gamboling on the lawn in the moonlight. The supernatural or rather subnatural ugliness of their faces, the length of legs and necks in some, and the apparent absence of both or either in others, made the spectators, although in one consent as to what they saw, yet doubtful, as I have said, of the evidence of their own eyes—and ears as well; for the noises they made, although not loud, were as uncouth and varied as their forms, and could be described neither as grunts nor squeaks nor roars nor howls nor barks nor yells nor screams nor croaks nor hisses nor mews nor shrieks, but only as something like all of them mingled in one horrible dissonance. Keeping in the shade, the watchers had a few moments to recover themselves before the hideous assembly suspected their presence; but all at once, as if by common consent, they scampered off in the direction of a great rock, and vanished before the men had come to sufficiently to think of following them.

My readers will suspect what these were; but I will now give them full information concerning them. They were of course household animals belonging to the goblins, whose ancestors had taken their ancestors many centuries before from the upper regions of light into the lower regions of darkness. The original stocks of these horrible creatures were very much the same as the animals now seen about farms and homes in the country, with the exception of a few of them, which had been wild creatures, such as foxes, and indeed wolves and small bears, which the goblins, from their proclivity toward the animal creation, had caught when cubs and tamed. But in the course of time, all had undergone even greater changes than had passed upon their owners, They had altered—that is, their descendants had altered—into such creatures as I have not attempted to describe except in the vaguest manner —the various parts of their bodies assuming, in an apparently arbitrary and self-willed manner, the most abnormal developments. Indeed, so little did any distinct type predominate in some of the bewildering results, that you could only have guessed at any known animal as the original, and even then, what likeness remained would be more one of general expression than of definable conformation. But what increased the gruesomeness tenfold, was that, from constant domestic, or indeed rather family association with the goblins, their countenances had grown in grotesque resemblance to the human. No one understands animals who does not see that every one of them, even amongst the fishes, it may be with a dimness and vagueness infinitely remote, yet shadows the human: in the case of these the human resemblance had greatly increased: while their owners had sunk toward them, they had risen toward their owners. But the conditions of subterranean life being equally unnatural for both, while the goblins were worse, the creatures had not improved by the approximation, and its result would have appeared far more ludicrous than consoling to the warmest lover of animal nature. I shall now explain how it was that just then these animals began to show themselves about the king's country house.

The goblins, as Curdie had discovered, were mining on— at work both day and night, in divisions, urging the scheme after which he lay in wait. In the course of their tunneling, they had broken into the channel of a small stream, but the break being in the top of it, no water had escaped to interfere with their work. Some of the creatures, hovering as they often did about their masters, had found the hole, and had, with the curiosity which had grown to a passion from the restraints of their unnatural circumstances, proceeded to explore the channel. The stream was the same which ran out by the seat on which Irene and her king-papa had sat as I have told, and the goblin-creatures found it jolly fun to get out for a romp on a smooth lawn such as they had never seen in all their poor miserable lives. But although they had partaken enough of the nature of their owners to delight in annoying and alarming any of the people whom they met on the mountain, they were of course incapable of designs of their own, or of intentionally furthering those of their masters.

[88]

THE COBS' CREATURES

For several nights after the men-at-arms were at length of one mind as to the facts of the visits of some horrible creatures, whether bodily or spectral they could not yet say, they watched with special attention that part of the garden where they had last seen them. Perhaps indeed they gave in consequence too little attention to the house. But the creatures were too cunning to be easily caught; nor were the watchers quick-eyed enough to descry the head, or the keen eyes in it, which, from the opening whence the stream issued, would watch them in turn, ready, the moment they left the lawn to report the place clear.

CHAPTER XIV

THAT NIGHT WEEK

DURING the whole of the week, Irene had been thinking every other moment of her promise to the old lady, although even now she could not feel quite sure that she had not been dreaming. Could it really be that an old lady lived up in the top of the house with pigeons and a spinning-wheel, and a lamp that never went out? She was, however, none the less determined, on the coming Friday, to ascend the three stairs, walk through the passages with the many doors, and try to find the tower in which she had either seen or dreamed her grandmother.

Her nurse could not help wondering what had come to the child—she would sit so thoughtfully silent, and even in the midst of a game with her, would so suddenly fall into a dreamy mood. But Irene took care to betray nothing, whatever efforts Lootie might make to get at her thoughts. And Lootie had to say to herself, "What an odd child she is!" and give it up.

At length the long looked-for Friday arrived, and lest Lootie should be moved to watch her, Irene endeavored to keep herself as quiet as possible. In the afternoon she asked for her doll's house, and went on arranging and rearranging the various rooms and their inhabitants for a whole hour. Then she gave a sigh and threw herself back in her chair. One of the dolls would not sit, and another would not stand, and they were all very tiresome. Indeed there was one that would not

[90]

even lie down, which was too bad. But it was now getting dark, and the darker it got the more exited Irene became, and the more she felt it necessary to be composed.

"I see you want your tea, princess," said the nurse: "I will go and get it. The room feels close: I will open the window a little. The evening is mild: it won't hurt you."

"There's no fear of that, Lootie," said Irene, wishing she had put off going for the tea till it was darker, when she might have made her attempt with every advantage.

I fancy Lootie was longer in returning than she had intended; for when Irene, who had been lost in thought, looked up, she saw it was nearly dark, and at the same moment caught sight of a pair of eyes, bright with a green light, glowering at her through the open window. The next instant something leaped into the room. It was like a cat, with legs as long as a horse's, Irene said, but its body no bigger and its legs no thicker than those of a cat. She was too frightened to cry out, but not too frightened to jump from her chair and run from the room.

It is plain enough to every one of my readers what she ought to have done—and indeed Irene thought of it herself; but when she came to the foot of the old stair, just outside the nursery door, she imagined the creature running up those long ascents after her, and pursuing her through the dark passages —*which, after all, might lead to no tower!* That thought was too much. Her heart failed her, and turning from the stair, she rushed along to the hall, whence, finding the front-door open, she darted into the court, pursued—at least she thought so—by the creature. No one happening to see her, on she ran, unable to think for fear, and ready to run anywhere to

[91]

elude the awful creature with the stilt-legs. Not daring to
look behind her, she rushed straight out of the gate, and up
the mountain. It was foolish indeed—thus to run farther and
farther from all who could help her, as if she had been seeking
a fit spot for the goblin-creature to eat her in at his leisure;
but that is the way fear serves us: it always takes the side of
the thing that we are afraid of.

The princess was soon out of breath with running up hill;
but she ran on, for she fancied the horrible creature just
behind her, forgetting that, had it been after her, such legs
as those must have overtaken her long ago. At last she
could run no longer, and fell, unable even to scream, by the
roadside, where she lay for sometime, half dead with terror.
But finding nothing lay hold of her, and her breath beginning
to come back, she ventured at length to get half up, and peer
anxiously about her. It was now so dark that she could see
nothing. Not a single star was out. She could not even tell
in what direction the house lay, and between her and home
she fancied the dreadful creature lying ready to pounce upon
her. She saw now that she ought to have run up the stairs at
once. It was well she did not scream; for, although very few
of the goblins had come out for weeks, a stray idler or two
might have heard her. She sat down upon a stone, and nobody but one who had done something wrong could have been
more miserable. She had quite forgotten her promise to visit
her grandmother. A rain-drop fell on her face. She looked
up, and for a moment her terror was lost in astonishment. At
first she thought the rising moon had left her place, and drawn
nigh to see what could be the matter with the little girl, sitting

alone, without hat or cloak, on the dark bare mountain; but she soon saw she was mistaken, for there was no light on the ground at her feet, and no shadow anywhere. But a great silvery globe was hanging in the air; and as she gazed at the lovely thing, her courage revived. If she were but indoors again she would fear nothing, not even the terrible creature with the long legs! But how was she to find her way back? What could that light be? Could it be—? No, it couldn't. But what if it should be—yes—it must be—her great-great-grandmother's lamp, which guided her pigeons home through the darkest night! She jumped up: she had but to keep that light in view, and she must find the house.

Her heart grew strong. Speedily, yet softly, she walked down the hill, hoping to pass the watching creature unseen. Dark as it was, there was little danger now of choosing the wrong road. And—which was most strange—the light that filled her eyes from the lamp, instead of blinding them for a moment to the object upon which they next fell, enabled her for a moment to see it, despite the darkness. By looking at the lamp and then dropping her eyes, she could see the road for a yard or two in front of her, and this saved her from several falls, for the road was very rough. But all at once, to her dismay, it vanished, and the terror of the beast, which had left her the moment she began to return, again laid hold of her heart. The same instant, however, she caught the light of the windows, and knew exactly where she was. It was too dark to run, but she made what haste she could, and reached the gate in safety. She found the house door still open, ran through the hall, and, without even looking into the nursery, bounded straight up the stair, and the next, and the next; then turning to the right, ran through the long avenue of silent rooms, and found her way at once to the door at the foot of the tower stair.

When first the nurse missed her, she fancied she was playing her a trick, and for some time took no trouble about her; but at last, getting frightened, she had begun to search; and when the princess entered, the whole household was hither and thither, over the house, hunting for her. A few seconds after she reached the stair of the tower, they had even begun to search the neglected rooms, in which they would never have thought of looking had they not already searched every other place they could think of in vain. But by this time she was knocking at the old lady's door.

CHAPTER XV

WOVEN AND THEN SPUN

"COME in, Irene," said the silvery voice of her grandmother.

The princess opened the door, and peeped in. But
the room was quite dark, and there was no sound of the spinning-wheel. She grew frightened once more, thinking that,
although the room was there, the old lady might be a dream
after all. Every little girl knows how dreadful it is to find a
room empty where she thought somebody was; but Irene had
to fancy for a moment that the person she came to find was
nowhere at all. She remembered however that at night she
spun only in the moonlight, and concluded that must be why
there was no sweet, bee-like humming: the old lady might be
somewhere in the darkness. Before she had time to think another thought, she heard her voice again, saying as before—

"Come in, Irene."

From the sound, she understood at once that she was not in
the room beside her. Perhaps she was in her bedroom. She
turned across the passage, feeling her way to the other door.
When her hand fell on the lock, again the old lady spoke—

"Shut the other door behind you, Irene. I always close the
door of my workroom when I go to my chamber."

Irene wondered to hear her voice so plainly through the
door; having shut the other, she opened it and went in. Oh,
what a lovely haven to reach from the darkness and fear through

which she had come! The soft light made her feel as if she were going into the heart of the milkiest pearl; while the blue walls and their silver stars for a moment perplexed her with the fancy that they were in reality the sky which she had left outside a minute ago covered with rainclouds.

"I've lighted a fire for you, Irene: you're cold and wet," said her grandmother.

Then Irene looked again, and saw that what she had taken for a huge bouquet of red roses on a low stand against the wall, was in fact a fire which burned in the shapes of the loveliest and reddest roses, glowing gorgeously between the heads and wings of two cherubs of shining silver. And when she came nearer, she found that the smell of roses with which the room was filled, came from the fire-roses on the hearth. Her grandmother was dressed in the loveliest pale-blue velvet, over which her hair, no longer white, but of a rich gold color, streamed like a cataract, here falling in dull gathered heaps, there rushing away in smooth shining falls. And even as she looked, the hair seemed pouring down from her head, and vanishing in a golden mist ere it reached the floor. It flowed from under the edge of a circle of shining silver, set with alternated pearls and opals. On her dress was no ornament whatever, neither was there a ring on her hand, or a necklace or carcanet about her neck. But her slippers glimmered with the light of the Milky-way, for they were covered with seed-pearls and opals in one mass. Her face was that of a woman of three-and-twenty.

The princess was so bewildered with astonishment and admiration that she could hardly thank her, and drew nigh with timidity, feeling dirty and uncomfortable. The lady was seated

"Come," and she still held out her arms.

on a low chair by the side of the fire, with hands outstretched to take her, but the princess hung back with a troubled smile.

"Why, what's the matter?" asked her grandmother. "You haven't been doing anything wrong—I know that by your face, though it *is* rather miserable. What's the matter, my dear?"

And still she held out her arms.

"Dear grandmother," said Irene, "I'm not so sure that I haven't done something wrong. I ought to have run up to you at once when the long-legged cat came in at the window, instead of running out on the mountain, and making myself such a fright."

"You were taken by surprise, my child, and are not so likely to do it again. It is when people do wrong things willfully that they are the more likely to do them again. Come."

And still she held out her arms.

"But, grandmother, you're so beautiful and grand with your crown on! and I am so dirty with mud and rain!—I should quite spoil your beautiful blue dress."

With a merry little laugh, the lady sprang from her chair, more lightly far than Irene herself could, caught the child to her bosom, and kissing the tear-stained face over and over, sat down with her in her lap.

"Oh, grandmother! you'll make yourself such a mess!" cried Irene, clinging to her.

"You darling! do you think I care more for my dress than for my little girl? Beside—look here!"

As she spoke she set her down, and Irene saw to her dismay that the lovely dress was covered with the mud of her fall on the mountain road. But the lady stooped to the fire, and taking from it, by the stalk in her fingers, one of the burning roses, passed it once and again and a third time over the front of her dress; and when Irene looked, not a single stain was to be discovered.

"There!" said her grandmother, "you won't mind coming to me now?"

But Irene again hung back, eyeing the flaming rose which the lady held in her hand.

"You're not afraid of the rose—are you?" she said, and she was about to throw it on the hearth again.

"Oh! don't, please!" cried Irene. "Won't you hold it to my frock and my hands and my face? And I'm afraid my feet and my knees want it too!"

"No," answered her grandmother, smiling a little sadly, as she threw the rose from her; "it is too hot for you yet. It would set your frock in a flame. Besides, I don't want to make you clean to-night. I want your nurse and the rest of the people to see you as you are, for you will have to tell them how you ran away for fear of the long-legged cat. I should like to wash you, but they would not believe you then. Do you see that bath behind you?"

The princess looked, and saw a large oval tub of silver, shining brilliantly in the light of the wonderful lamp.

"Go and look into it," said the lady.

Irene went, and came back very silently, with her eyes shining.

"What did you see?" asked her grandmother.

"The sky and the moon and the stars," she answered. "It looked as if there was no bottom to it."

WOVEN AND THEN SPUN

The lady smiled a pleased, satisfied smile, and was silent also for a few moments. Then she said—

"Any time you want a bath, come to me. I know you have a bath every morning, but sometimes you want one at night too."

"Thank you, grandmother; I will—I will indeed," answered Irene, and was again silent for some moments thinking. Then she said, "How was it, grandmother, that I saw your beautiful lamp—not the light of it only—but the great round silver lamp itself, hanging alone in the great open air high up? It was your lamp I saw—wasn't it?"

"Yes, my child; it was my lamp."

"Then how was it? I don't see a window all round."

"When I please, I can make the lamp shine through the walls—shine so strong that it melts them away from before the sight, and shows itself as you saw it. But, as I told you, it is not everybody can see it."

"How is it that I can then? I'm sure I don't know."

"It is a gift born with you. And one day I hope everybody will have it."

"But how do you make it shine through the walls?"

"Ah! that you would not understand if I were to try ever so much to make you—not yet—not yet. But," added the lady rising, "you must sit in my chair while I get you the present I have been preparing for you. I told you my spinning was for you. It is finished now, and I am going to fetch it. I have been keeping it warm under one of my brooding pigeons."

Irene sat down in the low chair, and her grandmother left her, shutting the door behind her. The child sat gazing, now at the rose-fire, now at the starry walls, now at the silvery light; and a great quietness came over her heart. If all the long-legged cats in the world had come rushing helter-skelter at her then, she would not have been afraid of them for a single moment. How this was, however, she could not tell;— she only knew there was no fear in her, and everything was so right and safe that it could not get in.

She had been gazing at the lovely lamp for some minutes fixedly: turning her eyes, she found the wall had vanished, for she was looking out on the dark cloudy night. But though she heard the wind blowing, none of it blew upon her. In a moment more, the clouds themselves parted, or rather vanished like the wall, and she looked straight into the starry herds, flashing gloriously in the dark blue. It was but for a moment. The clouds gathered again and shut out the stars; the wall gathered again and shut out the clouds; and there stood the lady beside her with the loveliest smile on her face, and a shimmering ball in her hand, about the size of a pigeon's egg.

"There, Irene; there is my work for you!" she said, holding out the ball to the princess.

She took it in her hand, and looked at it all over. It sparkled a little, and shone here and shone there, but not much. It was of a sort of gray whiteness, something like spun glass.

"Is this *all* your spinning, grandmother?" she asked.

"All since you came to the house. There is more there than you think."

"How pretty it is! What am I to do with it?"

"That I will now explain to you," answered the lady, turning from her, and going to her cabinet.

She came back with a small ring in her hand. Then she took the ball from Irene's, and did something with the two— Irene could not tell what.

"Give me your hand," she said.

Irene held up her right hand.

"Yes, that is the hand I want," said the lady, and put the ring on the forefinger of it.

"What a beautiful ring!" said Irene. "What is the stone called?"

"It is a fire-opal."

"Please, am I to keep it?"

"Always."

"Oh, thank you, grandmother! It's prettier than anything I ever saw, except those—of all colors—in your—Please, is that your crown?"

"Yes, it is my crown. The stone in your ring is of the same sort—only not so good. It has only red, but mine have all colors, you see."

"Yes, grandmother. I will take such care of it!—But—" she added, hesitating.

"But what?" asked her grandmother.

"What am I to say when Lootie asks me where I got it?"

"*You* will ask *her* where you got it," answered the lady smiling.

"I don't see how I can do that."

"You will though."

"Of course I will if you say so. But you know I can't pretend not to know."

"Of course not. But don't trouble yourself about it. You will see when the time comes."

So saying, the lady turned, and threw the little ball into the rose-fire.

"Oh, grandmother!" exclaimed Irene; "I thought you had spun it for me."

"So I did, my child. And you've got it."

"No; it's burnt in the fire."

The lady put her hand in the fire, brought out the ball, glimmering as before, and held it toward her. Irene stretched out her hand to take it, but the lady turned, and going to her cabinet, opened a drawer, and laid the ball in it.

"Have I done anything to vex you, grandmother?" said Irene pitifully.

"No, my darling. But you must understand that no one ever gives anything to another properly and really without keeping it. That ball is yours."

"Oh! I'm not to take it with me! You are going to keep it for me!"

"You are to take it with you. I've fastened the end of it to the ring on your finger."

Irene looked at the ring.

"I can't see it there, grandmother," she said.

"Feel—a little way from the ring—toward the cabinet," said the lady.

"Oh! I do feel it!" exclaimed the princess. "But I can't see it," she added, looking close to her outstretched hand.

"No. The thread is too fine for you to see it. You can only feel it. Now you can fancy how much spinning that took, although it does seem such a little ball."

"But what use can I make of it, if it lies in your cabinet?"

"That is what I will explain to you. It would be of no use to you—it wouldn't be yours at all if it did not lie in my cabinet. Now listen. If ever you find yourself in any danger—such, for example, as you were in this evening—you must take off your ring, and put it under the pillow of your bed. Then you must lay your forefinger, the same that wore the ring, upon the thread, and follow the thread wherever it leads you."

"Oh, how delightful! It will lead me to you, grandmother, I know!"

"Yes. But, remember, it may seem to you a very round-about way indeed, and you must not double the thread. Of one thing you may be sure, that while you hold it, I hold it too."

"It is very wonderful!" said Irene thoughtfully. Then suddenly becoming aware, she jumped up, crying—"Oh, grandmother! here I have been sitting all this time in your chair, and you standing! I *beg* your pardon."

The lady laid her hand on her shoulder and said:

"Sit down again, Irene. Nothing pleases me better than to see any one sit in my chair. I am only too glad to stand so long as any one will sit in it."

"How kind of you!" said the princess, and sat down again.

"It makes me happy," said the lady.

"But," said Irene, still puzzled, "won't the thread get in somebody's way and be broken, if the one end is fast to my ring and the other laid in your cabinet?"

"You will find all that arrange itself. I am afraid it is time for you to go."

"Mightn't I stay and sleep with you to-night, grandmother?"

"No, not to-night. If I had meant you to stay to-night, I should have given you a bath; but you know everybody in the house is miserable about you, and it would be cruel to keep them so all night. You must go down stairs."

"I'm so glad, grandmother, you didn't say—*go home*—for this is my home. Mayn't I call this my home?"

"You may, my child. And I trust you will always think it your home. Now come. I must take you back without any one seeing you."

"Please, I want to ask you one question more," said Irene. "Is it because you have your crown on that you look so young?"

"No, child," answered her grandmother; "it is because I felt so young this evening, that I put my crown on. And it occurred to me that you would like to see your old grandmother in her best."

"Why do you call yourself old? You're not old, grandmother."

"I am very old indeed. It is so silly of people—I don't mean you, for you are such a tiny, and couldn't know better—but it *is* so silly of people to fancy that old age means crookedness and witheredness and feebleness and sticks and spectacles and rheumatism and forgetfulness! It is so silly! Old age has nothing whatever to do with all that. The right old age means strength and beauty and mirth and courage and clear eyes and strong painless limbs. I am older than you are able to think, and—"

"And look at you, grandmother!" cried Irene, jumping up, and flinging her arms about her neck. "I won't be so silly again, I promise you. At least—I'm rather afraid to promise —but if I am, I promise to be sorry for it—I do. I wish I were as old as you, grandmother. I don't think you are ever afraid of anything."

"Not for long, at least, my child. Perhaps by the time I am two thousand years of age, I shall, indeed, never be afraid of anything. But I must confess that I have sometimes been afraid about my children—sometimes about you, Irene."

"Oh, I'm so sorry, grandmother!—To-night, I suppose, you mean."

"Yes—a little to-night; but a good deal when you had all but made up your mind that I was a dream, and no real great-great-grandmother. You must not suppose that I am blaming you for that, I daresay it was out of your power to help it."

"I don't know, grandmother," said the princess, beginning to cry. "I can't always do myself as I should like. And I don't always try. I'm very sorry anyhow."

The lady stooped, lifted her in her arms, and sat down with her in her chair, holding her close to her bosom. In a few minutes the princess had sobbed herself to sleep. How long she slept, I do not know. When she came to herself she was sitting in her own high chair at the nursery table, with her doll's-house before her.

CHAPTER XVI

THE RING

THE same moment her nurse came into the room, sobbing. When she saw her sitting there, she started back with a loud cry of amazement and joy. Then running to her, she caught her up in her arms and covered her dear little face with kisses.

"My precious darling princess! where have you been? What has happened to you? We've all been crying our eyes out, and searching the house from top to bottom for you."

"Not quite from the top," thought Irene to herself; and she might have added—"not quite to the bottom," perhaps, if she had known all. But the one she would not, and the other she could not say.

"Oh, Lootie! I've had such a dreadful adventure!" she replied, and told her all about the cat with the long legs, and how she ran out upon the mountain, and came back again. But she said nothing of her grandmother or her lamp.

"And there we've been searching for you all over the house for more than an hour and a half!" exclaimed the nurse. "But that's no matter, now we've got you! Only, princess, I must say," she added, her mood changing, "what you ought to have done was to call for your own Lootie to come and help you, instead of running out of the house, and up the mountain, in that wild—I must say, foolish fashion."

"Well, Lootie," said Irene quietly, "perhaps if you had a

big cat, all legs, running at you, you mightn't exactly know which was the wisest thing to do at the moment."

"I wouldn't run up the mountain, anyhow," returned Lootie.

"Not if you had time to think about it. But when those creatures came at you that night on the mountain, you were so frightened yourself that you lost your way home."

This put a stop to Lootie's reproaches. She had been on the point of saying that the long-legged cat must have been a twilight fancy of the princess's, but the memory of the horrors of that night, and of the talking-to which the king had given her in consequence, prevented her from saying that which after all she did not half believe—having a strong suspicion that the cat was a goblin; for the fact was that she knew nothing of the difference between the goblins and their creatures: she counted them all just goblins.

Without another word she went and got some fresh tea and bread and butter for the princess. Before she returned, the whole household, headed by the housekeeper, burst into the nursery to exult over their darling. The gentlemen-at-arms followed, and were ready enough to believe all she told them about the long-legged cat. Indeed, though wise enough to say nothing about it, they remembered with no little horror, just such a creature amongst those they had surprised at their gambols upon the princess's lawn. In their own hearts they blamed themselves for not having kept better watch. And their captain gave order that from this night the front door and all the windows on the ground floor should be locked immediately the sun set, and opened after upon no pretence whatever. The men-at-arms redoubled their vigilance, and for some time there was no further cause of alarm.

When the princess woke the next morning, her nurse was bending over her.

"How your ring does glow this morning, princess!—just like a fiery rose!" she said.

"Does it, Lootie?" returned Irene. "Who gave me the ring, Lootie? I know I've had it a long time, but where did I get it? I don't remember."

"I think it must have been your mother gave it you, princess; but really, for as long as you have worn it, I don't remember that ever I heard," answered her nurse.

"I will ask my king-papa the next time he comes," said Irene.

CHAPTER XVII

SPRING-TIME

THE spring, so dear to all creatures, young and old, came at last, and before the first few days of it had gone, the king rode through its budding valleys to see his little daughter. He had been in a distant part of his dominions all the winter, for he was not in the habit of stopping in one great city, or of visiting only his favorite country houses, but he moved from place to place, that all his people might know him. Wherever he journeyed, he kept a constant lookout for the ablest and best men to put into office, and wherever he found himself mistaken, and those he had appointed incapable or unjust, he removed them at once. Hence you see it was his care of the people that kept him from seeing his princess so often as he would have liked. You may wonder why he did not take her about with him; but there were several reasons against his doing so, and I suspect her great-great-grandmother had had a principal hand in preventing it. Once more Irene heard the bugle-blast, and once more she was at the gate to meet her father as he rode up on his great white horse.

After they had been alone for a little while, she thought of what she had resolved to ask him.

"Please, king-papa," she said, "will you tell me where I got this pretty ring? I can't remember."

The king looked at it. A strange, beautiful smile spread

like sunshine over his face, and an answering smile, but at the same time a questioning one, spread like moonlight over Irene's.

"It was your queen-mamma's once," he said.

"And why isn't it hers now?" asked Irene.

"She does not want it now," said the king, looking grave.

"Why doesn't she want it now?"

"Because she's gone where all those rings are made."

"And when shall I see her?" asked the princess.

"Not for some time yet," answered the king, and the tears came in his eyes.

Irene did not remember her mother, and did not know why her father looked so, and why the tears came in his eyes; but she put her arms round his neck and kissed him, and asked no more questions.

The king was much disturbed on hearing the report of the gentlemen-at-arms concerning the creatures they had seen; and I presume would have taken Irene with him that very day, but for what the presence of the ring on her finger assured him of. About an hour before he left, Irene saw him go up the old stair; and he did not come down again till they were just ready to start; and she thought with herself that he had been up to see the old lady. When he went away, he left the other six gentlemen behind him, that there might be six of them always on guard.

And now, in the lovely spring-weather, Irene was out on the mountain the greater part of the day. In the warmer hollows there were lovely primroses, and not so many that she ever got tired of them. As often as she saw a new one opening an eye of light in the blind earth, she would clap her hands with gladness, and, unlike some children I know, instead of pulling it, would touch it as tenderly as if it had been a new baby, and, having made its acquaintance, would leave it as happy as she found it. She treated the plants on which they grew like birds' nests; every fresh flower was like a new little bird to her. She would pay a visit to all the flower-nests she knew, remembering each by itself. She would go down on her hands and knees beside one and say "Good morning! Are you all smelling very sweet this morning? Good-bye!" And then she would go to another nest, and say the same. It was a favorite amusement with her. There were many flowers up and down, and she loved them all, but the primroses were her favorites.

"They're not too shy, and they're not a bit forward," she would say to Lootie.

There were goats too about, over the mountain, and when the little kids came, she was as pleased with them as with the flowers. The goats belonged to the miners mostly—a few of them to Curdie's mother; but there were a good many wild ones that seemed to belong to nobody. These the goblins counted theirs, and it was upon them partly that they lived. They set snares and dug pits for them; and did not scruple to take what tame ones happened to be caught; but they did not try to steal them in any other manner, because they were afraid of the dogs the hill-people kept to watch them, for the knowing dogs always tried to bite their feet. But the goblins had a kind of sheep of their own—very queer creatures, which they drove out to feed at night, and the other goblin-creatures were wise enough to keep good watch over them, for they knew they should have their bones by and by.

CHAPTER XVIII

CURDIE'S CLUE

CURDIE was as watchful as ever, but was almost getting tired of his ill-success. Every other night or so he followed the goblins about, as they went on digging and boring, and getting as near them as he could, watched them from behind stones and rocks; but as yet he seemed no nearer finding out what they had in view. As at first, he always kept hold of the end of his string, while his pickaxe left just outside the hole by which he entered the goblins' country from the mine, continued to serve as an anchor and hold fast the other end. The goblins hearing no more noise in that quarter, had ceased to apprehend an immediate invasion, and kept no watch.

One night, after dodging about and listening till he was nearly falling asleep with weariness, he began to roll up his ball, for he had resolved to go home to bed. It was not long, however, before he began to feel bewildered. One after another he passed goblin-houses, caves that is, occupied by goblin families, and at length was sure they were many more than he had passed as he came. He had to use great caution to pass unseen—they lay so close together. Could his string have led him wrong? He still followed winding it, and still it led him into more thickly populated quarters, until he became quite uneasy, and indeed apprehensive; for although he was not afraid of the *cobs*, he was afraid of not finding his way out.

[112]

But what could he do? It was of no use to sit down and wait for the morning—the morning made no difference here. It was all dark, and always dark; and if his string failed him he was helpless. He might even arrive within a yard of the mine, and never know it. Seeing he could do nothing better, he would at least find where the end of the string was, and if possible how it had come to play him such a trick. He knew by the size of the ball that he was getting pretty near the last of it, when he began to feel a tugging and pulling at it. What could it mean? Turning a sharp corner, he thought he heard strange sounds. These grew, as he went on, to a scuffling and growling and squeaking; and the noise increased, until, turning a second sharp corner, he found himself in the midst of it, and the same moment tumbled over a wallowing mass, which he knew must be a knot of the cobs' creatures. Before he could recover his feet, he had caught some great scratches on his face, and several severe bites on his legs and arms. But as he scrambled to get up, his hand fell upon his pickaxe, and before the horrid beasts could do him any serious harm, he was laying about with it right and left in the dark. The hideous cries which followed gave him the satisfaction of knowing that he had punished some of them pretty smartly for their rudeness, and by their scampering and their retreating howls, he perceived that he had routed them. He stood a little, weighing his battle-axe in his hand as if it had been the most precious lump of metal—but indeed no lump of gold itself could have been so precious at that time as that common tool—then untied the end of the string from it, put the ball in his pocket, and still stood thinking. It was clear that the cobs' creatures

[113]

had found his axe, had between them carried it off, and had so led him he knew not where. But for all his thinking he could not tell what he ought to do, until suddenly he became aware of a glimmer of light in the distance. Without a moment's hesitation he set out for it, as fast as the unknown and rugged way would permit. Yet again turning a corner, led by the dim light, he spied something quite new in his experience of the underground regions—a small irregular shape of something shining. Going up to it, he found it was a piece of mica, or Muscovy glass, called sheep-silver in Scotland, and the light flickering as if from a fire behind it. After trying in vain for some time to discover an entrance to the place where it was burning, he came at length to a small chamber in which an opening high in the wall revealed a glow beyond. To this opening he managed to scramble up, and then he saw a strange sight.

Below sat a little group of goblins around a fire, the smoke of which vanished in the darkness far aloft. The sides of the cave were full of shining minerals like those of the palace-hall; and the company was evidently of a superior order, for every one wore stones about head, or arms, or waist, shining, dull, gorgeous colors in the light of the fire. Nor had Curdie looked long before he recognized the king himself, and found that he had made his way into the inner apartment of the royal family. He had never had such a good chance of hearing something! He crept through the hole as softly as he could, scrambled a good way down the wall toward them without attracting attention, and then sat down and listened. The king, evidently the queen, and probably the crown-prince and the prime minister were talking together. He was sure of the queen by her shoes, for as she warmed her feet at the fire, he saw them quite plainly.

"That *will* be fun!" said the one he took for the crown-prince.

It was the first whole sentence he heard.

"I don't see why you should think it such a grand affair!" said his stepmother, tossing her head backward.

"You must remember, my spouse," interposed his Majesty, as if making excuse for his son, "he has got the same blood in him. His mother—"

"Don't talk to me of his mother! You positively encourage his unnatural fancies. Whatever belongs to *that* mother, ought to be cut out of him."

"You forget yourself, my dear!" said the king.

"I don't," said the queen, "nor you either. If you expect *me* to approve of such coarse tastes, you will find yourself mistaken. *I* don't wear shoes for nothing."

"You must ·acknowledge, however," the king said, with a little groan, "that this at least is no whim of Harelip's, but a matter of state-policy. You are well aware that his gratification comes purely from the pleasure of sacrificing himself to the public good. Does it not, Harelip?"

"Yes, father; of course it does. Only it *will* be nice to make her cry. I'll have the skin taken off between her toes, and tie them up till they grow together. Then her feet will be like other people's, and there will be no occasion for her to wear shoes."

"Do you mean to insinuate *I've* got toes, you unnatural

wretch?" cried the queen; and she moved angrily toward Harelip. The councilor, however, who was betwixt them, leaned forward so as to prevent her touching him, but only as if to address the prince.

"Your royal Highness," he said, "possibly requires to be reminded that you have got three toes yourself—one on one foot, two on the other."

"Ha! ha! ha!" shouted the queen triumphantly.

The councilor, encouraged by this mark of favor, went on.

"It seems to me, your royal Highness, it would greatly endear you to your future people, proving to them that you are not the less one of themselves that you had the misfortune to be born of a sun-mother, if you were to command upon yourself the comparatively slight operation which, in a more extended form, you so wisely meditate with regard to your future princess."

"Ha! ha! ha" laughed the queen, louder than before, and the king and the minister joined in the laugh. It was anything but a laughing matter to Harelip. He growled, and for a few moments the others continued to express their enjoyment of his discomfiture.

The queen was the only one Curdie could see with any distinctness. She sat sideways to him, and the light of the fire shone full upon her face. He could not consider her handsome. Her nose was certainly broader at the end than its extreme length, and her eyes, instead of being horizontal, were set up like two perpendicular eggs, one on the broad, the other on the small, end. Her mouth was no bigger than a small buttonhole until she laughed, when it stretched from ear to ear—

only to be sure her ears were very nearly in the middle of her cheeks.

Anxious to hear everything they might say, Curdie ventured to slide down a smooth part of the rock just under him, to a projection below, upon which he thought to rest. But whether he was not careful enough, or the projection gave way, down he came with a rush on the floor of the cavern, bringing with him a great rumbling shower of stones.

The goblins jumped from their seats in more anger than consternation, for they had never yet seen anything to be afraid of in the palace. But when they saw Curdie with his pick in his hand, their rage was mingled with fear, for they took him for the first of an invasion of miners. The king notwithstanding drew himself up to his full height of four feet, spread himself to his full breadth of three and a half, for he was the handsomest and squarest of all the goblins, and strutting up to Curdie, planted himself with outspread feet before him, and said with dignity—

"Pray what right have you in my palace?"

"The right of necessity, your majesty," answered Curdie. "I lost my way, and did not know where I was wandering to."

"How did you get in?"

"By a hole in the mountain."

"But you are a miner! Look at your pickaxe!"

Curdie did look at it, answering,

"I came upon it, lying on the ground, a little way from here. I tumbled over some wild beasts who were playing with it. Look, your majesty." And Curdie showed him how he was scratched and bitten.

[117]

The king was pleased to find him behave more politely than he had expected from what his people had told him concerning the miners, for he attributed it to the power of his own presence; but he did not therefore feel friendly to the intruder.

"You will oblige me by walking out of my dominions at once," he said, well knowing what a mockery lay in the words.

"With pleasure, if your majesty will give me a guide," said Curdie.

"I will give you a thousand," said the king, with a scoffing air of magnificent liberality.

"One will be quite sufficient," said Curdie.

But the king uttered a strange shout, half halloo, half roar, and in rushed goblins till the cave was swarming. He said something to the first of them which Curdie could not hear, and it was passed from one to another till in a moment the farthest in the crowd had evidently heard and understood it. They began to gather about him in a way he did not relish, and he retreated toward the wall. They pressed upon him.

"Stand back," said Curdie, grasping his pickaxe tighter by his knee.

They only grinned and pressed closer. Curdie bethought himself, and began to rhyme.

"Ten, twenty, thirty—
    You're all so very dirty!
    Twenty, thirty, forty—
    You're all so thick and snorty!

"Thirty, forty, fifty—
    You're all so puff-and-snifty!
    Forty, fifty, sixty—
    Beast and man so mixty!

"Fifty, sixty, seventy—
Mixty, maxty, leaventy—
Sixty, seventy, eighty—
All your cheeks so slaty.

"Seventy, eighty, ninety,
All your hands so flinty!
Eighty, ninety, hundred,
Altogether dundred!"

The goblins fell back a little when he began, and made horrible grimaces all through the rhyme, as if eating something so disagreeable that it set their teeth on edge and gave them the creeps; but whether it was that the rhyming words were most of them no words at all, for a new rhyme being considered more efficacious, Curdie had made it on the spur of the moment, or whether it was that the presence of the king and queen gave them courage, I cannot tell; but the moment the rhyme was over, they crowded on him again, and out shot a hundred long arms, with a multitude of thick nailless fingers at the end of them, to lay hold upon him. Then Curdie heaved up his axe. But being as gentle as courageous and not wishing to kill any of them, he turned the end which was square and blunt like a hammer, and with that came down a great blow on the head of the goblin nearest him. Hard as the heads of all goblins are, he thought he must feel that. And so he did, no doubt; but he only gave a horrible cry, and sprung at Curdie's throat. Curdie however drew back in time, and just at that critical moment, remembered the vulnerable part of the goblin-body. He made a sudden rush at the king, and stamped with all his might on his Majesty's feet. The king gave a most unkingly howl, and almost fell into the fire. Curdie then rushed into the crowd, stamping right and left. The goblins drew back howling on every side as he approached, but they were so crowded that few of those he attacked could escape his tread; and the shrieking and roaring that filled the cave would have appalled Curdie, but for the good hope it gave him. They were tumbling over each other in heaps in their eagerness to rush from the cave, when a new assailant suddenly faced him:—the queen, with flaming eyes and expanded nostrils, her hair standing half up from her head, rushed at him. She trusted in her shoes; they were of granite —hollowed like French *sabots*. Curdie would have endured much rather than hurt a woman, even if she was a goblin; but here was an affair of life and death: forgetting her shoes, he made a great stamp on one of her feet. But she instantly returned it with very different effect, causing him frightful pain and almost disabling him. His only chance with her would have been to attack the granite shoes with his pickaxe, but before he could think of that, she had caught him up in her arms, and was rushing with him across the cave. She dashed him into a hole in the wall, with a force that almost stunned him. But although he could not move, he was not too far gone to hear her great cry, and the rush of multitudes of soft feet, followed by the sounds of something heaved up against the rock; after which came a multitudinous patter of stones falling near him. The last had not ceased when he grew very faint, for his head had been badly cut, and at last insensible.

When he came to himself, there was perfect silence about him, and utter darkness, but for the merest glimmer in one tiny spot. He crawled to it, and found that they had heaved a slab against the mouth of the hole, past the edge of which a poor little gleam found its way from the fire. He could not move it a hair's breadth, for they had piled a great heap of stones against it. He crawled back to where he had been lying, in the faint hope of finding his pickaxe. But after a vain search, he was at last compelled to acknowledge himself in an evil plight. He sat down and tried to think, but soon fell fast asleep.

CHAPTER XIX

GOBLIN COUNSELS

HE must have slept a long time, for when he awoke, he felt wonderfully restored—indeed he felt almost well, and he was also very hungry. There were voices in the outer cave.

Once more then, it was night; for the goblins slept during the day, and went about their affairs during the night.

In the universal and constant darkness of their dwelling, they had no reason to prefer the one arrangement to the other; but from aversion to the sun-people, they chose to be busy when there was least chance of their being met either by the miners below, when they were burrowing, or by the people of the mountain above, when they were feeding their sheep or catching their goats. And indeed it was only when the sun was away that the outside of the mountain was sufficiently like their own dismal regions to be endurable to their mole-eyes, so thoroughly had they become disused to any light beyond that of their own fires and torches.

Curdie listened, and soon found that they were talking of himself.

"How long will it take?" asked Harelip.

"Not many days, I should think," answered the king. "They are poor feeble creatures, those sun-people, and want to be always eating. *We* can go a week at a time without food, and be all the better for it; but I've been told *they* eat two or

[122]

three times every day! Can you believe it?—They must be quite hollow inside—not at all like us, nine-tenths of whose bulk is solid flesh and bone. Yes—I judge a week of starvation will do for him."

"If I may be allowed a word," interposed the queen, "—and I think I ought to have some voice in the matter—"

"The wretch is entirely at your disposal, my spouse," interrupted the king. "He is your property. You caught him yourself. We should never have done it."

The queen laughed. She seemed in far better humor than the night before.

"I was about to say," she resumed, "that it does seem a pity to waste so much fresh meat."

"What are you thinking of, my love?" said the king. "The very notion of starving him implies that we are not going to give him any meat, either salt or fresh."

"I'm not such a stupid as that comes to," returned her Majesty. "What I mean is, that by the time he is starved, there will hardly be a picking upon his bones."

The king gave a great laugh.

"Well, my spouse, you may have him when you like," he said. "I don't fancy him for my part. I am pretty sure he is tough eating."

"That would be to honor instead of punish his insolence," returned the queen. "But why should our poor creatures be deprived of so much nourishment? Our little dogs and cats and pigs and small bears would enjoy him very much."

"You are the best of housekeepers, my lovely queen!" said her husband. "Let it be so by all means. Let us have our

[123]

people in, and get him out and kill him at once. He deserves it. The mischief he might have brought upon us, now that he had penetrated so far as our most retired citadel, is incalculable. Or rather let us tie him hand and foot, and have the pleasure of seeing him torn to pieces by full torchlight in the great hall."

"Better and better!" cried the queen and prince together, both of them clapping their hands. And the prince made an ugly noise with his hare-lip, just as if he had intended to be one at the feast.

"But," added the queen, bethinking herself, "he is so troublesome. For as poor creatures as they are, there is something about those sun-people that is *very* troublesome. I cannot imagine how it is that with such superior strength and skill and understanding as ours, we permit them to exist at all. Why do we not destroy them entirely, and use their cattle and grazing lands at our pleasure? Of course, we don't want to live in their horrid country! It is far too glaring for our quieter and more refined tastes. But we might use it for a sort of out-house, you know. Even our creatures' eyes might get used to it, and if they did grow blind, that would be of no consequence, provided they grew fat as well. But we might even keep their great cows and other creatures, and then we should have a few more luxuries, such as cream and cheese, which at present we only taste occasionally, when our brave men have succeeded in carrying some off from their farms."

"It is worth thinking of," said the king; "and I don't know why you should be the first to suggest it, except that you have a positive genius for conquest. But still, as you say, there is something very troublesome about them; and it would be

better, as I understand you to suggest, that we should starve
him for a day or two first, so that he may be a little less frisky
when we take him out."

> "Once there was a goblin
>   Living in a hole;
>   Busy he was cobblin'
>   A shoe without a sole.

> "By came a birdie:
>   'Goblin, what do you do?'
>   'Cobble at a sturdie
>   Upper leather shoe.'

> " 'What's the good o' that, sir?'
>   Said the little bird,
>   'Why it's very pat, sir—
>   Plain without a word.

> " 'Where 'tis all a hill, sir,
>   Never can be holes:
>   Why should their shoes have soles, sir,
>   When they've got no souls?' "

"What's that horrible noise?" cried the queen, shuddering
from pot-metal head to granite shoes.

"I declare," said the king with solemn indignation, "it's
the sun-creature in the hole!"

"Stop that disgusting noise!" cried the crown-prince vali-
antly, getting up and standing in front of the heap of stones,
with his face toward Curdie's prison.—"Do now, or I'll break
your head."

"Break away," shouted Curdie, and began singing again—

> "Once there was a goblin
>   Living in a hole,—"

"I really cannot bear it," said the queen. "If I could only
get at his horrid toes with my slippers again!"

"I think we had better go to bed," said the king.

"It's not time to go to bed," said the queen.

"I would if I was you," said Curdie.

"Impertinent wretch!" said the queen, with the utmost scorn in her voice.

"An impossible *if*," said his Majesty with dignity.

"Quite," returned Curdie, and began singing again—

> "Go to bed,
> Goblin, do.
> Help the queen
> Take off her shoe.

> "If you do,
> It will disclose
> A horrid set
> Of sprouting toes."

"What a lie!" roared the queen in a rage.

"By the way, that reminds me," said the king, "that, for as long as we have been married, I have never seen your feet, queen. I think you might take off your shoes when you go to bed! They positively hurt me sometimes."

"I will do just as I like," retorted the queen sulkily.

"You ought to do as your hubby wishes you," said the king.

"I will not," said the queen.

"Then I insist upon it," said the king.

Apparently his Majesty approached the queen for the purpose of following the advice given by Curdie, for the latter heard a scuffle, and then a great roar from the king.

"Will you be quiet then?" said the queen wickedly.

"Yes, yes, queen. I only meant to coax you."

"Hands off!" cried the queen triumphantly. "I'm going

to bed. You may come when you like. But as long as I am queen, I will sleep in my shoes. It is my royal privilege. Hare-lip, go to bed."

"I'm going," said Harelip sleepily.

"So am I," said the king.

"Come along then," said the queen; "and mind you are good, or I'll—"

"Oh, no, no, no!" screamed the king, in the most suppli-cating of tones.

Curdie heard only a muttered reply in the distance; and then the cave was quite still.

They had left the fire burning, and the light came through brighter than before. Curdie thought it was time to try again if anything could be done. But he found he could not get even a finger through the chink between the slab and the rock. He gave a great rush with his shoulder against the slab, but it yielded no more than if it had been part of the rock. All he could do was to sit down and think again.

By and by he came to the resolution to pretend to be dying, in the hope they might take him out before his strength was too much exhausted to let him have a chance. Then, for the creatures, if he could but find his axe again, he would have no fear of them; and if it were not for the queen's horrid shoes, he would have no fear at all.

Meantime, until they should come again at night, there was nothing for him to do but forge new rhymes, now his only weapons. He had no intention of using them at present, of course; but it was well to have a stock, for he might live to want them, and the manufacture of them would help to while away the time.

CHAPTER XX

IRENE'S CLUE

THAT same morning, early, the princess woke in a terrible fright. There was a hideous noise in her room—of creatures snarling and hissing and racketing about as if they were fighting. The moment she came to herself, she remembered something she had never thought of again—what her grandmother told her to do when she was frightened. She immediately took off her ring and put it under her pillow. As she did so, she fancied she felt a finger and thumb take it gently from under her palm. "It must be my grandmother!" she said to herself, and the thought gave her such courage that she stopped to put on her dainty little slippers before running from the room. While doing this, she caught sight of a long cloak of sky-blue, thrown over the back of a chair by her bedside. She had never seen it before, but it was evidently waiting for her. She put it on, and then, feeling with the forefinger of her right hand, soon found her grandmother's thread, which she proceeded at once to follow, expecting it would lead her straight up the old stair. When she reached the door, she found it went down and ran along the floor, so that she had almost to crawl in order to keep a hold of it. Then, to her surprise, and somewhat to her dismay, she found that instead of leading her toward the stair it turned in quite the opposite direction. It led her through certain narrow passages toward the kitchen, turning aside ere she reached it,

The goblins fell back a little when he began, and made horrible
grimaces all through the rhyme.

and guiding her to a door which communicated with a small back yard. Some of the maids were already up, and this door was standing open. Across the yard the thread still ran along the ground, until it brought her to a door in the wall which opened upon the mountain side. When she had passed through, the thread rose to about half her height, and she could hold it with ease as she walked. It led her straight up the mountain.

The cause of her alarm was less frightful than she supposed. The cook's great black cat, pursued by the housekeeper's terrier, had bounced against her bedroom door, which had not been properly fastened, and the two had burst into her room together and commenced a battle royal. How the nurse came to sleep through it, was a mystery, but I suspect the old lady had something to do with it.

It was a clear warm morning. The wind blew deliciously over the mountain-side. Here and there she saw a late primrose, but she did not stop to call on them. The sky was mottled with small clouds. The sun was not yet up, but some of their fluffy edges had caught his light and hung out orange and gold-colored fringes upon the air. The dew lay in round drops upon the leaves, and hung like tiny diamonds from the blades of grass about her path.

"How lovely that bit of gossamer is!" thought the princess, looking at a long undulating line that shone at some distance from her up the hill. It was not the time for gossamers though; and Irene soon discovered that it was her own thread she saw shining on before her in the light of the morning. It was leading her she knew not whither; but she had never in her life been out before sunrise, and everything was so fresh and cool and lively and full of something coming, that she felt too happy to be afraid of anything.

After leading her up a good distance, the thread turned to the left, and down the path upon which she and Lootie had met Curdie. But she never thought of that, for now in the morning light, with its far outlook over the country, no path could have been more open and airy and cheerful. She could see the road almost to the horizon, along which she had so often watched her king-papa and his troop come shining, with the bugle-blast cleaving the air before them; and it was like a companion to her. Down and down the path went, then up, and then down, and then up again, getting rugged and more rugged as it went; still along the path went the silvery thread, and still along the thread went Irene's little rosy-tipped forefinger. By and by she came to a little stream that jabbered and prattled down the hill, and up the side of the stream went both path and thread. And still the path grew rougher and steeper, and the mountain grew wilder, till Irene began to think she was going a very long way from home; and when she turned to look back, she saw that the level country had vanished and the rough bare mountain had closed in about her. But still on went the thread, and on went the princess. Everything around her was getting brighter and brighter as the sun came nearer; till at length his first rays all at once alighted on the top of a rock before her, like some golden creature fresh from the sky. Then she saw that the little stream ran out of a hole in that rock, that the path did not go past the rock, and that the thread was leading her straight up to it. A shudder ran through her from head to foot when she found that the thread was actually taking her into the hole out of which the stream ran. It ran out babbling joyously, but she had to go in.

She did not hesitate. Right into the hole she went, which was high enough to let her walk without stooping. For a little way there was a brown glimmer, but at the first turn it all but ceased, and before she had gone many paces she was in total darkness. Then she began to be frightened indeed. Every moment she kept feeling the thread backward, and as she went farther and farther into the darkness of the great hollow mountain, she kept thinking more and more about her grandmother, and all that she had said to her, and how kind she had been, and how beautiful she was, and all about her lovely room, and the fire of roses, and the great lamp that sent its light through stone walls. And she became more and more sure that the thread could not have gone there of itself, and that her grandmother must have sent it. But it tried her dreadfully when the path went down very steep, and especially when she came to places where she had to go down rough stairs, and even sometimes a ladder. Through one narrow passage after another, over lumps of rock and sand and clay, the thread guided her, until she came to a small hole through which she had to creep. Finding no change on the other side—"Shall I ever get back?" she thought, over and over again, wondering at herself that she was not ten times more frightened, and often feeling as if she were only walking in the story of a dream. Sometimes she heard the noise of water, a dull gurgling inside the rock. By and by she heard the sounds of blows, which came nearer and nearer; but again they grew duller and almost died away. In a hundred directions she turned, obedient to the guiding thread.

At last she spied a dull red shine, and came up to the mica-window, and thence away and round about, and right into a cavern, where glowed the red embers of a fire. Here the thread began to rise. It rose as high as her head, and higher still. What *should* she do if she lost her hold? She was pulling it down! She might break it! She could see it far up, glowing as red as her fire-opal in the light of the embers.

But presently she came to a huge heap of stones, piled in a slope against the wall of the cavern. On these she climbed, and soon recovered the level of the thread—only however to find, the next moment, that it vanished through the heap of stones, and left her standing on it, with her face to the solid rock. For one terrible moment, she felt as if her grandmother had forsaken her. The thread which the spiders had spun far over the seas, which her grandmother had sat in the moonlight and spun again for her, which she had tempered in the rose-fire, and tied to her opal ring, had left her—had gone where she could no longer follow it—had brought her into a horrible cavern, and there left her! She was forsaken indeed!

"When *shall* I wake?" she said to herself in an agony, but the same moment knew that it was no dream. She threw herself upon the heap, and began to cry. It was well she did not know what creatures, one of them with stone shoes on her feet, were lying in the next cave. But neither did she know who was on the other side of the slab.

At length the thought struck her, that at least she could follow the thread backward, and thus get out of the mountain, and home. She rose at once, and found the thread. But the instant she tried to feel it backward, it vanished from her touch. Forward, it led her hand up to the heap of stones— backward, it seemed nowhere. Neither could she see it as before in the light of the fire. She burst into a wailing cry, and again threw herself down on the stones.

CHAPTER XXI

THE ESCAPE

AS the princess lay and sobbed, she kept feeling the thread mechanically, following it with her finger many times up the stones in which it disappeared. By and by she began, still mechanically, to poke her finger in after it between the stones as far as she could. All at once it came into her head that she might remove some of the stones and see where the thread went next. Almost laughing at herself for never having thought of this before, she jumped to her feet. Her fear vanished; once more she was certain her grandmother's thread could not have brought her there just to leave her there; and she began to throw away the stones from the top as fast as she could, sometimes two or three at a handful, sometimes taking both hands to lift one. After clearing them away a little, she found that the thread turned and went straight downward. Hence, as the heap sloped a good deal, growing of course wider toward its base, she had to throw away a multitude of stones to follow the thread. But this was not all, for she soon found that the thread, after going straight down for a little way, turned first sideways in one direction, then sideways in another, and then shot, at various angles, hither and thither inside the heap, so that she began to be afraid that to clear the thread, she must remove the whole huge gathering. She was dismayed at the very idea, but, losing no time, set to work with a will; and with aching back,

[134]

and bleeding fingers and hands, she worked on, sustained by the pleasure of seeing the heap slowly diminish, and begin to show itself on the opposite side of the fire. Another thing which helped to keep up her courage was, that as often as she uncovered a turn of the thread, instead of lying loose upon the stones, it tightened up; this made her sure that her grandmother was at the end of it somewhere.

She had got about half way down when she started, and nearly fell with fright. Close to her ear as it seemed, a voice broke out singing—

> "Jabber, bother, smash!
> You'll have it all in a crash.
> Jabber, smash, bother!
> You'll have the worst of the pother.
> Smash, bother, jabber!—"

Here Curdie stopped, either because he could not find a rhyme to *jabber*, or because he remembered what he had forgotten when he woke up at the sound of Irene's labors, that his plan was to make the goblins think he was getting weak. But he had uttered enough to let Irene know who he was.

"It's Curdie!" she cried joyfully.

"Hush, hush!" came Curdie's voice again from somewhere. "Speak softly."

"Why, you were singing loud!" said Irene.

"Yes. But they know I am here, and they don't know you are. Who are you?"

"I'm Irene," answered the princess. "I know who you are quite well. You're Curdie."

"Why, how ever did you come here, Irene?"

"My great-great-grandmother sent me; and I think I've found out why. You can't get out, I suppose?"

"No, I can't. What are you doing?"

"Clearing away a huge heap of stones."

"There's a princess!" exclaimed Curdie, in a tone of delight, but still speaking in little more than a whisper. "I can't think how you got here, though."

"My grandmother sent me after her thread."

"I don't know what you mean," said Curdie; "but so you're there, it doesn't much matter."

"Oh, yes it does!" returned Irene. "I should never have been here but for her."

"You can tell me all about it when we get out, then. There's no time to lose now," said Curdie.

And Irene went to work, as fresh as when she began.

"There's such a lot of stones!" she said. "It will take me a long time to get them all away."

"How far on have you got?" asked Curdie.

"I've got about the half way, but the other half is ever so much bigger."

"I don't think you will have to move the lower half. Do you see a slab laid up against the wall?"

Irene looked and felt about with her hands, and soon perceived the outlines of the slab.

"Yes," she answered, "I do."

"Then, I think," rejoined Curdie, "when you have cleared the slab about half way down, or a little more, I shall be able to push it over."

"I must follow my thread," returned Irene, "whatever I do."

"What *do* you mean?" exclaimed Curdie.

"You will see when you get out of here," answered the princess, and then she went on harder than ever.

But she was soon satisfied that what Curdie wanted done, and what the thread wanted done, were one and the same thing. For she not only saw that by following the turns of the thread she had been clearing the face of the slab, but that, a little more than half way down, the thread went through the chink between the slab and the wall into the place where Curdie was confined, so that she could not follow it any farther until the slab was out of her way. As soon as she found this, she said in a right joyous whisper—

"Now, Curdie! I think if you were to give a great push, the slab would tumble over."

"Stand quite clear of it then," said Curdie, "and let me know when you are ready."

Irene got off the heap, and stood on one side of it.

"Now, Curdie!" she cried.

Curdie gave a great rush with his shoulder against it. Out tumbled the slab on the heap, and out crept Curdie over the top of it.

"You've saved my life, Irene!" he whispered.

"Oh, Curdie! I'm so glad! Let's get out of this horrid place as fast as we can."

"That's easier said than done," returned he.

"Oh, no! it's quite easy," said Irene. "We have only to follow my thread. I am sure that it's going to take us out now."

She had already begun to follow it over the fallen slab into the hole, while Curdie was searching the floor of the cavern for his pickaxe.

"Here it is!" he cried. "No, it is not!" he added, in a disappointed tone. "What can it be then?—I declare it's a torch. That *is* jolly! It's better almost than my pickaxe. Much better if it weren't for those stone shoes!" he went on, as he lighted the torch by blowing the last embers of the expiring fire.

When he looked up, with the lighted torch casting a glare into the great darkness of the huge cavern, he caught sight of Irene disappearing in the hole out of which he had himself just come.

"Where are you going there?" he cried. "That's not the way out. That's where I couldn't get out."

"I know that," whispered Irene. "But this is the way my thread goes, and I must follow it."

"What nonsense the child talks!" said Curdie to himself. "I must follow her, though, and see that she comes to no harm. She will soon find she can't get out that way, and then she will come with me."

So he crept once more over the slab into the hole with his torch in his hand. But when he looked about in it, he could see her nowhere. And now he discovered that although the hole was narrow, it was much larger than he had supposed; for in one direction the roof came down very low, and the hole went off in a narrow passage, of which he could not see the end. The princess must have crept in there. He got on his knees and one hand, holding the torch with the other, and crept after her. The hole twisted about, in some parts so low that he could hardly get through, in others so high that he could not see the roof, but everywhere it was narrow—far too narrow for a goblin to get through, and so I presume they never thought that Curdie might. He was beginning to feel very uncomfortable lest he could not see the end. The princess when he heard her voice almost close to his ear, whispering—

"Aren't you coming, Curdie?"

And when he turned the next corner, there she stood waiting for him.

"I knew you couldn't go wrong in that narrow hole, but now you must keep by me, for here is a great wide place," she said.

"I can't understand it," said Curdie, half to himself, half to Irene.

"Never mind," she returned. "Wait till we get out."

Curdie, utterly astonished that she had already got so far, and by a path he had known nothing of, thought it better to let her do as she pleased.

"At all events," he said again to himself, "I know nothing about the way, miner as I am; and she seems to think she does know something about it, though how she should, passes my comprehension. So she's just as likely to find her way as I am, and as she insists on taking the lead, I must follow. We can't be much worse off than we are, anyhow."

Reasoning thus, he followed her a few steps, and came out in another great cavern, across which Irene walked in a straight line, as confidently as if she knew every step of the way. Curdie went on after her, flashing his torch about, and trying to see something of what lay around them. Suddenly he started back a pace as the light fell upon something close by which Irene was passing. It was a platform of rock raised a few feet from the floor and covered with sheep skins, upon which lay two horrible figures asleep, at once recognized by Curdie as the king and queen of the goblins. He lowered his torch instantly lest the light should awake them. As he did so, it flashed upon his pickaxe, lying by the side of the queen, whose hand lay close by the handle of it.

"Stop one moment," he whispered. "Hold my torch, and don't let the light on their faces."

Irene shuddered when she saw the frightful creatures whom she had passed without observing them, but she did as he requested, and turning her back, held the torch low in front of her. Curdie drew his pickaxe carefully away, and as he did so, spied one of her feet, projecting from under the skins. The great clumsy granite shoe, exposed thus to his hand, was a temptation not to be resisted. He laid hold of it, and with cautious efforts, drew it off. The moment he succeeded, he saw to his astonishment that what he had sung in ignorance, to annoy the queen, was actually true: she had six horrible toes. Overjoyed at his success, and seeing by the huge bump in the sheep skins where the other foot was, he proceeded to lift them gently, for, if he could only succeed in carrying away the other shoe as well, he would be no more afraid of the goblins than of so many flies. But as he pulled at the second shoe, the queen gave a growl and sat up in bed. The same instant the king awoke also, and sat up beside her.

"Run, Irene!" cried Curdie, for though he was not now in the least afraid for himself, he was for the princess.

Irene looked once round, saw the fearful creatures awake, and like the wise princess she was, dashed the torch on the ground and extinguished it, crying out—

"Here, Curdie, take my hand."

He darted to her side, forgetting neither the queen's shoe nor his pickaxe, and caught hold of her hand, as she sped fearlessly where her thread guided her. They heard the queen give a great bellow; but they had a good start, for it would be some time before they could get torches lighted to pursue them. Just as they thought they saw a gleam behind them, the thread brought them to a very narrow opening, through which Irene crept easily, and Curdie with difficulty.

"Now," said Curdie; "I think we shall be safe."

"Of course we shall," returned Irene.

"Why do you think so?" asked Curdie.

"Because my grandmother is taking care of us."

"That's all nonsense," said Curdie. "I don't know what you mean."

"Then if you don't know what I mean, what right have you to call it nonsense?" asked the princess, a little offended.

"I beg your pardon, Irene," said Curdie; "I did not mean to vex you."

"Of course not," returned the princess. "But why do *you* think we shall be safe?"

"Because the king and queen are far too stout to get through that hole."

"There may be ways round," said the other.

"To be sure there might; we are not out of it yet," acknowledged Curdie.

[141]

"But what do you mean by the king and queen?" asked the princess. "I should never call such creatures as those a king and a queen."

"Their own people do, though," answered Curdie.

The princess asked more questions, and Curdie, as they walked leisurely along, gave her a full account, not only of the character and habits of the goblins, so far as he knew them, but of his own adventures with them, beginning from the very night after that in which he had met her and Lootie upon the mountain. When he had finished, he begged Irene to tell him how it was that she had come to his rescue. So Irene too had to tell a long story, which she did in rather a roundabout manner, interrupted by many questions concerning things she had not explained. But her tale, as he did not believe more than half of it, left everything as unaccountable to him as before, and he was nearly as much perplexed as to what he must think of the princess. He could not believe that she was deliberately telling stories, and the only conclusion he could come to was that Lootie had been playing the child tricks, inventing no end of lies to frighten her for her own purposes.

"But how ever did Lootie come to let you go into the mountain alone?" he asked.

"Lootie knows nothing about it. I left her fast asleep—at least I think so. I hope my grandmother won't let her get into trouble, for it wasn't her fault at all, as my grandmother very well knows."

"But how did you find your way to me?" persisted Curdie.

"I told you already," answered Irene;—"by keeping my finger upon my grandmother's thread, as I am doing now."

"You don't mean you've got the thread there?"

"Of course I do. I have told you so ten times already. I have hardly—except when I was removing the stones—taken my finger off it. There!" she added, guiding Curdie's hand to the thread, "you feel it yourself—don't you?"

"I feel nothing at all," replied Curdie.

"Then what can be the matter with your finger? I feel it perfectly. To be sure it is very thin, and in the sunlight looks just like the thread of a spider, though there are many of them twisted together to make it—but for all that I can't think why you shouldn't feel it as well as I do."

Curdie was too polite to say he did not believe there was any thread there at all. What he did say was—

"Well, I can make nothing of it."

"I can though, and you must be glad of that, for it will do for both of us."

"We're not out yet," said Curdie.

"We soon shall be," returned Irene confidently.

And now the thread went downward, and led Irene's hand to a hole in the floor of the cavern, whence came a sound of running water which they had been hearing for some time.

"It goes into the ground now, Curdie," she said, stopping.

He had been listening to another sound, which his practised ear had caught long ago, and which also had been growing louder. It was the noise the goblin miners made at their work, and they seemed to be at no great distance now. Irene heard it the moment she stopped.

"What is that noise?" she asked. "Do you know, Curdie?"

"Yes. It is the goblins digging and burrowing," he answered.

"And don't you know for what purpose they do it?"

"No; I haven't the least idea. Would you like to see them?" he asked, wishing to have another try after their secret.

"If my thread took me there, I shouldn't much mind; but I don't want to see them, and I can't leave my thread. It leads me down into the hole, and we had better go at once."

"Very well. Shall I go in first?" said Curdie.

"No; better not. You can't feel the thread," she answered, stepping down through a narrow break in the floor of the cavern. "Oh!" she cried, "I am in the water. It is running strong—but it is not deep, and there is just room to walk. Make haste, Curdie."

He tried, but the hole was too small for him to get in.

"Go on a little bit," he said, shouldering his pickaxe.

In a few moments he had cleared a large opening and followed her. They went on, down and down with the running water, Curdie getting more and more afraid it was leading them to some terrible gulf in the heart of the mountain. In one or two places he had to break away the rock to make room before even Irene could get through—at least without hurting herself. But at length they spied a glimmer of light, and in a minute more, they were almost blinded by the full sunlight into which they emerged. It was some little time before the princess could see well enough to discover that they stood in her own garden, close by the seat on which she and her king-papa had sat that afternoon. They had come out by

Curdie went on after her, flashing his torch about.

the channel of the little stream. She danced and clapped her hands with delight.

"Now, Curdie!" she cried, "won't you believe what I told you about my grandmother and her thread?"

For she had felt all the time that Curdie was not believing what she had told him.

"There!—don't you see it shining on before us?" she added.

"I don't see anything," persisted Curdie.

"Then you must believe without seeing," said the princess; "for you can't deny it has brought me out of the mountain."

"I can't deny we *are* out of the mountain, and I should be very ungrateful indeed to deny that *you* had brought *me* out of it."

"I couldn't have done it but for the thread," persisted Irene.

"That's the part I don't understand."

"Well, come along, and Lootie will get you something to eat. I am sure you must want it very much."

"Indeed I do. But my father and mother will be so anxious about me, I must make haste—first up the mountain to tell my mother, and then down into the mine again to acquaint my father."

"Very well, Curdie; but you can't get out without coming this way, and I will take you through the house, for that is nearest."

They met no one by the way, for indeed, as before, the people were here and there and everywhere searching for the princess. When they got in, Irene found that the thread, as she had half expected, went up the old staircase, and a new thought struck her. She turned to Curdie and said—

"My grandmother wants me. Do come up with me, and see her. Then you will know that I have been telling you the truth. Do come—to please me, Curdie. I can't bear you should think I say what is not true."

"I never doubted you believed what you said," returned Curdie. "I only thought you had some fancy in your head that was not correct."

"But do come, dear Curdie."

The little miner could not withstand this appeal, and though he felt shy in what seemed to him such a huge grand house, he yielded, and followed her up the stair.

CHAPTER XXII

THE OLD LADY AND CURDIE

UP the stair then they went, and the next and the next, and through the long rows of empty rooms, and up the little tower stairs, Irene growing happier and happier as she ascended. There was no answer when she knocked at length at the door of the workroom, nor could she hear any sound of the spinning-wheel, and once more her heart sank within her—but only for one moment, as she turned and knocked at the other door.

"Come in," answered the sweet voice of her grandmother, and Irene opened the door and entered, followed by Curdie.

"You darling!" cried the lady, who was seated by a fire of red roses mingled with white—"I've been waiting for you, and indeed getting a little anxious about you, and beginning to think whether I had not better go and fetch you myself."

As she spoke she took the little princess in her arms and placed her upon her lap. She was dressed in white now, and looking if possible more lovely than ever.

"I've brought Curdie, grandmother. He wouldn't believe what I told him, and so I've brought him."

"Yes—I see him. He is a good boy, Curdie, and a brave boy. Aren't you glad you have got him out?"

"Yes, grandmother. But it wasn't very good of him not to believe me when I was telling him the truth."

"People must believe what they can, and those who believe

[147]

more must not be hard upon those who believe less. I doubt if you would have believed it all yourself if you hadn't seen some of it."

"Ah! yes, grandmother, I daresay. I'm sure you are right. But he'll believe now."

"I don't know that," replied her grandmother.

"Won't you, Curdie?" said Irene, looking round at him as she asked the question.

He was standing in the middle of the floor, staring, and looking strangely bewildered. This she thought came of his astonishment at the beauty of the lady.

"Make a bow to my grandmother, Curdie," she said.

"I don't see any grandmother," answered Curdie, rather gruffly.

"Don't see my grandmother when I'm sitting in her lap!" exclaimed the princess.

"No I don't," said Curdie, almost sulkily.

"Don't you see the lovely fire of roses—white ones amongst them this time?" asked Irene almost as bewildered as he.

"No I don't," answered Curdie, almost sulkily.

"Nor the blue bed? Nor the rose-colored counterpane? Nor the beautiful light, like the moon, hanging from the roof?"

"You're making game of me, your royal Highness; and after what we have come through together this day, I don't think it is kind of you," said Curdie, feeling very much hurt.

"Then what *do* you see?" asked Irene, who perceived at once that for her not to believe him was at least as bad as for him not to believe her.

"I see a big, bare garret-room—like the one in mother's

cottage, only big enough to take the cottage itself in, and leave a good margin all round," answered Curdie.

"And what more do you see?"

"I see a tub, and a heap of musty straw, and a withered apple and a ray of sunlight coming through a hole in the middle of the roof, and shining on your head, and making all the place look a curious dusky brown. I think you had better drop it, princess, and go down to the nursery, like a good girl."

"But don't you hear my grandmother talking to me?" asked Irene, almost crying.

"No. I hear the cooing of a lot of pigeons. If you won't come down, I will go without you. I think that will be better anyhow, for I'm sure nobody who met us would believe a word we said to them. They would think we made it all up. I don't expect anybody but my own father and mother to believe me. They *know* I wouldn't tell a story."

"And yet *you* won't believe *me*, Curdie?" expostulated the princess, now fairly crying with vexation, and sorrow at the gulf between her and Curdie.

"No. I *can't*, and I can't help it," said Curdie, turning to leave the room.

"What *shall* I do, grandmother?" sobbed the princess, turning her face round upon the lady's bosom, and shaking with suppressed sobs.

"You must give him time," said her grandmother; "and you must be content not to be believed for a while. It is very hard to bear; but I have had to bear it, and shall have to bear it many a time yet. I will take care of what Curdie thinks of you in the end. You must let him go now."

"You are not coming, are you?" asked Curdie.

"No, Curdie; my grandmother says I must let you go. Turn to the right when you get to the bottom of all the stairs, and in that way you will arrive safely at the hall where the great door is."

"Oh! I don't doubt I can find my way—without you, princess, or your old grannie's thread either," said Curdie, quite rudely.

"Oh, Curdie! Curdie!"

"I wish I had gone home at once. I'm very much obliged to you, Irene, for getting me out of that hole, but I wish you hadn't made a fool of me afterward."

He said this as he opened the door, which he left open, and, without another word, went down the stairs. Irene listened with dismay to his departing footsteps. Then turning again to the lady—

"What does it all mean, grandmother?" she sobbed, and burst into fresh tears.

"It means, my love, that I did not mean to show myself. Curdie is not yet able to believe some things. Seeing is not believing—it is only seeing. You remember I told you that if Lootie were to see me, she would rub her eyes, forget the half she saw, and call the other half nonsense."

"Yes; but I should have thought Curdie—"

"You are right. Curdie is much farther on than Lootie, and you will see what will come of it. But in the meantime, you must be content, I say, to be misunderstood for a while. We are all very anxious to be understood, and it is very hard not to be. But there is one thing much more necessary."

"What is that, grandmother?"

"To understand other people."

"Yes, grandmother. I must be fair—for if I'm not fair to other people, I'm not worth being understood myself I see. So as Curdie can't help it, I will not be vexed with him, but just wait."

"There's my own dear child," said her grandmother, and pressed her close to her bosom.

"Why weren't you in your workroom, when we came up, grandmother?" asked Irene, after a few moments' silence.

"If I had been there, Curdie would have seen me well enough. But why should I be there rather than in this beautiful room?"

"I thought you would be spinning."

"I've nobody to spin for just at present. I never spin without knowing for whom I am spinning."

"That reminds me—there is one thing that puzzles me," said the princess: "how are you to get the thread out of the mountain again? Surely you won't have to make another for me! That would be such a trouble!"

The lady set her down, and rose, and went to the fire. Putting in her hand, she drew it out again, and held up the shining ball between her finger and thumb.

"I've got it now, you see," she said, coming back to the princess, "all ready for you when you want it."

Going to her cabinet, she laid it in the same drawer as before.

"And here is your ring," she added, taking it from the little finger of her left hand, and putting it on the forefinger of Irene's right hand.

[151]

"Oh, thank you, grandmother. I feel so safe now!"

"You are very tired, my child," the lady went on. "Your hands are hurt with the stones, and I have counted nine bruises on you. Just look what you are like."

And she held up to her a little mirror which she had brought from the cabinet. The princess burst into a merry laugh at the sight. She was so draggled with the stream, and dirty with creeping through narrow places, that if she had seen the reflection without knowing it was a reflection, she would have taken herself for some gypsy-child whose face was washed and hair combed about once in a month. The lady laughed too, and lifting her again upon her knee, took off her cloak and night-gown. Then she carried her to the side of the room. Irene wondered what she was going to do with her, but asked no questions—only starting a little when she found that she was going to lay her in the large silver bath; for as she looked into it, again she saw no bottom, but the stars shining miles away as it seemed in a great blue gulf. Her hands closed involuntarily on the beautiful arms that held her, and that was all.

The lady pressed her once more to her bosom, saying—

"Do not be afraid, my child."

"No, grandmother," answered the princess, with a little gasp; and the next instant she sank in the clear cool water.

When she opened her eyes, she saw nothing but a strange lovely blue over and beneath and all about her. The lady and the beautiful room had vanished from her sight, and she seemed utterly alone. But instead of being afraid, she felt more than happy—perfectly blissful. And from somewhere came the voice of the lady, singing a strange sweet song, of which she could distinguish every word; but of the sense she had only a feeling—no understanding. Nor could she remember a single line after it was gone. It vanished, like the poetry in a dream, as fast as it came. In after years, however, she would sometimes fancy that snatches of melody suddenly rising in her brain, must be little phrases and fragments of the air of that song; and the very fancy would make her happier, and abler to do her duty.

How long she lay in the water she did not know. It seemed a long time—not from weariness, but from pleasure. But at last she felt the beautiful hands lay hold of her, and through the gurgling waters she was lifted out into the lovely room. The lady carried her to the fire, and sat down with her in her lap, and dried her tenderly with the softest towel. It was so different from Lootie's drying! When the lady had done, she stooped to the fire, and drew from it her night-gown, as white as snow.

"How delicious!" exclaimed the princess. "It smells of all the roses in the world, I think."

When she stood up on the floor, she felt as if she had been made over again. Every bruise and all weariness were gone, and her hands were soft and whole as ever.

"Now I am going to put you to bed for a good sleep," said her grandmother.

"But what will Lootie be thinking? And what am I to say to her when she asks me where I have been?"

"Don't trouble yourself about it. You will find it all come right," said her grandmother, and laid her into the blue bed, under the rosy counterpane.

"There is just one thing more," said Irene. "I am a little anxious about Curdie. As I brought him into the house, I ought to have seen him safe on his way home."

"I took care of all that," answered the lady. "I told you to let him go, and therefore I was bound to look after him. Nobody saw him, and he is now eating a good dinner in his mother's cottage, far up the mountain."

"Then I will go to sleep," said Irene, and in a few minutes, she was fast asleep.

CHAPTER XXIII

CURDIE AND HIS MOTHER

CURDIE went up the mountain neither whistling nor singing, for he was vexed with Irene for taking him in, as he called it; and he was vexed with himself for having spoken to her so angrily. His mother gave a cry of joy when she saw him, and at once set about getting him something to eat, asking him questions all the time, which he did not answer so cheerfully as usual. When his meal was ready, she left him to eat it, and hurried to the mine to let his father know he was safe. When she came back, she found him fast asleep upon her bed; nor did he wake until the arrival home of his father in the evening.

"Now, Curdie," his mother said, as they sat at supper, "tell us the whole story from beginning to end, just as it all happened."

Curdie obeyed, and told everything to the point where they came out upon the lawn in the garden of the king's house.

"And what happened after that?" asked his mother. "You haven't told us all. You ought to be very happy at having got away from those demons, and instead of that, I never saw you so gloomy. There must be something more. Besides, you do not speak of that lovely child as I should like to hear you. She saved your life at the risk of her own, and yet somehow you don't seem to think much of it."

"She talked such nonsense!" answered Curdie, "and told

[155]

me a pack of things that weren't a bit true; and I can't get over it."

"What were they?" asked his father. "Your mother may be able to throw some light upon them."

Then Curdie made a clean breast of it, and told them everything.

They all sat silent for some time, pondering the strange tale. At last Curdie's mother spoke.

"You confess, my boy," she said, "there is something about the whole affair you do not understand?"

"Yes, of course, mother," he answered, "I cannot understand how a child knowing nothing about the mountain, or even that I was shut up in it, should come all that way alone, straight to where I was; and then, after getting me out of the hole, lead me out of the mountain, too, where I should not have known a step of the way if it had been as light as in the open air."

"Then you have no right to say that what she told you was not true. She did take you out, and she must have had something to guide her: why not a thread as well as a rope, or anything else? There is something you cannot explain, and her explanation may be the right one."

"It's no explanation at all, mother; and I can't believe it."

"That may be only because you do not understand it. If you did, you would probably find it was an explanation, and believe it thoroughly. I don't blame you for not being able to believe it, but I do blame you for fancying such a child would try to deceive you. Why should she? Depend upon it, she told you all she knew. Until you had found a better way of accounting for it all, you might at least have been more sparing of your judgment."

"That is what something inside me has been saying all the time," said Curdie, hanging down his head. "But what do you make of the grandmother? That is what I can't get over. To take me up to an old garret, and try to persuade me against the sight of my own eyes that it was a beautiful room, with blue walls and silver stars, and no end of things in it, when there was nothing there but an old tub and a withered apple and a heap of straw and a sunbeam! It was too bad! She *might* have had some old woman there at least who could pass for her precious grandmother!"

"Didn't she speak as if she saw those other things herself, Curdie?"

"Yes. That's what bothers me. You would have thought she really meant and believed that she saw every one of the things she talked about. And not one of them there! It was too bad, I say."

"Perhaps some people can see things other people can't see, Curdie," said his mother very gravely. "I think I will tell you something I saw myself once—only perhaps you won't believe me either!"

"Oh, mother, mother!" cried Curdie, bursting into tears; "I don't deserve that, surely!"

"But what I am going to tell you is very strange," persisted his mother; "and if having heard it, you were to say I must have been dreaming, I don't know that I should have any right to be vexed with you, though I know at least that I was not asleep."

"Do tell me, mother. Perhaps it will help me to think better of the princess."

"That's why I am tempted to tell you," replied his mother. "But first, I may as well mention, that according to old whispers, there is something more than common about the king's family; and the queen was of the same blood, for they were cousins of some degree. There were strange stories told concerning them—all good stories—but strange, very strange. What they were I cannot tell, for I only remember the faces of my grandmother and my mother as they talked together about them. There was wonder and awe—not fear, in their eyes, and they whispered, and never spoke aloud. But what I saw myself, was this: Your father was going to work in the mine, one night, and I had been down with his supper. It was soon after we were married, and not very long before you were born. He came with me to the mouth of the mine, and left me to go home alone, for I knew the way almost as well as the floor of our own cottage. It was pretty dark, and in some parts of the road where the rocks overhung, nearly quite dark. But I got along perfectly well, never thinking of being afraid, until I reached a spot you know well enough, Curdie, where the path has to make a sharp turn out of the way of a great rock on the left-hand side. When I got there, I was suddenly surrounded by about half-a-dozen of the cobs, the first I had ever seen, although I had heard tell of them often enough. One of them blocked up the path, and they all began tormenting and teasing me in a way it makes me shudder to think of even now."

"If I had only been with you!" cried father and son in a breath.

The mother gave a funny little smile, and went on.

"They had some of their horrible creatures with them too, and I must confess I was dreadfully frightened. They had torn my clothes very much, and I was afraid they were going to tear myself to pieces, when suddenly a great white soft light shone upon me. I looked up. A broad ray, like a shining road, came down from a large globe of silvery light, not very high up, indeed not quite so high as the horizon—so it could not have been a new star or another moon or anything of that sort. The cobs dropped persecuting me, and looked dazed, and I thought they were going to run away, but presently they began again. The same moment, however, down the path from the globe of light came a bird, shining like silver in the sun. It gave a few rapid flaps first, and then, with its wings straight out, shot sliding down the slope of the light. It looked to me just like a white pigeon. But whatever it was, when the cobs caught sight of it coming straight down upon them, they took to their heels and scampered away across the mountain, leaving me safe, only much frightened. As soon as it had sent them off, the bird went gliding again up the light, and just at the moment it reached the globe, the light disappeared, just the same as if a shutter had been closed over a window, and I saw it no more. But I had no more trouble with the cobs that night, or at any time afterward.

"How strange!" exclaimed Curdie.

"Yes, it is strange; .but I can't help believing it, whether you do or not," said his mother.

"It's exactly as your mother told it to me the very next morning," said his father.

"You don't think I'm doubting my own mother!" cried Curdie.

"There are other people in the world quite as well worth believing as your own mother," said his mother. "I don't know that she's so much the fitter to be believed that she happens to be *your* mother, Mr. Curdie. There are mothers far more likely to tell lies than that little girl I saw talking to the primroses a few weeks ago. If she were to lie I should begin to doubt my own word."

"But princesses *have* told lies as well as other people," said Curdie.

"Yes, but not princesses like that child. She's a good girl, I am certain, and that's more than being a princess. Depend upon it you will have to be sorry for behaving so to her, Curdie. You ought at least to have held your tongue."

"I am sorry now," answered Curdie.

"You ought to go and tell her so, then."

"I don't see how I could manage that. They wouldn't let a miner boy like me have a word with her alone; and I couldn't tell her before that nurse of hers. She'd be asking ever so many questions, and I don't know how many of them the little princess would like me to answer. She told me that Lootie didn't know anything about her coming to get me out of the mountain. I am certain she would have prevented her somehow if she had known it. But I may have a chance before long, and meantime I must try to do something for her. I think, father, I have got on the track at last."

"Have you, indeed, my boy?" said Peter. "I am sure you deserve some success; you have worked very hard for it. What have you found out?"

"It's difficult you know, father, inside the mountain, especially in the dark, and not knowing what turns you have taken, to tell the lie of things outside."

"Impossible, my boy, without a chart, or at least a compass," returned his father.

"Well, I think I have nearly discovered in what direction the cobs are mining. If I am right, I know something else that I can put to it, and then one and one will make three."

"They very often do, Curdie, as we miners ought to be well aware. Now tell us, my boy, what the two things are, and see whether we guess at the same third as you."

"I don't see what that has to do with the princess," interposed his mother.

"I will soon let you see that, mother. Perhaps you may think me foolish, but until I am sure there is nothing in my present fancy, I am more determined than ever to go on with my observations. Just as we came to the channel by which we got out, I heard the miners at work somewhere near—I think down below us. Now since I began to watch them, they have mined a good half mile, in a straight line; and so far as I am aware, they are working in no other part of the mountain. But I never could tell in what direction they were going. When we came out in the king's garden, however, I thought at once whether it was possible they were working toward the king's house; and what I want to do to-night is to make sure whether they are or not. I will take a light with me—"

"Oh, Curdie," cried his mother, "then they will see you."

"I'm no more afraid of them now than I was before," rejoined Curdie,—"now that I've got this precious shoe. They can't make another such in a hurry, and one bare foot will do for my purpose. Woman as she may be, I won't spare her next time. But I shall be careful with my light, for I don't want them to see me. I won't stick it in my hat."

"Go on, then, and tell us what you mean to do."

"I mean to take a bit of paper with me and a pencil, and go in at the mouth of the stream by which we came out. I shall mark on the paper as near as I can the angle of every turning I take until I find the cobs at work, and so get a good idea in what direction they are going. If it should prove to be nearly parallel with the stream, I shall know it is toward the king's house they are working."

"And what if you should. How much wiser will you be then?"

"Wait a minute, mother, dear. I told you that when I came upon the royal family in the cave, they were talking of their prince—Harelip, they called him—marrying a sun-woman—that means one of us—one with toes to her feet. Now in the speech one of them made that night at their great gathering, of which I heard only a part, he said that peace would be secured for a generation at least by the pledge the prince would hold for the good behavior of *her* relatives: that's what he said, and he must have meant the sun-woman the prince was to marry. I am quite sure the king is much too proud to wish his son to marry any but a princess, and much too knowing to fancy that his having a peasant woman for a wife would be of any material advantage to them."

"I see what you are driving at now," said his mother.

"But," said his father, "the king would dig the mountain to the plain before he would have his princess the wife of a cob, if he were ten times a prince."

"Yes; but they think so much of themselves!" said his mother. "Small creatures always do. The bantam is the proudest cock in my little yard."

"And I fancy," said Curdie, "if they once get her, they would tell the king they would kill her except he consented to the marriage."

"They might say so," said his father, "but they wouldn't kill her; they would keep her alive for the sake of the hold it gave them over our king. Whatever he did to them, they would threaten to do the same to the princess."

"And they are bad enough to torment her just for their own amusement—I know that," said his mother.

"Anyhow, I will keep a watch on them, and see what they are up to," said Curdie. "It's too horrible to think of. I daren't let myself do it. But they sha'n't have her—at least if I can help it. So, mother dear—my clue is all right—will you get me a bit of paper and a pencil and a lump of pease-pudding, and I will set out at once. I saw a place where I can climb over the wall of the garden quite easily."

"You must mind and keep out of the way of the men on the watch," said his mother.

"That I will. I don't want them to know anything about it. They would spoil it all. The cobs would only try some other plan—they are such obstinate creatures! I shall take good care, mother. They won't kill and eat me either, if they should come upon me. So you needn't mind them."

His mother got him what he asked for, and Curdie set out. Close beside the door by which the princess left the garden for the mountain, stood a great rock, and by climbing it Curdie got over the wall. He tied his clue to a stone just inside the channel of the stream, and took his pickaxe with him. He had not gone far before he encountered a horrid creature coming toward the mouth. The spot was too narrow for two of almost any size or shape, and besides Curdie had no wish to let the creature pass. Not being able to use his pickaxe, however, he had a severe struggle with him, and it was only after receiving many bites, some of them bad, that he succeeded in killing him with his pocket knife. Having dragged him out, he made haste to get in again before another should stop up the way.

I need not follow him farther in this night's adventures. He returned to his breakfast, satisfied that the goblins were mining in the direction of the palace—on so low a level that their intention must, he thought, be to burrow under the walls of the king's house, and rise up inside it—in order, he fully believed, to lay hands on the little princess, and carry her off for a wife to their horrid Harelip.

CHAPTER XXIV

IRENE BEHAVES LIKE A PRINCESS

WHEN the princess awoke from the sweetest of sleeps, she found her nurse bending above her, the housekeeper looking over the nurse's shoulder, and the laundry-maid looking over the housekeeper's. The room was full of women-servants; and the gentlemen-at-arms, with a long column of men-servants behind them, were peeping, or trying to peep in at the door of the nursery.

"Are those horrid creatures gone?" asked the princess, remembering first what had terrified her in the morning.

"You naughty little princess!" cried Lootie.

Her face was very pale, with red streaks in it, and she looked as if she were going to shake her; .but Irene said nothing—only waited to hear what should come next.

"How *could* you get under the clothes like that, and make us all fancy you were lost! And keep it up all day too! You *are* the most obstinate child! It's anything but fun to us, I can tell you!"

It was the only way the nurse could account for her disappearance.

"I didn't do that, Lootie," said Irene, very quietly.

"Don't tell stories!" cried her nurse quite rudely.

"I shall tell you nothing at all," said Irene.

"That's just as bad," said the nurse.

"Just as bad to say nothing at all as to tell stories!" ex-

[165]

claimed the princess. "I will ask my papa about that. He won't say so. And I don't think he will like you to say so."

"Tell me directly what you mean by it!" screamed the nurse, half wild with anger at the princess, and fright at the possible consequences to herself.

"When I tell you the truth, Lootie," said the princess, who somehow did not feel at all angry, "you say to me *Don't tell stories:* .it would appear that I must tell stories before you will believe me."

"You are very rude, my dear princess," said the nurse.

"You are so rude, Lootie, that I will not speak to you again till you are sorry. Why should I, when I know you will not believe me?" returned the princess.

For she did know perfectly well that if she were to tell Lootie what she had been about, the more she went on to tell her, the less would she believe her.

"You are the most provoking child!" cried her nurse. "You deserve to be well punished for your wicked behavior."

"Please, Mrs. Housekeeper," said the princess, "will you take me to your room and keep me till my king-papa comes? I will ask him to come as soon as he can."

Every one stared at these words. Up to this moment, they had all regarded her as little more than a baby.

But the housekeeper was afraid of the nurse, and sought to patch matters up, saying—

"I am sure, princess, nursey did not mean to be rude to you."

"I do not think my papa would wish me to have a nurse who spoke to me as Lootie does. If she thinks I tell lies, she had better either say so to my papa, or go away. Sir Walter, will you take charge of me?"

"With the greatest of pleasure, princess," answered the captain of the gentlemen-at-arms, walking with his great stride into the room. The crowd of servants made eager way for him, and he bowed low before the little princess's bed. "I shall send my servant at once, on the fastest horse in the stable, to tell your king-papa that your royal Highness desires his presence. When you have chosen one of these under-servants to wait upon you, I shall order the room to be cleared."

"Thank you very much, Sir Walter," said the princess, and her eye glanced toward a rosy-cheeked girl who had lately come to the house as a scullery-maid.

But when Lootie saw the eyes of her dear princess going in search of another instead of her, she fell upon her knees by the bedside, and burst into a great cry of distress.

"I think, Sir Walter," said the princess, "I will keep Lootie. But I put myself under your care; and you need not trouble my king-papa until I speak to you again. Will you all please to go away? I am quite safe and well, and I did not hide myself for the sake either of amusing myself, or of troubling my people. Lootie, will you please to dress me?"

CHAPTER XXV

CURDIE COMES TO GRIEF

EVERYTHING was for some time quiet above ground. The king was still away in a distant part of his dominions. The men-at-arms kept watching about the house. They had been considerably astonished by finding at the foot of the rock in the garden, the hideous body of the goblin-creature killed by Curdie; but they came to the conclusion that it had been slain in the mines, and had crept out there to die; and except an occasional glimpse of a live one they saw nothing to cause alarm. Curdie kept watching in the mountain, and the goblins kept burrowing deeper into the earth. As long as they went deeper, there was, Curdie judged, no immediate danger.

To Irene, the summer was as full of pleasure as ever, and for a long time, although she often thought of her grandmother during the day, and often dreamed about her at night, she did not see her. The kids and the flowers were as much her delight as ever, and she made as much friendship with the miners' children she met on the mountain as Lootie would permit; but Lootie had very foolish notions concerning the dignity of a princess, not understanding that the truest princess is just the one who loves all her brothers and sisters best, and who is most able to do them good by being humble toward them. At the same time she was considerably altered for the better in her behavior to the princess. She could not help seeing that she was no longer a mere child, but wiser than her age would account for. She kept foolishly whispering to the servants, however—sometimes that the princess was not right in her mind, sometimes that she was too good to live, and other nonsense of the same sort.

All this time, Curdie had to be sorry, without a chance of confessing, that he had behaved so unkindly to the princess. This perhaps made him the more diligent in his endeavors to serve her. His mother and he often talked on the subject, and she comforted him, and told him she was sure he would some day have the opportunity he so much desired.

Here I should like to remark, for the sake of princes and princesses in general, that it is a low and contemptible thing to refuse to confess a fault, or even an error. If a true princess has done wrong, she is always uneasy until she has had an opportunity of throwing the wrongness away from her by saying, "I did it; and I wish I had not; and I am sorry for having done it." So you see there is some ground for supposing that Curdie was not a miner only, but a prince as well. Many such instances have been known in the world's history.

At length, however, he began to see signs of a change in the proceedings of the goblin excavators: they were going no deeper, but had commenced running on a level; and he watched them, therefore, more closely than ever. All at once, one night, coming to a slope of very hard rock, they began to ascend along the inclined plane of its surface. Having reached its top, they went again on a level for a night or two, after which they began to ascend once more, and kept on at a pretty steep angle. At length Curdie judged it time to transfer his observation to another quarter, and the next night, he did not go to the mine at all; but, leaving his pickaxe and clue at home, and taking only his usual lumps of bread and pease-pudding, went down the mountain to the king's house. He climbed over the wall, and remained in the garden the whole night, creeping on hands and knees from one spot to the other, and lying at full length with his ear to the ground, listening. But he heard nothing except the tread of the men-at-arms as they marched about, whose observation, as the night was cloudy and there was no moon, he had little difficulty in avoiding. For several following nights, he continued to haunt the garden and listen, but with no success.

At length, early one evening, whether it was that he had got careless of his own safety, or that the growing moon had become strong enough to expose him, his watching came to a sudden end. He was creeping from behind the rock where the stream ran out, for he had been listening all round it in the hope it might convey to his ear some indication of the whereabouts of the goblin miners, when just as he came into the moonlight on the lawn, a whizz in his ear and a blow upon his leg startled him. He instantly squatted in the hope of eluding further notice. But when he heard the sound of running feet, he jumped up to take the chance of escape by flight. He fell, however, with a keen shoot of pain, for the bolt of a cross-bow had wounded his leg, and the blood was now streaming from it. He was instantly laid hold of by two or three of the men-at-arms. It was useless to struggle, and he submitted in silence.

"It's a boy!" cried several of them together, in a tone of amazement. "I thought it was one of those demons."

"What are you about here?"

"Going to have a little rough usage apparently," said Curdie laughing, as the men shook him.

"Impertinence will do you no good. You have no business here in the king's grounds, and if you don't give a true account of yourself, you shall fare as a thief."

"Why, what else could he be?" said one.

"He might have been after a lost kid, you know," suggested another.

"I see no good in trying to excuse him. He has no business here anyhow."

"Let me go away then, if you please," said Curdie.

"But we don't please—not except you give a good account of yourself."

"I don't feel quite sure whether I can trust you," said Curdie.

"We are the king's own men-at-arms," said the captain, courteously, for he was taken with Curdie's appearance and courage.

"Well, I will tell you all about it—if you will promise to listen to me and not do anything rash."

"I call that cool!" said one of the party laughing. "He will tell us what mischief he was about, if we promise to do as pleases him."

"I was about no mischief," said Curdie.

But ere he could say more he turned faint, and fell senseless on the grass. Then first they discovered that the bolt they had shot, taking him for one of the goblin creatures, had wounded him.

They carried him into the house, and laid him down in the hall. The report spread that they had caught a robber, and the servants crowded in to see the villain. Amongst the rest came the nurse. The moment she saw him she exclaimed with indignation:

"I declare it's the same young rascal of a miner that was rude to me and the princess on the mountain. He actually wanted to kiss the princess. *I* took good care of that—the wretch! And *he* was prowling about—was he? Just like his impudence!"

The princess being fast asleep, and Curdie in a faint, she could misrepresent at her pleasure.

When he heard this, the captain, although he had considerable doubt of its truth, resolved to keep Curdie a prisoner until they could search into the affair. So, after they had brought him round a little, and attended to his wound, which was rather a bad one, they laid him, still exhausted from the loss of blood, upon a mattress in a disused room—one of those already so often mentioned—and locked the door, and left him. He passed a troubled night, and in the morning they found him talking wildly. In the evening he came to himself, but felt very weak, and his leg was exceedingly painful. Wondering where he was, and seeing one of the men-at-arms in the room, he began to question him, and soon recalled the events of the preceding night. As he was himself unable to watch any more, he told the soldier all he knew about the goblins, and begged him to tell his companions, and stir them up to watch with tenfold vigilance; but whether it was that he did not talk quite coherently, or that the whole thing appeared incredible, certainly the man concluded that Curdie was only raving still, and tried to coax him into holding his tongue. This, of course, annoyed Curdie dreadfully, who now felt in his turn what it was not to be believed, and the consequence was that his fever returned, and by the time when, at his persistent entreaties, the captain was called, there could be no doubt that he was raving. They did for him what they could, and promised everything he wanted, but with no intention of fulfilment. At last he went to sleep, and when at length his sleep grew profound and peaceful, they left him, locked the door again, and withdrew, intending to revisit him early in the morning.

CHAPTER XXVI

THE GOBLIN MINERS

THAT same night several of the servants were having a chat together before going to bed.

"What can that noise be?" said one of the house-maids, who had been listening for a moment or two.

"I've heard it the last two nights," said the cook. "If there were any about the place, I should have taken it for rats, but my Tom keeps them far enough."

"I've heard though," said the scullery-maid, "that rats move about in great companies sometimes. There may be an army of them invading us. I heard the noises yesterday and to-day too."

"It'll be grand fun then for my Tom and Mrs. House-keeper's Bob," said the cook. "They'll be friends for once in their lives, and fight on the same side. I'll engage Tom and Bob together will put to flight any number of rats."

"It seems to me," said the nurse, "that the noises are much too loud for that. I have heard them all day, and my princess has asked me several times what they could be. Sometimes they sound like distant thunder, and sometimes like the noises you hear in the mountain from those horrid miners underneath."

"I shouldn't wonder," said the cook, "if it was the miners after all. They may have come on some hole in the mountain through which the noises reach to us. They are always boring and blasting and breaking, you know."

As he spoke there came a great rolling rumble beneath them, and the house quivered. They all started up in affright, and rushing to the hall found the gentlemen-at-arms in consternation also. They had sent to wake their captain, who said from their description that it must have been an earthquake, an occurrence which, although very rare in that country, had taken place almost within the century; and then went to bed again, strange to say, and fell fast asleep without once thinking of Curdie, or associating the noises they had heard with what he had told them. He had not believed Curdie. If he had, he would at once have thought of what he had said, and would have taken precautions. As they heard nothing more, they concluded that Sir Walter was right, and that the danger was over for perhaps another hundred years. The fact, as discovered afterward, was that the goblins had, in working up a second sloping face of stone, arrived at a huge block which lay under the cellars of the house, within the line of the foundations. It was so round that when they succeeded, after hard work, in dislodging it without blasting, it rolled thundering down the slope with a bounding, jarring roll, which shook the foundations of the house. The goblins were themselves dismayed at the noise, for they knew, by careful spying and measuring, that they must now be very near, if not under, the king's house, and they feared giving an alarm. They, therefore, remained quiet for awhile, and when they began to work again, they no doubt thought themselves very fortunate in coming upon a vein of sand which filled a winding fissure in

[175]

the rock on which the house was built. By scooping this away they soon came out in the king's wine-cellar.

No sooner did they find where they were, than they scurried back again, like rats into their holes, and running at full speed to the goblin palace, announced their success to the king and queen with shouts of triumph. In a moment the goblin royal family and the whole gobling people were on their way in hot haste to the king's house, each eager to have a share in the glory of carrying off that same night the Princess Irene.

The queen went stumping along in one shoe of stone and one of skin. This could not have been pleasant, and my readers may wonder that, with such skilful workmen about her, she had not yet replaced the shoe carried off by Curdie. As the king however had more than one ground of objection to her stone shoes, he no doubt took advantage of the discovery of her toes, and threatened to expose her deformity if she had another made. I presume he insisted on her being content with skin-shoes, and allowed her to wear the remaining granite one on the present occasion only because she was going out to war.

They soon arrived in the king's wine-cellar, and regardless of its huge vessels, of which they did not know the use, began as quietly as they could to force the door that led upward.

CHAPTER XXVII

THE GOBLINS IN THE KING'S HOUSE

WHEN Curdie fell asleep he began at once to dream. He thought he was ascending the mountain-side from the mouth of the mine, whistling and singing "*Ring, dod, bang!*" when he came upon a woman and child who were lost; and from that point he went on dreaming all that had happened since he met the princess and Lootie; how he had watched the goblins, and been taken by them, how he had been rescued by the princess; everything indeed, until he was wounded, and imprisoned by the men-at-arms. And now he thought he was lying wide awake where they had laid him, when suddenly he heard a great thundering sound.

"The cobs are coming!" he said. "They didn't believe a word I told them! The cobs'll be carrying off the princess from under their stupid noses! But they sha'n't! that they sha'n't!"

He jumped up, as he thought, and began to dress, but, to his dismay, found that he was still lying in bed.

"Now then I will!" he said. "Here goes! I *am* up now!"

But yet again he found himself snug in bed. Twenty times he tried, and twenty times he failed; for in fact he was not awake, only dreaming that he was. At length in an agony of despair, fancying he heard the goblins all over the house, he gave a great cry. Then there came, as he thought, a hand upon the lock of the door. It opened, and, looking up, he saw a lady with white hair, carrying a silver box in her hand, enter the room. She came to his bed, he thought, stroked his head and face with cool, soft hands, took the dressing from his leg, rubbed it with something that smelled like roses, and then waved her hands over him three times. At the last wave of her hands everything vanished, he felt himself sinking into the profoundest slumber, and remembered nothing more until he awoke in earnest.

The setting moon was throwing a feeble light through the casement, and the house was full of uproar. There was soft heavy multitudinous stamping, a clashing and clanging of weapons, the voices of men and the cries of women, mixed with a hideous bellowing, which sounded victorious. The cobs were in the house! He sprang from his bed, hurried on some of his clothes, not forgetting his shoes, which were armed with nails; then spying an old hunting-knife, or short sword, hanging on the wall, he caught it, and rushed down the stairs, guided by the sounds of strife, which grew louder and louder.

When he reached the ground floor he found the whole place swarming. All the goblins of the mountain seemed gathered there. He rushed amongst them, shouting—

> "One, two,
> Hit and hew!
> Three, four,
> Blast and bore!"

and with every rhyme he came down a great stamp upon a foot, cutting at the same time at their faces—executing, indeed, a sword dance of the wildest description. Away scattered the goblins in every direction,—into closets, upstairs, into chimneys, up on rafters, and down to the cellars. Curdie went on stamping and slashing and singing, but saw nothing of the people of the house until he came to the great hall, in which, the moment he entered it, arose a great goblin shout. The last of the men-at-arms, the captain himself, was on the floor, buried beneath a wallowing crowd of goblins. For, while each knight was busy defending himself as well as he could, by stabs in the thick bodies of the goblins, for he had soon found their heads all but invulnerable, the queen had attacked his legs and feet with her horrible granite shoe, and he was soon down; but the captain had got his back to the wall and stood out longer. The goblins would have torn them all to pieces, but the king had given orders to carry them away alive, and over each of them, in twelve groups, was standing a knot of goblins, while as many as could find room were sitting upon their prostrate bodies.

Curdie burst in dancing and gyrating and stamping and singing like a small incarnate whirlwind,

> "Where 'tis all a hole, sir,
>   Never can be holes:
> Why should their shoes have soles, sir,
>   When they've got no souls?
>
> "But she upon her foot, sir,
>   Has a granite shoe:
> The strongest leather boot, sir,
>   Six would soon be through."

The queen gave a howl of rage and dismay; and before she recovered her presence of mind, Curdie, having begun with the group nearest him, had eleven of the knights on their legs again.

[179]

"Stamp on their feet!" he cried, as each man rose, and in a few minutes the hall was nearly empty, the goblins running from it as fast as they could, howling and shrieking and limping, and cowering every now and then as they ran to cuddle their wounded feet in their hard hands, or to protect them from the frightful stamp-stamp of the armed men.

And now Curdie approached the group which, trusting in the queen and her shoe, kept their guard over the prostrate captain. The king sat on the captain's head, but the queen stood in front, like an infuriated cat, with her perpendicular eyes gleaming green, and her hair standing half up from her horrid head. Her heart was quaking, however, and she kept moving about her skin-shod foot with nervous apprehension. When Curdie was within a few paces, she rushed at him, made one tremendous stamp at his opposing foot, which happily he withdrew in time, and caught him round the waist, to dash him on the marble floor. But just as she caught him, he came down with all the weight of his iron-shod shoe upon her skin-shod foot, and with a hideous howl she dropped him, squatted on the floor and took her foot in both her hands. Meanwhile the rest rushed on the king and the bodyguard sent them flying, and lifted the prostrate captain, who was all but pressed to death. It was some moments before he recovered breath and consciousness.

"Where's the princess?" cried Curdie again and again.

No one knew, and off they all rushed in search of her.

Through every room in the house they went, but nowhere was she to be found. Neither was one of the servants to be seen. But Curdie, who had kept to the lower part of the house, which was now quiet enough, began to hear a confused sound as of a distant hubbub, and set out to find where it came from. The noise grew as his sharp ears guided him to a stair and so to the wine cellar. It was full of goblins, whom the butler was supplying with wine as fast as he could draw it.

While the queen and her party had encountered the men-at-arms, Harelip with another company had gone off to search the house. They captured every one they met, and when they could find no more, they hurried away to carry them safe to the caverns below. But when the butler, who was amongst them, found that their path lay through the wine cellar, he bethought himself of persuading them to taste the wine, and, as he had hoped, they no sooner tasted than they wanted more. The routed goblins, on their way below, joined them, and when Curdie entered, they were all, with outstretched hands, in which were vessels of every description, from sauce-pan to silver cup, pressing around the butler, who sat at the tap of a huge cask, filling and filling. Curdie cast one glance around the place before commencing his attack, and saw in the farthest corner a terrified group of the domestics unwatched, but cowering without courage to attempt their escape. Amongst them was the terror-stricken face of Lootie; but nowhere could he see the princess. Seized with the horrible conviction that Harelip had already carried her off, he rushed amongst them, unable for wrath to sing any more, but stamping and cutting with greater fury than ever.

"Stamp on their feet; stamp on their feet!" he shouted, and in a moment the goblins were disappearing through the hole in the floor like rats and mice.

[181]

They could not vanish so fast, however, but that many more goblin feet had to go limping back over the underground ways of the mountain that morning.

Presently however they were reinforced from above by the king and his party, with the redoubtable queen at their head. Finding Curdie again busy amongst her unfortunate subjects, she rushed at him once more with the rage of despair, and this time gave him a bad bruise on the foot. Then a regular stamping fight got up between them, Curdie with the point of his hunting knife keeping her from clasping her mighty arms about him, as he watched his opportunity of getting once more a good stamp at her skin-shod foot. But the queen was more wary as well as more agile than hitherto.

The rest meantime, finding their adversary thus matched for the moment, paused in their headlong hurry, and turned to the shivering group of women in the corner. As if determined to emulate his father and have a sun-woman of some sort to share his future throne, Harelip rushed at them, caught up Lootie and sped with her to the hole. She gave a great shriek, and Curdie heard her, and saw the plight she was in. Gathering all his strength, he gave the queen a sudden cut across the face with his weapon, came down, as she started back, with all his weight on the proper foot, and sprang to Lootie's rescue. The prince had two defenceless feet, and on both of them Curdie stamped just as he reached the hole. He dropped his burden and rolled shrieking into the earth. Curdie made one stab at him as he disappeared, caught hold of the senseless Lootie, and having dragged her back to the corner, there mounted guard over her, preparing once more to encounter the queen. Her face streaming with blood, and her eyes flashing green lightning through it, she came on with her mouth open and her teeth grinning like a tiger's, followed by the king and her bodyguard of the thickest goblins. But the same moment in rushed the captain and his men, and ran at them stamping furiously. They dared not encounter such an onset. Away they scurried, the queen foremost. Of course the right thing would have been to take the king and queen prisoners, and hold them hostages for the princess, but they were so anxious to find her that no one thought of detaining them until it was too late.

Having thus rescued the servants, they set about searching the house once more. None of them could give the least information concerning the princess. Lootie was almost silly with terror, and although scarcely able to walk, would not leave Curdie's side for a single moment. Again he allowed the others to search the rest of the house—where, except a dismayed goblin lurking here and there, they found no one—while he requested Lootie to take him to the princess's room. She was as submissive and obedient as if he had been the king. He found the bed-clothes tossed about, and most of them on the floor, while the princess's garments were scattered all over the room, which was in the greatest confusion. It was only too evident that the goblins had been there, and Curdie had no longer any doubt that she had been carried off at the very first of the inroad. With a pang of despair he saw how wrong they had been in not securing the king and queen and prince; but he determined to find and rescue the princess as she had found and rescued him, or meet the worst fate to which the goblins could doom him.

CHAPTER XXVIII

CURDIE'S GUIDE

JUST as the consolation of this resolve dawned upon his mind, and he was turning away for the cellar to follow the goblins into their hole, something touched his hand. It was the slightest touch, and when he looked he could see nothing. Feeling and peering about in the gray of the dawn, his fingers came upon a tight thread. He looked again, and narrowly, but still could see nothing. It flashed upon him that this must be the princess's thread. Without saying a word, for he knew no one would believe him any more than he had believed the princess, he followed the thread with his finger, contrived to give Lootie the slip, and was soon out of the house, and on the mountain-side—surprised that, if the thread were indeed her grandmother's messenger, it should have led the princess, as he supposed it must, into the mountain, where she would be certain to meet the goblins rushing back enraged from their defeat. But he hurried on in the hope of overtaking her first. When he arrived however at the place where the path turned off for the mine, he found that the thread did not turn with it, but went straight up the mountain. Could it be that the thread was leading him home to his mother's cottage? Could the princess be there? He bounded up the mountain like one of its own goats, and before the sun was up, the thread had brought him indeed to his mother's door. There it vanished from his fingers, and he could not find it, search as he might.

The door was on the latch, and he entered. There sat his mother by the fire, and in her arms lay the princess fast asleep.

"Hush, Curdie!" said his mother. "Do not wake her. I'm so glad you're come! I thought the cobs must have got you again!"

With a heart full of delight, Curdie sat down at a corner of the hearth, on a stool opposite his mother's chair, and gazed at the princess, who slept as peacefully as if she had been in her own bed. All at once she opened her eyes and fixed them on him.

"Oh, Curdie! you're come!" she said quietly. "I thought you would!"

Curdie rose and stood before her with downcast eyes.

"Irene," he said, "I am very sorry I did not believe you."

"Oh, never mind, Curdie!" answered the princess. "You couldn't, you know. You do believe me now, don't you?"

"I can't help it now. I ought to have helped it before."

"Why can't you help it now?"

"Because, just as I was going into the mountain to look for you, I got hold of your thread, and it brought me here."

"Then you've come from my house, have you?"

"Yes, I have."

"I didn't know you were there."

"I've been there two or three days, I believe."

"And I never knew it!—Then perhaps you can tell me why my grandmother has brought me here? I can't think. Something woke me—I didn't know what, but I was frightened, and I felt for the thread, and there it was! I was more frightened still when it brought me out on the mountain, for I thought it was going to take me into it again, and I like the outside of it best. I supposed you were in trouble again, and I had to get you out, but it brought me here instead; and, oh, Curdie! your mother has been so kind to me—just like my own grandmother!"

Here Curdie's mother gave the princess a hug, and the princess turned and gave her a sweet smile, and held up her mouth to kiss her.

"Then you didn't see the cobs?" asked Curdie.

"No; I haven't been into the mountain, I told you, Curdie."

"But the cobs have been into your house—all over it—and into your bedroom making such a row!"

"What did they want there? It was very rude of them."

"They wanted you—to carry you off into the mountain with them, for a wife to their Prince Harelip."

"Oh, how dreadful!" cried the princess, shuddering.

"But you needn't be afraid, you know. Your grandmother takes care of you."

"Ah! you do believe in my grandmother then? I'm so glad! She made me think you would some day."

All at once Curdie remembered his dream, and was silent, thinking.

"But how did you come to be in my house, and me not know it?" asked the princess.

Then Curdie had to explain everything—how he had watched for her sake, how he had been wounded and shut up by the soldiers, how he heard the noises and could not rise, and how the beautiful old lady had come to him, and all that followed.

"Poor Curdie! to lie there hurt and ill, and me never to know it!" exclaimed the princess, stroking his rough hand. "I would not have hesitated to come and nurse you, if they had told me."

"I didn't see you were lame," said his mother.

"Am I, mother? Oh—yes—I suppose I ought to be. I declare I've never thought of it since I got up to go down amongst the cobs!"

"Let me see the wound," said his mother.

He pulled down his stocking—when behold, except a great scar, his leg was perfectly sound!

Curdie and his mother gazed in each other's eyes, full of wonder, but Irene called out—

"I thought so, Curdie! I was sure it wasn't a dream. I was sure my grandmother had been to see you.—Don't you smell the roses? It was my grandmother healed your leg, and sent you to help me."

"No, Princess Irene," said Curdie; "I wasn't good enough to be allowed to help you: I didn't believe you. Your grandmother took care of you without me."

"She sent you to help my people, anyhow. I wish my king-papa would come. I do want so to tell him how good you have been!"

"But," said the mother, "we are forgetting how frightened your people must be.—You must take the princess home at once, Curdie—or at least go and tell them where she is."

"Yes, mother. Only I'm dreadfully hungry. Do let me

[187]

have some breakfast first. They ought to have listened to me, and then they wouldn't have been taken by surprise as they were."

"That is true, Curdie; but it is not for you to blame them much. You remember?"

"Yes, mother, I do. Only I must really have something to eat."

"You shall, my boy—as fast as I can get it," said his mother, rising and setting the princess on her chair.

But before his breakfast was ready, Curdie jumped up so suddenly as to startle both his companions.

"Mother, mother!" he cried, "I was forgetting. You must take the princess home yourself. I must go and wake my father."

Without a word of explanation, he rushed to the place where his father was sleeping. Having thoroughly roused him with what he told him, he darted out of the cottage.

CHAPTER XXIX

MASON-WORK

HE had all at once remembered the resolution of the goblins to carry out their second plan upon the failure of the first. No doubt they were already busy, and the mine was therefore in the greatest danger of being flooded and rendered useless—not to speak of the lives of the miners.

When he reached the mouth of the mine, after rousing all the miners within reach, he found his father and a good many more just entering. They all hurried to the gang by which he had found a way into the goblin country. There the foresight of Peter had already collected a great many blocks of stone, with cement, ready for building up the weak place—well enough known to the goblins. Although there was not room for more than two to be actually building at once, they managed, by setting all the rest to work in preparing the cement, and passing the stones, to finish in the course of the day a huge buttress filling the whole gang, and supported everywhere by the live rock. Before the hour when they usually dropped work, they were satisfied that the mine was secure.

They had heard goblin hammers and pickaxes busy all the time, and at length fancied they heard sounds of water they had never heard before. But that was otherwise accounted for when they left the mine; for they stepped out into a tremendous storm which was raging all over the mountain. The thunder was bellowing, and the lightning lancing out of a huge black cloud which lay above it, and hung down its edges of thick mist over its sides. The lightning was breaking out of the mountain, too, and flashing up into the cloud. From the state of the brooks, now swollen into raging torrents, it was evident that the storm had been storming all day.

The wind was blowing as if it would blow him off the mountain, but, anxious about his mother and the princess, Curdie darted up through the thick of the tempest. Even if they had not set out before the storm came on, he did not judge them safe, for, in such a storm even their poor little house was in danger. Indeed he soon found that but for a huge rock against which it was built, and which protected it both from the blasts and the waters, it must have been swept if it was not blown away; for the two torrents into which this rock parted the rush of water behind it united again in front of the cottage —two roaring and dangerous streams, which his mother and the princess could not possibly have passed. It was with great difficulty that he forced his way through one of them, and up to the door.

The moment his hand fell on the latch, through all the uproar of winds and waters came the joyous cry of the princess:—

"There's Curdie! Curdie! Curdie!"

She was sitting wrapped in blankets on the bed, his mother trying for the hundredth time to light the fire which had been drowned by the rain that came down the chimney. The clay floor was one mass of mud, and the whole place looked wretched. But the faces of the mother and the princess shone as if their troubles only made them merrier. Curdie laughed at sight of them.

"I never *had* such fun!" said the princess, her eyes twinkling and her pretty teeth shining. "How nice it must be to live in a cottage on the mountain!"

"It all depends on what kind your inside house is," said the mother.

"I know what you mean," said Irene. "That's the kind my grandmother says."

By the time Peter returned, the storm was nearly over, but the streams were so fierce and so swollen, that it was not only out of the question for the princess to go down the mountain, but most dangerous for Peter even or Curdie to make the attempt in the gathering darkness.

"They will be dreadfully frightened about you," said Peter to the princess, "but we cannot help it. We must wait till the morning."

With Curdie's help, the fire was lighted at last, and the mother set about making their supper; and after supper they all told the princess stories till she grew sleepy. Then Curdie's mother laid her in Curdie's bed, which was in a tiny little garret-room. As soon as she was in bed, through a little window low down in the roof she caught sight of her grandmother's lamp shining far away beneath, and she gazed at the beautiful silvery globe until she fell fast asleep.

CHAPTER XXX

THE KING AND THE KISS

THE next morning the sun rose so bright that Irene said the rain had washed his face and let the light out clean. The torrents were still roaring down the side of the mountain, but they were so much smaller as not to be dangerous in the daylight. After an early breakfast, Peter went to his work, and Curdie and his mother set out to take the princess home. They had difficulty in getting her dry across the streams, and Curdie had again and again to carry her, but at last they got safe on the broader part of the road, and walked gently down toward the king's house. And what should they see as they turned the last corner, but the last of the king's troop riding through the gate!

"Oh, Curdie!" cried Irene, clapping her hands right joyfully, "my king-papa is come."

The moment Curdie heard that, he caught her up in his arms, and set off at full speed, crying—

"Come on, mother dear! The king may break his heart before he knows that she is safe."

Irene clung round his neck, and he ran with her like a deer. When he entered the gate into the court, there sat the king on his horse, with all the people of the house about him, weeping and hanging their heads. The king was not weeping, but his face was white as a dead man's, and he looked as if the life had gone out of him. The men-at-arms he had brought

There sat his mother by the fire, and in her arms
lay the princess fast asleep.

with him, sat with horror-stricken faces, but eyes flashing with rage, waiting only for the word of the king to do something—they did not know what, and nobody knew what.

The day before the men-at-arms belonging to the house, as soon as they were satisfied the princess had been carried away, rushed after the goblins into the hole, but found that they had already so skilfully blockaded the narrowest part, not many feet below the cellar, that without miners and their tools they could do nothing. Not one of them knew where the mouth of the mine lay, and some of those who had set out to find it had been overtaken by the storm and had not even yet returned. Poor Sir Walter was especially filled with shame, and almost entertained the hope that the king would order him to be decapitated, for the very thought of that sweet little face down amongst the goblins was unendurable.

When Curdie ran in at the gate with the princess in his arms, they were all so absorbed in their own misery and awed by the king's presence and grief, that no one observed his arrival. He went straight up to the king, where he sat on his horse.

"Papa! papa!" the princess cried, stretching out her arms to him; "here I am!"

The king started. The color rushed to his face. He gave an inarticulate cry. Curdie held up the princess, and the king bent down and took her from his arms. As he clasped her to his bosom, the big tears went dropping down his cheeks and his beard. And such a shout arose from all the bystanders, that the startled horses pranced and capered, and the armor rang and clattered, and the rocks of the mountain echoed back the noises. The princess greeted them all as she nestled in her father's bosom, and the king did not set her down until she had told them all the story. But she had more to tell about Curdie than about herself, and what she did tell about herself none of them could understand except the king and Curdie, who stood by the king's knee stroking the neck of the great white horse. And still as she told what Curdie had done, Sir Walter and others added to what she told, even Lootie joining in the praises of his courage and energy.

Curdie held his peace, looking quietly up in the king's face. And his mother stood on the outskirts of the crowd listening with delight, for her son's deeds were pleasant in her ears, until the princess caught sight of her.

"And there is his mother, king-papa!" she said. "See—there. She is such a nice mother, and has been so kind to me!"

They all parted asunder as the king made a sign to her to come forward. She obeyed, and he gave her his hand, but could not speak.

"And now, king-papa," the princess went on, "I must tell you another thing. One night long ago Curdie drove the goblins away and brought Lootie and me safe from the mountain. And I promised him a kiss when we got home, but Lootie wouldn't let me give it to him. I would not have you scold Lootie, but I want you to impress upon her that a princess *must* do as she promises."

"Indeed she must, my child—except it be wrong," said the king. "There, give Curdie a kiss."

And as he spoke he held her toward him.

The princess reached down, threw her arms round Curdie's neck, and kissed him on the mouth, saying—

THE KING AND THE KISS

"There, Curdie! There's the kiss I promised you!"

Then they all went into the house, and the cook rushed to the kitchen, and the servants to their work. Lootie dressed Irene in her shiningest clothes, and the king put off his armor, and put on purple and gold; and a messenger was sent for Peter and all the miners, and there was a great and grand feast, which continued long after the princess was put to bed.

CHAPTER XXXI

THE SUBTERRANEAN WATERS

THE king's harper, who always formed a part of his escort, was chanting a ballad which he made as he went on playing on his instrument—about the princess and the goblins, and the prowess of Curdie, when all at once he ceased, with his eyes on one of the doors of the hall. Thereupon the eyes of the king and his guests turned thitherward also. The next moment, through the open doorway came the princess Irene. She went straight up to her father, with her right hand stretched out a little sideways, and her forefinger, as her father and Curdie understood, feeling its way along the invisible thread. The king took her on his knee, and she said in his ear—

"King-papa, do you hear that noise?"

"I hear nothing," said the king.

"Listen," she said, holding up her forefinger.

The king listened, and a great stillness fell upon the company. Each man, seeing that the king listened, listened also, and the harper sat with his harp between his arms, and his fingers silent upon the strings.

"I do hear a noise," said the king at length—"a noise as of distant thunder. It is coming nearer and nearer. What can it be?"

They all heard it now, and each seemed ready to start to his feet as he listened. Yet all sat perfectly still. The noise came rapidly nearer.

"What can it be?" said the king again.

"I think it must be another storm coming over the mountain," said Sir Walter.

Then Curdie, who at the first word of the king had slipped from his seat, and laid his ear to the ground, rose up quickly, and approaching the king said, speaking very fast—

"Please your Majesty, I think i know what it is. I have no time to explain, for that might make it too late for some of us. Will your Majesty order that everybody leave the house as quickly as possible, and get up the mountain?"

The king, who was the wisest man in the kingdom, knew well there was a time when things must be done, and questions left till afterward. He had faith in Curdie, and rose instantly, with Irene in his arms.

"Every man and woman follow me," he said, and strode out into the darkness.

Before he had reached the gate, the noise had grown to a great thundering roar, and the ground trembled beneath their feet, and before the last of them had crossed the court, out after them from the great hall-door came a huge rush of turbid water, and almost swept them away. But they got safe out of the gate and up the mountain, while the torrent went roaring down the road into the valley beneath.

Curdie had left the king and the princess to look after his mother, whom he and his father, one on each side, caught up when the stream overtook them and carried safe and dry.

When the king had got out of the way of the water, a little

[197]

up the mountain, he stood with the princess in his arms, looking back with amazement on the issuing torrent, which glimmered fierce and foamy through the night. There Curdie rejoined them.

"Now, Curdie," said the king, "what does it mean! Is this what you expected?"

"It is, your Majesty," said Curdie; and proceeded to tell him about the second scheme of the goblins, who, fancying the miners of more importance to the upper world than they were, had resolved, if they should fail in carrying off the king's daughter, to flood the mine and drown the miners. Then he explained what the miners had done to prevent it. The goblins had, in pursuance of their design, let loose all the underground reservoirs and streams, expecting the water to run down into the mine, which was lower than their part of the mountain, for they had, as they supposed, not knowing of the solid wall close behind, broken a passage through into it. But the readiest outlet the water could find had turned out to be the tunnel they had made to the king's house, the possibility of which catastrophe had not occurred to the mind of the young miner until he placed his ear close to the floor of the hall.

What was then to be done? The house appeared in danger of falling, and every moment the torrent was increasing.

"We must set out at once," said the king. "But how to get at the horses!"

"Shall I see if we can manage that?" said Curdie.

"Do," said the king.

Curdie gathered the men-at-arms, and took them over the garden wall, and so to the stables. They found their horses in terror; the water was rising fast around them, and it was quite time they were got out. But there was no way to get them out, except by riding them through the stream, which was now pouring from the lower windows as well as the door. As one horse was quite enough for any man to manage through such a torrent, Curdie got on the king's white charger, and leading the way, brought them all in safety to the rising ground.

"Look, look, Curdie!" cried Irene, the moment that, having dismounted, he led the horse up to the king.

Curdie did look, and saw, high in the air, somewhere about the top of the king's house, a great globe of light, shining like the purest silver.

"Oh!" he cried in some consternation, "that is your grand-mother's lamp! We *must* get her out. I will go and find her. The house may fall, you know."

"My grandmother is in no danger," said Irene, smiling.

"Here, Curdie, take the princess while I get on my horse," said the king.

Curdie took the princess again, and both turned their eyes to the globe of light. The same moment there shot from it a white bird, which, descending with outstretched wings, made one circle round the king and Curdie and the princess, and then glided up again. The light and the pigeon vanished together.

"Now, Curdie," said the princess, as he lifted her to her father's arms, "you see my grandmother knows all about it, and isn't frightened. I believe she could walk through that water and it wouldn't wet her a bit."

"But, my child," said the king, "you will be cold if you

[199]

haven't something more on. Run, Curdie, my boy, and fetch anything you can lay your hands on, to keep the princess warm. We have a long ride before us."

Curdie was gone in a moment, and soon returned with a great rich fur, and the news that dead goblins were tossing about in the current through the house. They had been caught in their own snare; instead of the mine they had flooded their own country, whence they were now swept up drowned. Irene shuddered, but the king held her close to his bosom. Then he turned to Sir Walter, and said—

"Bring Curdie's father and mother here."

"I wish," said the king, when they stood before him, "to take your son with me. He shall enter my bodyguard at once, and wait further promotion."

Peter and his wife, overcome, only murmured almost inaudible thanks. But Curdie spoke aloud.

"Please your Majesty," he said, "I cannot leave my father and mother."

"That's right, Curdie!" cried the princess. "*I* wouldn't if I was you."

The king looked at the princess and then at Curdie with a glow of satisfaction on his countenance.

"I too think you are right, Curdie," he said, "and I will not ask you again. But I shall have a chance of doing something for you some time."

"Your Majesty has already allowed me to serve you," said Curdie.

"But, Curdie," said his mother, "why shouldn't you go with the king? We can get on very well without you."

"But I can't get on very well without you," said Curdie. "The king is very kind, but I could not be half the use to him that I am to you. Please your Majesty, if you wouldn't mind giving my mother a red petticoat! I should have got her one long ago, but for the goblins."

"As soon as we get home," said the king, "Irene and I will search out the warmest one to be found, and send it by one of the gentlemen."

"Yes, that we will, Curdie!" said the princess.

"And next summer we'll come back and see you wear it, Curdie's mother," she added. "Sha'n't we, king-papa?"

"Yes, my love; I hope so," said the king.

Then turning to the miners, he said——

"Will you do the best you can for my servants to-night? I hope they will be able to return to the house to-morrow."

The miners with one voice promised their hospitality.

Then the king commanded his servants to mind whatever Curdie should say to them, and after shaking hands with him and his father and mother, the king and the princess and all their company rode away down the side of the new stream which had already devoured half the road, into the starry night.

CHAPTER XXXII

THE LAST CHAPTER

ALL the rest went up the mountain, and separated in groups to the homes of the miners. Curdie and his father and mother took Lootie with them. And the whole way, a light, of which all but Lootie understood the origin, shone upon their path. But when they looked round they could see nothing of the silvery globe.

For days and days the water continued to rush from the doors and windows of the king's house, and a few goblin bodies were swept out into the road.

Curdie saw that something must be done. He spoke to his father and the rest of the miners, and they at once proceeded to make another outlet for the waters. By setting all hands to the work, tunneling here and building there, they soon succeeded; and having also made a little tunnel to drain the water away from under the king's house, they were soon able to get into the wine cellar, where they found a multitude of dead goblins—among the rest the queen, with the skin-shoe gone, and the stone one fast to her ankle—for the water had swept away the barricade which prevented the men-at-arms from following the goblins, and had greatly widened the passage. They built it securely up, and then went back to their labors in the mine.

A good many of the goblins with their creatures escaped from the inundation out upon the mountain. But most of them soon left that part of the country, and most of those who remained grew milder in character, and indeed became very much like the Scotch Brownies. Their skulls became softer as well as their hearts, and their feet grew harder, and by degrees they became friendly with the inhabitants of the mountain and even with the miners. But the latter were merciless to any of the *cobs' creatures* that came their way, until at length they all but disappeared. Still—

"*But, Mr. Author, we would rather hear more about the Princess and Curdie. We don't care about the goblins and their nasty creatures. They frighten us—rather.*"

"*But you know if you once get rid of the goblins there is no fear of the princess or of Curdie.*"

"*But we want to know more about them.*"

"*Some day, perhaps, I may tell you the further history of both of them; how Curdie came to visit Irene's grandmother, and what she did for him; and how the princess and he met again after they were older—and how—But there! I don't mean to go any farther at present.*"

"*Then you're leaving the story unfinished, Mr. Author!*"

"*Not more unfinished than a story ought to be, I hope. If you ever knew a story finished, all I can say is, I never did. Somehow, stories won't finish. I think I know why, but I won't say that either, now.*"

THE END

[203]

AFTERWORD

The late nineteenth century saw the birth of the fantasy novel for children. Prior to this, most children's books, like *Goody Two-Shoes* and John Bunyan's *The Pilgrim's Progress*, had been written mainly for the purpose of moral instruction. Other books for children, such as William Roscoe's *The Butterfly's Ball* and Edward Lear's *Book of Nonsense*, were crafted solely for the sake of amusement. But the late nineteenth century saw the first efforts at combining the two, and one of the most successful and enduring of these early works was George MacDonald's *The Princess and the Goblin.*

Combining the adventurous elements of danger, mystery, and suspense with the moral values of faith, trust, and loyalty, MacDonald created a book as gripping as any of the popular "Penny Dreadfuls" of the day. Yet at the same time, MacDonald allowed his narrative to eloquently present his ideas, rather than forcing them upon his audience.

George MacDonald was born in 1824 in Aberdeenshire, Scotland. Although his mother died when he was only eight years old, Mac-Donald had a happy childhood, later saying that he "had never asked his father for anything...but it was given." When his father remarried seven years later, it was to a woman who was kind and loving to him and his three brothers, who in turn regarded her with much affection.

From these warm family memories MacDonald drew his parental figures for *The Princess and the Goblin.* Irene's all-wise, all-knowing, all-loving great-great-grandmother, who lives in a secret, magical place accessible only to those she chooses, evokes a timeless mother-figure who is always there when the child needs comfort or protection. Irene's King-Papa, who not only frequently embraces his beloved daughter but sheds tears of relief and joy when Curdie returns her to him, is the embodiment of the strong, caring, and protective father figure.

Interestingly, MacDonald included a less all-powerful, but no less loving, second set of parents in Curdie's mother and father. By trusting him to work by himself and to do what is right, Curdie's father shows great faith in his son. Curdie's mother gives her son the encouragement and guidance he needs to see his error in disbelieving Irene's seemingly impossible explanation of how she had rescued him. And it is the almost tangible love and warmth shared by Curdie and his parents that make Irene feel as comfortable in their humble cottage as in her great home. "How nice it must be to live in a cottage on the mountain!" says Irene, to which Curdie's mother replies, "It all depends on what kind your inside house is." In MacDonald's world, it is love and understanding that make a home special, not physical comforts.

MacDonald became a minister at the age of twenty-four, and although this career was short-lived—his unconventional viewpoints concerning church doctrine caused dissatisfaction among his congregation—his feelings about morality and faith can be clearly seen in his writings. In the early 1860s, as MacDonald began to discover his talent for fairy stories, he made friends with another minister, Charles Dodgson. Undecided whether or not to publish a story he had written about a friend's daughter, Dodgson asked MacDonald to read the story aloud to his children to see if they liked it. MacDonald's eleven children delighted in this new tale, his son Grenville declaring that he "wished there were 60,000 volumes of it." In this way, the MacDonald family played an important role in encouraging Dodgson (under the pseudonym of Lewis Carroll) to publish *Alice's Adventure in Wonderland*.

With the tremendous success of *Alice* in 1865, there was a sudden demand for more fairy stories. Two years later, MacDonald published his own collection of fantasy tales, titled *Dealings with the Fairies*, the most famous of these being "The Light Princess" and "The Golden Key." The following year, 1868, a new magazine for children called

[205]

Good Words for the Young appeared. Its first issue contained the initial installment of MacDonald's first fantasy novel for children, *At the Back of the North Wind*, which was issued in book form in early 1871. This tale of the poor, illiterate boy, Diamond, and his friendship with the magical North Wind is perhaps too sentimental and obvious in its religious and moral messages, particularly for modern readers. But MacDonald's imaginative imagery is still powerful, taking his readers on incredible flights of fancy.

In 1870 and 1871 *The Princess and the Goblin* was serialized in *Good Words for the Young*. Published in book form in the autumn of 1871, it was released at the same time as Lewis Carroll's *Through the Looking Glass*. (Interestingly, the first editions of both books bear the date of 1872 on their title pages). In this lengthy, sustained fairy story, Mac-Donald reaches his pinnacle as a writer for children. All of the powerful imagery and compelling characterizations of his earlier works are present, but with less overt symbolism and moralizing. As Humphrey Carpenter wrote in his *Secret Gardens: A Study of the Golden Age of Children's Literature* (Houghton Mifflin, 1985), *The Princess and the Goblin* "was in fact the first original British children's book to make an utterly confident, fresh use of such traditional materials as an old fairy spinning in a tower and a race of wicked dwarfs beneath a mountain." With these MacDonald creates a religious allegory for the Christian universe: The omnipotent, benevolent Grandmother lives up high where all is beautiful and only those who believe in her may find her; the wicked and nasty goblins live below where all is ugly and dangerous; and in between is the great house where mortals must choose between doing good or evil.

This marks the first truly successful combination of entertainment with moral instruction in children's literature. As Carpenter goes on to write, MacDonald created "an alternative religious landscape which a child's mind could explore and which could offer spiritual nourish-ment." Thus those who cried for the moral instruction of children as well as those who believed children's books should be more than instructional were both well served.

The Princess and the Goblin is also distinctive in that the traditional

[206]

role of women in fairy stories is also discarded by MacDonald. While Snow White, Rapunzel, and Sleeping Beauty all wait for their princes to rescue them, it is Irene who rescues Curdie when he is trapped by the goblins. And though she is unaccustomed to such work, she clears away the rocks behind which Curdie is imprisoned "with aching back, and bleeding fingers and hands." Unusual work for a princess!

Many authors have been strongly influenced by *The Princess and the Goblin*. Several times Rudyard Kipling refers to it as an influence on the title character's imagination in his short story, "Wee Willie Winkie." G. K. Chesterton wrote glowingly of it and J. R. R. Tolkien recalled it as one of his favorite books as a child. The nasty goblins in *The Hobbit* who lived beneath the Misty Mountains were no doubt inspired by MacDonald's tale. But perhaps most influenced of all was C. S. Lewis, who claimed MacDonald's *Phantastes* (a fantasy novel he wrote for adults) had "baptized" his imagination. Like MacDonald, Lewis sought to create an original mythic tale in which he could relate his own vision of Christianity. His seven "Chronicles of Narnia" were the result.

When *The Princess and the Goblin* was first issued in 1871, it was illustrated by Arthur Hughes. Using striking black-and-white engravings to show Irene, her grandmother, Curdie, and the goblins, Hughes created a masterful series of illustrations. But as the four-color printing process (which allowed for the economical printing of full color illustrations) came into common use in the early part of the twentieth-century, books illustrated in black-and-white began to lose favor. Children and parents alike clamoured for the bold and exciting illustrations of Arthur Rackham, Howard Pyle, Edmund Dulac, N.C. Wyeth, and their contemporaries. Publishers, eager to keep alive the stories that had delighted children in the past, sought out new illustrators to bring these books to life with full-color illustrations.

One of the more popular and successful of these artists was Jessie Willcox Smith. A student at Howard Pyle's "Brandywine School of American Illustration," whose alumni included N.C. Wyeth, Maxfield Parrish, and Elizabeth Shippen Green, Smith had already established a strong reputation as an illustrator of such children's

[207]

books as *A Child's Garden of Verses* by Robert Louis Stevenson and *Little Women* by Louisa May Alcott when she was asked to illustrate MacDonald's *At the Back of the North Wind*. The book was received so well that the following year, 1920, the publisher, David McKay, issued her newly illustrated edition of *The Princess and the Goblin*. Filled with lush, romantic images of Irene, Curdie, the grandmother and King-Papa, which are beautifully offset by the comically villainous goblins, Smith's suite of illustrations captured MacDonald's vision without limiting it.

George MacDonald is today considered one of the first great British fantasists for children, while Jessie Willcox Smith is respected as one of America's finest illustrators of children's books. In *The Princess and the Goblin*, the combination of their talents is as sure to excite young readers today as it did over sixty-five years ago.

—Peter Glassman

12 STEPS TO
LIVING
WITHOUT
FEAR

Other Books by Lloyd J. Ogilvie

THE OTHER JESUS
IF GOD CARES, WHY DO I STILL HAVE PROBLEMS?
MAKING STRESS WORK FOR YOU
ACTS, VOL. 5, COMMUNICATOR'S COMMENTARY
CONGRATULATIONS, GOD BELIEVES IN YOU!
THE BUSH IS STILL BURNING
WHEN GOD FIRST THOUGHT OF YOU
DRUMBEAT OF LOVE
LIFE WITHOUT LIMITS
LET GOD LOVE YOU
THE AUTOBIOGRAPHY OF GOD
LOVED AND FORGIVEN
LORD OF THE UPS AND DOWNS
IF I SHOULD WAKE BEFORE I DIE
A LIFE FULL OF SURPRISES
YOU'VE GOT CHARISMA
CUP OF WONDER
GOD'S BEST FOR MY LIFE
THE RADIANCE OF INNER SPLENDOR
GIFT OF FRIENDSHIP
GIFT OF LOVE
GIFT OF CARING
GIFT OF SHARING